History of Political Parties in Twentieth-Century Latin America

History of Political Parties in Twentieth-Century Latin America

Torcuato S. Di Tella

Transaction Publishers
New Brunswick (U.S.A.) and London (U.K.)

Third paperback printing 2007
Copyright © 2004 by Transaction Publishers, New Brunswick, New Jersey.

All rights reserved under International and Pan-American Copyright Conventions. No part of this book may be reproduced or transmitted in any form or by any means, electronic or mechanical, including photocopy, recording, or any information storage and retrieval system, without prior permission in writing from the publisher. All inquiries should be addressed to Transaction Publishers, Rutgers—The State University, 35 Berrue Circle, Piscataway, New Jersey 08854-8042.

This book is printed on acid-free paper that meets the American National Standard for Permanence of Paper for Printed Library Materials.

Library of Congress Catalog Number: 2003057350
ISBN: 0-7658-0181-7 (cloth); 1-4128-0510-4 (paper)
    978-0-7658-0181-4 (cloth); 978-1-4128-0510-0 (paper)
Printed in the United States of America

        Library of Congress Cataloging-in-Publication Data

Di Tella, Torcuato S., 1929-
  [Historia de los partidos politicos en América Latina, siglo XX. English]
    p. cm.
  Includes bibliographical references and index.
  ISBN 0-7658-0181-7 (alk. paper)
    978-0-7658-0181-4
  1. Political parties—Latin America—History. 2. Latin America—Politics and government—20th century. I. Title.

JL969.A45D513 2003
324.2'098'0904—dc21
                                          2003057350

Contents

Preface	ix
1. The Early Setting	1
Mexico, or the Reasons of Authoritarian Liberalism	1
Cuba: A Severely Guarded Boiler	3
The Caribbean and Central America	4
The South American Upper Tier	6
Peru Seeking a "Civilista" Right	8
Bolivia and Paraguay: A Structural Contrast	9
Brazil in the Times of "Café com Leite"	10
The Contrast between Chile and the River Plate Nations	11
2. Anarchism, Socialism, Revolutionary Nationalism: The Impact of the Mexican and Russian Revolutions	17
The Revolution in Mexico	18
The Impact in Peru: Aprismo and Mariátegui's Version of Marxism	22
In Bolivia and Paraguay Flammable Materials Accumulate	24
The Difficult Cuban Apprenticeship	26
Central America: Sandino's Saga	27
The Divergent Paths of Venezuela and Colombia	28
Ideological Mutations in Brazil: Nationalism and *Tenentismo*	29
Chile between Alessandri and Ibáñez: First Round	31
Political Evolution in Argentina: The Radical Party	33
The Uruguayan Model	37
3. The Military and Corporatist Onslaught: From the Thirties to the Second World War	43
Argentina in the "Década Infame"	44
The Beginnings of Varguismo in Brazil	46
Chile during the Popular Front: Contrast with Argentina	50

Post-Batlle Uruguay	53
The Effects of the Chaco War on Bolivia and Paraguay	55
Perú: Roots of the Antagonism between Military and Apristas	59
Ecuador, Colombia, and Venezuela	60
Mexico, from the Maximato to Cardenismo	63
The Revolution of 1933 in Cuba: Between Grau and Batista	63
Central America in Flames Demands a Theoretical Revision	65
4. The Postwar Dawn: Populism and Its Transformations	**71**
Peronist Argentina	72
Brazil: All Against Vargas	74
The Fall of Peronism and the Onset of Mass Praetorianism in Argentina	76
Uruguay, Paraguay, and Bolivia: Confronting Populism	80
Chile and the Second Coming of Ibáñez	84
Peru and Ecuador: Variants of Populist Strategy	86
Towards a Definition of Populism	89
Venezuela, Cuba, and Colombia: The Struggle Against Militarism	92
The PRI Consolidates Its Hold on Mexico	96
5. The Sixties and Seventies: From Revolution to Military Intervention	**99**
The "Peruvian Revolution"	100
Revolutionary Bolivia: No News from Paraguay	101
Brazil: Radicalization under Goulart and Military Coup	103
The Unstable Argentine Military Regimes	108
Christian Democracy and the Unidad Popular in Chile	111
The End of the Uruguayan Switzerland	114
The Democratic Experience in Colombia and Venezuela	116
In Mexico Social Tensions Accumulate	117
6. The Central American and Caribbean Cauldron	**121**
El Salvador	121
Guatemala	124
Honduras	126
Nicaragua	127
Costa Rica	130
Panama	132
Cuba	134
Dominican Republic	136
Haiti	138
Puerto Rico	139

Jamaica and Trinidad	139
Guiana and Surinam	141

7. The Workings of Democracy: From the Eighties to the New Century ... 147
    The Brazilian Transition ... 149
    Diversity of Transitions: Peru, Ecuador, Bolivia, and Paraguay ... 154
    The Unexpected Breakdown of the Argentine Dictatorship ... 164
    Political Openings in Uruguay and Chile ... 170
    Party Bipolarity under Attack in Venezuela and Colombia ... 173
    Mexico's Search for a Change ... 176

8. Continuity and Change in Latin American Party Systems ... 181
    (a) The Classical Conservative/Liberal Polarity ... 185
    (b) The Conservative/Liberal System Expanded towards Radicalism and Socialism ... 185
    (c) The Right/Left Polarity ... 186
    (d) Multiclass-Integrative Parties ... 187
    (e) Middle-Class Populist Parties ("Aprista") ... 188
    (f) Working-Class Populist Parties ("Peronist") ... 189
    (g) Working-Class Socialist Parties ("Social Democrat") ... 190
    (h) Social-Revolutionary Parties ("Fidelista") ... 192
    (i) Variants of Parties of the Right ... 193
    (j) Variants of Middle-Class Centrist Parties ... 194

Bibliography ... 197

Index ... 219

Preface

Long ago, it was said that men make their own history, but with the materials provided by society. This book is an attempt at studying the materials that Latin America has provided, during the twentieth century, and how they have been used by committed actors, particularly political parties. It so happens that a modern, democratic society is impossible without parties. Which may be a sorry state to be in, given their many and very well-known shortcomings. But the alternatives are even worse.

What I have attempted is to provide a basic narrative, divided into historical periods, and by countries, to help readers become acquainted in some depth with the actors of the drama. Parallel to the story, I seek sociological explanations, or rather hypotheses, so as to place in comparative perspective what is going on. The aim is to construct as systematically as possible an interpretation of the Latin American predicament. This must be grounded in general sociological theory and political science, but a focus on the way the many variables interact in the region, which given different initial conditions and combinations of factors, creates a peculiar idiosyncrasy.

In a sense, this is historical sociology, taking history as a quarry from which to extract a number of episodes that show the interaction of different actors, and the games played by them. I have described in detail some of the episodes, and have passed rather lightly over others, according to the bearing I believe they have on theoretical issues. Anyway, theory has been kept in the background, and I have given pride of place to the narrative, so as to avoid excessively vague generalizations. And I must admit that I have undertaken this trip in the time machine not only out of scientific curiosity but also to be better able to understand current and future events.

This is an expanded and updated version of a book originally published by the Fondo de Cultura Económica in Buenos Aires, in 1993, and reprinted in 1999. I have taken the opportunity of a stay as a visiting Tinker professor in Bolívar House at Stanford University to do the revisions and the translation, encouraged by the stimulating and friendly atmosphere created by its "jefa" and "subjefa," Terry Karl and Catherine Morrison, and by the whole staff, to whom go my heartfelt thanks. As for Transaction Publishers, I am deeply moved by their determination to commit my thoughts to paper rather than to the flames, and I suspect the hand of my old friend Irving Horowitz, is at it now as so often in the past.

Torcuato S. Di Tella
Buenos Aires
October 2002

1

The Early Setting

At the beginning of the twentieth century, Latin America seemed to be in the process of consolidating—with a few exceptions—as a successful extension of the West, finally administered in an efficient manner, leaving behind ages of civil war, *caudillismo,* and chronic instability. Seen from the theoretical perspective of evolutionary positivism, as stated in the very widely read books of Herbert Spencer, the continent was in an advanced transition from militarism to an industrial and civil society. From a Marxist point of view it, could be posited that imperialism was performing a progressive role, implanting capitalist economic structures, together with liberal institutions. An essential ingredient of those institutions was a system of political parties allowing the bourgeoisie to be represented, but also giving scope for the organization of the middle classes and the proletariat, which should prepare for the moment when the times might be ripe for them.

Less optimistic, of course, were the visions of classical conservative, or Catholic origin, for whom technological innovation was not an obvious good, nor did it necessarily produce social changes beneficial to all. Far from it; the deleterious effect of modernization on traditional mores and respect for hierarchical superiors might bring about chaos, not a civilized polity.

But let us see in more detail what the situation was in the various countries of the region in the early years of the twentieth century.

Mexico, or the Reasons of Authoritarian Liberalism

In Mexico, after the terrible convulsions of the Insurgencia (1810-1816) and the wars of Reform (1857-1860) and Intervention (1861-1867), an era of authoritarian but constitutional development had been inaugurated, overcoming the succession of military coups and popular rioting that had marked the nation's history. Porfirio Díaz's regime was heir to the radical liberalism of the earlier part of the nineteenth century, which had successfully waged the struggle against religious traditionalism and foreign conquest. Its great foundational symbol was the Constitution of 1857, paradigm of possible future developments, which for the moment it was necessary to apply parsimoniously. Power should be delegated to a paternalist and solid government, ruling over a basically apathetic majority, while watching the ever-present, dangerous activist minorities.

The only serious problem was that in order to avoid the national tendency to slip into civil war, an excessively personalist system had been created, based on the reelection indefinitely of Don Porfirio. The system, in practice, was one of single-party rule; as a matter of fact, it was not even possible to speak of a governing party. What really existed was the entourage of the president, made up of officials and some intellectuals, plus regional *caudillos* who were slowly being transformed into civilian administrators in an expanding economy.

The Catholic Church had been ostracized since the mid-century convulsions, but it was slowly returning to a position of respectability. It maintained an excellent liaison with the upper classes, and a correct relationship to the ruling circles. For the presidential elections of 1904, Díaz would be reelected once again, for the sixth time, which was not too much for a country under reconstruction, and he promised he would not insist. Formally, the governing party called itself Liberal, though it was quite different from its European namesakes, or even from the Conservatives of the Old World. But precisely in this—it could be argued—rested its claim to efficient adaptation to its difficult milieu.

Around the president, a brilliant intellectual group had been formed, imbued with the latest doctrines, and therefore known as the Científicos, a somewhat sarcastic name they finally adopted as their own. They included Finance Minister Yves Limantour, publicist Justo Sierra, and controversial author Francisco Bulnes, who had no qualms in overturning old clichés about the country's history. The Científicos, organized into a National Liberal Convention, had been in the forefront of the campaign to convince the general to take the presidency once more. Though in principle they were against unipersonal and excessively centralized government, given the existing social conditions they believed this was the only possible solution.[1]

There were some opposition groups of a more doctrinal liberal hue hoping to compete at least for positions of influence in Congress, so as to exert some control over the executive. At popular levels a more seriously stormy front was being created, with circumscribed but repeated outbursts of social protest in rural as well as urban and mining areas. Seen from the spheres of power, it was necessary not to lose too much time before enacting necessary reforms, and a search for new formulas was launched among the political class. But what aborted this effort was the firmly grounded fear, quite justified by the historical record, that any serious dissidence, once allowed to raise its head, would degenerate into uncontrollable violence, even if it started as a competition among gentlemen. And this is what happened.

Cuba: A Severely Guarded Boiler

In Cuba, the long-lasting Spanish rule had promoted impressive economic growth, though excessively concentrated on sugar, thus generating high occupational instability. Modernization and urban and educational development were considerably higher than in Mexico, and the Catholic Church less grounded in the hearts of the common people. A two-party system was formed, rather than a single, authoritarian regime, with Conservatives and Liberals rotating in office, depending on the favor they found in the mother country. The War of Independence, known as the Guerra de Diez Años (1868-1878) had seriously damaged business interests, also hampered by competition from the European sugar beet. Towards the end of the century, in 1895, the struggle was resumed, promoted by the Partido Revolucionario Cubano, founded by José Martí, who died in the first skirmishes, leaving a legacy of intellectual leadership and moral proselytizing.

Insurgency was firmly rooted among peasant groups and the lower middle classes, who spawned a guerrilla movement the Spanish authorities could not control. In fact, the revolutionary potential was very high on the island. Massive concentrations on sugar estates of a work force recently freed from slavery (1880) could instill fears of a rebellion along the lines of the one that had destroyed Haiti at the end of the previous century. Only strict security, and an unwritten pact among elites to water down their own internal conflicts could stave off this danger. However, this was not easily agreed to by everybody, because the relatively high level of education and the appalling oscillations in demand for labor of all kinds also impinged on the middle classes, which thus became a recruiting ground for ideological and political activists. To complicate matters, extensive immigration from Spain had created a commercial and industrial bourgeoisie which competed successfully with its native counterparts.[2]

The 1895 independence movement was on the verge of success, when the United States decided to intervene in order to avoid the kind of "caste war" that was on everybody's mind. They declared war on Spain in 1898 and quickly occupied the island. Despite annexationist tendencies, American public opinion, conscious of the need to keep good relationships with their southern neighbors, forced Congress to write a clause in the war declaration denying any intent to incorporate Cuba. However, an agreement was soon arrived at with the pro-independence forces on the island, also validated by Congress, adding a rider, known as the Platt Amendment, to the war declaration, authorizing the United States to intervene—without specifying any limits in time—to guarantee life, freedom, and property on the island. This clause became the basis for constant interference in Cuban affairs during the first three decades of the century.

Among partisans of the anti-Spanish insurgency there was a radical sector, based on those who had taken up arms, and a more moderate group of civilians and administrators. However, both had strong popular roots, given their record of opposing the Spanish government, and their rejection of any type of co-optation by the colonial authorities. American occupation lasted until 1902, when Tomás Estrada Palma, a well-respected personality, was elected president. Thus it seemed that Cuba joined, with a little delay, and under the protection of its elder uncle, the pattern of orderly progress which was spreading on the continent.

The Caribbean and Central America

In the rest of the Caribbean, instability was endemic. In the Dominican Republic a series of coups and violence had been temporarily halted by the strong government of General Ulises Heureaux, a man of color popular among the armed forces, who pacified the country and kept the elites quiet for a time. But after his assassination in 1899, agitation returned, and the United States was led to intervene, occupying the customs offices in order to ensure the recovery of their credits.[3]

Political conditions in Haiti were no better and were even more determined by personalist factions. A period which augured greater stability ended in 1902 in civil war and protracted anarchy, determining the United States to occupy the country in 1915, with French acquiescence.[4]

Central America was scarcely touched by the modernization that the rest of the continent was experiencing. The main exception was Costa Rica, strangely enough as a result of having been the Cinderella of colonial times due to its relative lack of Indian manpower. Thus, an independent subsistence peasantry was formed, and the elements of an alternance of factions in power laid. The Liberals had secured their cultural influence by closing down the clergy-dominated university. It took several decades to replace that old educational establishment with a new one, so that up to 1940 professionals were forced to have their training abroad.[5]

In the rest of Central America the two most populated countries were Guatemala and El Salvador, in contrast with the uninhabited Honduras and the more balanced Nicaragua. Guatemala had another peculiarity: its very high indigenous presence, almost half the total. This population was barely connected to the main centers of the country, and politically not very active. The whites and *ladinos* (mestizos or culturally assimilated Indians) cultivated mostly coffee in the fertile valleys, with Indian migrant manpower. Towards the south, near the Pacific coast, conditions were excellent for sugar and cotton, attracting deracinated workers from the highlands. On the other side of the mountains, in the strip of land reaching to the Atlantic, the swampy soil was only used for bananas. Several foreign companies were established, concentrating large numbers of workers, unwittingly creating conditions for class confrontation.

On the other hand, the Petén, the mostly low-lying northern part of the country, was sparsely populated, a haven for adventurers, including some

Indian colonizers, because lack of transportation made export agriculture impossible. In due time, however, new roads generated, as in some areas of the Altiplano, proletarianizing forces and the expulsion of old squatters by new commercial enterprises.

Modernization of Guatemala had been fostered by the iron dictatorship (1873-1885) of the Liberal Justo Rufino Barrios, confronting the Catholic Conservatives, and determined to destroy the remaining land-owning Indian communities, which were in the way of coffee capitalism. Barrios died in a war aimed at reconstructing the unity of Central America, and was succeeded by a classical Conservative/Liberal alternation, with constant military interferences, leading to another long dictatorship, also formally Liberal and quite developmental, of Manuel Estrada Cabrera (1898-1920).[6]

El Salvador, with an even denser population than the one existing in the settled part of Guatemala, had a very intermixed ethnic composition, so that the pure Indian sector was not numerous. Coffee was also predominant, having displaced, since the middle of the nineteenth century, the subsistence agriculture of the traditional landowning Indian communities. Towards the Pacific, new tropical plantations were established, as in Guatemala. Political competition, during the second part of the nineteenth century, had been highly unstable, with a constant rotation of military and civilian factions.[7]

In stark contrast with Guatemala and El Salvador, Honduras had an abundance of land and a small indigenous population. Most of its old inhabited area was dedicated to subsistence agriculture, with a large peasantry that had managed to keep its possessions. In the Atlantic lowlands, conditions were ripe for banana cultivation, as in Guatemala's similar area. The political system revolved around the bipolarity of a Liberal party, strong among urban and commercial sectors, and a National party, closely resembling the Conservatives.[8]

Nicaragua also had a relative abundance of land, but with a more diversified economy, including coffee, cotton, and sugar. In its big and underpopulated eastern lowlands, the Miskito Indians lived. They had passed through a period of British domination, converted to Protestantism, and were weakly connected to the rest of the country. The Nicaraguan geography facilitated the planning of a transoceanic canal, using the lakes of the western part, attracting many adventurers and the attention of the United States government. The political system was based on the classical confrontation of Conservatives and Liberals. Towards the end of the nineteenth century, José Santos Zelaya, a Liberal, came to power after overthrowing his Conservative predecessor, and inaugurated a rather long stretch of peace (1893-1909).

In Panama, independence was obtained in 1903, as a result of a separatist movement supported by North American intervention. After surrendering the canal the country was constituted, with an upper class of more recent origins than in most of the continent, more open to ambitious persons coming from any part of the world. Its strategic geographic and economic position augured a great future, which, in fact, was not attained, even though indices of modernization and educational attainment were quite high, second only to Costa Rica in the region. The treaty with the United States established the right of the northern power to intervene when necessary to ensure order. The result was that no army was organized, but only a police force called the Guardia Nacional, with little social prestige. The political system was based on a civilian tradition and few military coups (as in Colombia, of which it had been a part). The Liberal Party, already dominant when Panama was a province, continued to be hegemonic during the early decades, marked by the weak presence of the Catholic Church, as on the northern Colombian coast.[9]

The South American Upper Tier

Colombia

Colombia, with the new century, provided a deplorable example of regression to barbarism, in a civil war of unsurpassed cruelty, the so-called Guerra de los Mil Días (1899-1902). The political system, however, followed the classical lines, pitting a Conservative party, strong in the highlands and among the Catholic peasantry, against a very anticlerical Liberal party, with wide bases of support in commercial and professional circles, hegemonic on the Caribbean coast and among the black population. Liberalism had always had a moderate wing, and a radical and populist one, often quite at odds with each other, and that continued to be the case.[10]

The country had very low economic, urban, or industrial development, and its proletariat was not concentrated in mining or sugar enclaves, as in Mexico or Cuba. But its rural milieu, based since colonial times on a proliferation of medium-sized landowners, squatters, and more modest peasants distributed throughout its inaccessible geography, created permanent conflicts over possession of land. Local groups needed to associate at the national level for defensive purposes, creating clans linked as clientele to the two national parties. The virulence of political conflict thus reflected agrarian struggles, not necessarily of property holders against Indian communities (as in Mexico) or against erstwhile slaves (as in Cuba), but rather between sectors of middle and large rural *hacendados*. Each faction easily recruited followers among peons and clients, fueling village violence and civil wars. That is why people "were born Liberal or Conservative," because belonging to either of those bands was the costly but necessary insurance each Colombian had to take when coming into this world.[11]

One may wonder why this did not happen in other parts of Latin America to a similar extent. Even if in some other places such phenomena existed, Colombia had peculiarities not to be found elsewhere. First of all, the Indian population was not very numerous, and was soon either decimated or mixed, so a rather homogeneous ethnic pattern emerged, contrasting with such cases as Mexico, Ecuador, Peru, or Bolivia. There had also been very little slavery, except on the small Caribbean coast. And there was much fertile land, but in remote places, far from the influence of commercial or administrative centers, so that a high incentive was created for the establishment of Spanish settlers in self-enclosed, isolated places, managing medium and small plots dedicated to subsistence agriculture and a little interchange, including coffee. But when coffee was taken over by larger capitalist elements, displacing earlier occupants, towards the end of the nineteenth century, the reaction was intense.

The Conservative/Liberal duality was, of course, not completely clear-cut. Apart from the difference between moderates and radicals (*exaltados*), since 1880, a mutation had occurred among the more pragmatic sectors of Liberalism, creating a following for a political innovator, Rafael Núñez, who, having overcome his juvenile extremism, decided to seek a convergence with the opposite band. He thus created a new movement named Regeneración, which was in power, with some interruptions, between 1880 and 1894. His aim, in thus coalescing the opposing factions, was to form a solid single front, or at least a dominant one, so as to ensure governability, along Porfirio Díaz's path. But the social setting was very different from that of Mexico. In Colombia, despite continuous civil strife, there was never a massive subversive menace similar to the one existing in Mexico, as attested by its history, or potentially present in Cuba. Thus, the appetites of the various political factions were not so decidedly repressed by the consensus of the upper classes, and partisan bipolarity maintained itself, leading finally to the Guerra de los Mil Días, from which the Conservatives emerged victorious.[12]

Venezuela

Venezuela, during the time we are considering, was a very peripheral region of the continent, ravaged in the past by constant violence and civil war. Political conflicts had possessed a much more decidedly social and class-confrontation component than in Colombia, without reaching the intensity of Mexico. The necessity of establishing a dictatorial power in order to restrain the passions was thus felt much more in Venezuela than in Colombia. This power was not easily achieved, but in 1899 an era of civilian and military anarchy ended with the access of the so-called "Andean dynasty," a series of leaders from that area, whose first representative was Cipriano Castro, *caudillo* of the western state of Táchira. His authoritarian government (1899-1908) had to confront in 1902 an armed intervention by the main European powers, intent on collecting what was owed them, even if by unorthodox methods. As could be expected, the dictatorship was consolidated by the ensuing nationalist reaction, and by Latin American solidarity, crystalized in the Drago Doctrine, thus named after the Argentine magistrate who established the rather idealistic principle that debts should not be collected with gunboats or the threat thereof.[13]

Ecuador

In Ecuador, as in many other parts of the continent, there was also a protracted fight between Conservatives and Liberals, mixed with *caudillismo* and foreign intervention. The highland Sierra, with a great concentration of indigenous population, working on their own lands or on those of others, was the basis of Catholic Conservatism, with a very visible head in Quito. The Coast, represented by the port town of Guayaquil, was characterized by export-oriented plantations of cocoa beans, and had much greater social mobility and an ethnically mixed population with a black ingredient. It tended towards Liberalism in economics, politics, and religion. Partisan animosity was thus very marked, almost as in Colombia, and rooted in more clearly marked geographical and social differentiation. Towards the turn of the century the Liberals came to power with a *caudillo* with a popular following, Eloy Alfaro, who launched a radical program of secularization.[14]

Peru Seeking a "Civilista" Right

In Peru, a very agitated history was made more tragic by defeat in the War of the Pacific (1879-1883) against Chile. The oligarchy had always been very fractured, partly as a result of the division of the country into two regions: the Coast, ethnically very mixed and with intensively worked sugar and cotton areas (to which much later oil would be added), and the Sierra, predominantly Indian, with precapitalist *haciendas* and some important mining enclaves. The potential social and ethnic conflict had Mexican proportions, and had occasioned the deadly Túpac Amaru explosion at the end of the eighteenth century. But apart from that, never were there such intense confrontations as those witnessed in Mexico, and thus a system similar to the Porfiriato could never be established.

The nearest thing to a unification of the upper classes was the creation of the Civilista Party, in 1872, determined to finish with militarism, which tended to degenerate into destructive civil wars, or even worse, mutate into a menacing populism. *Civilismo* had difficulty in spawning constitutional governments, and was always threatened by some form of militarism.

The Civilistas, after a period of turmoil, acceded to the presidency in 1899, maintaining it up till 1912, when a division among their ranks facilitated changes. Thus, a populist anti-Civilista faction came to power, led by Guillermo Billinghurst, a large nitrate owner of Tarapacá, the lost province of the War of the Pacific. Billinhurst's popular support included a trade union movement of some weight, though quite moderate.[15]

Bolivia and Paraguay: A Structural Contrast

Bolivia

In Bolivia also, the new century witnessed a consolidation of a Conservative/Liberal polarity; this in a country where mining concentrations and the ethnic chasm, created ideal conditions for violence. The agitated decades prior to the War of the Pacific (when Bolivia, allied to Peru, lost its access to the Pacific) had seen a succession of civilian and military factions, often generating *caudillos*, especially among the middle ranks of the army, capable of mobilizing the masses. Probably in a somewhat exaggerated way, Alcides Arguedas, the Liberal historian, pinpointed this fact in his *History of Bolivia*, one of whose volumes was significantly titled *La plebe en acción*, referring especially to the administration of Manuel Belzú (1848-1855), an early authoritarian populist.[16]

Soon after the War of the Pacific, the silver economy was revived, which made possible a flowering of Conservative civilian rule, accompanied by the building of an infrastructure of railroads, roads and schools. Towards the end of the century this prosperity was decaying, together with the price of silver. A Liberal opposition was formed, with federalist orientations, leading to a revolution and access to power in 1899.[17]

The next twenty years saw the predominance of the Liberal Party, which soon forgot its federal schemes, and rode another wave of economic growth, always confined to the elites, fueled by tin mining. During this long period, Conservatism almost disappeared as a party, while following the First World War a dissident liberal nucleus was created, which finally took the form of the Republican Party. Thus the Conservative/Liberal formula was replaced by a Liberal/Republican one, performing a similar function.[18]

Paraguay

Paraguay, despite its poverty and geographic isolation, showed a marked contrast with Bolivia. Its ethnic composition was much more homogeneous, and its upper class almost exempt from aristocratic pretensions. The ease of migration to Argentina and the relative absence of large working-class concentrations contributed to a moderation of social conflict. The War of the Triple Alliance, waged by nationalist dictator Francisco Solano López against Argentina, Brazil, and Uruguay (1865-1870), had left a sequel of scarcely legitimated regimes in a ravaged country dominated by foreign powers. Soon a polarization developed between the Liberal Party, enemy of the national populist López tradition, and the Colorados, which were nearer to it. In 1904 a military coup inaugurated a long spell of Liberal hegemony, which seemed to set the country on the path of building a regime with formal liberties and some guarantees for those who did not oppose it too strenuously.[19]

Brazil in the Times of "Café com Leite"

Brazil, during the nineteenth century, had, like Cuba, a huge menacing slave population. The result was a strong upper-class control of potential dissidents from their own ranks, or from the middle classes. Monarchy helped consolidate this pattern. Since the beginning of the eighteenth century, through the Methuen Treaty between Great Britain and Portugal, the Brazilian economy had been very much connected with the rising imperial power. This made independence less of a trauma, in contrast to what happened in the more protectionist Hispanic areas. In fact, Brazil had practically no war of independence, and appeals from sectors of the elites to the masses were very moderate, or savagely repressed when they existed, mostly at provincial levels.[20]

Under monarchical rule there was a rotation of governing factions of Conservatives and Liberals, acting among an extremely reduced sector of the population. The war against Paraguay (1865-1870) raised the prestige of the armed forces, up to that moment very much under the control of government and of the upper classes. Finally, the proclamation of the Republic in 1889 was the result of military intervention, supported by sectors of the intelligentsia with Comtean positivist ideas. The new dispensation for several decades consisted of a variation of the Mexican system of single-party dominance, with the Republican Party solidly in power since 1894, after two transitional military presidencies.

The great difference with Mexico, though, was that in Brazil federalism was much stronger, due to the existence of four or five rival centers of power: the old sugar producing Northeast, decadent but still influential and with a large population; Minas Gerais, with a diversified agrarian economy; Rio de Janeiro, the capital and a coffee-growing region; Sao Paulo, increasingly taking first place in coffee production; and the militarized frontier society of Rio Grande do Sul. In each state, a local Republican Party was formed, only theoretically affiliated to a national organization. What existed, then, was a constellation of very autonomous local systems, based on parties which in practice were the only ones in each state.

Even so, it was necessary to avoid struggles for power which might lead to civil war—with the inevitable result of stimulating mass insurgencies—and so an unwritten pact was arrived at for alternation of the presidency between the two main states, Sao Paulo and Minas, in the so-called *política do café com leite*. In the country there were no important mining enclaves, and the agro-industrial ones, based on sugar, were diluted in the great mass of Brazil, so that structural bases for class confrontation were relatively scarcer than in Mexico or Cuba. If the sugar-producing Northeast, with high concentrations of former slaves, had been an independent country, certainly social tensions associated with its productive basis would have generated a kind of politics more in line with that of the Caribbean island.[21]

The strategy of cooptation followed by the ruling elites, together with the channeling of conflicts through the rivalry of states, diminished the likelihood of a dissident, progressive Liberal, or Radical alternative coming to life. In that sense, Brazilian politics were very resistant to the ideological or party innovations that were increasingly to be found in other sections of Latin America.[22]

The Contrast between Chile and the River Plate Nations

Chile

In the southernmost part of the continent, Chile reproduced, in marked contrast with Brazil, the European social structure and party systems. It had, in relative terms, a high urban, economic, and educational development, and an enviable institutional consolidation, within classical patterns of limited participation. Since early times, a Conservative/Liberal polarity arose, and towards the end of the nineteenth century, Liberalism made for a highly centralist and developmental experience under José Manuel Balmaceda (1886-1891), a more civilized version of the Liberal autocrats so common in the northern part of Latin America. He had to confront the resistance of the majority of the political class of his times, including sectors of his own highly divisible Liberal Party, which led to a civil war and his suicide.

The vitality of public freedoms, and the relative maturity of this society, facilitated the formation of political parties based on ever-wider sectors of the popular classes. The first one was the Radical Party, originally based on the mining old north (before the War of the Pacific), and it already had elected five deputies by 1863. In 1875, it had its first ministerial portfolio in a Liberal-dominated cabinet, and since then it was common to see its members occupying positions in coalition governments. This pattern was consolidated during the so-called Parliamentarian Republic which was born right after the civil war against Balmaceda, in 1891. The Radicals' first National Convention was held in 1888, with a representation of many local *asambleas*, a statute and a program, all of which set it apart from the other traditional parties.

To the left of the Radicals a Democratic Party was formed in 1888, following the model of European social democracy though in a more pragmatic fashion. One of is leaders and an early Congress representative was Luis Emilio Recabarren, a typographer and later founder of the Socialist Party (1912), together with a wide array of moderate mutual-help societies.

The mining centers of the north were an important basis for a confrontational politics, which was expressed through an early anarchist influence, and patterns of organization reminiscent of the French syndicalists. For the moment, however, the Radical Party was the main anti-status quo force, even if very heterogeneous, as it encompassed sectors with a socialist orientation, led by Valentín Letelier, and others with a more Liberal, laissez-faire, and market-oriented approach, represented by Enrique MacIver.[23]

Argentina

In Argentina, a political system similar to the Chilean could have been expected, closely resembling European models. The grounds for this assumption rest on its social structure, based on a temperate-climate agriculture, with a significant presence of a rural or small-town middle class, even if much weaker than in the United States or Australia. There had been also, in both countries, a relative absence of tropical plantation enclaves, with their slave populations, or of the ethnic chasms of Mexico and Peru. This could have led to a progression of Conservative, Liberal, Radical and Socialist parties. This was not exactly the case in Argentina, whose party system was already quite different from Chile's at the early time we are considering, and became increasingly so since the advent of Peronism during the Second World War.[24]

Basically, the disparity lies in the predominance of populism in Argentina, notoriously weak or most of the time absent in Chile. Argentina, with much more fertile land than Chile, and a more predominantly cattle-raising rather than agricultural pattern, had less of a peasant basis, which in those days was the classical popular component of conservatism. Instead of peasants, in the prosperous part of Argentina (and also Uruguay) since the early nineteenth century a rural proletariat existed, together with significant strata of semi-legal squatters, tenants, and sharecroppers, all of them with high geographical and some social mobility, little rootedness in local communities, and not much churchgoing. That relatively mobilized mass had been the support, during the early part of the nineteenth century, of the populist authoritarian federal *caudillos*, notoriously Juan Manuel de Rosas in Buenos Aires. After his overthrow in 1852, that tradition of mobilization remained dormant, and was partly coopted by new conservative forces. These, however, predominantly took the form of a unified conservative liberal oligarchy, organized into the Partido Autonomista Nacional (PAN) by President Julio A. Roca (1880-1886 and 1898-1904). This was the main political arm of the ruling classes, with positivist Spencerian ideas of progress, shunting aside the Catholic groups, unable to form a more classical conservative party. Roca's PAN was bent on rapid economic development with foreign capital, using mildly authoritarian methods, based more on ballot box juggling than open dictatorship. In a sense, this was an updated version of Mexico's Porfiriato.

Against this dominant coalition it was difficult to organize a moderate opposition party, rooted in the urban bourgeoisie or petty middle class, because those classes—in stark contrast with Chile—were massively foreign born and did not take up citizenship. Within the total population, in the early twentieth century, foreigners never amounted to more than 5 percent in Chile, against almost 30 percent in Argentina. In the largest urban centers and among active-age males the figures were much higher, reaching the level of 60 or 70 percent for commercial or industrial entrepreneurs, and for urban manual workers.

Turn-of-the-century Argentina, then, had the strange predicament that the two more strategic classes for the formation of a liberal regime were foreign-born, and did not take up citizenship, being thus deprived of the vote. Circulation of elites between economic activity and political leadership was less marked than in Chile, and probably this low presence of an involved bourgeoisie is one of the causes of the absence, or weakness, of an equivalent of the Chilean Liberal Party.

Bartolomé Mitre (president, 1862-1868) tried to create such a party, to oppose the abusive developmentalism of the PAN, but without much success at the polls, as most of his sympathizers were foreigners and lacked the vote. When Mitre finally put together an apparently winning coalition of oppositional groups, appealing to popular insurrection in 1890, he had a partial success, forcing the president to resign. But he was unable to consolidate his leadership with a solid party behind him, and most of his following deserted to the newly formed Radical Party, which had more *caudillista* and populist elements in its leadership than its Chilean namesake.[25]

In Chile, a contraposition was taking place between a Catholic Conservatism and an anticlerical Liberalism, to which a third contender was early added, the Radical Party, ready to participate in the corrupt game of elections, vote buying, clientelism, and coalition cabinets. In Argentina, the space occupied in Chile by Conservatism and Liberalism was preempted by the steamroller *desarrollismo* of the Partido Autonomista Nacional (PAN). The main opposition to this juggernaut was in the hands of the Unión Cívica Radical, much more populist, and less anticlerical, than its Chilean equivalent. So, instead of the Chilean dialectic between Conservatives and Liberals, in Argentina there was a counterpoint opposing a modernizing oligarchy to a radical populism.

Uruguay

In Uruguay the immigrant impact was similar to that in Argentina, and probably because of this the classical European or Chilean system was also not established. But Uruguay had a more modernized society (though less so than the province of Buenos Aires), lacking the archaic social bases of Argentina's interior provinces, which gave the PAN its winning edge. Thus a duality emerged between two historical factions, the Nacionales or Blancos, Catholic and conservative but with some rural populist elements, and the Colorados, urban, liberal-radical and associated with immigrant sectors.

These two political clans derived from early nineteenth-century factions, and both had roots in traditional *caudillismo*. Civil wars between them had been extremely violent, and created in the Uruguayan countryside a situation of insecurity that for decades retarded economic growth. Colorado dominance became total following the armed movement of General Venancio Flores in 1865. After a Blanco revolutionary attempt (1870-1872) a pacification pact was arrived at by which four departmental *jefaturas* (governorships, appointed by the national authorities), were given to the Blancos.

This was a way to grant the opposition access to some institutional levers, and dissuade it from resorting to arms. Among the Nacional or Blanco parties there was always a moderate, *acuerdista* sector, linked to the city "doctores," and a more confrontational one, capable of mobilizing the rural masses, which towards the end of the nineteenth century were led by Aparicio Savaria, a medium-sized landowner from the country's northeast. Savaria conducted two armed insurrections. The first one, in 1896, ended with an agreement by which he remained as a great power in the land, and his party acceded to six instead of only four *jefaturas*. He tried again in 1903-1904, but this time he met defeat and death. The country was quickly changing, and within the Colorado Party a mutation had occurred, under the leadership of José Batlle y Ordóñez, who inaugurated a period of growth which was eventually to convert Uruguay into "Latin America's Switzerland," but, alas, only for some golden decades.[26]

Notes

1. Daniel Cosío Villegas, ed., *Historia moderna de México*; Francisco Bulnes, *La guerra de Independencia: Hidalgo, Iturbide* and *El verdadero Juárez y la verdad sobre la intervención y el imperio*.
2. Rolando Mellafe, *La esclavitud en Hispanoamérica*; Nicolás Sánchez Albornoz, *La población de América Latina desde los tiempos precolombinos al año 2000*; Ramiro Guerra y Sánchez, *Azúcar y población en las Antillas*; Fernando Ortiz, *Contrapunteo cubano del tabaco y el azúcar*; Franklin W. Knight, *Slave Society in Cuba during the XIXth Century*; Herbert Klein, *Slavery in the Americas: A Comparative Study of Virginia and Cuba*; Manuel Moreno Fraginals, *El ingenio: el complejo económico social cubano del azúcar*.
3. Frank Moya Pons, *Manual de historia dominicana* and *La sociedad dominicana contemporánea*; H. Hoetink, *The Dominican People, 1850-1900: Notes for a Historical Sociology*.
4. James Leyburn, *The Haitian People*; David Nicholls, *From Dessalines to Duvalier: Race, Colour and National Independence in Haiti*.
5. James Dunkerley, *Power in the Isthmus: A Political History of Modern Central America*; Carolyn Hall, *El café y el desarrollo histórico-geográfico de Costa Rica*; Ciro F.S. Cardoso, "La formación de la hacienda cafetalera en Costa Rica"; Lowell Gudmunson, "Peasant, Farmer, Proletarian: Class Formation in a Small Holder Coffee Economy, 1850-1950"; Mitchell Seligson, *El campesino y el capitalismo agrario en Costa Rica*.
6. Héctor Pérez Brignoli, *Breve historia de Centroamérica*; Thomas Kairnes, *The Failure of Union: Central America 1824-1975*; Greg Grandin, *The Blood of Guatemala: A History of Race and Nation;* Severo Martínez Peláez, *La patria del criollo*.
7. Michael McClintock, *State Terror and Popular Resistance in El Salvador*, vol. 2 of *The American Connection*.
8. The United Fruit company had in 1954 26,000 employees. Alison Acker, *Honduras: The Making of a Banana Republic*, p. 85.

9. Sharon Phillips Collazos, *Labor and Politics in Panama: The Torrijos Years.*
10. Gerardo Molina, *Las ideas liberales en Colombia*; Luis Eduardo Nieto Arteta, *Economía y cultura en la historia de Colombia*; Jaime Jaramillo Uribe, *El pensamiento colombiano en el siglo XIX.*
11. Orlando Fals Borda, *Campesinos de los Andes: estudio sociológico de Saucío,* and *El hombre y la tierra en Boyacá: desarrollo histórico de una sociedad latifundista*; Marco Palacios, *El café en Colombia, 1850-1970.*
12. Indalecio Liévano Aguirre, *Rafael Núñez,* and his *Los grandes conflictos sociales y económicos de nuestra historia*; Orlando Fals Borda, *La subversión en Colombia.*
13. Mariano Picón Salas et al., *Venezuela independiente, 1810-1960*; Germán Carrera Damas, *Formulación definitiva del proyecto nacional: 1870-1900.*
14. José Gálvez, *Vida de Don Gabriel García Moreno.*
15. Jorge Basadre, *Historia de la República, 1822-1899,* and *La multitud, la ciudad y el campo en la historia del Perú*; Luis G. Lumbreras et al., *Nueva historia general del Perú*; Peter Blanchard, *The Origins of the Peruvian Labor Movement, 1883-1919*; Peter F. Klarén, *Peru: Society and Nationhood in the Andes.*
16. Alcides Arguedas, *Obras completas.*
17. The concept of federalism means in Latin America the opposite of what it meant in North American history. In the early United States the Federalist Party was in favor of stronger central government, trying to convert the Confederation into a Federation, through the Constitution of 1789. What in Latin America is called Federalism is nearer to the attitudes of the Antifederalists who opposed the 1789 Constitutional surrender of powers, or to the later states' rights approach, though without necessarily the latter's conservative implications.
18. Enrique Finot, *Nueva Historia de Bolivia;* Mariano Baptista Gumucio, *Historia Contemporánea de Bolivia, 1930-1978.*
19. Carlos Pastore, *La lucha por la tierra en el Paraguay*; Rafael Barrett, *Lo que son los yerbales paraguayos*; Juan E. O'Leary, *El Mariscal Solano López*; John Hoyt Williams, *The Rise and Fall of the Paraguayan Republic, 1810-1870*; Roberto Ares Pons, *El Paraguay del siglo XIX.*
20. Paula Beiguelman, *Formação política do Brasil*; Carl Degler, *Neither Black nor White: Slavery and Race Relations in Brazil and the United States*; Florestan Fernandes, *A integração do negro na sociedade de classes*; Richard Graham, "Causes for the Abolition of Negro Slavery in Brazil: An Interpretive Essay"; Raymundo Faoro, *Os donos do poder: formação do patronato político brasileiro*; José Murilo de Carvalho, *A construção da ordem: e elite política imperial*; Brasil Gerson, *O sistema político do Império*; Paulo Mercadante, *A consciencia conservadora no Brasil.*
21. Gilberto Freyre, *Casa grande y senzala*; Edgard Carone, *A Primeira República* and *A República Velha*; José Enio Casalecchi, *O Partido Republicano Paulista, 1889-1926*; Alberto Sales, *A pátria paulista.* Rio Grande do Sul was the main exception to the single-party Republican monopoly. There the oppositionist federalist Partido Libertador was a serious rival for power, grounded as it was in the separatist past of the so-called Republica Farroupilha of 1835-1845, and capable of mobilizing gaucho informal hosts, as in nearby Uruguay. See Alfredo Varela, *Revoluçoes cisplatinas: a República Riograndense.*
22. Edgar Rodrigues, *Os libertários*; Vamireh Chacon, *História das idéias socialistas no Brasil.*
23. Ricardo Donoso, *Las ideas políticas en Chile*; René León Echaiz, *Evolución histórica de los partidos políticos chilenos*; Alberto Edwards Vives, *La Fronda aristocrática en Chile*; Peter Snow, *El radicalismo chileno: historia y doctrina del Partido Radical*; Luis Palma Zúñiga, *Historia del Partido Radical.*

24. David Rock, *Argentina 1516-1987: From Spanish Colony to Alfonsín*; Nicolas Shumway, *The invention of Argentina*; Jean Borde and Mario Góngora, *Evolución de la propiedad rural en el valle del Puangue*; Rafael Baraona, Ximena Aranda and Roberto Santana, *Valle de Putaendo: estudio de estructura agraria*.
25. The Unión Cívica, formed in 1890 under Mitre's leadership, with the organizational cooperation of Leandro Alem, was split in 1891. On one side the Unión Cívica Nacional remained, under Mitre's leadership, as a liberal party. On the other, the Unión Cívica Radical, refusing any adaptation to the existing regime, was formed under Alem's inspiration and included his nephew, future president Hipólito Yrigoyen. See José S. Campobassi, *Mitre y su época*; José Landerberger and Francisco Conte, eds, *La Unión Cívica: origen, organización y tendencia*; Juan Balestra, *El 90: una evolución política argentina; Paula* Alonso, *Between Revolution and the Ballot Box: The Origins of the Argentine Radical Party*.
26. Alberto Zum Felde, *Proceso histórico del Uruguay: esquema de una sociología nacional*; Héctor Gros Espiell, *Esquema de la evolución constitucional del Uruguay*; Juan E. Pivel Devoto, *Historia de los partidos políticos en el Uruguay*; Washington Reyes Abadie, ed., *Crónica de Aparicio Saravia*; Juan A. Oddone, *La formación del Uruguay moderno: la inmigración y el desarrollo económico-social*.

2

Anarchism, Socialism, Revolutionary Nationalism: The Impact of the Mexican and Russian Revolutions

In Mexico, in 1910, the issue of Díaz's reelection came up again, despite all denials. Now the uneasiness among the middle classes led many to seek an alternative in General Bernardo Reyes, governor of Nuevo León. Further to the left, the anarchists, together with other people of varied ideological composition, basically heirs to the radical liberalism of the Juárez years, formed a Partido Liberal Mexicano (1906). This was very strange behavior for the libertarian current, of which Ricardo Flores Magón, in and out of jail and in exile in the United States, was the principal mentor. In fact, he belonged to a second generation of anarchists. The first one had been based among Mexico City artisans, along Proudhonian moderate lines. The new generation, formed toward the end of the century, was more violent, following international trends.[1]

In contrast with other countries like Argentina or Brazil, Mexican anarchists were not confined to foreign-born European groups, but had a strong local presence. These anarchists had been very active in 1906 in a strike at the huge copper mine of Cananea, an explosive working-class concentration in the extreme northwest, near the American border, where anticapitalist sentiments were mixed with anti-Yankee feelings. Later on, in 1907 and 1908, there was a wave of labor unrest in the textile centers of Veracruz state, situated in the industrial enclave of Orizaba, where a famous strike at the Río Blanco mill was severely repressed.[2]

Given these destabilizing forces, and the economic problems caused by the fall of silver prices, it was imperative in 1910 to appeal to Porfirio Díaz's patriotic sentiments and demand the supreme sacrifice of continuing at the rudder of a ship facing very stormy weather. Now, social conflict, ever more violent, was being compounded with regionalist dissidents like Bernardo Reyes, and the more ideological Francisco Madero, from a very wealthy Coahuila family in the northeast. The regime was able to thwart Reyes, sending him to a gilded exile as ambassador to France, but with Madero this strategy did not work. When he proclaimed his candidacy with the Partido Antirreleccionista, things started tumbling down, despite the sure manipulation of the ballot boxes which was the norm. Madero, after the trumped-up results were known, issued a revolutionary proclamation, and gathered some armed forces near the North American border.

The Revolution in Mexico

Surprisingly enough, the anarchists joined the cause of this progressive bourgeois, a fact to be taken into account also for the interpretation of other phenomena on the continent. Admittedly, there was a more principled sector of anarchists who refused such an alliance, and attempted a movement of their own, invading with very little success Baja California from exile in the United States. But the bulk of militants joined the "petty bourgeoisie," sure that once the shooting started it was impossible to foresee the consequences. The opposite argument, of course, was that if the anarchists became excessively involved they might become entangled in a political process with little resemblance to their original ideas.[3]

The social tensions predominant in Mexican society, especially in the numerous mining enclaves (copper and silver) and in the sugar areas around Cuernavaca, as well as in the textile centers in various parts of the country, facilitated the spread of revolutionary appeal, determining the downfall of Díaz, and later a very intensive and destructive civil war among the revolutionary factions. Under those circumstances, leadership was to a large degree of a military nature, not because it was based on career officers, but rather on people of the most varied origins who became leaders of irregular forces, like Álvaro Obregón and Plutarco Elías Calles.

The early spark of the armed rebellion, ignited by Madero, was concentrated along the northern border, from where supplies could come. The United States government took a position of neutrality, but in practice was prepared to scuttle Díaz, whose support of British rather than American oil companies, and dealings with the Japanese for a naval base in Baja California, were very irritating.

The regime was eroded from within, and it was incapable of organizing a determined fight to wipe out the rebel focus. Soon Díaz was convinced to abandon the country, and after an interim government, new elections duly set up Madero in the Palace. The armed struggle had been limited, mostly to the North, while in a few areas where Indian communities had been dispossessed by encroaching haciendas (especially in sugar-producing Cuernavaca) local rebellions also spread, in this case led by Indian smallholder Emiliano Zapata.

Madero had difficulty in containing the various forces which had converged in his support, trying to make concessions, advancing from his extremely moderate original platform, which was centered on the banning of reelection. He now included land redistribution, but only when concrete legal abuses by latifundistas could be proved. Agitation spread like wildfire, and the reaction from the Right was soon organized. Finally, in 1913, a coup by General Victoriano de la Huerta, after ten days of bombing and shooting in the capital city—the "Decena Trágica"—deposed Madero. A few days afterwards he was assassinated in jail, under the infamous "ley de fuga," which allowed the police to shoot prisoners who allegedly attempted to escape.

This generated an uproar, and resistance spread throughout the land. From the northeast ex- governor Venustiano Carranza, calling himself *Primer Jefe* of the Constitucionalista army, rallied moderate opinion and quite a few resources. In the center-north, cattle and horse dealer Pancho Villa led irregular bands, heading south. In the northwest, mostly in Sonora, Obregón and Calles abandoned their middle-class civilian pursuits to become military leaders. From the south, Zapata and his Indian followers converged on the capital city. Chaos ensued for several years. De la Huerta was soon deposed, but internecine fighting among the rebel armies continued. The anarchists who had created a central union organization named Casa del Obrero Mundial now formed red battalions, but surprisingly, in the factional fight, joined Venustiano Carranza against the agrarian rebels of Emiliano Zapata, disparaged because their religious superstition made them go to battle only if protected by numerous images and badges of the Virgin of Guadalupe.[4]

Finally, a Constitutional Convention was convened in 1917, establishing the right of workers to organize into unions, of peasants to own their lands, and, of course, prohibiting presidential reelection. Carranza was accepted as chief executive, up to 1920. At the moment of his succession, his attempt to remain in power generated a quick reaction, and his own death while fleeing. The new president was Alvaro Obregón, while both Villa and the Zapatistas remained somewhat shunted aside from the centers of power.

In those days, the political party spectrum was very complex and shifting, with intense regional variations, in part a reflection of the predominance of armed factions. During Obregón's administration (1920-1924) his support was called the Partido Liberal Constitucionalista, which purported to represent the early, moderate reformist mentality of Francisco Madero. The party, becoming excessively independent from its new mentor, proposed in 1921 the adoption of a parliamentary regime, which did not endear it to the chief executive. Obregón then joined forces with a Partido Cooperativista, bent on more radical changes. This party became a majority in Congress, but when the succession was launched, it made the mistake of not supporting the official candidate, Calles, which led to its early demise and dissolution.[5]

The new president, Calles, then, giving new life to the progressive program, surrounded himself with people from a Partido Laborista, where Luis Morones and other erstwhile anarchist union leaders converted to pragmatism were active.

Meanwhile, violence was returning to the land. Since 1926 there had been a break between Calles and the Catholics. To confront a spate of anticlerical measures, the Church opted for a suspension of religious services throughout the country, obviously seeking to inflame its flock and prepare for armed resistance. This measure was particularly effective in Jalisco and Michoacán, where a rural and small-town "ranchero" middle class was quite strong, and extremely religious. Agrarian redistributive pressure was often directed against them, in order not to antagonize excessively the large and still powerful landowners.

Armed rebellion did take place, igniting a prolonged and extremely destructive and cruel civil war, which only ended in 1929, through the intervention of the Pope and American Catholics. The Cristero war, as it was called, reproduced the scenes of the Vendée of the French Revolution, classical in its violence and for demonstrating the strong roots of conservative and antirrevolutionry ideas.

In defense of their traditional mode of life, the middle peasants were prepared to ally themselves with anybody who would help against the government. Thus the bases were laid for a strong current of popular conservatism in some areas of traditional Mexican society, which again manifested itself during the Second World War in the Sinarquismo—a more urban party—and in the Partido de Acción Nacional (PAN), founded in 1944, including not only rightist Catholic and pro-fascist elements, but also the remaining moderates of the early times of the revolution.[6]

One of the more prestigious intellectuals who joined this cause was José Vasconcelos, who had had a distinguished role in the educational policy of Obregón, and who moved towards a moderate version of liberalism, and then towards fascism, interpreted as a form of "developmental dictatorship," deemed imperative for countries at the stage of evolution of Mexico.

But to go back to the narrative: in 1928 Obregón, always a powerful, almost mythical revolutionary figure, presented himself for reelection, which after one intervening period was then legal (it was banned later through a constitutional amendment). The Laboristas, as their predecessors the Cooperativistas, again made a mistake and opposed Obregón, who nevertheless won his return to the presidential chair, but Destiny would not have it. A bullet from a Catholic fanatic, incensed by the Cristero massacres, killed him, causing a power vacuum which could only be filled by Calles, who was finishing his term in office and thus could not be reelected immediately.[7]

Under the circumstances, Calles passed from being a subordinate of Obregón, to become the self-proclaimed Jefe Máximo de la Revolución. He remained a power behind the throne, manipulating things so that the presidential position (now extended from four to six years) was held by three different nonentities under provisional arrangements. This time was appropriately called the Maximato (1928-1934).

To secure his control, Calles created what up to then had been astonishingly absent from this revolutionary experience: a single revolutionary party, single at least in the sense of unifying all favorable forces. The new party, calling itself first Partido de la Revolución Mexicana, changed its name twice, ending up as the Partido Revolucionario Institucional (PRI), which was dominant up to the end of the twentieth century, its fate being for the first time put in jeopardy in the July 2000 elections.

The PRI, as quintessential to the Mexican regime as the Communist Party was to the Soviet Union, was much slower in its growth and consolidation. It was never legally a single party, but the use and abuse of power made challenges ineffectual, both from the conservative PAN and from the sectarian Left. In the PRI, the various preexisting factions were incorporated, including the main trade union and peasant confederations. Hence the semi-corporatist organization of the party, which had at its beginning three branches: labor, peasantry, and military. Soon reality forced it to create a fourth branch, the "popular" one, whose name hid the fact that it was made up of the least popular members, that is, bureaucrats, careerists, and new entrepreneurs who were profiting from the rather corrupt regime. Economic growth was, in any case, quite strong, especially since the thirties, reaching during the seventies Asian Tiger levels, only to stagnate later on.

The PRI was based on a wide multi-class coalition, wherein the most dynamic forces of Mexican society could be found. True enough, on election day the ballot boxes seldom reflected the truth. In outlying rural areas the usual practice, given the absence of opposition representation at the polling stations, was to mark the non-voters as having come, and, of course, voted in the correct way. Given widespread land distribution, protection of labor rights, and unionization, most probably the PRI did have popular support, and it would have gained a majority even if ballots had been honestly counted. But in that case its weaknesses might have been revealed, for example in low voter turnout, or occasional victories of an opposition deemed to be scarcely loyal. More serious than distortion of electoral results was the heavy hand used against serious opponents, especially among the popular classes, which cast doubts about the prevalence of human rights, except among a privileged minority living in Mexico City.[8]

However, despite these and other dark spots, the PRI remained for long the paradigm of a party of multiclass national integration, nominally and often in practice oriented towards radical social change, as under Lázaro Cárdenas's presidency (1934-1940), when foreign oil companies were expropriated and land distribution achieved its maximum momentum. Such parties are typically formed as a result of social revolution or of an anticolonial struggle, representing on one hand the main pro-change forces, and on the other the new elites that benefit from the altered circumstances. From this perspective, the PRI is in a class—allowing for different social contexts—with the ruling Communist parties from Western Europe to China, including Castro's Cuba, and with the national revolutionary structures at the helm in many Arab and African countries, as well as India's Congress Party.[9]

The Impact in Peru: Aprismo and Mariátegui's Version of Marxism

The impact of the Mexican Revolution was particularly intense on the young student leader Víctor Raúl Haya de la Torre, who, expelled from Peru by a dictatorial government, arrived in Mexico, on his way to complete his training in Europe, in 1924. It was the end of Obregón's presidency, with Vasconcelos spreading the gospel of culture from the Ministry of Education, and a vast array of economic, social, and cultural initiatives. It seemed that finally Latin Americans had found the right autochthonous formula, based on the struggle of the masses, rather than on the intellectual elites' tendency to follow uncritically European models of a liberal or a socialist hue. Now it was possible to emulate, on the rest of the continent, a model generated in the region. Besides, Peru's social structure was quite similar to that of Mexico, even if with less economic development, and a somewhat less violent history.

Haya formed in Mexico the Alianza Popular Revolucionaria Americana (APRA), as an ideological nucleus and basis for the launching of a new International, competitive with the more rigid Second (social democratic) and Third (communist). The new movement would base itself on a multiclass alliance with worker and peasant support but, given the weakness of these classes, under the leadership of a third component, the middle strata. These, in Latin America, were mostly part of the dispossessed and exploited majority, and not a support of the existing order, as in Europe. Thus, at least, Haya saw their role, and continued to expand his ideas in a series of books from the thirties, when he was able to return to Peru to organize the local section of the Apra, the Partido del Pueblo, taking advantage of a brief interlude of democracy.[10]

Haya's thought shows the strong impact of Marxism, melded with social democratic and Fabian elements absorbed while he was a student at Oxford, and he didn't miss an opportunity to attend the debates of the House of Commons, watching the incredible verbal fencing of the leaders of the only parliament which actually functioned in the world. Influenced by the eclectic intellectual climate of England, he claimed, polemically against Leninism, that even if in developed nations one could think of a revolutionary party of the proletariat, that was impossible in regions scarcely touched by industrialism.

Could it be said, then, that the order of the day was a "bourgeois revolution"? Not exactly, because the bourgeoisie, excessively submissive to imperialism, did not have the clout to take power on its own. What was imperative was to create a new political instrument, equivalent to the one that had been forged by Lenin, but under different conditions. An alliance of the downtrodden masses, under the leadership of the middle classes, could come to control the state, and from there launch a program of economic growth and social change, including, as in Mexico, land reform, industrialization, and social welfare.

The economic program, however, in Haya's view, had to take a page from Marx's classical analyses, or even from Lenin's early works, like *The Development of Capitalism in Russia*, rather than from the practice of the Soviet leader. These theoretical texts asserted that in the absence of intense capitalist growth it was impossible to establish socialism, so that only a bourgeois revolution was on the agenda. But the bourgeoisie, in countries of the periphery, was not capable of coming to power on its own, and feared agitating the masses. That is why Lenin stressed that their work had to be done for them, but at a price, which in the Soviet experience turned out to be confiscatory.

The socialist elite, which for Lenin should form the leadership of a party of "professional revolutionaries," recruited among whichever social milieux, would exert power in a transitory manner, without becoming a new class, putting the private entrepreneurs to work at what they knew, that is, the production of goods and services. They would continue to be the owners, thus retaining a lot of social influence, but would be shorn of political power. History showed that this delicate equilibrium was not achieved in the Soviet Union, and finally the bourgeoisie had its assets expropriated, while the revolutionary party became, in a manner not predicted by the theory, the kernel of a new dominant class, the state bureaucracy.

For Haya, a more explicit alliance had to be formed, including the middle class, though not the bourgeoisie, which was far too implicated in the status quo. The whole should be welded together through a powerful state apparatus. In order to accelerate economic development it was necessary to enroll the collaboration of foreign capitalists, who certainly could not be cajoled into working under duress. Admittedly, Haya used to say that the international plutocrats have as much need to invest abroad as the countries of the periphery have of receiving their resources. To come to an understanding with such powerful gentlemen would not be easy, of course, and Haya took on that task through his own political skills and his followers.[11]

Haya posited the need for what he called the "state of the four powers," as an instrument in making different social groups cooperate, even if conflictually, in a common effort. The Fourth Power would be economic, expressing itself through a corporative body, with "qualitative" representation of capital and labor, including sectors of the intelligentsia, or institutions like the armed forces, without excluding foreign capital. It was better to have them inside than plotting outside, he thought, and thus control the influence which they would exert in any case. In a sense, with this entity the absence of an electorally significant conservative party was compensated for. The trade unions were of course also given an assured number of delegates, apart from those they could garner through the popular political parties, and surely more pragmatically oriented.

José Carlos Mariátegui, the Marxist thinker who died at an early age in 1930, developed an alternative set of ideas, at the beginning in cooperation with Haya, and then in opposition to him. Mariátegui emphasized the central role of the Indians in the future changes Peru could envision, and in turn the Indian problem depended on the solution given to the property structure in land. In his *Siete ensayos de interpretación de la realidad peruana* (1928) he stated his position, which diverged from that of other Marxists, who believed that such an exploited and downtrodden population could not become the basis for a successful revolt in the absence of a previous vigorous capitalist development. Mariátegui, straying quite far from the generally accepted doctrines, believed that under the leadership of a dedicated elite, strongly imbued with a set of values, even fanatical in its convictions, revolutionary changes could be brought about. He added that the habits of social cooperation the Indians had inherited from the time of the Incas, and maintained in their surviving landholding communities, would help the transition to a socialist society.[12]

The Socialist Party he worked toward setting up at the end of the twenties joined, under his prodding, the Third International, and after his death (1930) changed its name to Communist. But in this party for long the orthodox followers of Soviet dictates branded him a "populist," displacing him from the pantheon of revered masters. The fact that he freely used George Sorel's ideas, as a basis for a voluntaristic interpretation of history, did not help.[13]

Both Haya de la Torre and Mariátegui founded what became political religions in Peru, creating social forces whose strength depended on their capacity to generate messianic collective feelings. This had little to do with the social democratic or the Leninist ideas they were predicated on. On the other hand, when Haya criticized the Latin American Marxists for their espousal of a revolution based only on the working class he was missing his aim. In fact, his observations applied more to the social democrats than to the Communists, as the latter based their work on the formation of a disciplined elite, with methods and experiences quite alien to Karl Marx's theoretical arsenal. Haya in effect coincided with them in realizing the urgency of that task, though he never succeeded in forming such a tightly knit group. He added—in this, coinciding with Mariátegui—the need to create a mystique, but he did it his own way, through a personality cult of which he himself was the object, a mutation of the traditional role of the *caudillo* in the region, and foreign to Mariátegui's ideas.

In Bolivia and Paraguay Flammable Materials Accumulate

In Bolivia the Conservative/Liberal alternation which had been typical of the cycle of silver and the beginnings of the era of tin mining (1880-1920), with only one violent interruption—the Federal Revolution of 1899—came to an end in 1920. That year the grievances of dissident liberal circles, organized rather recently in the Republican Party, were channeled through the barracks. The military, in any case, was still reticent to assume political power openly, so they immediately transferred it to the Republicans. From the internal struggle within this new group Bautista Saavedra emerged victorious (1921-1925), at the head of a sector his rivals dubbed "personalista," equating it with Yrigoyen's fraction of the Radical Party in Argentina. His main adversary, Daniel Salamanca, formed a "Genuino" sector, more oriented towards traditional legalism and free trade. So the bipolarity which had started as Conservative/Liberal, and was later replaced by a Liberal/Republican one, now took the form of two fractions of the same Republican Party opposed to one another.

Saavedra started a program of social reform, with popular support, particularly among the artisan "cholos," (mixed bloods) confronting the upper classes, and organized his followers in a militia under the name of Guardia Republicana. In the very important mining areas trade union organization began in earnest, made easier by the great masses of manpower which could be found there. The Left had some influence among the working class, and it created several short-lived socialist parties. Near Oruro a mining union federation was established, which launched a general strike in 1923, harshly repressed in an episode which degenerated into a massacre. Saavedra made up for this with other progressive measures, applied in the urban sector, where most of his partisans could be found.

Saavedra tried unsuccessfully to remain in power at the end of his mandate, but he was deposed, and after an interval replaced by his erstwhile heir apparent Hernán Siles Reyes (1926-1930). Siles started a new Partido Nacionalista, with a reformist youth full of socialist ideas, many of whom would later form the leadership of the Movimiento Nacionalista Revolucionario (MNR), among them Enrique Baldivieso, Augusto Céspedes, Carlos Montenegro, and Víctor Paz Estenssoro.

Further to the left were the Moscow-oriented Partido de Izquierda Revolucionaria (PIR), and the Trotskyite Partido Obrero Revolucionario (POR), started in exile in Argentina. In a Third National Labor Congress in Oruro the usual struggles between anarchists and Communists had priority over other matters. Also at this time there was an important Aprista influence, and a great impact of books by Mariátegui and by the Argentine socialist José Ingenieros. In general, the diffusion of Marxist ideas and trade union experience was much more widespread in Bolivia than what might have been expected given its marked underdevelopment.[14]

This was not the case of Paraguay, where social tensions were less evident, and trade unionism extremely weak. With some interruptions, Liberal party hegemony, initiated in 1904, maintained itself up to the end of the War of the Chaco (1932-1935) which pitted this country against Bolivia for control of oilfields situated in the ill-defined hinterland between their settled areas. The war broke out during the presidency of Eusebio Ayala (1932-1936), who took the opportunity to unify the various Liberal factions, and tried to establish a dialogue with the Colorados. But this internal peace would not survive the tragedies of the war, one of the few that was lost by both sides, or so their public opinions claimed in order to demand punishment of the responsible political elites. Neither Bolivia nor Paraguay would ever be the same.[15]

The Difficult Cuban Apprenticeship

In Cuba, the government of order and progress of Estrada Palma (1902-1906) faced a crisis toward the end of his administration, discovering the dire need to remain in power, for which purpose he formed the Partido Moderado, and started harassing the opposition. The abuses accompanying his reelection provoked an armed uprising of the Liberal Party, more solidly based on membership quite experienced in the anti-Spanish struggle. The situation was very delicate, because, to quote Secretary of War William Taft, in less than ten days 200,000,000 dollars worth of American property could go up in flames.[16]

To stem the almost sure victory of the rebels, who might ignite a broad social revolution beyond their intentions (as happened a few years later under similar circumstances in Mexico), the United States decided to intervene, under the provisions of the Platt Amendment, and occupied the island for a further three years (1906-1909). The presidential elections of 1908 were won by José Miguel Gómez (1909-1913), a hero of the War of Independence, and leader of the Liberal Party, or more precisely of its "miguelista" wing, with much sympathy among the black population. During his time he had to confront, however, a rebellion by the Partido Independiente de Color, founded in 1909, one of the few in Latin America explicitly describing itself as ethnically based. That party had been banned in 1910 under a law expressly prohibiting such appeals, due to their potential role in stimulating a "guerra de colores." The Partido Independiente de Color also menaced the bases of support of the Liberals among the lower strata. The repression was very violent, costing some 3,000 lives.

At the end of Gómez's term American influence dissuaded him from seeking reelection, and in a relatively free competition the oppositional Conservative Party came to office, with its candidate Mario Menocal. In his own case, he got away with being reelected (1916), which was constitutionally permitted, though frowned upon. But in order to accomplish his maneuver he had to overcome an armed Liberal insurrection, which for the moment seemed to overwhelm the country, provoking partial American interventions.[17]

During the twenties, both Aprismo and Communism were widely diffused among Cuban intellectuals, and trade unionism took root, with the formation of national federations of railwaymen, sugar workers, and cigar makers, federated into the Communist-influenced Confederación Nacional Obrera de Cuba

(CNOC). National politics was particularly corrupt, and the usual alternation between Liberals and Conservatives found little enthusiasm among the new generations coming out of the universities, in many cases from downwardly mobile upper classes dislodged by new large-scale and more modern American investors. The sugar industry had had its moment of glory during the First World War and its aftermath, with prices of up to twenty-two cents a pound in 1922, dipping catastrophically that same year to a paltry four cents.[18]

In 1920, Menocal tried to be reelected a second time, but this was too much for his American tutors, who forced an alternation. Moreover, there was the fact that public opinion signaled Liberalism as a sure winner. Menocal, however, grabbed the opportunity created by a splinter group of the Liberal Party, led by Alfredo Zayas, calling itself the Partido Popular Cubano (PPC). Immediately Menocal decided to support Zayas, with the understood proviso of a return of the favor after four years. For Zayas this was easily conceded, as in Cuba four years was equivalent to infinity. The ploy succeeded, and thus Conservative influence was perpetuated under Liberal garb.

The trouble was that the United States pretended to moralize Cuban politics, which was strange, since they didn't do the same with their own Southern states. The fact is that, as Secretary of State Bainbridge Colby said, "free and honest elections are essential for the maintenance of a government attuned to the defense of life, property and individual freedoms." In other words, free elections were a guarantee against armed insurrection, with its attendant disasters.[19]

The influence of Uncle Sam forced Zayas to form a so-called "honest cabinet," but soon enough the island's habits overwhelmed any puritan intentions its mentors may have had. Anyway, the persistent pressure forced free competitive elections in 1924, which were won by Gustavo Machado, a Liberal businessman who had made a fortune after participating in the War of Independence. Apparently, relatively peaceful party alternation in office was taking root. Machado started a program of social reforms, but the recurring crisis of the sugar economy would push him towards new political schemes of an authoritarian bent.

Central America: Sandino's Saga

Another country where the influence of the Mexican Revolution was strongly felt, combined with Aprista and Marxist ideas, was Nicaragua. During the twenties, a nineteenth-century-type civil war was raging between Conservatives and Liberals, as though taken directly from García Márquez's *Cien Años de Soledad*. Among the irregular sectors of the Liberal forces was Augusto César Sandino, a peasant of relatively comfortable, though extramarital, origins. As a young man, he was forced to migrate to several places in Central America, finally reaching the Gulf oil regions of Mexico. He returned bearing with him the images of the Revolution, as Haya de la Torre had, though interpreting them at a less sophisticated intellectual level.

Sandino was able to recruit a strong armed following, acting under very traditional and primitive conditions, and little ideological concern for most of its members. When the leader of the Liberal insurrection came to an agreement with his Conservative opponent, in 1927, Sandino refused to lay down arms and continued the fight, with a more radicalized program, though unable to form a permanent political party.

The Nicaraguan civil war had caused the intervention of American Marines, who had to confront Sandino in a civil war of national proportions. When, in 1933, after a new political pact giving power to the erstwhile rebellious Liberals, foreign troops withdrew, Sandino considered his aims partially fulfilled, and returned to civilian life, determined to cooperate in democratic reconstruction with the chief of the Guardia Nacional, Anastasio Somoza. Cooperation did not last long, and the following year Sandino was assassinated in an ambush, while the regime veered towards a more repressive pattern. Many decades later, new protest movements would use Sandino's name and some of his ideas, though in a very different social context.[20]

In the rest of Central America the twenties didn't bring much novelty. In Guatemala the dictatorship of Estrada Cabrera ended with an army coup in 1920, and a brief stretch of Conservative/Liberal alternation was inaugurated, till in 1931 General Jorge Ubico assumed power in a more authoritarian way, in the trail of Barrios and Estrada. In Honduras, the alternation between Nationals (i.e., conservatives) and Liberals was replaced by the long tyranny of Tiburcio Carias Andino, a man of humble origins who, in association with the National Party, and with the support of the United Fruit Company, tried to imitate other authoritarian regimes in the region, and was at the helm from 1932 to 1948. In El Salvador, coffee produced times of prosperity for the middle and upper classes, together with disruption and displacement of small-scale producers, also affected by the high demographic pressure. The crisis of the early thirties would add to this process, generating in 1932 a peasant rebellion with the participation of the Communist Party, to which we will return.

The Divergent Paths of Venezuela and Colombia

In Venezuela, Cipriano Castro transferred power to Juan Vicente Gómez (1908-1935), another member of the "Andean Dynasty," who initiated a long regime of stark repression, centralization, and economic development, made more dynamic by the growth of the oil industry during the twenties. Towards the latter part of his many years in office, in 1928, a student rebellion broke out, under the leadership of a group of Marxist intellectuals and students, among them Rómulo Betancourt and the Communist Party leader Gustavo Machado. Betancourt was forced into exile in Costa Rica, where he joined the local Communist Party, which was quite independent from Moscow dictates. He would later be one of the founders of Acción Democrática (born in 1937 with the name of Partido Democrático Nacional), with ideas and internal organization quite similar to those of the Peruvian APRA, even if adapted to a country with greater ethnic homogeneity and higher economic and educational development.[21]

In Colombia, the Conservative/Liberal polarity was classical, and after the Guerra de los Mil Días (1899-1902), it reasserted itself in a more peaceful fashion, under Conservative hegemony. Liberalism, trying to renew itself, considered during the twenties the need to adopt "social," eventually socialist ideas, or at least to embrace programs of social reform and labor rights. On its side, Conservatism consolidated its ideological Catholic roots, along the lines of the papal encyclical *Quadragessimo anno* (1931). Among independent youth sectors, socialist ideas were also being adopted, as reflected in the doctorate thesis of Jorge Eliécer Gaitán, *Las ideas socialistas en Colombia*, of 1924.

Gaitán oscillated for long, together with many of the members of his generation, between independent Socialist activity and infiltration into the receptive Liberal Party. The Aprista alternative also offered itself, which was one of the models Gaitán tried to emulate when he split the Liberal Party in 1946 to form his own organization, under strong personalized and charismatic leadership, though remaining as a wing of the old party. Colombia, in any case, did not offer conditions favorable to an Aprista experience, due to its lack of large rural or mining working-class concentrations, except to some extent among the coastal banana workers. Even the main cities were more evenly distributed in population than in other countries, so that a sizeable and organizable proletariat had not yet appeared.[22]

Ideological Mutations in Brazil: Nationalism and *Tenentismo*

In Brazil, the ideological influences from other parts of the continent were not very marked. Single-party Republican hegemony continued, with the main exceptions of Sao Paulo and Rio Grande do Sul, where a certain diversity existed. In Sao Paulo the domination of the Partido Republicano Paulista was mildly challenged by the Partido Democrático, a sort of progressive Liberalism of heterogeneous composition. Rio Grande do Sul, with a social structure more similar to that of Uruguay, and therefore more prone to party competition than the rest of Brazil, had long experience of violent republican struggles against the Empire, and of internal discords. Now, the Partido Republicano Riograndense, of positivist and quite authoritarian convictions, was confronted with a more popular and federalist Partido Libertador.[23]

In the rest of the country there was a notable absence of middle-class moderate reform parties along the lines of the Chilean and Argentine Radicales, or the Peruvian Apristas. This was a consequence of the political weakness of the middle strata, and of the deflection of political passions via regionalist conflicts, which let steam off a more class-based confrontation. The single-party regimes dominant in each state actually hid a nationwide bipolarity between a coalition centered on Sao Paulo, and another one based on Minas Gerais, both with shifting membership and strategies, but coexisting through the "café com leite" arrangement of rotating the presidency between the two major states. Among younger sectors, especially among professional classes and the armed forces, this system was becoming increasingly discredited.

Typically, the agitation for some changes was felt principally among army junior officers, in what came to be called *tenentismo*. An uprising in 1922 in Rio de Janeiro was immediately crushed, with several people killed. More complex was a similar event in 1924, based in Sao Paulo and Rio Grande do Sul. The rebels controlled São Paulo for a few days, establishing contacts with some working-class groups, but soon the central authorities hit back and the rebels had to escape towards the deep interior of the country. They formed what came to be known as the "Prestes Column," after the name of its main leader. A few hundreds strong, for three years they roamed various parts of Brazil, always persecuted, and aiming not so much at starting a massive revolt, which was unthinkable, but at least to arouse the moral conscience of the nation.[24]

The ideas under which they operated were extremely heterogeneous, and quite contradictory. They formed a strange combination of liberal democratic conceptions with others of an authoritarian or Mussolinian cast, the latter interpreted as "developmental dictatorship," that is, more or less as a later generation viewed Nasserism. Given the difficulty of forming competitive and efficient political parties in a country of the periphery, it was believed that an element of authoritarianism was necessary, as well as a more genuine representation via corporativism. Political parties, under Brazilian conditions, could only lead to the domination of the local feudal clans, through their vast clientelistic connections, capable of giving them a trumped-up congressional majority. So it was better to use the "qualitative" corporatist structures of representation, because even the universal vote simply hid the hegemony of the landed oligarchy. Under corporatism, not only the influence of the local landed elites was to be eliminated, also the danger of appeal to the masses by demagogic politicians would be arrested.

Ideas of this type had already been developed by Alberto Torres, a writer and practical politician of liberal convictions, who was governor of the state of Rio de Janeiro (1898-1900), and remained very active during the first two decades of the century. In his case, a fascist influence could not be argued, and his general attitude was that of liberal constitutionalism, and also clearly antiracist, a minority position among the Brazilian elites.[25]

His disciple Francisco José Oliveira Vianna would re-elaborate these concepts, in his case from a clearly authoritarian and supposedly scientific racist perspective. In his early *Populações meridionais do Brasil* (1920) he diagnosed the social setting allowing the persistent power of the local, falsely liberal oligarchical elites. At the same time, Oliveira Vianna argued that the agricultural working population provided a basically docile mass, which in principle secured social peace, but only if its manipulation by feuding local elites could be avoided. And this could only be done by a strong central government. Somewhat different was the situation among the more aggressive mounted *gaúchos* of the south, and the *sertanejos* of the arid northwest, easily recruited into the hosts of civil wars.[26]

The ideas of Torres and Oliveira Vianna were already having an impact on wide sectors of the reading public, including the armed forces, during the twenties. Later on, during the thirties, their prestige increased, their works were reprinted, and other writers followed in their footsteps, providing the basis for legitimation of Vargas's Estado Novo established in 1937.

Chile between Alessandri and Ibáñez: First Round

In Chile, the Conservative/Liberal set was already enlarged to include Radicalism and Socialism, and therefore there was less space—or need—for an Aprista party, or a multi-class integrative one along Mexican lines. Political structures were more clearly linked to social classes, particularly among their leadership and activist elements.

Chile was, in its central region, a small Mediterranean Europe, and in the south a wool-producing and also mining Australia, while in the north there were more typically Latin American mining enclaves (not that these could not be found also in the Old Continent, especially in coal). Early anarchism, socialism, and its intermediate forms, like revolutionary syndicalism of French Sorelian roots, became, under Chilean conditions, especially in the northern and southern extremes, very confrontational. A widespread series of strikes marked the early years of the century, and they were violently repressed, notably in the famous massacre at the Santa María school in Iquique, where thousands of miners had taken refuge after deserting their nitrate fields up in the mountains (1907).

In 1912, typographer and journalist Luis Emilio Recabarren, abandoning a long militancy in the Democratic Party, had founded the Partido Socialista Obrero, very closely linked to the main trade union organization. The party, in any case, took a lot of time before it had a significant presence at the polls, though when it finally reached that stage, in the early thirties, it retained it. Its two successor formations, the Socialists and the Communists, as often bickering as in alliance, usually encompassed about a third of the electorate.[27]

Before that happened, the popular mass followed, during the twenties, the banners of Arturo Alessandri, from a progressive sector of the Liberals, who in association with the Radicals and the Democrats won the presidency in 1920. The Lion of Tarapacá—as he was called—enjoyed a solid popularity, which was not diminished by his calling his followers "mi querida chusma" (my dear rabble). Among his projects there was a Labor Code and a set of social security measures intended to put the country at the level of the more advanced societies of its time. He also wanted to create, through a changed constitution, a strong executive, to replace the rudderless and shifting governing coalitions of the República Parlamentaria inagurated after the overthrow of Balmaceda in 1891.

The Chilean Parliamentary experience competes with the French Third and Fourth Republics as an epitome of weak government and endless making and unmaking of coalitions. Without falling into an authoritarian alternative—as was being explored in Brazil by the *tenentes* and later by Vargas—Alessandri emphasized the need to strengthen the Presidency in order to create a firm governing structure and incorporate a dose of state prodding if the economy was to pass from its agrarian to an industrial phase. He encountered the solid resistance of traditional Conservatives and of the majority of his own Liberal Party, as could be expected. Also the Socialist left mistrusted him, fearing an excessive intervention into trade union affairs.[28]

In 1924 an interruption of the constitutional process took place, as a result of uneasiness among the armed forces, in a complex process in which two sectors of the military converged. One, mostly of high-ranking officers, wished to control what it considered demagogic excesses of the president, and also to increase their own salaries. The other sector, including Carlos Ibáñez, Marmaduke Grove, and more junior comrades, by contrast, wanted to put into effect Alessandri's social reforms, but without his agitational side. Ideologically, they were as eclectic as Brazil's *tenentes*.

Ibáñez, inspired by the Mussolinian example, soon emerged at the top during the military interregnum, displacing his rival Grove. He strongly repressed the Marxist working-class movement, and tried to co-opt other unions or create new ones, as well as launching a political force which disclaimed the name of "party," the Unión Social Republicana de Asalariados de Chile (USRACH) so as to get legitimacy through the ballot box. In a different sort of country, he could have become an early Vargas or a Perón, but it didn't happen. With the impact of the world economic crisis, he lost credibility and was deposed in 1931 through a reaction from both right and left, as well as center.[29]

Nothing remained of Ibáñez's attempt at creating a new authoritarian popular party. A provisional junta took over, seeing to the holding of elections, but a strange phenomenon then occurred, revealing the intensity of social tensions under the surface. A sector of the marines rebelled, and together with other armed forces, some of Ibañista loyalty, declared a Socialist Republic, which lasted a few weeks, and tried to put much of the nation's private property in the hands of the government. This was enough to convert most of the dominant classes to the rule of law as understood in the capitalist West. A moderate sector of the Socialist Republic leaders took over, and convened elections, which saw a tug of war between the Left, now led by Grove, who had been adopted by a reborn Socialist Party, and a Right, headed by the now toothless Lion of Tarapacá, who won the contest anyway. The Radicals were divided, and soon went into opposition.

The second presidency of Arturo Alessandri (1932-1938) saw the consolidation of the two-pronged Conservative/Liberal Right. On the left, the old Partido Socialista of Recabarren had converted to Communism in the early twenties. After going underground during the dictatorship it reemerged, though shorn of several of its components, which formed a new Socialist Party, with many nationalist and Aprista currents, and a military man, Grove, as its leader. There was a notable absence of social democratic theoreticians, though the Socialists' practice was quite moderate, and often starkly anticommunist.[30]

Political Evolution in Argentina: The Radical Party

If Chile had Australian elements in its south, Argentina was, directly, an Italian Australia, or could have become one with a bit more luck. The difference lay, among other things, in that immigrants to Australia came all, at one time, from the most industrially advanced country in the world, and did not lose their nationality when landing. The transition to independence was very gradual, and was undertaken under the control of British institutions. The transference of population, even if transoceanic, was more like an internal migration, a mutation of the old country into a new nation.

In Argentina, masses of people also came, proportionally as many as to Australia, but without much protection apart from the one given by their consulates, which they were not prepared to abandon in exchange for the very flimsy guarantees provided by Argentine laws. On the other hand, European immigrants came with the "aristocracy of the skin," white people in a still heavily mestizo country, and they felt—and actually occupied a position—above the motley assortment of gauchos, peons and other manual workers of the local population. The immigrant could easily jump over them, and even feel the equal or the superior of a large sector of the impoverished middle classes of the interior.

It is useful here to contrast this situation with what was occurring in the United States. There, apart from the fact that the proportion of foreigners never reached more than half the Argentine figures, the vast majority of Italians and other Southern or Eastern Europeans remained in the lower rungs of the social pyramid, only a notch above the black population, which at the time of mass migration was mostly confined to the South. Not only the old Yankee middle class, but also the native working class occupied positions above the mass of newcomers. This forced them to adapt to the rules of the game as defined by the nation they were entering.

North American institutions afforded more serious guarantees than the Argentinean, and therefore the immigrants were attracted to the acquisition of citizenship, which they got in their great majority (70 percent against 3 percent in Argentina), and which was necessary in order to obtain some benefits.

Also political parties were active in recruiting, but if their Río de la Plata counterparts did not engage widely in that practice, it was not because they were less imaginative, but because the immigrants rejected their entreaties.

It is true that among the Argentine ruling class there were sectors who feared an excessive influx of new citizens, who might alter the existing political system, or introduce new revolutionary ideologies. But an inspection of the literature of the times shows that, apart from this fact, among the new communities there was a clear resistance to political incorporation, considered rhetorically a betrayal of their fatherland, and in practice a bad deal. On the other hand, local elites, even if they certainly distrusted the massive waves of new entrants, were divided as to their effects. And they certainly had no qualms about the incorporation of the more successful immigrants, who had made it into the bourgeoisie.

An added result of the situation of the foreigners in Argentina was a certain disparagement which they felt towards the country they were settling in. They did love the land, but especially if empty of natives. And this attitude was of course transmitted to a couple of generations, with the usual exception of those who overreacted and became more nationalist than the locals, as also happened in the United States. Most probably this is the source of a large literature of uprootedness and lack of identity which has been dominant for decades.

The typical situation, prevalent in countries like the United States at the time, of the native discriminating against the foreigner, was reversed in Argentina, where it was the foreigners who discriminated against the natives (except the very upper classes and some of their intellectual hangers-on, of course), that is, they discriminated what in time became the country of their own children, and their children inherited those attitudes. A Borges nightmare, indeed.

In synthesis, it can be said that the social amalgam of the foreigners with the local population was successful, because they did not experience the social discrimination their peers suffered in North America. By contrast, the political amalgam was far from unproblematic. By not taking up citizenship they weakened the representation of two social classes strategic for a process of democratic development: the urban bourgeoisie and the skilled proletariat.[31]

At the working-class level, the "Australian" traits of Argentina could have led to expect the growth of a reformist Labor movement. That is, a more solid and moderate version of the Chilean scenario. But what happened was an early anarchist presence, and the formation of a Socialist Party with weak links to its social base, which in its majority did not possess citizenship, not because anybody denied it to them, but because they preferred to opt out.[32]

A paradox was present in the ideological-party spectrum. The enormous preponderance of foreigners and their children in the prosperous part of the country caused their political preferences to be similar to those prevalent in Europe. But the "political country" was much more archaic than its productive base, and in the still quite significant interior things were quite different. When that reservoir of a more native working population came to the large cities as a result of industrialization and other push-pull factors, the transformation of the electorate inevitably had to introduce more nationalist patterns into political action.[33]

Argentine Radicalism, born in 1891 as a dissidence from the front organized by Bartolomé Mitre in the unsuccessful 1890 revolution, also had to confront a voting population which was more traditional than what could be surmised by looking at the nation's economic development. It is thus that it retained more charismatic, *caudillista,* and other old-style characteristics than its Chilean counterparts. Its incorporation into the political system was, on the other hand, more traumatic, accompanied by several attempts at armed rebellion. The transition to a more genuine democracy was the handiwork of the last ancien régime president, Roque Sáenz Peña, who, despite having come to power through the usual abuses, established secret voting, representation of minorities, and other guarantees. Of course, he thought his side could win, despite those measures, at the price of giving the opposition—Radicals and Socialists—a sizeable representation in Congress.

Sáenz Peña believed that the opposition was based on activist minorities, but that the mass of the population, especially those of the more Creole interior, formed a malleable silent majority, and would continue to vote, even under free conditions, for their hierarchical superiors. What was essential was to force them to go to the polls, and thus penalties for not voting were incorporated into the law.

It is significant that in his 1910 bid for the presidency, Sáenz Peña had already emphasized three legally binding obligations as the bases for institutional reconstruction. One was for children to undergo complete primary schooling, a traditional tenet, which to a large extent was aimed at the assimilation of the immigrant mass, so as to prevent the country from becoming a congeries of foreign enclaves which might at some future date claim independence as the Texans had done.

The second obligation was universal male military service, which sought not only to form a powerful army, but also to homogenize the immigrant communities, withdrawing their sons from the exclusively familial environment and the influence of their Old World communities, often settled in compact neighborhoods or rural areas.

The third obligation, the main novelty introduced by Sáenz Peña, was the legal requirement to vote, so as to incorporate the lower rungs of the social pyramid into the national system, overcoming apathy and regionalism.[34]

The president was introducing these reforms in a context that was quite menacing. During the early part of the century the revolutionary potential was very high, higher than a retrospective look, excessively impressed by the saga of the bountiful Pampas, would lead one to believe. True enough, Argentina was becoming one of the seven or eight richest countries of the world, in per capita terms. But meanwhile, the social tensions and the costs of the saga were quite high. For the immigrants the trauma of deracination defies the imagination, and it generated, in lean times, masses of unemployed, many of them men having come alone, without their families, easy prey to anarchist preachers, especially when they addressed them in their own languages.

An important urban mass existed, then, without nationality nor a vote, but harboring resentment and a potentially violent mood. They might easily meld with the leftist activists, or with the Radicals, continually plotting some armed insurrection. To give vent to these pressures it was advisable to loosen the safety valves, many reformist conservatives thought, opening the door so that the Radicals and the moderate Socialists would pass, leaving outside the firebrands and the unassimilable groups. It would also be convenient to facilitate the adoption of citizenship by the more prosperous immigrants, but this attempt did not succeed.[35]

It is quite probable that the Mexican example contributed to the conversion to reform of a good sector of the Argentine conservative liberal leadership. The Porfiriato was a rigid version of the Argentine so-called "unicato," that is, the dominance of the institutional system by the president. It was equally based on a positivist conception, bent on modernizing the country under strict elite control. Those elites were very powerful, but certainly not omnipotent, and thus they had to be careful. Mexico showed what could happen if adequate measures were not taken in time. Admittedly, in Argentina reelection had been outlawed by the Constitution, and nobody seriously pretended to change that provision, enacted as a reaction to the protracted rule of Juan Manuel de Rosas in the early part of the nineteenth century. However, the need to look for a new candidate every six years was a source of constant turbulence. It is also true that the standard of living was much higher than in Mexico. But it was far from obvious that social revolutions only happen in poor countries, and the widespread Marxist doctrines maintained rather the contrary.

General Julio A. Roca, the country's elder statesman, during his later years (he died in 1914) showed his concern about the Mexican example, where a sort of moderate Radical, Francisco Madero, had unleashed the tigers, and soon he was surrounded, however unwillingly, by anarchists and dispossessed Indian masses. In Argentina there was no dearth of anarchists, and instead of Indians there were European immigrants, which could be even worse from a conservative perspective. The aborted 1905 Russian revolution was there to warn carefree optimists. And the 1917 events set the prairie on fire.[36]

The fact is that Argentine conservatism had, since those days, two variants, the *aperturista* and the traditionalist. The *aperturista* was represented in 1916, when the first presidential elections under the new law were to be held, by Lisandro de la Torre, head of a newly formed Partido Demócrata Progresista.

The traditionalists were based in the rich rural areas of Buenos Aires province, where the dominant force was Marcelino Ugarte's Conservative Party. Their discords facilitated the victory of Hipólito Yrigoyen, leader of the Unión Cívica Radical, now conducted by its more "Intransigent" sector, which had dislodged the moderates led by Bernardo de Irigoyen (no relative of Hipólito).

Radicalism in power, even if in no way revolutionary, was quite mobilizational, and it appealed increasingly to mass agitation, enough to alarm the conservatives. Admittedly, these tended to sleep lightly, but the fact is that they were confronting the sudden invasion of the spheres of power by an uncouth group of upstarts with the capacity to stir the masses into action. Argentine Radicalism would have been much more moderate, and indeed stronger, if it had encompassed enough sectors of the urban bourgeoisie. But these, mostly foreigners, saw the game from the outside, marveling at what was happening in the "país político."[37]

The Uruguayan Model

In Uruguay, since the end of the nineteenth century a progressive group had been formed within the Colorado Party, led by José Battlle y Ordóñez, son of a military man who had been president of the Republic. His followers, known as Batllistas, are often considered to be the equivalents of the Yrigoyenistas on the other side of the Plata. But in fact there are many differences. If anything, they were nearer to Chile's Radicalism, though they didn't follow that model too closely either.

In some measure, Coloradismo, as a whole party, was and is nearer to the Liberals, or to Argentina's followers of Bartolomé Mitre, but with a greater capacity to keep its "radical" components inside the fold. The Colorados were part of the old regime, having been at the helm of affairs for decades, including, through some of their factions, the time of the militarist rule of Lorenzo Latorre and Máximo Santos (1876-1886). That is, they would represent, at the same time, the "régimen" and the "causa," as the Argentine Radicals called the oligarchic governments and their own movement, respectively. Batlle began his *cursus honorum* within the "régimen," fulfilling positions as that of chief of police of one of the departamentos (districts) in 1887, and afterwards became a member of the Senate and president of that body.

In 1903, during the usual succession crisis, the reformist forces got the upper hand, and Batlle was appointed president, by a Congress elected through open suffrage. The negotiations in such an elitist body are too complex to describe here, but they merit being incorporated in a world anthology of political bargaining.[38]

In fact, the Uruguayan Blanco/Colorado bipolarity hid a more basic proliferation of factions, reminiscent of the Tory/Whig setup in Great Britain. The executive was impotent before a Congress where those factions were represented, and where respect for political rivals was based on their capacity to recruit armed support for an uprising. The *coparticipation* system, established since 1872, which gave the control of some *departamentos* to those who were out of power, had as a result if not as a purpose, precisely to facilitate such uprisings, on the basis of local policemen, jail guards, and even the toughened members of fire brigades, and thus to force any government to respect the opposition.

One of the first tasks of Batlle's government was to stem a rebellion by Aparicio Saravia (the second one he commanded), which lasted several months (1903-1904) and ended with the death of its leader and several thousand victims, dead and wounded. Once militarily consolidated, Batlle decided to finish with the coparticipation system, eliminating the Blanco control of several departamentos, leaving only two in the hands of a friendly faction of that political family.

He could then dedicate himself more fully to social reform. He began to garner support and sympathies among trade unionists, socialists, and even anarchists. Batllismo, like Chilean Radicalism but even more so, had an important leftist component, and probably this fact delayed the growth of a Socialist movement with enough support in the ballot boxes.

For the 1907 election, Batlle managed to set up a weak candidate, who would not dispute his return to power four years later. This happened according to plan, and during his second presidency (1911-1915) Batlle proceeded on the road of social reform, secularization, and rule of law that transformed Uruguay into "the Switzerland of Latin America." The role of the state in managing public utilities and other productive enterprises was expanded, prompting the accusation of being "socialist" which was common among local and foreign conservative circles.[39]

When finishing his second term it was not so easy to maintain the system of give and take he had used before, so he decided to create, by a constitutional amendment, a collective executive power, the Colegiado, modeled on the unimpeachable Swiss example. Executive power would be exercised, in rotation, by the various members of that body. This could be interpreted as a democratic step forward, or also as an attempt to break the presidential chair if he was not going to use it. Thus, he could remain as a power behind the throne, controlling *sine die* his own party.

The full Colegiado project, however, did not go through, because in the Constitutional Convention elected in 1916 his opponents, who included the whole Blanco Party and quite a few traditional Colorados, got a majority. Intense political bargaining ensued, and an intermediate solution was adopted. A National Administrative Council would be adopted (that is, the new name for the Colegiado), but including one third of its members from the opposition, and it would control only the technical ministries. The president, who continued to exist, would manage the Defense, Interior and Foreign Relations portfolios. Also, secret suffrage was established, and a representation of one third of the seats for the opposition in each departamento was guaranteed. Batlle's successor, Feliciano Viera (1915-1919), was a moderate Colorado, who decided to give the country (or the conservative classes) a respite, stopping the reforms for a while. Thus the so-called "alto de Viera" was inaugurated, contributing to the pacification of internal tensions, which were mounting.[40]

During the twenties, Colorado hegemony continued, though with Blanco participation in the Administrative Council. In 1927, the presidency was won by Juan Campisteguy, an erstwhile Batllista militant who had veered towards decidedly moderate if not conservative positions, and had cultivated good relationships with the military. Rumors of possible armed coups were beginning to circulate, and one of their aims was to eliminate the Colegiado, seen as an obstacle to efficient government. The coming international economic crisis would give a more cutting edge to their arguments.

Notes

1. Juan Gómez Quiñones, *Porfirio Díaz, los intelectuales y la revolución*; James D. Cockcroft, *Intellectual Precursors of the Mexican Revolution, 1900-1913*.
2. John M. Hart, *El anarquismo y la clase obrera mexicana, 1860-1931*.
3. François Xavier Guerra, *México, del Antiguo Régimen a la Revolución*; Alan Knight, *The Mexican Revolution*; Ramón Ruiz, *The Great Rebellion, Mexico, 1905-1924*; Stanley Ross, *Francisco Madero: Apostle of Mexican Democracy*.
4. Fabio Barbosa Cano, ed., *La CROM, de Luis Morones a A.J. Hernández*; Rosendo Salazar, *La Casa del Obrero Mundial*.
5. Héctor Aguilar Camín, *La frontera nómade*; John Womack, *Zapata y la Revolución Mexicana*; Enrique Krauze, *Venustiano Carranza, puente entre siglos*.
6. Jean Meyer, *La Cristíada*; Enrique Krauze, *Plutarco Elías Calles*; Jennie Purnell, *Popular Movements and State Formation in Revolutionary Mexico: The Agraristas and Cristeros of Michoacán*.
7. Enrique Semo et al., eds., *Historia de la cuestión agraria mexicana*; Barry Carr, *El movimiento obrero y la política en México, 1910-1929*. There were also many regionalist parties, some of them with advanced Socialist goals.
8. Pablo González Casanova, *La democracia en México*; José Luis Reyna and Richard S. Weinert, eds., *El autoritarismo en Mexico*; Enrique Krauze, *Caudillos culturales en la Revolución Mexicana*; José Vasconcelos, *Memorias*; Roderick Camp, *Intellectuals and the State in Twentieth Century Mexico*.
9. See Robert A. Dahl, ed., *Regimes and Oppositions*.
10. Luis A. Sánchez, *Haya de la Torre y el Apra*; Felipe Cossío del Pomar, *Haya de la Torre, el indoamericano*; Eugenio Chang Rodríguez, *La literatura política de González Prada, Mariátegui y Haya de la Torre*; Julio Cotler, *Clases, Estado y nación en el Perú*.
11. Víctor Raúl Haya de la Torre, *Obras completas*. A good synthesis can be found in his *Treinta años de aprismo*. See also Harry Kantor, *Ideología y programa del movimiento aprista*; Robert Alexander, ed., *Aprismo: The Ideas and Doctrines of Víctor Raúl Haya de la Torre*; Thomas M. Davies and Víctor Villanueva, eds., *Trescientos documentos para la historia del APRA*.
12. José Carlos Mariátegui, *Obras*; José Aricó, ed., *Mariátegui y los orígenes del marxismo latinoamericano*; Sheldon B. Liss, *Marxist Thought in Latin America*;

Harry E. Vanden, *National Marxism in Latin America, José Carlos Mariátegui's Thought and Politics*. See also Mariátegui, "Sentido heroico y creador del socialismo," in *Defensa del Marxismo*, pp. 71-74. This book, posthumously published, gathers articles written during the decade of the twenties for various periodicals.
13. "Henri de Man y la 'crisis' del Marxismo," and "El problema de las elites."
14. Enrique Finot, *Nueva historia de Bolivia*; Mariano Baptista Gumucio, *Historia contemporánea de Bolivia*; Herbert S. Klein, *Orígenes de la Revolución Nacional boliviana, la crisis de la generación del Chaco*; Fernando Campero Prudencio, ed., *Bolivia en el siglo XX: la formación de la Bolivia contemporánea*.
15. Policarpo Artaza, *Ayala, Estigarribia y el Partido Liberal*.
16. Quoted in Louis A. Pérez Jr, *Cuba under the Platt Amendment, 1902-1934*, p. 104; see also Allan Reed Millett, *The Politics of Intervention, The Military Occupation of Cuba, 1906-1909*.
17. John Dumoulin, *Azúcar y lucha de clases, 1917*.
18. Julio Antonio Mella, *Qué es el ARPA* [sic]; Erasmo Dumpierre, *Mella, esbozo biográfico*; Sheldon Liss, *Roots of Revolution: Radical Thought in Cuba*.
19. Quoted in Pérez, *Cuba under the Platt Amendment*, p. 181; see also his *Army Politics in Cuba, 1898-1958*; and Jorge Domínguez, *Cuba, Order and Revolution*.
20. William Kamman, *A Search for Stability: United States Diplomacy toward Nicaragua, 1925-1933*; Sergio Ramírez, *El pensamiento vivo de Sandino*; Gregorio Selser, *Sandino, general de hombres libres*.
21. William Roseberry, *Coffee and Capitalism in the Venezuelan Andes*; Arturo Sosa Abascal et al., *Gómez, gomecismo y antigomecismo*; Luis Salamanca, ed., *Los pensadores positivistas y el gomecismo*; Arturo Sosa Abascal y Eloi Lengrand, *Del garibaldismo estudiantil a la izquierda criolla: los orígenes marxistas del proyecto AD, 1928-1935*; Robert Alexander, *Rómulo Betancourt and the Transformation of Venezuela*; Rómulo Betancourt, *Venezuela, política y petróleo*.
22. Gerardo Molina, *Las ideas liberales en Colombia*; Roberto Herrera Soto, ed., *Antología del pensamiento conservador en Colombia*.
23. José Enio Casalecchi, *O Partido Republicano Paulista, 1889-1926*; Alfredo Varela, *Revoluções cisplatinas: a República Riograndense*.
24. Maria Cecília Spina Forjaz, *Tenentismo e Aliança Liberal, 1927-1930*; Paulo Sérgio Pinheiro, *Estratégias da ilusão: a revolução mundial e o Brasil, 1922, 1935*.
25. Alberto Torres, *A organização nacional*, and *O problema nacional brasileiro*; Barbosa Lima Sobrinho, *Presença de Alberto Torres*.
26. Francisco José Oliveira Vianna, *Evolução do povo brasileiro*, *O idealismo daConstituição* and *Instituções políticas brasileiras*.
27. Hernán Ramírez Necochea, *Historia del movimiento obrero en Chile, antecedentes, siglo XIX*; Sergio González Miranda, *Hombres y mujeres de la Pampa: Tarapacá en el ciclo de expansión del salitre*; Alejandro Witker, *Los trabajos y los días de Recabarren*; José Bengoa, *Historia del pueblo mapuche: siglo XIX y XX*.
28. Jaime Eyzaguirre, *Chile durante el gobierno de Errázuriz Echaurren, 1896-1901*; Julio Heise González, *Chile, el período parlamentario*; Arturo Alessandri, *Recuerdos de gobierno*; Ricardo Donoso, *Alessandri, agitador y demoledor*; Claudio Orrego et al., *Siete ensayos sobre Arturo Alessandri Palma*; René Millar Carvallo, *La elección presidencial de 1920*.
29. Ernesto Wurth Rojas, *Ibáñez, caudillo enigmático*; René Montero Moreno, *La verdad sobre Ibáñez*; George Strawbridge, *Ibáñez and Alessandri: The Authoritarian Right and the Democratic Left in XXth Century Chile*.
30. Frederick Nunn, *Chilean Politics, 1920-1931: The Honorable Mission of the Armed Forces*; Ignacio Sosa, *Conciencia y proyecto nacional en Chile, 1891-1973*; Carlos Charlín, *Del avión rojo a la República Socialista*.

31. For various and often contrasting views on the role of immigration see Herbert Klein, "La integración de inmigrantes italianos en Argentina y los Estados Unidos"; Hilda Sábato and Ema Cibotti, "Inmigrantes y política, un problema pendiente" and *Hacer política en Buenos Aires, Los italianos en la escena pública porteña, 1860-1880*; Hebe Clementi, *El miedo a la inmigración*; Fernando Devoto and Gianfausto Rosoli, eds, *La inmigración italiana en la Argentina* and by the same *L'Italia nella società argentina*; Carl Solberg, *Immigration and Nationalism: Argentina and Chile, 1890—1914*.
32. Jeremy Adelman, ed., *Essays in Argentine Labor History, 1870-1930*.
33. Karen L. Remmer, *Party Competition in Argentina and Chile: Political Recruitment and Public Policy, 1890-1930*.
34. Alfredo Díaz de Molina, *José Figueroa Alcorta, de la oligarquía a la democracia, 1898-1928*; Alfredo Etkin, *Bosquejo de una historia y doctrina de la Unión Cívica Radical*; Manuel Gálvez, *Vida de Hipólito Yrigoyen*.
35. Iaacov Oved, *El anarquismo y el movimiento obrero en la Argentina*.
36. Plácido Grela, *El grito de Alcorta, historia de la rebelión campesina de 1912*; Miguel Angel De Marco and Oscar Luis Ensinck, *Historia de Rosario*.
37. Ricardo Caballero, *Hipólito Yrigoyen y la revolución radical de 1905*; Roberto Etchepareborda, *Tres revoluciones, 1890, 1893, 1905*; David Rock, *El radicalismo argentino, 1890—1930*; Hebe Clementi, *El radicalismo, nudos gordianos de su economía*, and *El radicalismo, trayectoria política*; Leonardo Paso, *Historia del origen de los partidos políticos en la Argentina, 1810-1918*.
38. Milton I. Vanger, *José Batlle y Ordóñez, el creador de su época, 1902-1907*.
39. The opinions of British representatives during a somewhat later period can be seen in Gerardo Caetano and Raúl Jacob, *El nacimiento del terrismo, 1930-1933*, vol 1, chapter 14. See also Jorge Balbis et al., *El primer batllismo, cinco enfoques teóricos*.
40. Milton I. Vanger, *El país modelo*; José Pedro Barrán and Benjamín Nahum, *Historia rural del Uruguay moderno*, and *Batlle, los estancieros y el imperio británico*.

3

The Military and Corporatist Onslaught: From the Thirties to the Second World War

The year 1930 is pivotal in Latin American history due to the number of regime changes that took place at that time or in its proximity as a result of the world economic crisis. The changes, however, were quite different in the various countries. The case of Argentina is typical of the generally accepted image of what happened that year. A popular government was overthrown by military intervention backed by the conservative classes, who attempted to create a system of limited participation, which preferably did not depend on elections, adopting some version of the corporatist institutions established in Italy.

Radicalism, in power since 1916, had seriously eroded the electoral strength of the conservative parties, with the occasional help of a central "intervención" in the provinces. The Right had already presented itself divided in the 1916 elections, and had always been based on an array of quite autonomous provincial machines. In the Radical Party, a moderate wing emerged, almost as if to replace the vanishing relevance of the true-blood conservatives. This sector was called Antipersonalista, meaning anti-Yrigoyenista. Its symbolic figure was Yrigoyen's successor, Marcelo T. de Alvear, handpicked by the old man because of his relative detachment from politics, and lack of real roots in the country, or so it seemed to him. Alvear proved more difficult to deal with than expected, and after two years in power stimulated a division by his friends, the nicknamed "galeritas," though he did not formally join them. Yrigoyen, when Alvear's administration was finishing (1928), prepared himself for the classical return to power, this time with a much more agitational and populist message. He won by a wide margin, his main opposition having been the Antipersonalista Radicals.[1]

After the defeat this sector came to an agreement with what remained of classical Conservatism, and with a group separated from the Socialist Party, forming a *concordancia*. This heterogeneous grouping consolidated itself due to the mismanagement both of the polity and the economy by the ailing

Yrigoyen. On the other hand, his decision to nationalize a large part of the recently implanted but growing oil industry, even if it was backed by a sector of the military, antagonized the business community. Finally, the coup led by General José Félix Uriburu in late 1930 had little difficulty in overthrowing the discredited government, with the support of a wide gamut of public opinion.

Argentina in the "Década Infame"

Within the provisional regime there were two factions. One, led by Uriburu himself, wished to create a corporatist regime, without political parties, or with a single, official party or "movement," as in the fascist countries. The other faction was associated with a longer national tradition, and preferred a return to the old days of conservative preponderance, if necessary with the help of some ballot box juggling, but without destroying the liberal institutions that promised to put Argentina, at some future date, at the level of the more advanced nations. Many believed that in the absence of the supposed corruption and clientelism of the Yrigoyen administration the silent majority would once again impose itself.[2]

Uriburu tried to coopt the leader of the progressive wing of the Conservatives, Lisandro de la Torre, who had already been their candidate in 1916, but to no avail, despite his personal friendship and some vacillations by the seasoned politician, who had been moving somewhat to the left.

So the regime was pressed by public opinion into holding elections. To test the mood of the people, a provincial consultation was convened in the province of Buenos Aires, and as it again favored the Radicals, it was immediately invalidated. The UCR then adopted the same attitude it had assumed during the pre-1916 ancien régime, of abstention from the polls, hoping to delegitimize the government and prepare conditions for an intervention from friends among the armed forces. The government, now clearly in the hands of the non-corporatist sector, soon called national elections. Given the abstention of the Radicals, and with the help of some vote-rigging, it defeated the opposition, formed by the alliance of the Partido Demócrata Progresista with the Socialist Party. The victorious candidate, General Agustín P. Justo, of Antipersonalista Radical origins, was accompanied by the son of the eponymous figure of Argentine conservatism, Julio A. Roca, who represented the old provincial factions, united and christened Partido Demócrata Nacional.

A new conservative stage was thus initiated, with an acceptable level of public freedoms, though numerous abuses, and the established practice of electoral fraud, especially in the province of Buenos Aires. Working-class organizations, which had been in the main anarchist during the very early part of the century, and later had taken the road of moderate syndicalism, now became, for the most part, Socialist, with a significant and growing Communist sector.

The spectrum of political parties at the time, then, had a certain similarity with the Chilean, and therefore the European pattern: a conservative (Demócrata Nacional) party on the right; a fraction of the Radicals (Antipersonalistas) and the Demócrata Progresistas performing to some extent the role of the Liberals; the very moderate and normally majoritarian Radicals in the center, with a capacity to incorporate voters from the popular strata; and a Left formed by the Socialists and Communists.

There were two important differences with Chile, however. First of all, the Right did not possess the capacity of their trans-Andean counterparts to win free competitive elections, even if buying a few votes, but without actually putting them in the ballot boxes. On the other hand, the Left was much more reduced to the main urban centers, especially the city of Buenos Aires. It lacked such outlying working-class bastions as the mining, meat-packing, and sheep-raising areas in the extreme north and south of Chile, which gave the Left a national dimension. The social composition of the country was also responsible for the more European cultural and ideological orientation of its population.

Even if the immigration impact was being absorbed, through the new generation, still the percentage of foreigners, without the vote, was very high among the bourgeoisie and the urban working class. But the interior of the country, usually peripheral in terms of economic weight and political power (despite the provincial origin of most presidents) was acquiring a greater say, its population being mobilized via the impact of mass communications, and an increasing number of its people moving to the large and medium urban centers, where their condition as "criollos," often ethnically mixed, made them feel discriminated against. In Chile, this phenomenon did not exist with a similar intensity, because the working class of that country was more homogeneous than the Argentinian, due to the much-reduced presence of the foreign element.[3]

The conservative governments of the thirties have been stigmatized by nationalist and leftist critics, and branded with the name of "década infame," both because of their fraudulent practices and their attempts to integrate the country as much as possible into the British Commenwealth. However, that strategy was to a large extent dictated by the condition of the world economy. This is the case of the famous (or infamous) Roca-Runciman Pact (1933), which allowed free access to British industrial products and coal, in exchange for the permission to export a large amount of top-quality meat, which otherwise would not have been able to overcome protective imperial tariffs benefiting Australian producers. This opening to Great Britain—some pundits claimed that Argentina had become "the sixth dominion"—sidetracked the interests of local industrialists, and also those of North American exporters.

The world crisis, however, forced the government to adopt economic planning policies, inspired by the erstwhile Independent Socialist Federico Pinedo, now converted into a conservative czar of the economy. The scarcity of foreign exchange, moreover, made imports more difficult and dearer, thus compensating local industrial producers for the ill effects of the Roca-Runciman pact.

The industrial bourgeoisie was becoming increasingly concerned about its future, as it did not have much standing among the existing array of political parties. Most commercial or middle-class sectors, either conservative or radical, agreed that the primary-product export model, which had been so successful in the past, had to be returned to as soon as possible. The Left was also resistant to protectionist schemes, which it thought would mostly benefit parasitic capitalist groups, like the sugar barons of Tucumán, who on top of everything paid the worst salaries in the country.

While political parties and a large sector of well-to-do public opinion were not favorable to industrial protectionism, the same cannot be said about the industrialists themselves, the nationalist intellectuals, mostly of a rightist cast of mind, and last but not least the armed forces. The military's motives were obvious, as industry was an essential component of a rearmament policy, considered necessary in order to prepare for eventual involvement in the coming world conflict, and in order to compete with Brazil and Chile. Among the intellectuals there were many, often of decaying traditional families, whose conservatism had led them, since the early part of the century, to react against the cosmopolitanism and new habits brought in by endless waves of immigrants. Thus a "nacionalista" sector was formed, motivated not only, as in other countries, by antiimperialist sentiments, but also by their resistance against what they believed to be the immigrants' potentially revolutionary propensities. Nationalism then, which in many parts of the less developed world takes a leftist coloring, in Argentina was at the beginning clearly rightist, with falangista and fascist overtones. There was also a leftist nationalism, with such figures as Manuel Ugarte, a dissident from the Socialist Party, but voices such as his were a small minority within their ideological sphere.

As for the popular masses, they were the ones to support the worst consequences of the crisis, especially their less skilled strata, often internal migrants, with little if any social protection. All things considered, conditions were being created for a historical mutation of the political party scheme, which happened with the rise of Peronism, a subject we will return to.

The Beginnings of Varguismo in Brazil

In Brazil, there was also a violent change of regime in 1930, with almost opposite characteristics to those of the Argentine phenomenon, though some of its social actors were similar. The implicit pact of "café com leite" required the transfer of power to Minas Gerais, but given the seriousness of the crisis the Paulista elite was not prepared to abandon its control over national economic policy. The country was thus thrust into the dangerous waters of political competition. The opposition selected Getúlio Vargas, governor of Rio Grande do Sul, a member of the local Republican Party, put forward by the Minas people in order not to appear too arrogant. He also had the support of a minor state of the northeast, where he picked his running mate. The official Paulista candidate, sure enough, won in most states.

Civic outrage was felt among wide sectors of the public, including the local opposition groups in Sao Paulo and Rio Grande do Sul. *Tenentismo*, mostly in exile, was added, and it had some sympathy among other military men. The very federal nature of the country, which included the existence of heavily armed local police, facilitated resistance. This started in Rio Grande, where the federal garrison was quickly surrounded, and arms were distributed to the populace. In Minas Gerais a similar situation materialized, and civil war started, with the immediate participation of the experienced *tenentes*. After a very short confrontation the revolutionary forces had the upper hand, partly because the high military command in Rio de Janeiro decided it was better to give in rather than risk a major conflagration; they were also to some extent influenced by *tenentista* ideas, and impressed by the need for change.

Thus Vargas's provisional government was inaugurated, which therefore was not the result of a military coup as in Argentina, but rather of a regional insurrection with popular support and the participation of *tenentes* returning from exile. Nationalist intellectuals and junior officers imbued with some version of authoritarian developmentalist ideas were present in both cases, but with a decidedly more progressive bent in Brazil where they rose against the traditional oligarchy rather than a popular party in power.

The Left, in general, did not support the insurrection, but a certain number of its members soon joined the new regime, seeing the possibilities of reform that were being opened, in however unorthodox a manner. Luis Carlos Prestes, the *tenentista* chieftain who had adhered to Communism during his days in Buenos Aires, declined to join the Vargas forces, and was sent by his comrades for training to Moscow, where he would remain several years. He eventually became the leader of his party, but could never dispel the suspicions of old militants and some bureaucrats that he harbored populist, petty-bourgeois ideas, a consequence of his military upbringing.[4]

The new provisional government, which lasted four years, sent *interventores* to practically all states, using mostly the *tenentes*. In Minas Gerais, whose government had been part of the revolutionary coalition, it wasn't necessary to send an *interventor*, but Francisco Campos, national minister of education and native of that state, organized a militarized legion, clearly inspired by fascist models. More pragmatic was the medical doctor Pedro Ernesto Batista, who headed the Federal District (Rio de Janeiro), very much oriented towards progressive social reforms. João Alberto Lins de Barros, of the *tenentista* group, was *interventor* in Sao Paulo, and he also organized there a legion, rather than a political party. In the capital city a Clube Tres de Outubro (celebrating the date of the revolution) was organized, a sort of modern version of the Jacobin Club with a different ideology. It purported to be the general staff of the pro-change forces, mostly associated with *tenentismo*, seeking to make sure radical reforms were adopted and a unified national political party or movement created. This, given the federal nature of the country (despite centralized provisional institutional practices) was a very difficult task, at which they didn't succeed.[5]

Soon conflicts emerged with the traditional forces of the state of Sao Paulo, where João Alberto managed to antagonize not only the coffee interests but also the Partido Democrático and the industrialists, as well as much liberal public opinion, orchestrated through the Establishment newspaper *O Estado de São Paulo*. Finally a revolt erupted, with constitutionalist slogans, as a protest against the permanence of the supposedly provisional government. In this rebellion there were some separatist components, never fully eliminated from Paulista politics, but the main object was a return to constitutional practices, which hopefully might also allow a return to Paulista dominance, or at least of the old "café com leite" pattern. In this adventure the support of both Rio Grande do Sul parties was also obtained, even of Vargas's own Republicans, whose other leaders were jealous of his predominance and centralist orientations.[6]

Civil war demanded immense efforts on both sides, and this time it lasted a few weeks more than the 1930 uprising. The national government emerged victorious, but it had to accelerate the convocation of the Constituent Assembly. The problem was how to elect this body in order to ensure a majority for the supporters of the new regime. After much debating it was decided to do it through universal secret male suffrage except for illiterates, but adding 20 percent of "functional" representatives of professional, cultural, business, and labor associations. This corporatist element was expected to provide a solid sector of pro-government votes, as its leaders could be easily coopted, even in the labor area, subject to strong manipulation in order to stem leftist tendencies. In the Constituent Assembly, through these and other methods, a governmental majority was created, via the wide panoply of local parties and legions of the most diverse kind. The Constitution which was finally adopted, in any case, followed quite standard liberal formulas, leaving aside the corporatist features some of its members wished to introduce. The same Assembly, for the first time as an exceptional measure, elected Vargas president for a four-year mandate, but reelection was not permitted.[7]

Under the guarantees of the new dispensation, the Communists organized a front, called Aliança Nacional Libertadora (ANL), with the returned Prestes at its head. This party acquired rapid popularity, particularly in the urban areas, and had non-negligible support among some *tenentes* or other lower ranks influenced by Prestes.

With these bases, the last attempt of the class-confrontationist policy of the International was implemented in Brazil. The armed uprising broke out in November 1935, in Rio de Janeiro and the northern cities of Recife and Natal, where thanks to Prestes's contacts some barracks fell to the rebels. Popular mobilization, however, failed to materialize, and the loyal troops pitilessly bombarded the foci of resistance. Prestes was soon found and sent to jail, where we would remain for the following ten years.[8]

The right within the regime was strengthened as a response to the revolt, which for all they knew might be attempted again. On the other hand, throughout the land a Catholic and nationalist reaction was underway, led by Plínio Salgado. He had organized in 1932 the Associação Integralista Brasileira (AIB), directly patterned after the German model, with a capital Greek sigma letter as its symbol of unity. Their program included social legislation and a corporatist organization of Congress, with a single party at its helm, and a very vertical, hierarchical organization. It had important support among the German and Italian immigrant communities of southern Brazil, among the army high command, the bourgeoisie, the nationalist intelligentsia, and many Catholic circles, particularly during its early stages, when its totalitarian character was not yet fully manifest.[9]

In 1937 the new elections were approaching, and the trouble was that Vargas could not be legally reelected. Oppositionists rightly feared a last-minute maneuver to remain in power. The main candidate, José Américo de Almeida, an early revolutionist of 1930, was identified with liberal and democratic positions, a mildly critical heir to the regime. Official circles had been up to then unable to form a unified pro-government party. The chaotic array of local forces continued in existence, resisting centralized discipline. Given the uncertainty about the future under a new leader, the allegedly always-present Communist menace, and the unfathomable attitudes of the Integralistas, Vargas decided to cut the Gordian knot and stage a palace coup, in November 1937.

He dissolved Congress and inaugurated the so-called Estado Novo, clearly inspired by the corporatist doctrines espoused by writers like Alberto Torres, Oliveira Vianna, and the younger Antonio José Azevedo do Amaral. The more concrete institutional model was provided by the Mussolinian Italian regime. Thus, a new Constitution was directly given by the chief executive, establishing a new "functional" system of representation, combined with the more classical liberal one, filtered through indirect two-stage elections, and the banning of political parties. In fact, though, invoking exceptional circumstances, the application of the Constitution was postponed, and a personal dictatorship established. The Estado Novo, in contraposition to the Italian fascist model, did not provide for a single party, but banned them all. Other social conditions also differentiated both regimes. In Brazil the subversive menace, though it couldn't be ignored, never had the immediacy it had acquired in the European setting, where it was supported by a strong Marxist party and a vigorous trade union organization. In consequence, Vargas never succeeded in creating a single party during the Estado novo regime, so as to acquire control of mass mobilization. Integralism, which was far from loyal to him, did not perform this role, because of its extremism. When towards the end of the Second World War Vargas did obtain enough popular support, this was of a type quite opposite to the Italian or German cases, as he seriously antagonized the very upper class which had accompanied him during the early stages of the Estado Novo.[10]

Integralism, incensed at being left aside under the new dispensation, and overly optimistic about the extent of its support among influential circles, attempted a coup de main in 1938. It almost succeeded in kidnapping Vargas in his residence, but the Army was loyal to the regime, and rescued him. Since then Integralism decayed, and lost many of its sympathizers, increasingly aware of the "excesses" of the Nazis, and adopting more orthodox conservative positions.

The new attitudes being spawned at the time in Argentina among industrialists, nationalist intellectuals, the military, and the new masses of recently urbanized workers, also had their counterparts in Brazil. In those days, that country's industrial base was smaller than that of Argentina, taken in absolute terms, and much weaker in per capita terms, even if the greater dimensions of its internal market augured a brighter future. The enormous amount of the impoverished population in the backward states constituted an endless source of cheap and malleable manpower, not easily unionized nor readily recruited into leftist parties. On the other hand, though, a pauperized mass, both in its places of origin and in those where it tended to migrate, might one day erupt in deadly violence, as witnessed by the Mexican case. For that, of course, that mass needed the leadership of disgruntled elites, likely to be generated among the middle strata with relatively high education.

In Argentina, the numerous and prosperous middle class was quite capable of absorbing and moderating its dissident members. The urban workers had trade union experience which gave them a countervailing power but deprived them of revolutionary potentialities. The solid party system also tended to channel in a nonviolent way most social conflicts, and it would have done so even more clearly if the ruling groups had been open to some form of political fair play.

To put it in a nutshell, the Argentine social structure set, against the dominant classes, some serious rivals, among the middle and lower strata, capable of fighting for pieces of the pie, but without realistic prospects of social revolution. In Brazil, by contrast, the propertied classes had a superficially more solid situation, as they did not have to confront strong popular associations and trade unions. But they lived beside a sleeping giant, which might one day awake, shaking off the many Lilliputians swarming over its body.[11]

Chile during the Popular Front: Contrast with Argentina

In Chile, the solidity of the domination of the capitalist classes was intermediate between what was the case in Argentina and in Brazil. Chile's social structure was quite similar to the Argentinian, though with a somewhat lower standard of living, and with many areas of vicious social confrontation. But Chile's institutional development and associative experience was equal if not superior to that of its neighbor, and the same could be said of education, except at the primary level. The result was that the Chilean middle class performed less of a moderating role than in Argentina, and did harbor more dissatisfied elites. Its archetypical Radical Party, however, was basically moderate and centrist. As for the Left, it was stronger in Chile than in Argentina, and more maximalist in its programs, which resulted in the predominance of the Communist over the Socialist party, and the diffusion of antireformist attitudes in the latter.

The high urbanization of the country, and the prevalence, since early times, of a social policy, meant that it was impossible to speak of a sleeping giant, as in Brazil. The main concern of the Chilean upper classes was that the popular forces, even if using constitutional channels, were very strongly organized and confrontationist, at least in their speech, and in the attitudes of their activist minorities.

The Chilean political scenario, normalized after 1932, was again agitated at the end of Alessandri's second term (1932-1938), partly due to the news coming from Europe. If in France and in Spain Popular Fronts were being formed to fight against fascism, why couldn't a similar thing be tried in South America? It could, and for the 1938 elections the Radicals, Socialists, and Communists joined forces in a Popular Front to oppose the conservative candidate, and won by a slight difference, putting their man, Pedro Aguirre Cerda, in the Moneda.

The passions stirred by the campaign were greater than ordinary, and were accompanied by ominous signs. Some extremists had organized a "Naci" Party (short for National Socialist, hispanicizing the German appellative), a weaker version of the Brazilian Integralists. Rejected by the traditional Right, they campaigned on their own, and at a given moment they were on the verge of staging a successful coup de main against the outgoing president. Alessandri ordered a pitiless repression, as a result of which several dozen youths of the better families of Chilean society lay dead, in many cases shot without due process after having surrendered.

The worst of it all was that the presidential candidate of this lunatic group was General Ibáñez, who had unsuccessfully tried to come back to the fore through practically every political grouping in the country, except—for the moment—the Left. As a reaction to the repression, Ibáñez and the party that supported him decided to give their votes to the Popular Front. After all, González von Marées, the "Naci" leader, argued that they were also part of the anticapitalist Left. Worse confusions were still to come.

The Popular Front formed a cabinet with the Radicals and Socialists, while the unacceptable Communists supported from Congress. Alarm was widespread among the Right, national and foreign. The government's measures, however, were not at all extreme. Far from it, caution was taken not to irritate the landowning classes. Thus, agrarian reform was not mentioned, nor was unionization stimulated in the countryside, where in times of harvest it could seriously harm production. A strong impulse was given to industrialization, with state promotion channeled through the Corporación de Fomento de la Producción (CORFO), and some advances were achieved in the areas of social security and unionization.[12]

The Chilean example was particularly taken into consideration in Argentina, where the possibility of reproducing it in order to fight the ruling Concordancia was obvious. The Socialist Party became the most enthusiastic promoter of this scheme, despite its traditional distrust of Radicalism, and its decided opposition to Communism. It so happened that in the Unión Cívica Radical the reticence against such a coalition was very great, as the party had always rejected such negotiations, preferring to stand alone, as true representative of the people. The beginning of World War II, with the German-Soviet pact, made further attempts in this direction impossible, but they were resumed after 1941. They were about to be finalized, when in June 1943 a military coup completely changed the panorama.

The coup had, at its inception, the support of the same group of military and nationalist intellectuals who had been behind the 1930 intervention, with the economic Right passively acquiescing. The vacillations among the latter group were due to the fact that now, in contraposition to the Uriburu *pronunciamiento*, the overthrown regime was not a popular but a conservative one.

The succession of General Justo, in 1938, had been canonical in its use of fraud and intimidation, exerted against none other than Marcelo de Alvear, now leading the main branch of the Radical Party, and enjoying the sympathies if not the open support of the Left, as a lesser evil than a continuation of a corrupt conservative regime. The fact that such a decidedly moderate, almost conservative man as Alvear was considered unacceptable by the system has often been considered as a sign of political blindness. To reject open and loyal competition against him was in fact a bit suicidal, though it could be always argued that behind him lurked a whole array of more dangerous characters, notably the "Intransigentes" of his own party, and that he would be soft on the repression of Communism and trade union agitation. However, the selection by the official party, always heading the Concordancia coalition, of Roberto Ortiz, an antipersonalista Radical, recalled the times of Roque Sáenz Peña, because apparently the new president was determined to stop the fraudulent practices that had allowed him to occupy his post.

Ortiz immediately did start an operation of political house cleaning. In 1940 he intervened the province of Buenos Aires, after the scandal of a recent election won by the usual methods. Equally important, that same year he guaranteed a fair national legislative renewal, with the result that the opposition got the majority in the Lower House. But evil omens once again reasserted themselves, and the president became incapacitated due to an incurable illness, of which he soon died. Thus, the hope for a really competitive race in late 1943 faded away The vice president Ramón Castillo, an old-style conservative, was determined to seat Robustiano Patrón Costas, a sugar baron and hard-line traditional politician in the Casa Rosada by any means.[13]

The new elections in the province of Buenos Aires, held under his supervision, were again fraught with fraud. As for the ensuing presidential contest, Patrón Costas, sure to win, was seen as excessively pro-Allies, and this was not good for the burgeoning industrialist and military forces, and much less for the nationalist intellectuals, who preferred a more neutralist policy. The main point in dispute was what should be done after the war, when a foreseeable influx of foreign consumer goods might spell disaster for the greenhouse enterprises and also for their employees.

Under these conditions the 1943 military coup was prepared, as a result of contradictory forces. Reception was also mixed, as some expected it to return the country soon to democratic practices, while others hoped for a new regime along corporatist and protectionist lines. The latter group soon got the upper hand, making it difficult for progressive, liberal or Radical forces to support the supposedly provisional regime.[14]

Post-Batlle Uruguay

In Uruguay, Colorado hegemony was maintained throughout the twenties, even if ever more closely challenged by the Blancos or Nacionales, who under the leadership of Luis Alberto de Herrera combined an appeal to the ideological and economic Right, with the mobilization of nationalist and popular sentiments. The system, controlled by Batlle up to his death in 1929, thereafter was left to fend for itself.

The electoral law, known as the Ley de Lemas, allowed citizens to vote at the same moment for the party of their preferences ("Lema"), and for the internal faction they fancied. Then all votes given to the same party would be added up, so that the elected official might have had fewer direct votes than some of his rivals. The purpose of this arrangement was to avoid the fatal results of party divisions. But it had the side effect of allowing many different bed-fellows to coexist in the same broadly defined party or "Lema." Within the Colorado family there was an important conservative sector, known as Riverista after the name of a nineteenth-century *caudillo*, which was unhappy with the "excessive" reforms of the Batllistas. Within Batllismo there were also contrasting opinions about the usefulness of the Colegiado, and about the "road to socialism" the party was allegedly taking. In the 1930 election, after Batlle's death, a vacuum of power was generated, which was filled by the nomination of Gabriel Terra, a politician with a long career in the Colorado Party who cultivated excellent relations with the business community and could show a good record of public administration.

In the Blanco Party the great majority followed Luis Alberto de Herrera, and in 1926 almost put him in the presidential chair. But opposition to his leadership was also strong, because of his intransigence and authoritarian propensities. He had been instrumental in the self-defeating expulsion from the party of a left-leaning group, the Radicalismo Blanco, which might have provided the necessary votes for the party's coming to power in 1926. Herrera's Blanco opponents, based on the prestigious newspaper *El País*, formed the Nacionalista Independiente sector. More to the left, but still within the common fold, Carlos Quijano, future director of the widely read and very leftist weekly *Marcha*, organized an Agrupación Nacional Democrático-Social. In the Colorado Party there was also an extreme leftist faction, very interested in the Soviet experiment, led by Julio C. Grauert.

The economic crisis of 1930 shook the national political scene. Among the Colorados the reformist tendencies, frozen since the "alto de Viera," were reactivated. The Right, closely linked to the Riverista Colorado faction, organized a National Committee for Economic Vigilance. This pressure group, supported by most business sectors, was clearly launched for political action, though avoiding partisanship, and cultivating friends in both parties. On the other side, the reform cause was promoted by a pact, which its critics dubbed "*pacto del chinchulín*" (a very tasty part of any self-respecting barbecue) between the Batllistas, who still included Terra, and the Independiente Blancos. The latter were offered several official positions in exchange for their support of a continued progress of reforms about whose advisability they were not very convinced. Projects on hand included advances in the area of social security, retirement pensions, and minimum salaries, as well as a widening of the area of public ownership, especially by creating the ANCAP, a state monopoly in oil refinement and sale.

In the subsequent confrontation the opposition successfully concentrated its fire on the vulnerable Colegiado, which was opposed not only by Riveristas and Herreristas, but by President Terra himself, who was thus abandoning the Batllista fold, of which, in any case, he had been only a peripheral member. Terra then resorted to a coup d'état, dissolving Congress in 1933. He convened immediately a Reform Convention, which was elected with the abstention of the Batllistas and Blancos Independientes, and was thus deprived of much legitimacy.

The new Constitution strengthened the executive, eliminating the Colegiado, and it created a Senate which gave nearly equal representation to the majority and the minority, in effect maintaining the old system known as "Coparticipación," but now without an apportionment of Departamento Jefaturas. Terra was reelected under the new provisions (1934-1938), and at the end of his mandate the democratic system reasserted itself, with the return to participation by Batllistas and Blanco Independientes. In fact, yesterday's abstentionists were now able to elect Alfredo Baldomir (1938-1942), initiating a new period of reform-oriented rule. However, factional oscillations again left the executive without a Congressional majority in 1942, and Baldomir then resorted to the same weapon earlier used by Terra, including another Reform Convention providing a return to the Colegiado. It also eliminated coparticipation in the Senate, which was going to be elected by the whole nation in a single district, through proportional representation, a very unorthodox way of electing such a body.

Terra's and Baldomir's coups were relatively *blandos* (soft) if judged by continental standards, and were quickly corrected with a return to normality, reminiscent if at all of De Gaulle's accession to power in France in 1958. They did reveal a profound uneasiness, but they were not accompanied by any serious repression. In contrast to the French case, however, in Uruguay the process was not accompanied by a radical mutation in the party system, which might have helped to channel in a clearer way the existing tensions.[15]

The Effects of the Chaco War on Bolivia and Paraguay

In Bolivia and Paraguay the Chaco War (1932-1935) generated permanent alterations in their political systems. Up to then both countries had been controlled, for decades, by governments of a Liberal orientation, with little popular participation. In Bolivia, to the classical Conservative/Liberal duality a Republican Party had been added since 1920, under the leadership of Bautista Saavedra, and later of Hernán Siles, forming a sort of equivalent of the Radicals of the Southern Cone. Siles attempted, like his predecessor, to remain in power beyond legal limits, but he failed in the face of a very determined civilian and military opposition. Thus in 1930 a "corrective" and short-lived military coup soon returned power to a more conservative-liberal sector of the Republican Party, headed by the austere Daniel Salamanca (1931-1934).

Salamanca was involved in the Chaco War, adopting at the beginning very bellicose attitudes. Military defeats prompted a rebellion, led by war hero Captain Germán Busch. But the military were still reticent to take power directly, so they simply forced the transmission of power to the vice president, a nonentity who had his tenure extended up to the moment peace was signed (1934-36).

During this interregnum the return of soldiers from the front heated up the political scene. Busch formed a Legion of Veterans (ex-Combatientes, LEC), of which he was supreme chief. Among intellectuals leftist ideologies spread like wildfire, and a Confederación Socialista de Bolivia (CSB) was formed, with many militants from Siles's Nacionalismo (the name he had given to his faction of the Republican Party), under the direction of Enrique Baldivieso, who cultivated good relationships with the armed forces. Trade unions had ampler scope for organizing, and the Federaciones Obreras del Trabajo were reactivated in several centers, especially the mining areas and the skilled artisans of La Paz, who staged a very serious strike.

Given the altered circumstances Busch decided to intervene again, but always without taking first place. He persuaded Colonel David Toro, his senior, to fill the role of chief executive, at the head of a military junta. The strange thing was that in order to justify the takeover the new authorities promised to implement a program of "state socialism," with the cooperation of the "leftist parties," which were plentiful. Finally, the bugbear of generations of conservative thinkers (mainly Alcides Arguedas and Franz Tamayo) was coming into being: the alliance of the Army and the People.[16]

The new government was supported by the wide gamut of parties of the Left, which included the populist-oriented CSB of Baldivieso (soon renamed Socialist Party); the youth groups which had surrounded Siles and his Nacionalismo, headed now by Carlos Montenegro and his Célula Socialista Revolucionaria; and the typographer Waldo Alvarez, who had been the leader of the general strike that had spearheaded the second armed intervention of Germán Busch, and to whom now the Ministry of Labor was given. To this mixture was added also the participation of the old Saavedra, who was still active and wished to add this new hue to his colors, founding a Partido Republicano Socialista, later renamed Partido de la Unión Republicana Socialista (PURS), which despite its name was a right-of-center group.

Further to the right could be found the bulk of the military, who were not very clear about what socialism meant, and who founded several secret masonic-type lodges, like the Razón de Patria (RADEPA) and the lesser-known Estrella de Hierro. In the mining business, which strangely enough was in Bolivian hands, magnates like Mauricio Hochschild and Carlos Víctor Aramayo tried to exert their influence on government, competing with their colleague and large investor Simón Patiño.

As an organ of the socialist intelligentsia, its more pragmatic sector founded the daily *La Calle* in 1936, where Armando Arce, Augusto Céspedes, Carlos Montenegro, and Víctor Paz Estenssoro tried to interpret the new times to a disoriented public opinion and, not least, to themselves. The group was connected to Baldivieso's CBS, and supported very decidedly the Spanish Republic during the Civil War. However, the policy of alliances led them to privilege contacts with the barracks and to fraternize with people who scarcely espoused leftist ideologies but were determined to confront the foreign-backed oligarchy, mainly the "Rosca" of the three tin mining magnates, one of whom happened to be Jewish, and the other a native Indian.

David Toro's government persecuted anarchist and Communist activists, and signed an agreement with an Italian mission in order to reform the local police. It also tried to include corporatist bases of representation into a new Constitution being written at the time. Of more weight was the decision, prompted by the power behind the scenes, Busch, to expropriate the Standard Oil fields.

In July 1937, Busch finally overcame his scruples, ditched and exiled Toro, and took for himself the main office. He convened another Reforming Convention, at which only the official party, christened Frente Unico Socialista, presented itself. The new body confirmed Busch as president, with Baldivieso as his second in command. As a reaction to these apparently inexplicable events, among the Right an activist group was formed, of clear Nazi inspiration, led by Oscar Unzaga de la Vega, who created the Falange Socialista Boliviana, rooted in his native Cochabamba, the less Indian area of the mountainous part of the country. The "socialist" appellative did not help correct matters, as its sources of inspiration were Chile's Nacional Socialista party led by Jorge González von Marées, and the Spanish Falange's creator José Antonio Primo de Rivera.

The more moderate Right, following the Argentine example, formed a "Concordancia," centered on the Liberals (whose principal figure was the prestigious writer Alcides Arguedas), the Republicanos Genuinos (of the recently deceased Salamanca) and the Saavedrista faction of Republicanos, renamed PURS. The government tried to form a Partido Democrático Socialista, with Montenegro, Paz Estenssoro, and Céspedes, but the initiative did not take root. The proliferation of political parties displaying the word "socialist," real or imaginary, clear or confused, was staggering.

Given the difficulty of unifying public opinion through democratic means, Busch opted in April 1939 for a coup d'état, proclaiming his dictatorship, supported by the Veterans of the LEC, and with his socialist friends, beginning with the vice president Baldivieso. Appearing on the balcony of the Palacio Quemado, in front of a great multitude, Busch had no better idea than to salute them raising rather stiffly his right arm, putting in evidence either his pragmatism or rather his mental instability, which would lead him some time later to commit suicide.[17]

The dictatorship quickly approved a Labor Code, forced mining entrepreneurs to sell their export-earned dollars at low official prices, and it was planning to set up a tin refinery. On the other hand, it committed excesses, such as condemning Mauricio Hochschild to death because of his violations of exchange rules, even if after an agonizing cabinet session he was pardoned. According to Augusto Céspedes, who would later become the ideologue of the Movimiento Nacionalista Revolucionario that staged the very radical 1952 revolution, the dictatorship, after its attacks on the mining "Rosca" was converted from "fascist and minoritarian" to "nationalist and popular." Whatever the case may be, after Busch's suicide power was taken back by the armed forces, who displaced vice president Baldivieso, launching an electoral process ending in the accession of General Enrique Peñaranda, a conservative liberal, who did not lack the support of some socialist faction.

In 1941 the now self-proclaimed "Socialistas Independientes" of *La Calle* decided to form a more massively based political party, or rather "movement," the Movimiento Nacionalista Revolucionario (MNR). Paz Estenssoro, Céspedes, and Montenegro were its main lights, together with José Cuadros Quiroga, who wrote an inaugural manifesto. In it he proposed a number of progressive policies, but as a token of his pragmatism and moderation he did not mention agrarian reform, expropriation of foreign companies, or the extension of the vote to illiterates. He did make general declarations against imperialism and condemned false democracy, international socialism, and for good measure Judaism. This latter inclusion did not help the international image of the new movement, already beclouded by its collaboration with Busch's dictatorship, and the stamp of "fascist" stuck to it.

In Paraguay things could not be more different, though there also the impact of the war was strongly felt. The Liberal government of Eusebio Ayala (1932-1936) had been relatively successful in the conduct of the war, but not enough for his critics, who complained of having been deprived of the fruits of victory. Both Ayala and his chief of staff General José Félix Estigarribia were considered weak in accepting pacification in 1935, which had been brought about through the efforts of Argentina's foreign minister, who subsequently earned the Nobel Prize. These discontents erupted in February 1936, when the war hero Major Rafael Franco staged a coup and became the supreme power in the land, putting together an extremely heterogeneous group of collaborators.

Typically, people with a mentality akin to Brazil's *tenentismo* were numerous in the armed forces. In the cabinet, such confessed Marxists as Anselmo Jóver Peralta (who would later evolve towards Aprismo) rubbed shoulders with fascists and Nazi sympathizers such as ministers of the interior Gomes Freire Esteves and of agriculture Bernardino Caballero, including also the Colorado dissident Juan Stefanich. Stefanich would later develop his "solidaristic" ideology, giving intellectual backing to a new political movement, Febrerismo, which had been founded to support the revolution of that month. Febrerismo, after revising some of its earlier foundations, evolved also towards Aprista-type conceptions, finally becoming a member of the Socialist International. This movement was originally based on an association of war veterans, as its Bolivian equivalents who tried to impose state socialist solutions through authoritarian rule.

The new regime soon declared itself identified with the "totalitarian" processes then dominant in Europe, without much distinction between the German and the Russian varieties. A Labor Department and a Committee for Civilian Mobilization were created, but the degree of social agitation and involvement of disaffected intellectuals was much lower than in Bolivia, possibly because the number of aspiring educated people was smaller, and they lacked support among a concentrated working class. On the other hand, the ethnic structure of the country was much more homogeneous, and easy migration to Argentina reduced tensions at all levels.

One year after it was started, another military coup finished with this experiment, and inaugurated a period of military regimes with partial Liberal involvement. In 1939 General Estigarribia, returning to the country after a gilded exile as diplomatic representative, staged yet another coup, but died in an aviation accident in 1940. After a chaotic intermezzo, General Higinio Morínigo rose to the top, with a classical barracks dictatorship, but obtaining the support of some sectors of the Colorado party which gave him an aura of popularity.[18]

Perú: Roots of the Antagonism between Military and Apristas

In Peru the crisis of 1930 saw the emergence of a military junta that proposed to return the country to democracy after the long *Oncenio*, the eleven-year authoritarian but civilian rule of Augusto Leguía. Their leader was Colonel Luis Sánchez Cerro, who attempted to remain in power through rigged elections. Of very modest origins, and of a strongly *cholo* complexion, he posed as a man of the people, forming a Unión Revolucionaria, clearly personalist, competing with a more genuinely populist party, Haya de la Torre's Apra.

Apristas were convinced that they won the 1931 elections, and that fraud kept them in second place. The fact is that they had planned armed resistance and sought out some military allies. The plot proceeded swiftly, and when it burst out the following year the rebels were able to control for a few days the city of Trujillo, in the sugar-producing north, where they had a very large number of adherents. But other foci failed to come out in time, and eventually the army surrounded them. In the ensuing chaos several jailed officers were killed. The retribution was incommensurate: thousands of their militants were forced to dig their own graves and shot into them, in what came to be called the "Massacre of Trujillo." Thus the ancestral enmity between the Apristas and the armed forces, and by extension the upper classes, was born.

Vengeance was swift to come, and in 1933 Sánchez Cerro was shot dead by an Aprista militant. The party, of course outlawed, continued to consolidate its underground and exile organizations, with Haya de la Torre usually trying to perform a moderating role over the youthful impulses of his followers. A few years afterwards another Aprista bullet cut short the life of the owner of the conservative newspaper *El Comercio*, which since then swore never to refer to the "criminal sect" in its pages, not even in the police news section.[19]

In 1939, when renovation was due, the very wealthy and Civilista banker Manuel Prado was made president (1939-1945). The World War atmosphere favoring democracy had an impact on him, and at the end of his mandate he accepted staging a free election, though of course without the Apristas, despite the fact that Haya de la Torre, fully solidary with the Allies, had evolved in a very moderate direction, seeking support among progressive and labor circles in the United States, whose vehement anti-Communist stance he shared.

Aprismo had extended to the whole of Peru, but particularly to some enclaves where a labor force of often recent rural origin was concentrated. This was the case of the sugar areas of Northern Peru, where the famous "Aprista bastion" was to be found in the departamentos of Libertad and Lambayeque, around the city of Trujillo. There a few large enterprises, foreign and nationally owned, had displaced the numerous petty producers, and also some of the old family-held large farms, impinging on peripheral members of the upper classes, like Haya de la Torre himself. In Cerro de Pasco, copper, lead, and silver mining also created an Aprista labor concentration.[20]

Trade unionism had an early development in the city of Lima, since the mid-nineteenth century, along moderate, mutual-help lines. Anarchism started being relevant towards the early part of the twentieth century, and in 1919 led two massive general strikes. In a sense, Leguía's *Oncenio* dictatorship was an answer to this popular challenge. Now Aprismo was the heir to these traditions, and many anarchists joined the new movement, which was becoming a synthetic amalgam of trade union activists with university students, intellectuals, and a provincial middle class which had difficulty surviving the competition of national or international capitalism.[21]

Mariátegui's Socialist Party, renamed Communist after the death of its founder, had a tightly knit organization, but not much electoral force, partly because most of the time it was outlawed (but so was Aprismo). Prado, however, allowed them more freedom, in order to erode the Aprista bases, though without much success. Their enthusiasm for the Peruvian leader who apparently was conducting the country towards redemocratization led them to bestow on him the basically undeserved title of the "Peruvian Stalin."

Ecuador, Colombia, and Venezuela

Ecuador

In Ecuador the classical Conservative/Liberal polarity, often interrupted by military coups, started confronting serious problems, which erupted in 1924 in a violently repressed strike in Guayaquil with a cost of a thousand lives. The search for new solutions was under way and found receptive minds among junior officers of a *tenentista* mentality. The "July Revolution" (1925) they sponsored maintained itself in power up to 1931, introducing progressive social legislation. However, it was overcome by the ripples of the 1930 world economic crisis, and it was ended through the intervention of more classically oriented officers, who allowed the Liberal Party a return to power, through far from fair elections.[22]

Against this fraudulent Liberalism a wide resistance was formed, led by José María Velasco Ibarra, a Catholic provincial politician linked to the Conservative Party, but with his own electoral bases in Guayaquil. Street agitation forced the ruling Liberals to grant competitive elections, from which Velasco Ibarra came out as the new president (1933-1934), a position he would return to for half a dozen times, never for very long periods. Velasco's early support was extended to incorporate a dangerous plebeian component from the more urban mestizo Coast (which contrasted with the conservative and Indian Quito and mountainous interior). The Left and the intellectuals, for their own reasons, opposed Velasco Ibarra, who was becoming a paradigmatic, almost caricatured symbol of populism. He decided, in front of intense opposition from right and left, to declare himself dictator, a perfect excuse for the military, still mostly Liberal, to depose him.

Several years of instability ensued, up to 1940, when a new election gave Velasco the opportunity to present himself again, this time with the support of the Left. The Liberal-inclined rulers rigged the election in favor of their candidate. Velasco attempted an armed insurrection, but with no results, and was forced into exile.

Colombia

In Colombia, Conservative hegemony, dating from the Thousand Days War, confronted the classical stumbling block: a division within party ranks, overconfident of their dominance, and riddled by internal discord. Thus it was that a very moderate Liberalism could seat Enrique Olaya Herrera, then ambassador to Washington (1930-1934). The 1930 crisis did not have, then, in Colombia the military denouement which accompanied it in so many other places, though the tempests it unleashed were probably partly responsible for the Conservative division.

Within the Liberal Party an elite bent on rapid social change was formed, headed by Alfonso López Pumarejo (1934-38 and 1942-1945) in what he called the "Revolución en Marcha." Trade unionism was not very strong, but there were Liberal nuclei within it, which together with the Communists supported a program of moderate land reform, industrialization, and social legislation. As it was impossible to have himself reelected, in 1938 López selected low-profile Eduardo Santos as his successor, hoping to have the favor returned, which is what happened four years later. López then continued, at a somewhat diminished pace, his policy of reforms and industrialization, during the critical war years.[23]

Now it was the turn of the Conservatives to despair about returning to power given the protracted Liberal hegemony, unless, of course, a division within their ranks set in. Jorge Eliécer Gaitán was the man responsible for this turn of political fortunes. As we have already seen, he had socialist ideas early on but oscillated between promoting them through independent organization or by infiltration within a larger structure. He had finally opted to work within Liberalism, but internal infighting led him to divide the party, which therefore had two candidates in 1946. Gaitán was surrounded by young leftist intellectuals and activists, and he developed a remarkable capacity to stimulate the masses to paroxisms of enthusiasm. He had adopted some elements of Aprista ideology, and was an admirer of Haya de la Torre, but his movement never had the solidity nor the ideological underpinnings of the Peruvian model. What he did have was charisma and *verticalista*, hierarchical organization.

As a result of the division, the Conservative Mariano Ospina Pérez won the elections, even if with considerably less than half the electorate, and thus was somewhat delegitimized. Political violence, quite usual in Colombia's history (though not generally accompanied by military coups) finally exploded when Gaitán, who had meanwhile returned to a reunited Liberal fold, was assassinated in 1948. Popular reaction set up a wave of destruction, in the famous *Bogotazo*, where a few hundred people lost their lives and many their property, in the event itself and in the unending vendettas that followed it, reaching out to the remotest villages. Thus the so-called Violencia was started, a bloodbath that claimed two or three hundred thousand victims during the next decade. This violence, as usual in the country's history, pitted clans of property holders or squatters against each other, together with their clienteles. It was not, therefore, basically a struggle of the dispossessed against the propertied, even if with time it acquired some of those traits.[24]

In parallel to the way Liberalism had experienced a move to the left, among the Conservative ranks a symmetrical shift took place, but towards the more extreme right, of Francoist persuasion. The leader of this sector was Laureano Gómez, who had started his career as a progressive Conservative concerned with applying the social doctrine of the Church, and later evolved towards corporatism. In the 1950 renewal of national authorities, the Liberal Party abstained, in the time-hallowed tradition of facilitating an armed uprising by first deligitimizing the regime. Gómez was elected by the Conservatives, and soon dissolved Congress and governed in an authoritarian and personalist manner. This of course intensified the Violencia, and it also helped divide Conservatives, many of whom preferred more classical forms of government. Finally, in 1953 General Gustavo Rojas Pinilla cut the Gordian knot, deposed Gómez, and started a "Roman dictatorship," with the acquiescence of most moderate sectors of both parties, who hoped that with this strong medicine the country might be pacified, and the various factions brought to reason.

Venezuela

In Venezuela, the regime of Juan Vicente Gómez, consolidated by the oil bonanza, did not budge during the 1930 crisis. But death undid what politicians could not break, and in 1935 the succession issue was opened, amid popular outbursts of violence, as if to celebrate the event. General Eleazar López Contreras, a member of the innermost kernel of the regime, was the anointed successor (1935-1941), trying to introduce some reforms, and organizing a political party that was not much more than a dependency of the Ministry of the Interior. The same policy was continued by Isaías Medina Angarita, who was presumed to be a less forceful personality, and was expected not to obstruct López Contreras's return in due time. In 1945, however, the worldwide enthusiasm for democracy reached Venezuela, and prompted a group of military men to stage a coup, in combination with Acción Democrática, whose leaders had returned from exile at the death of Gómez. The transitory military regime prepared for fair elections, so as to start a new era of legitimized institutional progress.

Mexico, from the Maximato to Cardenismo

In Mexico as well, the 1930 crisis did not much affect the institutional system created by the revolution and consolidated by Calles, the Jefe Máximo. The trauma, if at all, had occurred in 1928, when at the end of Calles' administration he was expected to favor the return of his predecessor, Alvaro Obregón, which is what he did. But Obregón was immediately shot by a Catholic fanatic. Calles found himself then at the helm of affairs, but incapable of occupying the dead man's shoes. He opted for the organization of a solid ruling party, the Partido Revolucionario Mexicano, which after a couple of changes of name, though not of habits, became the Partido Revolucionario Institucional (PRI). He also promoted three successive low-profile men to occupy provisionally the presidential chair, during the six years he had to wait before doing it himself. This period is known as the Maximato (1928-1934).

At the end of the Maximato, Mexican experience advised caution on the subject of reelection, and so Calles preferred to support another minor figure, General Lázaro Cárdenas, who was duly elected. Cárdenas, however, soon showed his teeth, and after a confrontation sent his erstwhile chief into exile, beginning a radicalized phase of the Revolution, with a dynamic program of land distribution, struggle against the Church, and finally nationalization of oil fields and refineries.

With this policy the regime was regilding its laurels, enabling it to coopt many sectors of the Left, and to consolidate its prestige among urban workers and peasants. Trade unionism, with leaders like Luis Morones and Fidel Velázquez, abandoned its radical past, and joined wholeheartedly the governing party, of which it became one of its formally established branches. Corruption also set in, and governmental tutoring was exerted with a heavy hand, even though always some dissident trade union and peasant groups did exist.

During the radical changes in property structure brought about by Cárdenas, grumbling of disaffection spread among the military and upper classes, even if most of these were by now of revolutionary origin. Cárdenas, however, to stem this discontent, managed the traditional pendulum, and selected as his successor the much more moderate General Manuel Ávila Camacho (1940-1946).

The Revolution of 1933 in Cuba: Between Grau and Batista

In Cuba, the government of Gustavo Machado (1925-1933) had begun with the best reformist auspices, which had earned it the support of the American Federation of Labor, intent on creating a friendly trade union movement on the island. However, increasing abuses in the field of public liberties turned various national political forces and international labor against him. To counteract this trend Machado tried a consolidation of traditional parties, that is, his own Liberals plus Zayas' splinter group and the Conservatives, in what came to be known as Cooperativism, a Cuban version of the Argentine and Bolivian Concordancia.

In the opposition another Liberal group arose, Carlos Mendieta's Unión Nacionalista, and many others proliferated, increasingly determined to use violence against a dictatorship hardly covered by legal forms. Among these new groups pride of place was taken by one calling itself simply ABC, recruited among university sectors, and the more leftist Directorio Estudiantil Universitario (DEU). There was also a veterans' organization, the Movimiento de Veteranos y Patriotas, some of whose participants increasingly veered towards the left.[25]

The crisis of the thirties hit an economy already rocked by low prices, and generated uncontrollable revolutionary forces, clearly perceived by North American observers, who considered most of them as potentially Communist, not necessarily because of their ideology but as a result of pressures they would face should they achieve power in a violent context. The danger was sufficiently imminent to prompt the newly installed Franklin Roosevelt to send Sumner Wells as a mediator to persuade Machado to relinquish power in an orderly transition.

The envoy, applying the Platt Amendment, convened the three traditional parties forming the Cooperativista coalition, plus the new groupings, especially the Unión Nacionalista of Mendieta and the ABC, to propose alternatives, and he also met with General Alberto Herrera, chief of the armed forces, just in case.

Finally, through the pressure of the general, Machado was forced to resign, passing on power to the scarcely respected Carlos Céspedes, in August 1933, opening an unpredictable Pandora's box. After a few days the non-commissioned officers, under the direction of Sergeant Fulgencio Batista, mutinied, demanding better salaries. Officers, seeing themselves surpassed by this movement, opted for a strategic withdrawal, and left the control of the barracks in the hands of the rebellious ranks, hoping to capitalize on the inevitable backlash of civil society.

But the opposite happened. The rebels found themselves surrounded by enthusiastic civilian activists, from the Directorio Estudiantil to all forms of the Left except the Communist Party, and became masters of the situation by omission. Shocking an incredulous public opinion, and the sorcerer's apprentice Sumner Wells, they appointed a provisional junta which quickly designated Professor Raúl Grau San Martín as president, with an extremely progressive, actually quite radical cabinet bent on changing things from the root, including of course an agrarian reform, aimed against what was mostly North American property.

The sergeants and their troops surrounded the National Hotel where the officers had taken refuge, and forced them to surrender, while Grau distributed 400 promotions to officer positions to those who up to the previous days had been despised minor ranks. The feared "communism" was showing its head, surprisingly enough under the cloak of an agitation of the military. Not for long, though. Soon enough, both the North Americans and the local Right understood that their hopes had to be pinned on Batista. After a few interviews he was convinced of the advisability of a corrective coup, in January 1934, putting more moderate persons in lieu of Grau San Martín.

After a time of ruling from behind the scenes, Batista decided to set himself forth as a candidate in free elections, held under the newly proclaimed constitution, at that time hailed as one of the more progressive in the world, independently of whether it could be applied or not. Batista won the race and behaved as a dyed-in-the-wool democrat (1940-1944). These years, marked by the world war, saw a convergence of progressive opinion around Batista, who nominated two Communists to ministerial positions, the first such act on the continent. This could not help producing some alarm in Washington, already concerned about the coming to power of the Popular Front in Chile (1938), though there at least the Communists were kept out of the ministries. The internal opposition was represented by Grau, who had organized a political party, the Revolucionario Auténtico, which bore the same name as Martí's in order to mark its roots, and oriented itself in what may be called an Aprista-like direction, though with less organizational or ideological solidity. Grau had to compete with Batista, who was capable of channeling a good sector of the popular classes behind his charismatic leadership and his image of a "man of the people," a sort of Cuban Sánchez Cerro, in contrast with the more cultivated Grau.

Trade unionism had an important presence, numerically based especially on the unstable and seasonal sugar industry labor force, and with more organizational clout among railwaymen and cigar workers, a classical Cuban activity where a skilled proletariat was gathered. The very numerous unemployed intelligentsia and students provided an enviable recruiting ground for the more diverse political innovators, as long as they could demonstrate their anti-status quo credentials.

Central America in Flames Demands a Theoretical Revision

In Central America, during the thirties, two phenomena of special theoretical interest took place in the struggle against conservative and foreign domination. One was in Nicaragua, with Sandino, beginning in the twenties as we have already seen, and ending with the assassination of the rebel chief in 1934. The other one was the revolutionary attempt in El Salvador, led by the Communist Party in 1932.

In this latter country, demographic pressure was intense, combined with the onslaught of capitalist coffee producers on the peasantry. A succession of civilian rulers, showing little respect for the rights of the opposition, alternated in power from the end of the First World War throughout the twenties.

Finally, one of them, Pío Romero Bosque (1927-1931), opted for regime liberalization, taking advantage of coffee prosperity which still lasted during the early part of his mandate, even if afterwards prices hit bottom during his last two years in office. The ensuing crisis activated the popular, trade union, and peasant sectors, which took the opportunity of relaxed controls to start organizing. At the same time a significant Communist Party was created, and participated in a massive demonstration in the streets of San Salvador, on May 1st 1930. At the electoral level, a Labor Party was also formed, led by a moderate but populist politician, Arturo Araujo, who won the elections in 1931.

Social agitation continued during his term in office, generating great alarm within the Right. Peasants in the west began multitudinous protests with violent aspects, while the Communist Party, under the direction of Farabundo Martí, tried to channel that insurgency. Facing the increasing threat of mass violence, the armed forces overthrew Araujo, replacing him with the vice president, General Maximiliano Hernández Martínez, who had evolved towards conservative positions. A few weeks afterwards, the feared Communist revolt burst out, but with poor planning and delays. Apparently, these were partly due to the frantic but unsuccessful efforts to find allies among junior sectors of the armed forces.

Repression was swift, easily overcoming resistance from the ill-coordinated rebel groups, some of which had been able to retain control of certain towns for a few days. Immediately after the resistance had been put down a witch hunt was undertaken. After a month some 30,000 people had lost their lives, according to reports of the time, in what came to be known as *La Matanza*, an early version of what would become commonplace in later decades.[26]

During the long regime of General Hernández Martínez (1931-1944) the security forces, divided into an urban police and a rural national guard, became the main armed branch of the government, more central than the army itself. On the other hand, the president got himself systematically reelected, using a political party with no real support, and with the help of a volunteer armed militia whose fascist inspiration was obvious. His excesses finally set him on a collision course with the armed forces and with the United States, concerned about the Axis sympathies of the regime. So a military coup overthrew the dictator, initiating a stage of military anarchy.

In Nicaragua, Anastasio Somoza, chief of the National Guard, strengthened his position to the point of defying Juan Bautista Sacasa (1932-1936), and supporting a general strike in early 1936 organized by the Nicaraguan Partido Trabajador (PTN), heavily influenced by the Communists. The Third International, in those days, and equally so its local representatives, rejected any involvement with subversive violent activities, favoring the Popular Front tactic of cooperation with the "petty bourgeoisie," however defined, maybe including people like Somoza, who in fact persistently tried to get the support of popular groups throughout the early part of his career.[27]

Somoza having achieved the top post in 1936, he soon prepared his future reelection by a change in the Constitution, for which he again approached the

PTN. In 1944 the Communist Party (now renamed Socialista Nicaragüense) once more supported Somoza, rejecting any cooperation with a general strike aimed at unseating him. This attitude, based on the solidarity of Somoza with the Allies, and on his confrontation against the Conservatives, was similar to the one that led their counterparts in Peru to support Prado, or in Costa Rica Calderón Guardia, a subject we will come to presently.[28]

In Panama also, there was a challenge to the traditional status quo, even if of a much lesser caliber than in Nicaragua or El Salvador. Since the twenties a political group was formed, around the brothers Arnulfo and Harmodio Arias, known as Acción Comunal, oriented towards social reform combined with anti-Yankee sentiments and some racism towards blacks, many of them immigrants from the British Caribbean. This group obtained military support to depose the existing authorities, and organized a new party, Liberal Doctrinario, apparently a mutation of the old stem, and at the beginning it was so in effect, under the presidency of Harmodio (1932-1936). After a family squabble his post was taken by friendly Juan Denóstenes Arosemena (1936-1940), to fall finally into the hands of the younger brother, Arnulfo, venturing into new, populist waters.

Symbolically, Arnulfo changed the name of the party, now christened Nacional Revolucionario (PNR), with a new ideology, "Panameñismo," a mixture of Aprismo and of the newly rising Peronism, and became the main antagonist of the upper classes for decades, before the access of Torrijos to power towards the end of the sixties.[29]

From a theoretical point of view, events in Salvador were such as to make Karl Marx turn in his grave, supposing he was resting quietly in it after the Russian Revolution. For Russia, however, Trotsky had argued that in that peripheral but very populous country great concentrations of manpower could be found, of unsuspected proportions, despite the general level of underdevelopment. According to statistics the percentage of the industrial labor force working in large-scale enterprises was greater than in Germany, a fact that explained the high level of class-consciousness that according to Trotsky existed among workers in Russia. Of course Trotsky left aside the enormous peasant population, over which the industrial sector floated, highly concentrated, no doubt, but forming a relatively small iceberg in the peasant sea.

However, the fact that in countries of the periphery great concentrations of manpower might exist is something that should be taken into account in any attempt to interpret the presence of diverse types of political parties. In Latin America, the equivalent of the industrial concentrations formed in tsarist Russia by foreign capital and the state were the mining and agri-business enclaves, especially sugar, and in lesser scale bananas and cotton. Coffee—dominant in the Salvadoran countryside, apart from subsistence agriculture—did not give rise to such concentrations, rather creating a middle stratum with infinite gradations, from small propertyholders to tenants and sharecroppers. There were, however, two important factors to take into account in El Salvador, namely, the avidity for land of large capitalist developers, and the demographic pressure which kept proletarianizing increasing numbers of peasants, sending many to the cities as internal migrants. But in order for a rebellion to materialize, it was necessary to have a leadership element brought from outside the popular classes.

In the Latin American countries certain factors are present, which may explain the formation of anti-status quo elites capable of giving leadership to the masses. Admittedly, from a classical Marxist point of view it could be argued that the Salvadoran upheaval of 1932 was premature, and therefore destined to failure. It is probably true that the insurgency of 1932 was in effect untimely, but by the same token so were later events in Cuba or Nicaragua. However, these uprisings, even if flying in the face of Marx's theoretical concepts, were successful and did wipe out most of the capitalist classes.

The international evidence makes it quite clear, in fact, that revolutionary tendencies do not derive from what happens among the working class, but are rather based on tensions generated at other levels, and not necessarily among the peasantry. To analyze them it is necessary to take into account the following characteristics of societies like those of Central America, and many others on the continent:

1. Structural dualism, due to the co-existence of notably underdeveloped areas and more modernized centers, usually associated with foreign investment and imported technology.[30]
2. Urbanization and educational levels generating a greater supply of people aspiring to middle- or upper-status jobs than what the economy can provide. The result, combined with the previous point, is a complex social stratification which spawns a plethora of dissatisfied groups among the middle or higher strata.[31]
3. Intense internal migrations, and other forms of social mobilization not accompanied by a comparable capacity to organize autonomous working-class associations of a trade union or a political kind.[32]
4. A concentration of economic power in foreign enterprises, and in national groups allied to them, generating a lack of legitimacy, especially among the discontented middle classes, which otherwise might provide a conservative buffer.

These factors, present in a very different manner in the various countries, will be taken into account in the analyses of the coming chapters, in order to understand how their interaction generates different models of social change and of political representation of societal interests.

Notes

1. The "intervención" was a constitutional provision that allowed the federal government to abrogate local authorities when the latter were deemed to be unable to uphold

The Military and Corporatist Onslaught   69

the rule of law. The decision had to be taken by Congress, but during its long recess the Executive could do it.

2. The concept of "movement" has been given a central theoretical role by various and contradictory ideological schools of thought, as representing a more genuine expression of popular sentiments than political parties, without their complex structures of intermediation that distort the popular will. See Susan Eckstein, ed., *Power and Popular Protest: Latin American Social Movements*; Joe Foweraker, *Theorizing Social Movements*; Antonio Escobar and Sonia E. Alvarez, eds., *The Making of Social Movements in Latin America, Identity, Strategy and Democracy*, and the same with Evelina Dagnino, eds., *Cultures and Politics, Politics and Cultures*.

3. Horacio Sanguinetti, *Los socialistas independientes*; Alberto Ciria, *Partidos y poder en la Argentina moderna, 1930-1946*.

4. Eurico de Lima Figueiredo, ed., *Os militares e a revolução de 30*; Virgílio A. de Melo Franco, *Outubro 1930*; Boris Fausto, *A revolução de trinta, historiografia e história*; Edgard Carone, *O PCB*; Leoncio Martins Rodrigues, "O PCB, os dirigentes e a organizaçao."

5. Octavio Malta, *Os tenentes na revolução brasileira*.

6. João Alberto Lins de Barros, *Memórias de um revolucionário*.

7. Michael Conniff, *Urban Politics in Brazil, The Rise of Populism, 1925-1945*; Ángela Maria de Castro Gomes, ed., *Regionalismo e centralização política, partidos e Constituinte nos anos 30*.

8. Ricardo Antunes, *Classe operária, sindicatos e partido no Brasil, da revolução de 30 até a Aliança Nacional Libertadora*; Stanley Hilton, *A rebelião vermelha*; Moacyr de Oliveira Filho, *Um operário no poder: a insurreição comunista de 1935 vista por dentro*.

9. Hélgio Trindade, *O Integralismo: o fascismo brasileiro na década de 30*; Sandra McGee Deutsch, *'Las derechas', The Extreme Right in Argentina, Brazil and Chile, 1890-1939*.

10. Aspásia Camargo et al., *O golpe silencioso: as origens da república corporativa*; Hélio Silva, *A ameaça vermelha: o plano Cohen*; Robert M. Levine, *O regime de Vargas: os anos críticos, 1934-1938*; Kenneth Erikson, *The Brazilian Corporative State and Working Class Politics*; Philippe Schmitter, *Interest Conflict and Political Change in Brazil*.

11. Warren Dean, *A industrialização de Sao Paulo*; Wilson Cano, *Raízes da concentração industrial em São Paulo*.

12. Federico Gil, *El sistema político de Chile*; Weston Agor, *The Chilean Senate*; Benny Pollack, "The Chilean Socialist Party, Prolegomena to its Ideology and Organization."

13. Comisión de Homenaje, *El Presidente Ortiz y el Senado de la nación*.

14. Raúl Larra, *Mosconi, general del petróleo* and *El General Baldrich y la defensa del petróleo argentino*; Enrique Mosconi, *La batalla del petróleo*.

15. Germán Rama, *El club político*; Gerardo Caetano and Raúl Jacob, *El nacimiento del terrismo, 1930-1933*. See vol. 1, pp. 223-234 for a statistical correlation between the business leadership and that of the Herrerista and Riverista sectors of both main parties.

16. Porfirio Díaz Machicao, *Historia de Bolivia: Toro, Busch, Quintanilla*.

17. Regarding fascist ideas in Busch and other military men, see Baptista, *Historia contemporánea*, p. 484.

18. It must be said that the Paraguayan Colorado Party has no connection or resemblance to its Uruguayan namesake.

19. Orazio Ciccarelli, *The Sánchez Cerro regime in Peru, 1930-1933*; Vincent C.Peloso, *Peasants on Plantations, Subaltern Strategies of Labor and Resistance in the Pisco Valley*.
20. Dirk Kruijt and Menno Velinga. *Labor Relations in Multinational Corporations: The Cerro de Pasco Corporation in Peru (1902-1974)*.
21. Peter Klarén, *Modernization, Dislocation, and Aprismo, Origins of The Peruvian Aprista Party, 1870-1932*; Michael J. Gonzales, *Plantation Agriculture and Social Control on Northern Peru, 1875-1933*; Imelda Vega Centeno, *Aprismo popular, mito, cultura e historia*, and *Ideología y cultura en el aprismo popular*.
22. George Blanksten, *Ecuador, Constitutions and Caudillos*; John Martz, *Ecuador: Conflicting Political Culture and the Quest for Progress*; Miguel Murmis, ed., *Clase y región en el agro ecuatoriano*.
23. Alvaro Tirado Mejía, *Aspectos políticos del primer gobierno de Alfonso López Pumarejo, 1934-1938*.
24. Mariano Arango, *Café e industria, 1850-1930*; Robert H. Bates, *Open-Economy Politics: The Political Economy of the World Coffee Trade*; Luis Ospina Vásquez, *Industria y protección en Colombia*; Arturo Alape, *El Bogotazo, memorias del olvido*; Germán Guzmán Campos, Orlando Fals Borda and Eduardo Umaña Luna, *La violencia en Colombia*; John Booth, "Rural Violence in Colombia, 1948-1963."
25. James O'Connor, *The Origins of Socialism in Cuba*.
26. Roque Dalton, *Miguel Mármol, los sucesos de 1932 en El Salvador*; Joaquín Méndez, *Los sucesos comunistas en El Salvador*; David Browning, *El Salvador, Landscape and Society*; Thomas P. Anderson, *Matanza, El Salvador's Communist Revolt of 1932*; Michael McClintock, *State Terror and Popular Resistance in El Salvador*; Rollie Poppino, *International Communism in Latin America, A History of the Movement, 1917-1963*; Sheldon B. Liss, *Radical Thought in Central America*.
27. James Dunkerley, *Power in the Isthmus*.
28. See Dunkerley, pp. 113 n.62, 123 and 156 n.26. Also Roosevelt, who privately thought that Somoza was "an s.o.b... but on the right side," had kind words for him, and invited him to visit Washington.
29. Stephen C. Ropp, *Panamanian Politics, From Guarded Nation to National Guard*; Collazos, *Labor and Politics in Panama*.
30. During the sixties it became fashionable to condemn "dualism," as though this approach asserted that the modern and the archaic sectors of the economy were separate worlds, with no interaction. Thus Rododolfo Stavenhagen, in his *Siete tesis equivocadas sobre América Latina*, argued that as there was an exploitation of the labor force of the less developed areas by enterprises of the modern sector, thus reducing salaries because of the unlimited provision of low wage workers, it was incorrect to refer to a "duality," it being necessary to consider the whole economy as an integrated system. Of course one must do this, and some extreme version of the dualism theory are not valid, as those originated by the creator of the concept N.N. Boeke, in his studies of the then Dutch Indies. However, the existence of a strong discontinuity in the social structure of Latin American countries is more marked than in the First World, and must be taken into account to explain its political characteristics.
31. Ted Robert Gurr, *Handbook of Political Conflict: Theory and Research*; Sheldon Stryker and Anne Statham Macke, "Status Inconsistency and Role Conflict." For a historian's use of the concept of status inconsistency, see Laurence Stone, "The English Revolution."
32. Karsten Paerregaard, *Linking Separate Worlds, Urban Migrants and Rural Peru*; Pierrette Hondagneu-Sotelo, *Gender Transitions, Mexican Experiences of Immigration*.

4

The Postwar Dawn: Populism and Its Transformations

During the Second World War, Argentina underwent quantitative and qualitative changes of enormous significance. The first impact of the international conflict over its economy was negative, because transport difficulties reduced the purchases of foreign buyers and made provision of semi-finished industrial imputs almost impossible. But after a couple of years everything began to be produced locally, at whatever cost, stimulating new investment and intensive use of existing capital stock. This unexpected and unplanned protection widened the gamut of locally produced goods, and the earnings of industrialists, among whom a large group of new entrepreneurs was generated, all of them threatened by the Damocles sword of the end of the war.

Under these conditions the succession of late 1943 was being prepared, always within the dominant conservative group, which would without any doubt try to perpetuate itself through fraud. The more traditionalist, change-averse faction of the Partido Demócrata Nacional took the upper hand, with its candidate Robustiano Patrón Costas, sugar baron from the north. Though he was also an industrialist, and in need of protection, this was of a very different kind from the one needed by the new entrepreneurs who were substituting manufactured imports.

Protection against Brazilian or Caribbean sugar was an easy thing to get, and it had been granted for decades. For the new interests, on the other hand, the prospect was to confront the main world economic powers after the war, and that didn't allow them much peace of mind. Patrón Costas was not likely to support the kind of protection they required, and he also happened to be quite pro-British, which made things worse. The fact was that within the existing array of political parties it was very difficult for the newly created industrialist groups to find a receptive audience for the huge tariff barriers they demanded as a matter of life or death.

Opposition to the regime was being formed, as we saw in the previous chapter, possibly a moderate version of the Popular Front that had come to power in 1938 in Chile. In Argentina such a coalition would have to incorporate Radicals, Socialists, Communists, and the small and regional Demócrata Progresistas. In the Unión Cívica Radical, which knew it could muster a majority without any outside help, there was strong resistance to this combination. The death of its respected leader Marcelo de Alvear in 1942 unleashed an internal contest between the moderate Unionista faction, ready for dialogue, and the Intransigentes, led by Amadeo Sabattini, who cultivated Yrigoyen's image of inaccessibility and doctrinal purity. Among younger militants there were quite a few, like Moisés Lebensohn and Arturo Frondizi, who leaned towards a quite radical leftism. But none of the forces considering the formation of a coalition were very much sensitized to the issue of protectionism. This was unattractive to the commercial or agrarian middle classes which made up the bulk of the Radicals' strength, or to the labor aristocracy associated with Socialism, all of whom preferred to have access to cheap and good quality products, of whatever origin, rather than swelling the profits of insatiable local capitalists. It also happened that economic liberalism was very strongly rooted among the more diverse political and social circles, even on the Left, where many preferred not to interfere with the forces of world capitalism, deemed to be more capable of promoting quick development, and therefore the preconditions for socialism.

When in 1943 a coup was staged by a military lodge (GOU, Grupo Obra de Unificación) of colonels and other middle-ranking officers, among them Juan Domingo Perón, the scenario suddenly changed. The increasingly wide sectors which did not have representation in the previous party system found finally a conduit for their concerns. There was a convergence of industrialists in need of all-out protection, military wishing to consolidate an armaments-producing capability, nationalist and Catholic intellectuals concerned with the potentially subversive effects of the foreseeable postwar unemployment, and new masses of mostly unskilled workers employed in the ramshackle but very profitable new factories.[1]

Peronist Argentina

During the first year or two of the military regime (1943-1944) the interest of the manufacturers in supporting the industrialization policy, strongly encouraged by the government, was evident. But by 1945 businessmen of all sorts were alarmed by Perón's determination to arouse the masses in order to use them as a battering ram against his otherwise stronger opponents among the landowning, commercial, and financial circles, closely connected with foreign interests. Most probably Perón had in mind a multi-class integrative party, following models which might go from Italian fascism, seen as "developmental dictatorship," to the Mexican PRI, which became prestigious after Cárdenas's imposing series of revolutionary reforms and assertion of sovereignty against North American oil companies. The paradoxical fact is that despite his authoritarian nationalist background he ended up spawning a very different political movement from what he envisaged in his early attempts. His aim was to unify the dynamic sectors of Argentine society at all class levels, especially the manufacturers, the technicians, the middle class, and the skilled workers. With such a solidaristic party he expected to stem the class struggle he believed would intensify after the war, and thus he would create the preconditions for attempting a continental hegemonic project.

But destiny would not have it. The majority of the upper and middle classes did not approve of his ideas and methods. The church and the armed forces, mostly favorable at the beginning, grew increasingly restive at the mobilizationist traits of his regime, which also alienated even those industrialists who were profiting from his economic policies. Finally, what started as an attempt at class harmony, ended up arousing the most intense experience of class confrontation in Argentina's history.[2]

In his quest for popular support, Perón approached the leaders of the existing trade unions, among whom he first found strong resistance, but later on an increasing number of allies. The renewal and expansion the working class was undergoing at the time, partly fed by internal migration, facilitated the change of loyalties. The many old leaders who remained irreconcilable with the new predicament lost contact with the culturally transformed masses, and were replaced by more pliable new men.[3]

The price of acquiring these new friends was to alienate some of his early supporters, including many of his military comrades and especially the industrialists, who were finding their authority in the workplace challenged. When in early October 1945 a palace coup ousted him from his official positions and confined him to a military hospital, popular reaction was swift to come. With quite spontaneous enthusiasm—and the leniency of the nationalist sectors of the army and police—an immense crowd gathered in the Plaza de Mayo demanding Perón's return, and did not disperse till their idol was freed and returned to positions of power.

The politicians who had been trying to create an oppositionist front against the ruling conservatives continued to confront the new authorities, and eventually did form the alliance, the Unión Democrática, in 1946. The Demócratas Nacionales were not invited, because of their bad record, even if most of them supported it. But what might have been, in the idea of its early promoters, a version of the various Popular Fronts organized in Europe and Chile, became a different type of convergence mostly based on upper- and middle-class elements, because the majority of the masses were conquered by the "coronel del pueblo y general de la nación," Juan D. Perón.

In early 1946, basically free elections were held, giving Perón a handsome, though not overwhelming victory (55 against 45 percent) over the Unión Democrática. During his years in power (1946-1955) Perón consolidated the industrial development of the country, establishing a strict protectionism which, given the high diversity of war-induced new establishments, found it impossible to determine which lines to promote. The main utilities and public services were converted into state enterprises, following models which at the time were being adopted throughout Europe, and were strongly favored by social democratic or labor parties. The public administration of these large-scale activities, however, became a source of outrageous clientelism and corruption. Work discipline was also weakened in private businesses, which could scarcely resist any union demand, always supported by the government, at least during the first years. Popular standards of living and social security soared, creating a climate of extended prosperity, only to be threatened during the later part of the regime, as a result of the reduction in the value of Argentine exports.

In the cultural field, the University was transformed into an extension of the state, with most independent academics expelled and exiled, and primary and secondary education used as a means of propaganda for the regime, especially after the death of Perón's very popular wife, Evita, who was transformed into a hallowed icon. Practically all newspapers were either coopted or suppressed, and the same happened to radio stations.

Brazil: All Against Vargas

In Brazil during the Estado Novo dictatorship an important industrial growth had taken place, also under the protection afforded by World War II. In the urban centers the situation had some similarities to that in Argentina, as the very numerous workers recently arrived from the far interior made up a very pliable mass for the launching of a populist movement. The temptation to take the path of mass mobilization was irresistible, partly stimulated by the Peronist example. But this generated the gut reaction of the wealthier strata, not only due to the democratic preferences some of their members might have had, but because of the Brazilian elites' inveterate fear of any type of popular agitation.[4]

Finally in 1945 Vargas was forced to grant free elections, leaving aside the never-applied formulas of the Estado Novo, and pledging he would not be a candidate. He then formed two political parties destined to continue his work. One, rural and moderate if not conservative, was called Social Democrático (PSD), and was mostly based on local elites of the less-developed states. The other one, Trabalhista Brasileiro (PTB), was intended to channel the popular- and working-class forces that were being aroused by his policies, organized from the top down in official trade unions with little if any autonomy, but a lot of popular endorsement. Vargas's more enthusiastic followers, branded as *queremistas* ("we want Vargas") demanded his permanence in power, or else his reelection. The opposition formed a União Democrática Nacional, significantly with the same name as the Argentine anti-Peronist coalition, but in this case forming a single party, where the conservative/liberal groups were dominant, even if they included some student and "antifascist" left support. With time, the UDN would become clearly the main conservative party of the country, while its Argentine namesake dissolved, leaving its members to follow their own routes.[5]

During the agitated month of October 1945, when the short-lived military putsch against Perón had taken place, followed by his triumphal return on October 17, in Brazil a *golpista* disposition spread among civilian and military anti-Vargas groups, concerned lest the dictator should attempt to perpetuate himself in power, as he had done in 1937. The coup, which found scarcely any resistance, in fact occurred, but with only preventive purposes, so that the elections, envisaged for the end of the year, were maintained.

Despite the obvious sympathy of the majority of the military for the UDN candidate, he lost in the contest, against General Eurico Gaspar Dutra, who had been minister of war, and though he had been alienated by what seemed to be Vargas's attempt to remain in power, he now became reconciled and got the support of the old man's followers. The idea, of course, was for Vargas to be able to return after five years.

During the *queremista* agitation, and the liberalization that accompanied the preparation for elections, the Communist Party was legalized, and Prestes freed. His comrades supported the popular pro-Vargas agitation, chastened by what had happened to the Argentine party, isolated from the working class as a result of its opposition to Perón. However, in the 1945 elections they did launch an independent candidate, who got a good 10 percent of the electorate, a senator, and several members of the Lower House. In 1947 they again obtained good results in the legislative elections, especially in Sao Paulo and other industrial areas. Dutra's government (1946-1951) saw to it to stop this trend, outlawing the party, which never again got much support at the ballot boxes, though it retained important areas of influence among trade unions, infiltrating the officially controlled labor organizations.[6]

In 1950, Vargas's candidacy, promoted by the PTB, swept the country, despite not having been supported by a large chunk of the more conservative PSD. The anti-Vargas UDN got a sizeable vote but lost. Now, in his "second coming," Vargas posed as a punctilious democrat, moving decidedly to the left, even if he could not control the corruption and other excesses committed by his partisans, who often violently menaced the main opposition leaders.

Vargas's ideology had gone through a radical mutation, or so it seemed if one took literally his declarations. In one of them he stated that there were two forms of democracy, one of which was "liberal and capitalist . . . based on inequality," while the other was "socialist democracy, or the democracy of the workers," for which he would fight. In the state elections of 1947 he had gone to the length of allowing himself to be photographed together with Prestes. His victory in 1950, even if it did not have the explicit support of the Communist Party, did drag in many of its militants and sympathizers.[7]

The Right and the military had to appeal to their greatest reserves of forbearance to tolerate the return of the dictator they had helped to unseat, who did not make things more palatable with his socialist declarations, which might not be credible but alarmed many people. In fact, Varguismo was undergoing a mutation which was also underway in several other cases on the continent, where fascistic movements became radicalized towards some form of left nationalism and socialism.

Vargas wished to take a further step in the direction of social reform and redistribution, naming his protégé, João Goulart, a well-known mass agitator, as Minister of Labor. The resistance from the business community and the military created again a *golpista* atmosphere. This was augmented by the undeniable spread of corruption and occasional violence against opposition journalists, so that the high command of the armed forces asked Vargas in 1954 to withdraw for a few months from his post, in order to allow the Judiciary to clean up things. Realizing that he was finally against the wall, Vargas decided to adopt a historical gesture, and after writing a political testament he committed suicide, hoping that popular wrath would explode, and help create a new type of society. The impact was emotionally very great, but nothing like the upheaval he expected. Anyway he succeeded in averting the military takeover which was contemplated by his accusers.

Vargas's vice president replaced him, and soon elections were held, when the by now more solid alliance of PSD and PTB paved the way for Juscelino Kubitshek's victory at the polls. The process was not very smooth, though, because rumors of armed intervention to stop this event were rife. This prompted a nationalist, pro-Varguista faction of the army to execute another "preventive" coup, this time against the Right, ensuring the holding of elections within constitutional parameters. Teixeira Lott, the loyal general, in doing this, was positioning himself as a friend of the people, maybe for future use, if the occasion arose.[8]

The Fall of Peronism and the Onset of Mass Praetorianism in Argentina

In Argentina, the party structure set up by Perón was also plural in its beginning, as in Brazil. There were the so-called Independents, recruited from among nationalist and other right-wing intellectuals. Then, particularly in the interior, there were some Conservative leaders and the co-opted Radicals, who had organized a Unión Cívica Radical (Junta Renovadora), equivalent in a sense to the Brazilian PSD. Then, with pride of place, there was the Partido Laborista, obviously akin to the PTB but with a stronger union base. It was started by some experienced labor leaders, like phone worker Luis Gay, leader of the minoritarian syndicalist trade union federation, and packinghouse organizer Cipriano Reyes, who had been a rival of the Communist-dominated main union in that field. Argentine Laborismo, though theoretically patterned after its British model, in fact never had much autonomy, and once Perón was elected he ordered the dissolution of all party structures that had taken him to power, purportedly to avoid internal bickering, which was widespread. He then ordered their fusion into a Partido Único de la Revolución Nacional, later rechristened Peronist, or Justicialista, very directly subordinated to his commands.

The intense social and political confrontation existing in the country soon led Perón to curtail civic liberties, especially after a *razzia* of independent newspapers in 1950. Prosperity, generated by high export prices, and full employment fueled by a protected industry, guaranteed a high wage level for several years.

Towards the beginning of Perón's second term (1952), made possible by an amendment to the Constitution, economic problems appeared, as a result of diminishing export prices, excessive public expenditure, and mismanagement of public monies. The Church began to withhold its support, so as to avoid being caught in a crisis of the regime, and it started training trade union leaders loyal to Catholic rather than Peronist doctrine. In doing this it was touching a very sensitive nerve, and the government retaliated with a divorce law, support for Pentecostals, and other similar measures, in an increasing escalation, which even led to Peron being excommunicated.

At the same time, entrepreneurial forces were becoming concerned with the permanent populist and agitational attitudes of the government, even if some ruling circles were trying to adopt more moderate policies. The opposition, seeing the shift in loyalties of the military, intensified its contacts in that area. Finally, in 1955 conditions were created for a coup attempt, culminating in June with the bombardment of the Plaza de Mayo and the death of some 400 members of the crowd that had gathered there to defend the regime. Perón urged revenge, and soon the ecclesiastical Curia office and the four main churches of the city of Buenos Aires were up in flames.

Already two years earlier (1953), in reaction to a bomb planted at a mass Peronist gathering, which caused a few deaths, the incensed crowds went on a rampage and burned the Jockey Club and the headquarters of the Radical and the Socialist parties. Finally, in September 1955 another armed movement succeeded in overturning Perón, who had to seek exile in Paraguay.

Thus a three-year period known as the "Revolución Libertadora" was started, with the initial support of practically all anti-Peronist forces (excepting the Communists but including non-party Catholic groups), convoked to form a civilian Advisory Council. Since then, and for eighteen years, Peronism would be almost permanently outlawed, or only temporarily admitted as long as it behaved and agreed to remain a minority. Its militants answered by forming violent action groups in order to prepare the return to power via civilian agitation and cultivation of their remaining military friends. The process generated the worst episodes of violence the country had known since the midnineteenth century. Guerrilla groups were eventually formed, like the

Montoneros and a few others, while at the same time Marxists created their own. In the next chapter we will return to this subject.

In Argentina, the military regime that overthrew Peronism in 1955 had a very short first stage, under Catholic and nationalist General Eduardo Lonardi, when a policy of coexistence with the hopefully reconstructed Peronists was attempted. But the more clearly liberal sectors of the victorious coalition soon got the upper hand through General Pedro E. Aramburu and Admiral Isaac Rojas, both supported by a majority of Radicals and Socialists, who attempted to dismantle the totalitarian structures which, in their view, had made the persistence of Peronism possible. A number of *intervenciones* and violent takeovers of union locals ensued, often by old leaders who, in most cases were unable to maintain themselves due to rank and file resistance.

In 1956, a civilian uprising of Peronist activists with the cooperation of a few military officers was nipped in the bud, with the shooting, unaccompanied by any judicial process, of a couple dozen militants, including General Juan José Valle. Within the civilian anti-Peronist coalition some fissures began to show, till a serious break occurred within the Unión Cívica Radical, the clearly main anti-Peronist force in the country, and therefore the obvious heir of the Libertadora regime.

One group, known as Intransigente (UCRI), led by Arturo Frondizi, adopted more progressive programs, and sought to "integrate" amenable sectors of the overthrown regime. In such an alliance the UCRI would perform the role of representative of the "national bourgeoisie," an entity to which much theoretical store was given at the time. Thence came the name of *desarrollismo* given to this approach, which beginning from a semi-Marxist foundation ended up increasingly conservative.

The other branch of the Radicals, the UCR del Pueblo (UCRP), led by Ricardo Balbín, was more adamantly anti-Peronist, and found a positive echo among the conservative and centrist liberals (almost shorn of party representation) and the older sectors of the Socialist Party.

In 1958, elections were convened, with the Peronists out of the game, invalidated because of their totalitarian character. Frondizi, in the face of the political vacuum thus created, intensified his "integracionista" efforts and his criticisms of the Libertadora military regime, and finally signed a pact with Perón, who gave the votes he controlled in exchange for relegitimation and a future equivalent favor.

With the votes loaned by his erstwhile adversary, Frondizi entered the Casa Rosada, foiling the plans of the Revolución Libertadora leaders, who for a while harbored the idea of invalidating the whole process, but finally decided to accept it and wait for a better opportunity.

In the new government, inaugurated in 1958, tensions appeared immediately between the demands of the Peronists and the limitations which obviously hung over the president. This caused a violent break between the occasional allies, leaving Frondizi in a situation of extreme instability, because even if he maintained control of Congress (where no Peronists had entered) his social bases would be fatally eroded. He was challenged by a trade union movement he had put in the hands of the Peronists, and from the economic Right, the military, and the center and left liberals, including, of course, Balbín's UCRP. However, and despite continuous military demands and interferences—often acknowledged and accepted—Frondizi attempted to engage in an independent foreign policy. He went to the length of having secret interviews with Che Guevara, with disastrous effects, because he did not gain acceptance from the Left (including increasingly radicalized Peronists) and he irritated the Right, which was in the process of coming nearer to him.

In the 1962 congressional and provincial gubernatorial elections Frondizi thought the right moment had come to "normalize" the country's political system. He allowed the registration of various makeshift provincial "neo-Peronist" parties, generally quite moderate, and tried to channel the conservative and ant-Peronist vote to himself. This was a difficult operation, because that sector of public opinion had been more oriented towards the UCRP, and abhorred Frondizi's methods in coming to power over the shoulders of the Peronist giant. Now Frondizi was allowing the Peronists a relatively free expression, a very risky operation, even if intended to show the country that they could be defeated.

The ploy almost succeeded, because the UCRI outpaced the UCRP as the nucleus of the mostly right-of-center anti-Peronist electorate, though not enough to defeat the Peronists, who came out on top in several provinces, including strategic Buenos Aires. There they got 40 percent, much less than their historic levels, signaling that if their enemies united they could defeat them. However, that union was difficult to establish. The worst of it was that now the Peronists would control the police of the very populous industrial belt of the city of Buenos Aires (which was part of the province) and thus might demur at controlling the foreseeable excesses of labor agitators, maybe producing a second October 17.

Conservative and military spheres were alarmed, even if looking at things from a long-term perspective the fact that Peronism, throughout the country, got considerably less than 50 percent of the vote meant that changes were underway. Admittedly, this low vote might have been due to the fact that Perón himself was barred from being a candidate, and that his followers didn't have much access to the media, while divisionism among their ranks was rampant. Finally, after a few weeks of frantic negotiations, a coup was engineered, but trying to maintain some legal forms, so that the vice president, José María Guido, was made to replace Frondizi, while Congress was shut down.[9]

Uruguay, Paraguay, and Bolivia: Confronting Populism

Uruguay

In Uruguay there was no equivalent of the Argentine or Brazilian phenomena. This is probably linked to the character of the country, almost a city-state, without much industry or mining or agribusiness concentrations. The Uruguayan prosperity of the times created a strong middle-class mentality throughout. Rather than rural-urban migrations, the pattern was one of out-migration to nearby Argentina. Population grew older, there wasn't much renewal in patterns of life, and memories and traditional prestige were kept alive. Thus the hegemony of the Colorado and Blanco parties was maintained, with a very small sector occupied by the Socialist and Communist Left, which anyway did have a dominant presence in the trade unions. Conditions were not ripe for populism, neither among the popular nor among the middle and upper strata, where there was ample space for elite accommodation and for the co-optation of dissident groups. Later on, things would change, but never favoring populism, rather some form of socialist politics.

For the moment, in lieu of populism, a progressive faction of the Colorado Party was consolidated, led by Luis Batlle Berres, nephew of the old *caudillo*. At the end of his mandate (1947-1951) a constitutional change was sanctioned, reintroducing the canonical version of the Colegiado executive. Now there would be no longer a president, but a chairman of the collective body, rotated every year. This time Herrerismo, normally opposed to such innovations, supported the change, so as to get at least a taste of power, and the possibility of later changing the system from within.

Luck accompanied this calculation, and in 1958 the Blanco Party triumphed, always under the leadership of Luis Alberto de Herrera, though he could only occupy the position of chairman of the Colegiado, and that for just one year. His designation was helped by a nominally Colorado faction, the so-called Ruralismo, led by Benito Nardone, better known as Chicotazo (Whiplash), who through a popular radio program whipped up the sentiments of the rural and small-town middle classes. On the other hand the industrial development of the times brought into the cities quite a few internal migrants—nothing comparable to Argentina, of course—who were more responsive to the traditionalist appeal of the Blancos than to the more modernized arguments of the Colorados.[10]

Paraguay

Paraguay also didn't have the conditions necessary for the formation of a classical populism, due to non-existent concentrations of manpower, in stark contrast with Bolivia. In Bolivia also there was a strong differentiation between the Europeanized middle class and the Indian mass, still linked to its ancestral communities. In Paraguay, ethnic mixing had been intense since early colonial times, and the result was a much more homogeneous country. Migration, as in Uruguay, went rather towards the outside, that is, Argentina, rather than engrossing its own cities, which did not change so much their demographic composition or their historical memories, again resembling Uruguay and contrasting most notably with Brazil. One effect of this was the permanence of loyalties to the old Colorado and Liberal parties. The Colorados did have some elements of nationalist populism, associated with the tradition of the López dynasty and the disasters of the War of the Triple Alliance, generating a resentment of truly Irish proportions.

The Morínigo regime (1940-1948) had to confront a serious challenge in the 1947 civil war against a coalition of Liberal and Febrerista forces which also had the backing of the small but well-organized Communist Party. In order to survive, Morínigo had to mobilize his Colorado Party allies, till then rather passive. But factional infighting again put him at peril, and after a period of military anarchy another strong and more lasting regime came to power, headed by General Alfredo Stroessner (1954). Now Coloradismo became unequivocally the governing party, with elements of populism, and sympathies in Argentina, where Peronist nationalists shared their devotion to the memory of the López saga. That populist ingredient, however, was much smaller than in Argentina, the degree of authoritarianism much greater, and Stroessner's popularity, though it existed, partially channeled via the Colorado Party, could never be equated with Perón's. Stroessner's regime became increasingly terrorist, even though keeping some democratic formalities, granting the Liberals a minor role as a permitted opposition. A more open enmity came from the Febreristas, and from some Colorado factions pushed out of the seats of power.[11]

Bolivia

In Bolivia, civilian convulsions were much more plentiful than in Paraguay. The nationalist mentality which had been expressed through Busch and Toro reemerged in late 1943, in a military coup of the Razón de Patria (RADEPA) lodge together with the Movimiento Nacionalista Revolucionario (MNR), which established General Gualberto Villarroel in the Palacio Quemado (1943-1946).

The cabinet included members of the MNR, plus other independent socialists and some trade unionists, particularly the miners, led by Juan Lechín, a man of non-working class origins, son of a ruined Arab merchant. The Lechinista Federación Sindical de Trabajadores Mineros de Bolivia (FSTMB) fought against the old Marxist and anarchist unionism, slowly replacing it in the workers' preferences. In the rural sector, generally not very much cultivated by the Left, a first Peasant Congress was convoked, with strong participation by indigenous activists. It adopted a radical land reform program and demanded the extension of the vote, but it did not get much of a hearing in ruling circles.

In the government there were also members of the military Right, self-defined as Independents. The opposition was centered on a Unión Democrática (1944) joining the conservative Concordancia with the crypto-communist PIR, who justified that partnership on the supposedly fascist traits of the regime. In November 1944, a coup was attempted against Villarroel, counting for its success on the support of the Unión Democrática and such leftist groups as the PIR plus some trade unionists. In repressing this plot the government incurred many excesses, including the execution of dozens of people, some from the more traditional upper-class families, mixed with labor leaders and Marxist militants. This "massacre of Chuspipata" was one more in many such episodes of Bolivia's history, but given the nature of the victims it marked the ruling circles with fire and lost them the support of moderate groups and the economic Right, not to mention the extreme Left.

The ensuing agitation weakened the regime, and finally a wave of strikes by teachers, students, railwaymen, and building workers culminated in July 1946 in a massive tumult which overcame police cordons and, profiting from the indecision of the armed forces, entered into the Palace and assassinated Villarroel, hanging him from a lamppost as a warning to tyrants.

The country then returned to a very limited form of democracy, with a competition between the Liberal and the Republican-Socialist (PURS) parties, the latter being a mutation of Saavedrismo, which had been a progressive force in the twenties and was still alive, though now quite conservative. During this time (1946-1952) the traditional ruling elites were blind to the surge of social tensions, not only among the working class and the peasantry, but also, and equally important if not more lethal, among sectors of the middle classes and the intelligentsia.

When in 1951 the MNR, finally allowed to take part in the very limited-franchise elections, won a majority, a military coup ensued, to invalidate the process, but the military had to face an immense popular protest. Miners, with their dynamite charges, and the sympathy of significant sectors among the police and the armed forces, still loyal to Villarroel's memory, overcame, in a short civil war, the forces of the three-pronged oligarchy, with its mining enterprises, its landowners, and its political parties. The Marxist Left (the PIR) was caught in a quandary. Its anti-Villarroel and therefore anti-MNR stance led it to support the liberal government, against what was still considered a fascist, or in the best of cases, a national bourgeois faction quite willing to repress workers with even greater violence than the less rabid liberals and conservatives. But votes flowed to that creature, and so did most of the popular organizations, whether industrial, mining or rural.

The MNR in power paved the way for Víctor Paz Estenssoro (1952-1956) to inaugurate an era of radical reforms as the continent had never seen since the Mexican Revolution. He expropriated the latifundia, the tin mines belonging to the three national companies known as "la Rosca," and the foreign-owned oilfields (which had been reprivatized after Busch's takeover), while severe limits were set to the expansion of the military forces. Internal social tension was kept at a high pitch, even if opposition forces had a paltry presence at the polling booths, now open to all adults. The traditional parties of the liberal right and center practically disappeared, while the newly arisen Falange Socialista Boliviana took their place, and underemphasized its pro-Nazi origins, coming to represent in due time most of the non-MNR middle and upper classes.

Within the MNR, probably as a consequence of this vacuum, a division set in, between Paz Estenssoro and charismatic union leader Juan Lechín. Further to the left, there were still the Stalinist PIR and the Trotskyite POR, with some labor bases and the support of sectors of the intelligentsia.

In 1956, given the constitutional impossibility of having Paz Estenssoro reelected, the more moderate and low-profile Hernán Siles Suazo was asked to fill the post, with the understanding that he would pass it on again to Paz, as he actually did, in 1960. Resentful of this perpetuation, some hopefuls within the MNR, like Walter Guevara Arce, split openly, forming the MNR Auténtico. On the other hand, in order to better control the armed forces, an MNR military cell was formed, commanded by generals René Barrientos and Alfredo Ovando.

At this stage, the Bolivian Revolution had lost much of its reformist zeal, after having helped to create a national bourgeoisie, closely associated to the right wing of the ruling party, as in Mexico with the PRI. Economic conditions, though, did not allow a consolidation of Mexican proportions, and the opposition both from the Right and the Left kept its pressure, even if deprived of votes.

In 1964, efforts were under way to avoid the foreseeable succession crisis. A constitutional change allowed the reelection of the experienced leader, but this fanned the flames of discontent within the party, and Juan Lechín broke away with his own Partido Revolucionario de Izquierda Nacionalista (PRIN). Bowing to conservative and military pressure Paz selected as his running mate General Barrientos, and won at the polls by a wide margin. But it was becoming obvious that Barrientos was the Trojan horse within the regime, and after a few months he led a coup, together with the other military MNR leader, Alfredo Ovando.

At the moment of the coup, Lechín, in a flurry of Machiavellian strategy, attempted to become the civilian support of the new authorities, and approached the palace at the head of his working-class supporters, only to be received with a fusillade. Soon afterwards he was exiled, and his Central Obrera Boliviana outlawed. Barrientos, at the beginning sharing power with Ovando, formed a new political force, purportedly heir to the discredited MNR, getting the collaboration of an incredible array of ideological groups, from the anemic Stalinist PIR to some old socialist groups of the times of Busch, and Guevara Arce's dissident MNR. His conservative character was evidenced when he had to confront miners' strikes, repressed in what came to be know as the "massacre of San Juan," perpetrated by air attacks against mining towns and neighborhoods of La Paz. Things were getting ugly in the Altiplano.

In 1966, Barrientos tried to legitimize his position through trumped-up elections, while most political forces abstained. In any case, he posed as the continuator of the changes initiated by the 1952 revolution, cultivating the support, if not of the workers, at least of the much more numerous peasants, especially their better-off sectors.

Chile and the Second Coming of Ibáñez

In Chile, the Popular Front had undergone a series of internal crises, but had basically maintained the pattern of Radical presidents, and cabinets where members of the Left were present, especially Socialists. In 1946 Gabriel González Videla was elected, but this time with the open support of the Communists, to whom he gave two ministries. This was the second time such a thing was done on the continent, after the example set by Batista in Cuba in 1940. But the honeymoon with the Left did not last long, and partly due to Cold War influences, González Videla expelled his allies and outlawed the party, striking off its militants from the electoral rolls, as in Brazil.

His administration ended without much glory, leaving his party shorn of much of its classical popular support. The Right was always there as an alternative, and the Left was usually able to muster a third of the electorate, though now acrimony between Socialists and Communists made their cooperation impossible. The unforeseen outcome was that General Ibáñez, apparently a political corpse, came back to life, as a hope for those who had lost faith in political parties, including many who had recently joined the electorate, whether by migrating from the countryside to the cities, or by becoming more alert through the increased impact of the mass media. Of great effect also was the news coming from Argentina about prosperity and popular well-being under the aegis of a strong military father figure.

Ibáñez, despite his condemnation of "partidocracia," became associated with a small party created some time before, the Agrario Laborista (PAL), with a name reminiscent of those that had been created by Perón and Vargas. He also involved a faction of the decaying Partido Democrático (its "National" wing, PADENA). But more important than these rubber stamps was the support he obtained from a faction of the Socialist Party, which split for the occasion.

One minority Socialist sector, together with the outlawed Communists, carried Salvador Allende, a man with some experience in Popular Front cabinets, as their candidate. But the greater part of the party, renamed Socialista Popular (PSP), opted for supporting Ibáñez, seen as a Chilean version of Perón. The Argentine ruler was at the time being reevaluated in radical circles on the continent, as a better alternative to old-fashioned social democratic models, deemed to be slavishly copying European experiences. This support involved most of the political leftist militants, including many who had sympathized with the Communists, all of whom overcame their previous resistance against a man who had been a dictator, severely repressed organized labor, and gone to the extent of being a candidate of the Nacional Socialista ("Naci") party in 1938.

Ibáñez won by a landslide, wiping out the independent Left, shamed into 5 percent by the electorate. Apparently, this was something similar to what had happened in the neighboring country, where Perón had also put an end to the influence of the Left. There was one difference, though, in that Ibáñez had the Trojan horse of the Socialists among his cohorts, and Chile's social structure was not Argentina's.[12]

When, after two years of having inaugurated his term in office, Ibáñez confronted a period of lean years, the Socialists broke away, taking with them most of the popular support. The ageing president, a lame duck when he still had four years ahead of him, survived amidst continued crises, and alliances with the Right. And this was the end of Ibañismo.

It is interesting to contrast the formation of the military-trade union coalition in Argentina, between Perón and his Partido Laborista, with that in Chile between Ibáñez and the Socialistas Populares. The latter was an explicitly planned alliance between clearly independent forces in a climate of public liberties, and within a social setting that did not favor a charismatic role for the leader. In Argentina, on the other hand, a veritable political fusion had occurred, and the electorate no longer belonged to the old trade unionists and dissident members of the Left who had accompanied Perón in his bid for power. So Perón, when he clashed with the leaders of the Laborista Party, kicked them out with great ease, and kept authoritarian and *verticalista* control of his renamed Peronist Party.

After Ibáñez the traditional "three tier" system reasserted itself. On the Right, about a third of the electorate was located, favoring two parties with nineteenth-century roots, the Conservatives and the Liberals, who eventually were reunited into a National Party. On the Left, another third of the public gave their preferences, in almost equal proportions, to the Communist and the Socialist parties (the latter often divided), plus some rubber stamps like what remained of the old Demócratas. In the center Radicalism was being slowly replaced by Christian Democracy, which merits a longer treatment.

During the thirties, a politicized and reform-oriented youth had grown up in Catholic milieux, often of quite upper-class origins. The classical confrontation between religious and anticlerical factions made it unthinkable for Catholic militants to affiliate with the "lay arc" spanning from the Liberals to the Radicals and further away to the Marxists. So they had to operate within the Conservative Party, where they formed a very innovative and autonomous youth section, with leaders like Eduardo Frei Montalva, Bernardo Leighton, and Radomiro Tomic.The ideas held by these young activists reached from the social doctrine of the Church to models inspired by Iberian and Mussolini-like authoritarianism, seen as a radical shortcut for social change. In other words, they appeared to be a civilian reproduction of some of the Brazilian *tenentes*, but in a very different social context.

Towards the mid-thirties they separated from the old Conservative fold, and formed their own party, the Falange Nacional, a name that clearly denotes their contradictory beliefs. Soon, however, they sloughed off their early corporatist inclinations, and became just one more center party, engrossed in the unending game of building and destroying congressional majorities. During the 1950s, a further change ripped the Conservative Party, when a not-at-all-youthful sector, with Social Christian ideas, broke away and later joined the Falange, giving birth to the Christian Democratic Party (1958). This was the political formation that started replacing the Radicals in the preferences of the middle classes, which did not need to display any longer their anticlerical attitudes, given the important changes the Catholic Church was undergoing,.[13]

The operation of this three-tier system, at the end of Ibáñez's term, gave the upper hand to the Right, which had as its representative Jorge Alesandri, the totally tamed son of the Lion of Tarapacá. The Left came a close second, again putting up Allende as its candidate, with a united front of Socialists, Communists, and small fragments of the Demócrata Party.[14]

Peru and Ecuador: Variants of Populist Strategy

Peru

In Peru, the conservative government of Manuel Prado (1939-1945) granted free elections, but, of course, without legalizing the Aprista Party. So Haya de la Torre decided to support independent center candidate José Luis Bustamante y Rivero, who thus achieved the presidency. Apristas, who got into Congress under Bustamante's colors, made up the largest bloc in the House, led by the old man, who controlled things from behind the scenes, and had evolved markedly towards moderation, determined to cooperate with progressive sectors in the United States, especially the trade unions and the left wing of the Democratic Party.

But cooperation with Bustamante proved difficult. The rebel traditions of Aprismo got the upper hand, despite being reined in by Haya, and were responsible for a wave of strikes and some subversive attempts, topped by the uprising of Navy marines in the port of Callao. Bustamante then outlawed Apra, repression ensued, and finally the armed forces intervened, led by General Manuel Odría (1948-1956).

Odría, following Spanish Falangista models, had the support of the local and the international conservative forces, and benefited from years of economic prosperity, which allowed him to start some social policies. Lima and other main cities grew, harboring a large population of shantytown dwellers.

The building of low-price housing in those areas, even if insufficient, allowed Odría to gain some popularity. Towards the beginning of the fifties, he tried to reproduce the Argentine model, in a continental context where erstwhile dictators like Vargas and Ibáñez were returning in democratic and popular guise. But Peru's conditions were different, partly because a deeply rooted populism which was not prepared to cooperate with him was already in existence

Odría fell then between two stools, because he failed to obtain a really significant popular following, but he antagonized the upper classes, who were alarmed at the prospect of a repetition of Perón's excesses. The Right suddenly rediscovered its democratic convictions (provided they did not involve an Aprista victory), and in 1956 forced the dictator to convoke free elections, a move also supported by the United States, desirous of cleaning up its backyard, to show the difference with the horrors occurring in the Soviet area. Free competition, that is, but without the Apristas.

The Right was presenting Prado again with a good record but few if any votes of his own. On the left several parties squabbled with each other, but also with few predicaments. The great vacuum was the one created by Apra's absence. Odría thought he, or rather his delegated man (as he accepted being out of the race) might gather a good portion of popular preferences, especially in the Lima *barriadas*, which happened only in a very small scale. The new rising star was that of Fernando Belaúnde Terry, an architect who formed a new party, Acción Popular, with traits similar to those of Christian Democracy. It had a solid grounding among prosperous professional groups with a social conscience, and reaching out to the broad masses. He obviously was trying to replace Apra, posing as a more realistic and moderate alternative.

Many believed that the Apra would support Belaúnde, but it didn't happen that way. Haya's argument was that with Belaúnde, an inexperienced man at the helm of a hastily-put-together force, the Bustamante y Rivero episode would be reenacted. The rabidly anti-Aprista military and upper classes would consider Belaúnde a pawn in the hands of the much stronger Apra, and then would intervene to stop the process. To have the verdict of the ballot boxes honored, it was better to combine votes with money, and therefore he ordered his loyal followers to support Prado, among whose lists some Apristas would be included. Prado could not be accused of eventually becoming a tool in the Apristas' hands, because he had, if not many votes, a solid economic backing to help him hold his own. In this way Haya hoped to divide the field of his enemies, splitting the civilian Right from the military. To end with the domination of the armed forces it was convenient to strike a pact with the capitalist interests, in their relatively more liberal expression. Something like the struggle, during the World War, against fascism.

This strategy was highly condemned in leftist circles, and also by Aprista militants, many of whom abandoned the party to form an Apra Rebelde, which soon became a guerrilla force. But Prado won the election, the Apristas got some seats in Congress and many mayoralties (which were then appointed by the Executive) and strengthened their labor organizations. The price of this so-called Convivencia was, for the Apra, to scuttle its more extreme militants, and for the Right to accept the demise of the Aprista ghost, tolerating their accession to office six years hence.[15]

Ecuador

In Ecuador, Velasco Ibarra had created a political force which was a caricature of Aprismo, with much less cohesion, discipline, and ideological backing. Guayaquil, with its heterogeneous population and its upper class of very recent origin, gave more scope for a populist experience than the conservative, heavily Indian Sierra surrounding Quito. Velasco did form a movement with nationwide characteristics, overcoming to some extent the deep-seated regional animosities, but its organizational structure was rather shallow. The future had in store for him an incredible series of brief periods in power and violent overthrows. Though most of the time he did irritate sectors of the Right (others supported him), he never formed a political force with the challenging capacity against the established order which other populisms had on the continent.

In the previous chapter we saw Velasco, overthrown and exiled in 1934, trying to come back through apparently free elections in 1940. When fraud stopped him he attempted to lead a popular insurrection, with support among the military. But this was easier said than done, and he failed miserably. However, he made a new attempt in 1944. As this was sure to be equally thwarted, popular wrath exploded in Guayaquil, and this time with echo among the armed men. After some fighting, a junta took over, with the support of a motley array of Velasquistas, dissident Liberals, Conservatives, Communists, and Independent Socialists.

This was Velasco's greatest day, when he was able to defeat the oligarchy through what came to be known as "the Glorious 28th of May Revolution." Within the military, there was ferment not totally different from that of the Brazilian *tenentes*, but in this case also fueled by frustration at the loss to Peru of much Amazonian territory, after a short war. Parallels can also be found with the reaction in Bolivia and Paraguay to the Chaco War, though in this case the conflict had been much more circumscribed, and was stopped by inter-American intervention.[16]

Velasco, now in the presidential palace, gave great scope to his leftist friends, who soon overreached themselves, and were set aside. They were replaced with a new political force led by Carlos Guevara Moreno, another popular leader from Guayaquil, who wanted to apply "Peronist" concepts. After two years Velasco, tired of his friends' infighting, decided to stage a coup d'état, dissolving Congress and assuming dictatorial control of the administration (1946). But the armed forces did not approve, and forced him to resign, replacing him with his vice president, appointed by a compliant Congress.

When authority had to be renovated, in 1948, a Liberal-led coalition headed by Galo Plaza won by a small margin against the Conservatives. Galo Plaza was the model ruler for the North American observers. He was a successful businessman, respectful of institutional constraints, the polar opposite of Velasco Ibarra. So respectful he was, that after four years he had no alternative but to accept the verdict of the polls, and let a rejuvenated Velasco Ibarra back at the helm of affairs, this time with the financial support of Perón, and of various populist forces, including his own and that of Guevara Moreno, apart from the fascist-oriented Agrupación Nacionalista Ecuatoriana (ARNE).

This time—the third—he was able to finish his term (1952-1956) and when it ended he supported the Conservatives, who had adopted the Social Christian appellation, and put Camilo Ponce in the presidency. Apparently the country was slowly evolving towards the consolidation of democracy and of orderly change of governments.

However, the 1960 election took place in the new climate created by the Cuban Revolution, which affected the entourage of the old *caudillo*. He ran again, with a coalition spanning from some Catholic conservative groups to radical leftists, forgetting the clashes he had had with them in the past. There was also a more classical leftist formula, sponsored by the Communist Party and some Socialist and Guevara Moreno populists, but many flocked to Velasco's banners, in order to stop the "greater evil" of Washington's protégé Galo Plaza, who was also running.

Things went once again through the usual routine: Velasco president, a wide program of social change, irritation among the easily alarmed Right, military coup after one year (1961), and completion of the term by the vice president. But soon enough, to obviate the danger of ungovernability, the military took power directly in 1963, which they would keep up to 1968. And this time they had ideas of their own, as they had been increasingly convinced that important changes were necessary in order to avoid greater and dangerous ones. But finally public opinion forced them to hold free elections, which were again won by Velasco Ibarra, this time with the support of rival/friend Guevara Moreno's populism based on Guayaquil. In that town, a new leader, Assad Bucaram, had emerged, and was considered a dangerous man, despite, or rather because, of his image of integrity, and his capacity to mobilize the barrios. But the wheel of fortune had not stopped spinning, and rather rapidly too, as those who persist in this story will learn.

Towards a Definition of Populism

By now it is high time to have a closer look at the nature of this oft-used concept, populism, which in recent years has become almost a four-letter word to designate irresponsible economic policies. It is also applied to conservative politicians who appeal to popular feelings and prejudices, and has been tacked on to such otherwise unimpeachably Establishment personalities as Ronald

Reagan and Margaret Thatcher. Though one should not quarrel about names, this exceedingly wide usage is not fruitful, because it can end by applying to almost any politician capable of winning an election.[17]

In contrast, fascism, often adept at mobilizing the masses, is best considered as a different breed, though it has points of contact with what can be properly called populism. The latter concept, as it was developed in the social sciences during the sixties, refers to political expressions which have a capacity to instigate large masses of poorly organized people into action against the privileges of the better-off, even if often a section of the ruling classes joins, or even creates or leads, the movement.

The radical-right parties that have proliferated in several European countries, from France to Austria, also often branded populist, should again be put in another category, because they are not aimed against the dominant groups but rather against underprivileged ones they see as threatening. They do appeal to parts of the native working class, and they antagonize the liberal bourgeoisie and intelligentsia, but their enemies are not to be found mostly among the upper classes. In fact, they are nearer to fascism, but in order to avoid terminological terrorism they should be branded rather "radical nationalists" or "radical Right," as the case may be. Anyway, they should not be mixed with the populist phenomena we are now considering, which combine sharp anti-status quo attitudes with a leadership basically derived from disgruntled minorities from the middle or upper strata.

Populism, thus, tends to take the place of what would be a social democratic or labor party—or the American Democratic Party—if cultural and economic conditions were more mature. In a developing country, social tensions are likely to generate a very troubled and insecure section even among the middle and upper layers of the pyramid, including, of course, the military and the clergy, in search for new ways to cope with their predicament. Their very strategic presence in the popular coalition does make a difference with the social democratic or labour patterns.[18]

Summarizing the above analysis, populism may be defined as a political movement based on a mobilized but not yet autonomously organized popular sector, led by an elite rooted among the middle and upper echelons of society, and kept together by a charismatic, personalized link between leader and led, the result, in turn, of widespread social and cultural traits often found on the periphery. Depending on how these factors operate, different forms of populism emerge, mostly as a result of the type of anti-status quo elites involved. Some of those factors are also present in first world countries, but on the periphery they operate with far greater intensity. It is possible to hypothesize that once social conditions turn towards a more urban, educated, and secular pattern, populism may be deprived of some of its breeding grounds, and be replaced by some form of social democracy, whether through an internal mutation, or by losing its electoral support to a new challenger to its left.[19]

Parallel to the slow demise of populism, one may expect also a growth of self-proclaimed Conservative parties, by that or any other name. Populism robs the Right of its potential clientele among some of the poorer strata of the population in rural or peripheral urban areas, and among regionalist-oriented middle strata and leadership cadres. This is paradoxical, because populism is usually the main antagonist of the conservative parties, which exist almost everywhere, even if they do not get many votes. Conservatism and populism do have quite distinct core constituencies, the former among the majority of the well-to-do, and the latter among the more urbanized working class. Those two core constituencies happen to be also the same for modern conservative and social democratic parties. In between, a lot of intermediate sectors, often quite unsophisticated in their political attitudes, fluctuate. Traditional conservatism often lacks, in Latin America, the capacity to coopt the middle classes, or sizeable sectors of the rural or urban poor. Thus, the middle classes go their own way, becoming the backbone of center parties, while the poorer strata remain available for populist mobilization from above. As society evolves, and what may be called political culture develops, associationist practices spread, creating alternatives to populism on the left.

A strong conservative party or alliance is very likely to have a sizeable sector with authoritarian tendencies, reflecting the attitudes dominant among its constituency. Nevertheless, it performs a positive role in democratization, precisely because it provides means of legitimate expression to those sectors, which are forced to mingle with others of their basic conservative persuasion, but more prepared to engage in consensual politics. It would be almost tautological to say that a strong Conservative party, if fully sharing democratic values, would perform a positive role in maintaining them. The less obvious hypothesis is that even a not very democratically oriented party can perform that role, because of the way it funnels and blends basic class interests and feelings into the political arena. Similar considerations apply to the Left: it is a generally confirmed fact that when it has an ample electorate it tends to moderation, even if it usually includes a minority of authoritarian elements.

A political system capable of channeling the tensions existing in any economically developed democracy needs at least two mechanisms of interest: articulation and aggregation. On one side, a party where the entrepreneurial classes will feel comfortable, knowing that it will defend their interests and can occasionally win an election. On the other, a party linked to the trade unions and other popular sectors.[20]

Generally the former can be called the "party of the Right," and the latter the "Left" or "Popular party." These terms can be challenged, as often the popular party will have many conservative traits (as is typically the case with Peronismo), and the party voted by the entrepreneurs may also get the support of the intelligentsia as a second best. But under whatever names, the expression of those two sets of interests, that is, the entrepreneurs and the working class, is necessary for the consolidation of democracy, once a certain level of economic and cultural development has been attained. Populism should be seen as a rather crude form of expressing those interests, under conditions of relative social primitivism.

Venezuela, Cuba, and Colombia: The Struggle Against Militarism

Venezuela

In Venezuela, Gómez's more liberal successors' regime was ended by a military coup by young officers, with the full support of the Aprista-like Acción Democrática Party. Free elections gave an overwhelming majority to this party, with a very radical program of social change, including land reform and educational changes that could only lead to a frontal clash with the Catholic Church. The Communist Party reemerged from clandestinity, but without much electoral presence. Labor unions were mostly controlled by Acción Democrática, with a quite smaller leftist presence. A Christian Democratic Party was formed in the opposition, under the name of Comité de Organización Política Electoral Independiente (COPEI), led by Rafael Caldera, who had evolved from early authoritarian attitudes towards a more mainstream alignment with contemporary European models

After two years of a transitional government by a military junta, Rómulo Gallegos, a respected novelist but inept politician, was elected, though the real power behind the throne remained Rómulo Betancourt, founder of Acción Democrárica and its undisputed leader. The regime, known as the Trienio (1945-1948), witnessed very high social polarization. The local conservative forces, together with the church and the oil corporations, and the blessing of the United States, finally paved the way for a military coup.

Thus a long dictatorship was inaugurated, under the command of General Marcos Pérez Jiménez, one of the plotters of 1945, who benefited from years of oil bonanza. Rural-urban migration created an enormous belt of poverty around Caracas, despite the government's attempts to alleviate it by construction of cheap housing. The process echoed to some extent the contemporaneous Peruvian events, and Pérez Jiménez had some success in cultivating popular support among the barrios, as his colleague Odría, but without being able to compete with Acción Democrática.

Acción Democrática's strength, however, like the Apra's, did not lie so much in the larger cities' proletariat as in the mining concentrations, in this case oil, and among the provincial middle classes and the peasants, who had benefited from a moderate land reform. The capital city's more prosperous middle class, by contrast, did not favor a mobilizational approach to politics, but preferred the Christian Democrats, or other groups split from Acción Democrática.

In January 1958 the wave of cleaning-up the backyard that had already disposed of Odría (1956) and of Colombia's Rojas Pinilla (1957), reached

Pérez Jiménez, who was toppled by a combined civic-military movement. Now Betancourt could come back to power, exerting it more directly than the previous time, and he was prepared to do it in an extremely cautious way, like Haya de la Torre, with whom he had a close relationship. This meant a decidedly anticommunist position, openness to foreign investments, and a break with the leftist elements within his own party. With this mental set, Betancourt got together with the leaders of the main parties (COPEI and other middle-of-the-road groups) except the Communists, and including the main business association (Fedecámaras). They came to an agreement to respect each other's positions, trying to cooperate in government whenever possible and avoid the confrontations of the Trienio. The negotiation was known as the Pacto de Punto Fijo, after the name of the home of one of the signers.

Betancourt thus achieved his ambitions (1959-1964), but his party lost its left wing, which formed the Movimiento de Izquierda Revolucionaria (MIR), soon converted to guerrilla activity under Fidel Castro's prompting. The Christian Democrat COPEI became the main opposition, mosty center-right, against AD's center-left, with occasional presence of smaller parties. Venezuela was well on its way to becoming a paragon of democracy in an otherwise very agitated continent.[21]

Cuba

Towards the years we are covering the force which hypnotized the Left was Fidel Castro, who had incredibly overpowered the northern Goliath and his local minions. Batista's first government (1940-1944), scrupulously respectful of democratic principles, had been followed by the hegemony of the Partido Revolucionario Cubano Auténtico (PRCA) of Raúl Grau San Martín, who was president from 1944 to 1948, followed by Carlos Prío Socarrás (1948-1952). Both of them, in contrast with Batista, adopted an adamant anticommunist stance, fully immersed in the Cold War mentality. They eroded Communist domination of the labor movement, substituting their own party's stalwarts, who became increasingly corrupt and violent. New forces, invoking the tradition of Martí, led by Senator Eduardo Chibás, formed the Partido del Pueblo, also known as Ortodoxo, one of whose rank and file members was young Fidel Castro. Chibás had a wide impact on public opinion through his radio program, where he inveighed against all forms of corruption and abuse of power. Despairing of a change by other means, he sought to create a major impact and moral revulsion by committing suicide during his radio transmission, becoming a martyr but without really changing very much the social and political panorama. Except, maybe, in firing people like Fidel Castro to even more determined action.

At the end of Prío Socarrás's period, a reelection of Grau San Martín was in the offing, but this was cut short by a coup d'état by Batista (1952-1958), who started a dictatorial regime not exempt from some populist trappings, based on the unimpeachable record of his 1940-1944 term. At this time the labor movement in Cuba was internally quite divided, among the followers of Batista, who claimed to be a local Perón, those of the Revolucionario Auténtico Party, akin to Aprismo, and the Communists. The Ortodoxos of the self-immolated Chibás, were stronger among students than among the working class.

Batista, who had recourse to increasingly violent and repressive measures, was one of the dictators on the waiting list for "clean up" as the fifties wore on. A guerrilla movement started by Fidel Castro and a few other militants succeeded in maintaining a focus, and developing roots among the peasant population, though always on a small scale. The challenge didn't seem mortal, and the rebellion could be equated with those raging in Peru and Venezuela, which were eventually wiped out. But when the United States government decided to promote a change, Batista's days were numbered. Castro's guerrilla movement received help from the exiled Prío Socarrás and from other American sources, while the United States government curtailed arms support for the dictator. This was a clear signal to a wide sector of civilian and military opinion, and finally the regime crumbled, against the surging wave of Castro's followers.

On the very first day of 1959, Castro was master of Havana, inaugurating a regime which seemed to be a slightly more radical version of such popular revolutionary parties as the Apra and Acción Democrática, or the Bolivian MNR. In fact, Fidel received support from Betancourt, and the initial blessing of Haya de la Torre, but soon they were going to pull apart, to a large extent due to a shortsighted policy on the part of the American government. Castro's own revolutionary group, named Movimiento 26 de Julio, came to banish other forces, adopting the Communist name after merging with the Partido Socialista Popular, the local name of their new allies. Tensions persisted between the two components of the new party, but they were eventually subsumed under Fidel Castro's charismatic and quite *verticalista* leadership.[22]

Colombia

In Colombia the *Violencia* had prompted a military intervention in 1953, with passive support among moderate members of both parties, by General Gustavo Rojas Pinilla, who after a few years achieved quite a widespread pacification. This success stimulated demands for a return to the Constitution. For Rojas the temptation was strong to remain in power, so as to be able to launch the social reforms necessary if a permanent solution to the violence was to be found. In this process, Rojas surrounded himself with leftist advisors, including Antonio García, leader of a minuscule Socialist Party, and many Gaitanistas, trying also to follow on Perón's steps. This required forming his own political party, not an easy task.

The fact is that, in an even starker way than Peru's Odría, he managed to alarm the conservative classes, without getting much support from the have-nots, most of whom were still rural and not yet highly mobilized. He fell victim to a coup by his own comrades, preceded by a widespread civilian resistance, strikes and lockouts. In contrast with Peru, though, rather than a menacing Aprista movement a very strongly rooted two-party system existed. To avoid the renewal of violent confrontations, Conservatives and Liberals agreed, in a Pacto de Benidorm (a Spanish locality where they met in exile) to share power for a very long time. Even recalcitrant Laureano Gómez, now converted to democracy, signed this pact, and so did practically the entire political class of the country, except the surviving Gaitanistas and disorganized Pinillistas.

The pact stipulated that during sixteen years the top job would alternate between the two parties, while all ministries, congressional seats, and local authorities would be equally shared by them. The arrangement, with constitutional force, was approved by a referendum. In effect, and by agreement, democratic elections were eliminated, though the formality was maintained, in order to select from the various alternative candidates of the party whose turn it was. After sixteen years of this system, its application was extended for a further four years, so that only in 1978 did the first openly competitive elections take place.[23]

The first ruler of the so-called Frente Nacional regime was the Liberal Alberto Lleras Camargo, who had to implement, among other things, legal proceedings against Rojas Pinilla. After passing through those proceedings, and posing as a victim of revenge, Rojas did resurface, and finally organized his own party, or movement, the Alianza Nacional Popular (ANAPO), trying to profit from the memories of his stint in power, and the erosion of the new system. The lack of enthusiasm for it was responsible for a low participation on election day, often less than 50 percent of potential voters.

In 1970, when it was the turn of the Conservatives, a limiting situation presented itself. Taking advantage of a legal loophole as to who could claim to be a Conservative, Rojas Pinilla registered his candidacy as within the fold of that political family. It so happened that at the time the party was seriously divided between its official candidate Misael Pastrana, and another one, the son of Laureano Gómez, Álvaro, who had become an enemy of the Front arrangement, and was veering towards the radical Right, but with anti-status-quo overtones.

Pastrana got the votes of all the Liberals who cared to go to the polls, and of the official Conservatives. But the nominally Conservative vote was divided in three, that is, Pastrana, Gómez and Rojas. Rojas obtained some 40 percent of the grand total, clearly less than the sum of the others, but only a bit less than Pastrana. Or so they said, but the Pinillistas never believed it, and maintained that they had been robbed of the prize. This was the main challenge the Frente received in its history. Soon afterwards the ANAPO slid into a clearly minoritarian position, and led by the general's daughter, it retained for a time some strength, especially in the barriadas of Bogotá, but eventually disappeared.

It would be necessary to wait a couple of decades for another serious challenge to the two-party system, but meanwhile violence was coming back, partly fanned by Pinillista extremists, who formed a guerrilla group called Movimiento 19 (M-19), in memory of the day of the stolen elections, April 19, 1970. The seeds of violence, which had not been eradicated from Colombian soil, sprang again, with a greater class content. As in other parts of the continent, Marxist guerrillas became a permanent feature of vast areas, and even upper-class priests like Camilo Torres led some of them. Ominously, narcotraffic was also taking hold, and entering into strange coalitions with other subversive forces.

The PRI Consolidates Its Hold on Mexico

In Mexico, the revolutionary regime, increasingly integrative of various tendencies and interest groups, retained its grip on power, and led a very successful economic development, even if very unevenly distributed. Ávila Camacho was succeeded by Miguel Alemán (1946-1952), while the party hegemony reached its maximum expression. The PRI systematically won elections with considerable ballot-box stuffing, but probably it would have won anyway, even if an honest count had been held. The people running the system claimed that if real competition existed passions would be fanned, and they always kept in mind Porfirio Díaz's reproach to Madero, while boarding the ship for exile, about the danger of unleashing the tigers of his native land. In the same way as Adenauer exclaimed, in postwar Germany, "keine experimenten!" Mexicans were made to proceed very slowy on the path of genuine democratization, if at all.

PRI domination was based on its revolutionary tradition, which earned it a lot of popular support, and on its experience of rapid economic growth. The new entrepreneurs would have preferred a less radical phraseology, but anyway they mostly accepted the regime, from which they were profiting, in legal and illegal ways. Some of their more principled members, however, favored the Partido de Acción Nacional (PAN), of Catholic and Vasconcellian roots, which identified with the Madero phase of the regime, and in fact expressed mostly conservative and free enterprise sectors.

A great part of the entrepreneurial class was quite conscious that free-market nostrums could not be applied to a country at the stage of development of Mexico, where state intervention, and a determined protectionism, were necessary in order to allow the launching of an industrialization process. Besides, the nation's violent traditions made it advisable to have a party in power which had showed its capacity to mediate and filter popular demands, conceding something to them, both in reality and at a verbal level. This interfered somewhat with rural capitalist development, as investors were wary of *agrarista* unrest, periodically revived, but in the comercial, financial, and industrial areas things were much quieter. As long as rates of growth came close to the two-digit mark, there was no problem. As for the Left, a proliferation of parties only reached small minorities of the intelligentsia and the workers, and was severely crushed when it raised its head more menacingly outside of the Federal District.

Notes

1. Robert Potash, *Perón y el GOU, los documentos de una logia secreta,* and his *El ejército y la política en la Argentina*; Alain Rouquié, *Poder militar y sociedad política en la Argentina*; Manuel Mora y Araujo and Peter Smith, eds., *El voto peronista*; José Vazeilles, *Los socialistas.*
2. Adolfo Dorfman, *Cincuenta años de industrialización en la Argentina, 1930-1980*; Dardo Cúneo, *Comportamiento y crisis de la clase empresaria*; Cristina Lucchini, *Apoyo empresarial en los orígenes del peronismo*; Jorge Schvarzer, *Empresarios del pasado: la Unión Industrial Argentina.*
3. This is a highly controversial subject. See Gino Germani, *Política y sociedad en una época de transición: de la sociedad tradicional a la sociedad de masas,* chs. 4 and 9, and "El surgimiento del peronismo, el rol de los obreros y los migrantes internos"; Miguel Murmis and Juan Carlos Portantiero, *Estudios sobre los orígenes del peronismo*; Juan Carlos Torre, *Perón y la vieja guardia sindical*; Joel Horowitz, *Argentine Unions, the State, and the Rise of Perón, 1930-1945.*
4. Fernando Henrique Cardoso, *Ideologías de la burguesía industrial en sociedades dependientes: Argentina y Brasil*; Christian Buchrucker, *Nacionalismo y peronismo, la Argentina en la crisis ideológica mundial, 1927-1955.*
5. Maria Vitória Benevides, *A UDN e o udenismo*; Lucia Hippolito, *De raposas e reformistas: o PSD e a experiência democrática brasileira*; Ángela de Castro Gomes, *A invenção do trabalhismo*; Edgard Carone, *Movimento operário no Brasil, 1877-1944.*
6. Jean-Pierre Bernard et al., *Tableau des partis politiques en Amérique du Sud,* p. 136.
7. Paulo Brandi, *Vargas, da vida para a história,* pp. 204-205 and 211; Maria Celina Soares D'Araújo, *O segundo governo Vargas, 1951-1954: democracia, partidos e crise política*; John W.F. Dulles, *Getúlio Vargas, biografia política.*
8. Gláucio Dillon Soares and Nelson do Vale Silva, "Urbanization, Race and Class in Brazilian Politics."
9. Robert Alexander, *Labor relations in Argentina, Brazil and Chile*; Eugenio Kvaternik, *Crisis sin salvataje: la crisis político-militar de 1962-63.*
10. Gustavo Varela, *De la República liberal al Estado militar: Uruguay 1968-1973.*
11. Paul Lewis, *Paraguay under Stroessner,* and his *Socialism, Liberalism and Dictatorship in Paraguay.*
12. Paul Drake, *Socialism and Populism in Chile.*
13. George Grayson, *El Partido Demócrata Cristiano Chileno*; M. Fleet, *The Rise and Fall of Chilean Christian Democracy*; Timothy R. Scully, *Rethinking the Center: Cleavages, Critical Junctures and Party Evolution in Chile.*
14. James Petras and Maurice Zeitlin, *El radicalismo político de la clase trabajadora chilena*; Jorge Barría, *El movimiento obrero en Chile.*
15. Francisco Miró Quesada, *La ideología de Acción Popular*; Carlos Valenzuela, *Frustraciones y realidades políticas en América Latina: del APRA al MNR*; Víctor Villanueva, *La tragedia de un pueblo y un partido*; Daniel Castro, ed., *Revolutions and Revolutionaries: Guerrilla Movements in Latin America.*
16. Pablo Cuvi, *Velasco Ibarra: el último caudillo de la oligarquía*; Silvia Vega Ugalde, *La gloriosa: de la revolución del 28 de mayo de 1944 a la contrarrevolución*

velasquista; Agustín Cueva, *El proceso de dominación política en el Ecuador*, and his articles "Interpretación sociológica del velasquismo," and "Ecuador, 1925-1975"; Rafael Quintero, *El mito del populismo en el Ecuador*; Felipe Burbano de Lara and Carlos de la Torre Espinosa, eds., *El populismo en el Ecuador*.
17. Rudiger Dornbusch and S. Edwards, eds., *The Macroeconomics of Populism in Latin America*.
18. For the concept of neocorporativism, meaning a state-sponsored recognition of sectorial interests as participants in policy making, see Gerhard Lehmbruch and Philippe Schmitter, eds., *Patterns of Corporatist Policy Making*; Philippe Schmitter and Gerhard Lehmbruch, eds., *Trends Toward Corporatist Intermediation*; Philippe Schmitter and J. Grot, *Corporative Sisyphus*.
19. The concept of social mobilization is used in different forms in the literature. Here it is defined as the breakdown of traditional loyalties and controls linking the popular strata to those above them. See Karl Deutsch, "Social mobilization and political development" and Gino Germani, *Política y sociedad en una época de transición*. Other authors, like Charles Tilly, in his *From Mobilization to Revolution*, use the concept of social mobilization to indicate a confrontationist activity that demands among other things organization and shared ideas as to goals. For that type of phenomena I prefer to use the word political mobilization. A political mobilization implies a previous state of social mobilization, which is something that happens to people, an external force acting on them. It sets them free from traditional constraints, but as they still lack much experience in organizing themselves autonomously they require leadership from above. See also Douglas Madsen and Peter Snow, *The Charismatic Bond: Political Behavior in Times of Crisis*; regarding the formation of coalitions, William Riker, *The Theory of Political Coalitions*, and Barbara Geddes, *Politician's Dilemma: Building State Capacity in Latin America*. See also Ghita Ionescu and Ernest Gellner, eds. *Populism: Its Meanings and National Characteristics*; Michael L. Conniff, *Latin American Populism in Comparative Perspective;* Adam Przeworski, *Capitalism and Social Democracy*.
20. See also Philippe Schmitter and Terry Lynn Karl, "What Democracy Is, and Is Not."
21. John Duncan Powell, *Political Mobilization of the Venezuelan Peasant*; Philip B. Taylor Jr, *The Venezuelan Golpe de Estado of 1958: The Fall of Marcos Pérez Jiménez*; John D. Martz, *Acción Democrática: Evolution of a Modern Political Party in Venezuela*; René Salgado, "Economic Pressure Groups and Policy-Making in Venezuela: The Case of Fedecámaras Reconsidered."
22. Andrés Suárez, *Cuba: Castroism and Communism, 1959-1966*; Maurice Zeitlin, *Revolutionary Politics and the Cuban Working Class*.
23. Robert Dix, *Colombia: The Political Dimensions of Change*; Richard Sharpless, *Gaitán of Colombia: A Political Biography*; Antonio García, *La rebelión de los pueblos débiles*; Elmo Valencia, *Libro rojo de Rojas*; Felipe Echavarría Olazaga, *Colombia, una democracia indefensa: la resurrección de Rojas Pinilla*; John A. Booth, "Rural Violence in Colombia, 1948-63."

5

The Sixties and Seventies: From Revolution to Military Intervention

When Manuel Prado's second term (1956-1962) finished, free elections were held, this time with full Aprista participation, with the result that Haya de la Torre won the race by a small margin over Belaúnde Terry, Odría arriving in third place. But the tug of war between the Apra and the Right and the military was not finished. At the same time, guerrilla activity was rife, including dissident Aprista groups. The military, confronting this scenario, decided to intervene, claiming abuses on the part of Prado's government in favor of Apra.

A junta was thus established, which quickly organized a return to civilian rule, a strategy Alfred Stepan has called *moderating*, that is, purportedly only aimed at correcting some malfunctionings of the electoral system, rather than founding a new authoritarian regime. The idea was to transfer power to another more amenable group of civilian politicians, hopefully more sensitized to the needs of capital accumulation. This is what happened: within a year a new popular verdict gave a slight majority to Belaúnde Terry, who was thus inaugurated. In the new Congress, the Apra, incensed by this manipulation of results, played a determinedly obstructionist role, even in joint actions with Odría, whose party, in any case, did not survive for long.[1]

During the brief span of military rule, there were rumors of a presumed "Nasserism" among some officers. This current of opinion, in fact, had been growing, especially among intelligence specialists, who were looking for radically new strategies to fight simultaneously the subversive and the Aprista challenges. They came upon the scarcely original idea that radical changes were necessary in order to root out discontent. Seen from this perspective, the short-sighted conservative classes, who opposed reforms, were as dangerous to the existing social order as those who went to the mountains to destroy it. On the other hand, in order to institute the contemplated radical changes, it was necessary to suppress for a long time any party competition, as well as constitutional freedoms.

What had happened was that the military, during their fight against the guerrillas, had been forced to get into closer contact with the "real Peru" than ever before, and they came to understand the revolutionaries' concerns, if not to share them. In any case, a mental mutation was taking place among those who were believed to be the guard dogs of the oligarchy.

In 1968, when only a few months were left before the end of Belaúnde's administration, an almost sure Aprista victory was forecasted, due to the natural erosion of popularity of the incumbents. The military, still determined to bar the way to the Apristas, decided this time to intervene before and not after the foreseeable electoral result. They took as a justification a scandal linked to an oil concession given to an American company, based on an eleven-page contract from which the last page had been mysteriously withdrawn. The coup took place, thus invalidating the whole complex strategy Haya de la Torre had spun as a means to foil his adversaries, who proved to be harder and more resourceful that what he had imagined.

The "Peruvian Revolution"

The new regime of the "Peruvian Revolution" was led by General Manuel Velasco Alvarado, who was one of the officers more genuinely convinced of the need for the proposed reforms. Many items from the more radical Aprista platforms were adopted and put into effect, taking also points from the leftist parties' programs. Solid support was obtained from the intelligentsia—national and Latin American—who didn't put much store in the values of "formal bourgeois democracy." Some Aprista leaders were involved with the new regime, which, after all, was enacting some of their more cherished projects, even if under a different political system, one of whose purposes, and not the least of them, was precisely to destroy the bases of Aprista strength.

The new rulers delivered the mostly archaic and inefficient latifundia in the Sierra region to agrarian communities, as in Mexico, though now as a concession from above, not a violently hard-won conquest. They also took over the sugar enterprises, converting them into cooperatives run by their workers with some state surveillance. In this case, the aim was not so much to increase productivity as to erode the Aprista hold over the workers of that industry. Existing foreign-owned mining concerns were also nationalized, though an area for new private international investment was maintained. For most industrial businesses an "industrial community" was created, by which the work collective (not the individual workers) were to receive in shares a percentage of profits, till they came to own 49 percent of the total share capital.

The state also expropriated national circulation newspapers, beginning with *El Comercio*, giving them to journalists' cooperatives, or other associations like trade unions, peasant federations, and the like. Under the direction of an erstwhile Aprista militant a national Sistema Nacional de Movilización Social (SINAMOS) was created, in charge of establishing connections between the national or local authorities and the various popular groups, residential units or work communities. This "participatory" dialogue was supposed to supersede the discredited functioning of parties—which were closed down—and of Congress, seen as mere institutional smokescreens for the domination of the capitalists.

The convergence with many of the theories, and above all the gut feelings, of vast sectors of the intelligentsia was appalling. For many, the Peruvian Revolution was a more practical alternative to the Cuban way, among other reasons because the military supported it. But few challenged the elimination of competitive elections, fearing to be branded as old-style liberals.

The interesting feature of the new regime was that it didn't attempt to create a political party, either because it didn't believe in such a thing, or because it was not able to do it. Actually, the SINAMOS never got off the ground. The preexistence of a populist movement, still very much rooted among the popular classes, probably was one of the main reasons for the fiasco. This fact should be contrasted with the success a similar military group had, some years earlier, in Argentina, in launching a permanent new movement, despite its equally strong anti-party ideological convictions. Admittedly, the two countries were very different, and at the time Peru was not going through a stretch of prosperity, as Perón enjoyed.

The early years of the Peruvian regime were relatively prosperous, and they had rather ample support in middle- and upper-class public opinion, which welcomed the disappearance of the Aprista menace, and hoped to partake in the spoils the regime was so widely generating. In a sense, what was occurring was a repetition, in a much less violent context, under strict hierarchical control and without mass mobilization, of the Mexican Revolution, which had proved to be an efficient method of generating wealth for those who knew how to adapt.

However, and precisely because the destruction of a whole old dominant class had not occurred, as in Mexico, the regimentation of public opinion behind the new authorities was never very complete. After a few years the reticence of investors, the difficulty in establishing authority in the new socialized enterprises, and the hostility of the liberal sectors of public opinion, combined with an ecological disaster caused by the withdrawal of the *anchovetas* deep into the Pacific, hitting mortally the fish fertilizer industry, spelled the end of the regime.[2]

Revolutionary Bolivia: No News from Paraguay

In Bolivia, the Barrientos coup (1964) inaugurated a twenty-year period of utter chaos and oscillating strategies by all political actors. Barrientos had combined military authoritarianism with peasant support, but a fatal aviation accident cut short this experience. His vice president, a civilian, despite his former socialist connections, was taken to be a representative of the Rosca by the rural activists, who proclaimed General Ovando "peasant leader," towards the end of that same year 1969, aiming at revitalizing the military-peasant pact started by Barrientos and tarnished by his own repressive policies on the labor front.

Given this new orientation, Lechín's Confederación Obrera Boliviana (COB) gave its support to the revolutionary government of the armed forces, while the repressive apparatus was being dismantled. A wide civilian group, including sectors of the MNR, leftwing social Christians, and the Socialist Marcelo Quiroga Santa Cruz, cooperated in the cabinet. One of its first decisions was to again nationalize oil production, which had been given as a concession to Gulf by Barrientos.

The persistence of social confrontation in the mines, plus peasant mobilization dating from the 1952 revolution, and the uneasiness of the intelligentsia, stimulated the most unprejudiced search for solutions among the guardians of public order, precisely in order to be able to maintain it, though often disturbing it in the process. At a certain moment the accumulation of pressures on Ovando led him to resign. In the ensuing chaos, a coup within the coup took place, led by General Juan José Torres, an admirer of the Peruvian Revolution, supported by a general strike. Bolivians then attempted to apply a more radical version of what was happening in the neighboring country, also without incorporating most members of the popular party, in this case the MNR, who thought of themselves as the real inventors of the model.

The new authorities convened a Popular Assembly which was to perform consultative roles. There, the extreme left got a sizeable representation, including the recently established Partido Socialista, Lechín's Partido Revolucionario de Izquierda Nacional (PRIN), and the Trotskyite Partido Obrero Revolucionario (POR) who had Guillermo Lora as its guide. To this were added splinter groups from the MNR or from Christian Democracy, the latter having formed a Movimiento de Izquierda Revolucionaria (MIR).

The Assembly resounded with the echoes of the eighteenth-century Parisian Convention, or Lenin's Soviets. Forceful occupation of factories, the remaining privately owned landed estates, and even research and university centers, were everyday happenings, creating a situation which could have easily gotten out of control. Finally, a right-wing sector of the armed forces put an end to this agitation, inaugurating a long dictatorial rule by General Hugo Banzer Suárez, in August 1971. This time he was supported by the majority faction of the MNR, led by Paz Estenssoro, and by the Falange (FSB). Both "historic" organizations had been out of power during the hectic recent years, and were seen as heralding a return to moderation and normality, despite their traditional enmity.[3]

In 1974, a second stage in Banzer's rule was initiated, with a cancellation of the agreement with the MNR and FSB, the banishment of all party activity, the intervention of most trade unions, and a commitment to redemocratize the country in six years' time. Banzer's years in power, contrasting with the previous disorder, were accompanied by economic growth, stability, North American support and international investment.

In Paraguay, meanwhile, not much happened, at least nothing seriously capable of rocking the solid dictatorship of General Stroessner, who, as we have seen, did enjoy some elements of popular support, via the Colorado Party. One of the bases of his popularity was a very dynamic policy of land distribution, which seen in statistical tables seems descriptive of the proceedings in Mexico. This was done using the ample reserves of state property, and was unaccompanied by adequate credit or technological support, but it did create an ample group of thankful smallholders, usually the sons of the older *campesinos* settled around Asunción, who thought that this was better than nothing.[4]

Brazil: Radicalization under Goulart and Military Coup

In Brazil, quick growth, opening to foreign investment, and monumental constructions under Juscelino Kubitshek (1956-1961), builder of Brasilia, were changing the country, but the country faced the usual problem of succession, still under the effect of the crisis caused by Vargas's suicide. It will be recalled that at the time constitutional normality had been saved by a preemptive coup organized by General Teixeira Lott, a member of the nationalist, that is, broadly speaking Varguista, section of the armed forces. Now it was time to repay him, not only out of *noblesse oblige*, but in order to cement a friendship that would be a guarantee against future upheavals, as those that were ravaging Argentina. So, despite being a bad speaker and incapable of arousing public enthusiasm, Lott became the candidate of the Varguista coalition of the Partido Social Democrático (PSD) and Partido Trabalhista Brasileiro (PTB). This hardly stimulating choice was compensated by his running mate, firebrand João Goulart, who could attract activists and others among the masses who needed a charismatic figure.

The opportunity was taken hold of by the União Democrática Nacional (UDN), which suddenly saw the light at the end of the tunnel. It decided to coopt a maverick political *condottiere* from Sao Paulo, Jánio Quadros, who at the head of a personalist following had become mayor of the city, with a broom as his very explicit symbol. There was also a third candidate, Adhemar de Barros, a Paulista former collaborator of Vargas, who had formed his own populist party, based on his native state. The election was very balanced, and the results appalling: Quadros won the presidency, and Goulart the vice presidency, positions that at the time were voted for separately. The worst had happened, in terms of political stability.[5]

Basically, despite some verbal excesses of the candidate, it was a conservative victory, won at the price of coopting a heterodox political figure, who presumably would know how to keep his place. But far from it, Quadros pretended to leave his mark on history, adopting innovatory internal and foreign policies, inspired by Charles de Gaulle, who was capable of withdrawing from NATO and meeting Mao Tse Tung without raising an excessive outcry. Thus, among other things, Quadros invited and honored Che Guevara, and he adopted some more concrete decisions on economic matters. The business community felt betrayed and deprived of the fruits of what after all had been *their* electoral victory as much as the president's.

It was pointless labor to try to convince the Right that these were only concessions, necessary to consolidate a national leadership so closely menaced by Goulartismo. The resistance among civilian and military sectors was adamant, and led to a demand for change, as those that every couple of months were made in Argentina and obediently put into effect by Frondizi.

Quadros didn't want to follow that example, and resisted. Without going to the length of Vargas, he resigned, hoping to be asked to remain in office, especially because the prospect of Goulart coming to replace him was really ominous for the Establishment. Attempts were made to dissuade him but with no results. The motives for his stubbornness are not known, but the image of De Gaulle internally exiled in Colombey-les-Deux-Églises was surely on his mind. The fact is that Quadros was caught at his own game, his resignation accepted, and Goulart recalled from continental China, where we was conducting a suspicious study tour.

The armed forces decided that such a man was incapable of occupying the executive post, but a faction, not by chance posted in Rio Grande do Sul (Goulart's home state), and headed by a nationalist general, resisted the attempted coup, and prepared for armed confrontation. At this moment the experienced political class started frantic negotiations to avoid the possibility of a protracted civil war, with the always-feared fatal consequences. They decided to adopt a Parliamentary regime, allowing Goulart to occupy the Palace of the Alvorada, but in the sorry role of a European chief of state. Thus the country was pacified.[6]

The traits of the Brazilian electorate were such, that the same people who for the national executive post chose a firebrand like Goulart, at the state and municipal levels would vote for local notables, usually very moderate and cooptable by the Establishment. Thus a conservative majority existed in Congress, including many members of the Varguista coalition, notably its PSD wing.[7]

But Brazil is not Europe, and Goulart, once at the helm, started pulling the strings till he managed to call for a plebiscite to confirm or annul the new dispensation. Predictably, a majority decided, in January 1963, to return to strong executive rule, with the argument that even if Parliamentarism was the method adopted in most highly developed countries, precisely for that reason it was inappropriate in Latin America, where it could only consolidate the local oligarchical or clientelistic clans.

So now Goulart could use the formidable power of the Brazilian presidency, were he found himself surrounded by an extremely heterogeneous group of leftist activists, ranging from the Moscow-oriented Communist Party to other fractions following the inspiration of Mao Tse Tung, or of Fidel Castro, mixed with independent leftists, Trabalhistas and bourgeois nationalists. By contrast, the Varguista right, that is, the PSD, which was based among local notables, was increasingly concerned, as much if not more than the anti-Varguista UDN, a more modern party based on the upper and middle classes of the industrially advanced areas. Those two parties, though rivals, had a majority in Congress, and thus could block Goulart's plans, but street agitation was another matter.[8]

Goulart's program included radical land reform, expropriating with little if any compensation the best-located latifundia, productive or not. He stimulated the formation of "groups of eleven," sets of armed people ready to overcome the expected violent resistance of the landowners. In the Northeast, especially in sugar-producing Pernambuco, armed Ligas Agrarias were active, led by Francisco Julião, from the small Socialist Party, but well connected to the local Trabalhistas' leftist leader, Miguel Arraes.

The intended reforms, as they did not have much hope of passing through Congress, were left in the hands of popular agitation, which was extended to the lower ranks of the armed forces, reaching down to non-commissioned officers and privates. Goulart and his entourage hoped in this manner to make an impact on public opinion, reaching the remotest places, and get a majority in the future Congress. The more enthusiastic were already preparing for an armed uprising, with wide mass mobilization and connection with a military faction, if at all possible.[9]

All this agitation occurred in a political context in which the governorships of the three main federal units, São Paulo, Minas Gerais, and Guanabara (Rio de Janeiro) were in the hands of the UDN or the by now right-wing oppositionist Adhemar de Barros. The Catholic Church, which also felt menaced by the proposed reforms in the educational system, and had many sectors closely linked to the upper classes, joined the opposition, organizing massive demonstrations with empty pots and pans and other accoutrements of the ritual.

Finally, in early 1964 a coup led by General Humberto Castelo Branco, with strong civilian support from the middle and of course upper classes, took place. To cover appearances, it did not dissolve Congress (where it had a friendly majority) but only purged it of its more extreme elements, mostly from the PTB and some Marxists. After this cleanup the ritual was performed of having this body elect Castelo Branco president of the Republic. At first political parties were not touched, except the avowedly Marxist ones, and violent repression, though it existed, never reached the levels of contemporary or later Argentine or Chilean phenomena.

A series of "Institutional Acts" were consecrated in the new Constitution, of 1967, which allowed under its aegis future decisions by the executive, overruling the normal functioning of the three powers. To prevent populist phenomena, usually associated with the election of the chief executive, it was decided that this process would be indirect, and performed by the Congress, even if the president would retain most powers, so that the regime could not be described as parlamentarian. On the other hand, in order to avoid fragmentation, all elected representatives were forced to come together into two parties, one supporting the government, Aliança Renovadora Nacional (ARENA), and the other performing the role of a loyal opposition, the Movimento Democrático Brasileiro (MDB). The idea was to achieve in due time conditions for the operation of a two-party system, along North American or European lines.

In the pro-government ARENA, most members of the UDN and a majority of the PSD were registered, plus several regionalist groups. Most Trabalhistas (except those ousted, who formed an Auténtico extra-parliamentary group) and a minority of PSD members joined the MDB. What had actually happened, to make the 1964 coup possible, was a split in the Varguista alliance, with its right wing joining the more classical conservatives. A new era was being inaugurated, Varguista banners falling from the hands of the PSD and being taken up by the PTB, whose more radical members, anyway, were moving towards the left.

Governors also had to be elected in an indirect manner, by the local legislatures. In 1965, before these dispositions were enacted, there had been direct local elections in several states, where the opposition was triumphant. Now, with the new electoral system, in 1966 pro-government leaders won practically all the contests. Towards the end of the year (1966) official candidates for the Lower House also came on top in the only direct elections sanctioned by the Constitution, though a large number of people abstained from participation, annulled their votes (7 percent) or voted blank (14 percent).

Despite these distortions, during the whole duration of the military regime (1964-1985) Congress was in operation (with the exception of a few months in 1969), and elections by secret vote held to fill national and state legislative posts and municipal authorities, the voter always having the choice of ARENA or MDB. The governmental candidates usually had a majority, without ballot box stuffing, though there was at the beginning a total lack of freedom of the press, and an atmosphere of intimidation. At some point, the government, in order to consolidate its majority, resorted to the *cédula única*, that is, people had to opt for the ARENA or MDB lists, where legislative and municipal positions were part of an indivisible slate. In this manner it was thought that the voter, desirous of having a municipal authority with good connections, capable of getting support for local improvements, would vote for the ARENA notables, whom anyway he knew and usually respected, while he didn't know nor cared for the state or national legislators included in the *cédula única*.

This ploy, widely condemned by the opposition as undemocratic, was effective, given the nature of the electorate, which could be influenced by such considerations, because, strictly speaking, nobody was stopping them from choosing the MDB list.

Castelo Branco was followed by Artur da Costa e Silva in 1967, through a decision of Congress. However, internal currents existed within the governmental majority, namely, as was often the case in other parts of the region, between a nationalist, authoritarian but somewhat reformist wing, and another one more oriented towards openness to foreign capital and cooperation with the United States. In 1968 an intensified oppositional activity, fired in part by the events in Paris and the anti-Vietnam War agitation, accompanied by a wave of strikes, caused a sort of internal coup, which the president himself implemented, through Institutional Act No. 5, known as AI-5, which gave to the executive the power to dissolve Congress, purge it of some members (*cassação*), or postpone its sessions.

Costa e Silva's illness forced an early succession, which benefited the hard-line candidate General Emílio Garrastazu Médici, a result of intense deliberation among the military top brass, but sanctioned by Congress, where the ARENA was only too eager to follow military suggestions.

Médici's administration (1969-1974) was the more repressive regime, accompanied by tortures and a strict censorship of the press. Popular resistance generated urban guerrilla activity, led by erstwhile Communist leader Carlos Marighela and by Carlos Lamarca, an army captain who followed Prestes' trajectory, though the old leader now favored non-violent action and infiltration of the MDB. After some very provocative actions, including the kidnapping of two foreign diplomats, the movement was destroyed, with the death of its two heads. On the other hand, the Catholic Church became increasingly disaffected, and among its middle and also some of its high levels a very radical theology of liberation extended its influence.[10]

In 1974, Congress, always after consultations with the military, elected General Ernesto Geisel (1974-1979), of the *aperturista*, that is, the open-to-change wing of the armed forces, who started a process of normalization. That same year, legislative elections with quite a considerable freedom of the press and of association were held, allowing the MDB a major presence, especially in the larger cities, though the ARENA retained its majority, based on the vast rural or small-town interior. The grip of the military on power was consolidated by the astonishing success of the industrialization drive, accompanied by a pragmatic combination of protectionism, subsidies and state prodding, which reached Asian Tiger proportions, peaking in growth rates of 11 percent a year.

The Unstable Argentine Military Regimes

In Argentina, the attempt to incorporate Peronism as a minority in a civilian government failed with Frondizi's overthrow in 1962. A short-lived military government ensued (1962-1963), with vice president José María Guido as a figurehead. During that time, two armed confrontations took place, with tanks on the streets but only a few dead, between the "Azul" and the "Colorado" factions. The former, led by General Juan Carlos Onganía, aimed at reproducing, from more solid positions, Frondizi's policy of integrating the amenable sections of the outlawed movement. The Colorados were more anti-Peronist, and they believed in the continued necessity to ban the country's majority party, seen as fascist but also as potentially falling under the control of its more radical, Fidelista elements, as was happening in Brazil with Goulart.

Onganía failed in his attempt at becoming the candidate of a broad coalition of moderate Peronists and nationalist and Catholic factions, including splinter groups from the Christian Democratic, Radical (UCRI) and Socialist parties. As it proved impossible to weld all these elements together, the prohibition of Peronism was maintained, causing its adherents to vote blank, getting a fourth of the electorate. With somewhat less than that, Arturo Illia, the Unión Cívica Radical del Pueblo (UCRP) candidate, came into office, but highly delegitimized and vulnerable to popular agitations of any kind. These the Peronists pitilessly fostered, together with their controlled trade unions, including factory occupations and taking of hostages.

The Peronist hardliners had undertaken for quite some time sabotage activities and other violent forms of what was called the *Resistencia*, to create revolutionary conditions permitting the return of their leader, probably in alliance with a sector of the armed forces. Paradoxically, the right wing of Peronism, well connected with the nationalist sectors of the armed forces, was an essential component of this plan. In fact, this convergence didn't happen, but the hope of some day instituting it explains many of the ensuing Peronist strategies, fired by the memory of the founding days of the movement.

In 1967, elections to renew Congress and to select provincial governors were scheduled, equivalent to those that had spelled Frondizi's ruin. There were still two years to go for the presidential contest, but the likelihood that the Peronists would again win the race was seen as catastrophic. In effect, it would give them legitimacy, and would be very difficult to resort again to annulling the results. So, as happened in Peru in 1968 (with the second veto of Apra), a coup was engineered just a few months before and not after the elections, and using an ad hoc argument, which many members of the public could believe. This was that Illia was stalling the country, never deciding on a set course of action, allowing security to deteriorate, and garbage to accumulate because he did not repress the strikes efficiently enough.

Here a strange convergence of strategies took place. Peronism, at the time, was deeply divided between those who were prepared to obey whatever directives Perón gave, and another labor-based group, led by metalworker Augusto Vandor and needle trades' José Alonso, who preferred to use their bargaining power to become at least a recognized pressure group within the country, whatever happened to the old leader's electoral ambitions.

Perón, of course, had his own ideas, and was preparing to use his more radicalized followers for a frontal attack against his military and civilian enemies. Some of those youths were of Peronist extraction, but most were recruited from among university students or young professionals, until recently quite foreign to the Peronist movement, but who were now discovering unsuspected revolutionary potentialities in it. These people formed a guerrilla organization named Montoneros, and a surface structure, the Juventud Peronista. One of their aims was to get rid of reformist union bureaucrats, who, conscious of having been thus selected, responded in kind.

Now the divisions within Peronism were becoming more complex, almost unfathomable. There were the trade union structures, led by strongmen with little respect for democratic values, and with their own paramilitary groups. On the other, the Montoneros, and, occasionally allied with them in their common dislike for the trade unionists, the provincial Peronist Party leaders, often quite moderate, but ready to adopt pragmatically any course of action. Inside Perón's own entourage there were extreme rightist groups, some of them of fascist or even Nazi persuasion, in uneasy coexistence with the more leftist ideological elements that had been recruited by John William Cook. The best-known representative of the rightist group, very close to Perón and his wife Isabelita, was their own private secretary José López Rega.

When the 1966 coup took place, putting Onganía in the presidential chair, the military's aim was to prevent the foreseeable Peronist victory at provincial, and in two years' time national level. The main enemy was Perón himself, and some sectors of his surrounding, especially of course the leftist and Montonero elements, but not at all the labor leaders. These, therefore, felt confident enough to appear in the ceremony of empowerment, believing that a tactical alliance could be built between the military and the moderate labor leaders, against the Left (Peronist or Marxist) and the centrist and middle-class Radical Party, leaving in the cold Perón himself and many of his electorally inclined followers. But soon reality disposed of these illusions, and the orthodox economic policy adopted by Onganía's civilian advisers antagonized the trade unionists and many other popular sectors.

As time passed, Peronism, now more or less reunited after the labor leaders' faux pas, built an opposition coalition of unsuspected strength against the regime of the so-called Revolución Argentina (1966-1973). The main political party, with strong labor roots, together with leftist activists of all sorts and right-wing paramilitary formations, assailed the government giving it no respite. It was as though in Italy at about that time there had been a coalition of the Red Brigades with the Socialist and Communist parties, plus the fascist terrorists.

The Revolución Argentina was also destabilized by its own internal struggles, to a large extent due to contrasting tactics as to how to deal with the Peronist menace. In 1969 a general strike in Córdoba, the second largest city and a center of new industries, promoted by leftist leaders within and outside Peronism, was soon transformed into a major episode of violence, known as the Cordobazo, a name reminiscent of the much earlier Bogotazo in Colombia. This showed that the struggle could become a mass phenomenon.[11]

The ruling groups in the regime were split by the usual confrontation between those who thought a "social opening" should be tried in order to let off some steam, and those who set store by an increased repression. Onganía was among the former, even if the dividing line between both schools of thought was not at all neat.

The tension escalated to the point that after one year of the event, when another protest in Córdoba erupted, General Norberto Levingston, of the Intelligence area, forcefully replaced Onganía. He intended to combine repression with a policy not necessarily of *apertura*, but of industrial promotion, which would be better received by labor and even by sectors of the intelligentsia than the previously dominating orthodox free market measures. It even seemed that the Peruvian model might be reproduced in Argentina. But after one year, again dissension had the better of the ruling circles, and Levingston was in turn displaced by General Alejandro Lanusse (1971), from the conservative-liberal sector of the army, who decided to head towards normalization, legalizing all political parties, though forbidding Perón himself to be a candidate.

In these elections (1973) the regime was incapable of presenting someone with any possibilities of winning the race. In contrast with the Brazilian pattern, the man anointed by the authorities, an obscure air chief, got only 2 percent of the preferences. The Right and Center-Right parties put together another candidate, Francisco Manrique, also a military man, who had been in charge of social policies during the dictatorship, and who had later broken away, but probably did channel a lot of pro-regime opinion. These various factions of the Right reached in total somewhat less than 20 percent. The Radical Party was also rather unsuccessful, barely exceeding that mark, quite below its traditional achievements. Peronism, by contrast, swept the polls with its candidate, the obscure Héctor Cámpora, collecting half the total vote, and supported by a coalition with small parties, the Christian Democrats, some Socialists and what remained of Frondizistas, all of them internally divided and having split from their former organizations. There was also an independent Left, based on an alliance of the Intransigente Party with a fraction of the Christian Democrats, plus the Communists, totaling some 10 percent of the poll.

Peronism's access to power was celebrated with a mass gathering in the Plaza de Mayo, where from the balcony Cámpora was saluting in the company of Salvador Allende and the Cuban Osvaldo Dorticós on representing Fidel Castro, none of which assuaged the fears of the Right and the military. The Plaza was full of guerrilla groups, a good dozen of them, all temporarily pacified, though on the night of the sameday they went to the Villa Devoto jail to liberate the political prisoners kept there. The Peronist Right was also apprehensive about a palace coup by the leftist and Montonero sectors of their own movement, who to a large extent had surrounded Campora, despite his conservative origins. Cámpora was selected by Perón precisely because of his very low profile.

In order to regain the conditions for strong government and legitimacy, Perón persuaded Cámpora to resign, thus forcing new elections, held late that same year 1973. In them the Left decided to join the popular will, and vote for Perón, who, unable to decide between running mates, chose his wife Isabelita and got 62 percent of the total poll. Once in government, Perón attempted a national pacification, with a famous embrace with long-time opposition leader Ricardo Balbín. But soon the guerrilla groups, mainly the Montoneros and the Marxist Ejército Revolucionario del Pueblo (ERP), continued the fight, clashing not only with the regular army but also with various paramilitary squads and trade union special task forces.

On the death of Perón, in mid-1974, his wife replaced him, but proved unable to ride the wild horse. Kidnapping on all sides, persecution, and torture became rampant, and finally the armed forces intervened, believing they could conduct the anti-subversive fight better without civilian interference. Thus a military dictatorship was installed (1976-1983), continuing the repressive and state terrorist practices of Isabelita's term, and finally liquidating the guerrillas, but unable to launch the impressive economic growth that had accompanied the experience of their Brazilian peers, or even of Pinochet's last years in power.[12]

Christian Democracy and the Unidad Popular in Chile

In Chile, when Conservative/Liberal Jorge Alessandri was finishing his term (1958-1964), the prospect of a Socialist victory was on everybody's mind. The Right did not have a suitable candidate, and suffered the natural erosion of unfulfilled expectations. Christian Democracy formed a third ideological family, with quite a few votes, though usually arriving in third place. Finally the Right decided to step aside and support Eduardo Frei Montalva, the moderate leader of the Christian Democrats, with the unwritten understanding, or rather hope, that they would oblige next time. Thus Frei was consecrated with almost two-thirds of the electorate, but Allende, who was again a candidate, got some more percentage points than the previous time, positioning himself as a potential winner if the union of his opponents were to give way.

Frei's government, despite its origins, was one of significant social change, undertaking robust land reform and housing programs. It benefited from U.S. support through the Alliance for Progress, intent on consolidating what was called Revolución en Libertad. The conservative classes, who had been instrumental in bringing Frei to power, felt disappointed, and prepared themselves for a fight in 1970, again under Jorge Alessandri, who had become an elder statesman, and had always been a prominent industrialist in the sawmill and paper business. Christian Democracy, far from honoring a pact that after all it had never signed, set up its most leftist available candidate, Radomiro Tomic, to compete with Allende, who was once more heading the Unidad Popular. This was a repetition of previous coalitions, plus some leftist factions of the Christian Democrats (Izquierda Cristiana and Movimiento de Acción Popular Unitaria, MAPU) and the Radicals (the main party, which had lost a wing to the right and another to the left, the Izquierda Radical). Outside of the coalition the extremist Movimiento de Izquierda Revolucionaria (MIR) favored a more determined confrontationist policy and occasional violence, but never engaged in guerrilla activities. Allende won, by a very small margin, getting some 37 percent of the vote against Alessandri's 35 percent, leaving Tomic far behind. Allende had won, but the electorate, in its majority, was averse to his projects.

As no candidate had an absolute majority, the decision was up to Congress, which had not been renovated at the time, but was about two years old. Thus, its decision would not be considered very legitimate, even if proportions were more or less the same as those recently expressed. There was a very strong tradition that Congress validated the candidate who had come out on top, but it was not legally binding. In this case, feelings against the winning candidate ran high. But Christian Democracy wished to consolidate its progressive image, rubbing out the impression caused by its having come to power through the embrace of the Right. So finally an agreement was reached with Allende by which he committed himself to respect constitutional rights, to assuage doubts as to the depth of liberal convictions among his followers.

The early months of the Unidad Popular government were rather quiet, but soon there was an upsurge of radical demands by its followers, accompanied by appropriations of ranches and factories. Many businesses were passed to the dominion of the state, without Congressional approval, taking advantage of an almost-forgotten provision of the Socialist Republic which had somehow remained on the books. Also the executive's control over prices and wages allowed it to throttle most enterprises, including private schools which thus went into receivership or into the hands of the state. On the extremes of the political spectrum the MIR vied with the major parties in fanning the flames of popular enthusiasm. And among the main partners of the coalition, the Socialists were overreaching themselves so as to surpass their partners/rivals the Communists in revolutionary single-mindedness. It was very difficult for Allende and his closest collaborators to restrain the militants, who were convinced that a Cuban-style overhaul of society could be accomplished by legal means. This required a majority, which in some elections the Unidad Popular was approaching, reaching 44 percent. At the same time, though, the opposition and the Catholic Church were being welded into an understanding, to impeach Allende. The president's entourage was also suspected of plotting some violent takeover, with the help of military friends who might be inspired by the Peruvian example.

The opposition to Allende took to the streets, with paramilitary groups being formed, and a movement of small-scale entrepreneurs, among them the strategic truck owners, determined to stop the country, and relying on the United States for help. In this atmosphere, the traditionally disciplined armed forces took the road of a coup d'état, knowing they could count on the sympathy of a majority of the population, and of the Christian Democratic Party, whose leaders at the beginning believed it would only by a brief "corrective" intervention, soon handing over control to them. In fact, the coup was accompanied by harsh repression, and it lasted almost two decades (1973-1990).[13]

The political stability of the Chilean dictatorship, which had Augusto Pinochet at its helm throughout, without any serious risk of being undercut from within, should be contrasted with the chaotic succession of factions in Argentina, where *all* military regimes (1943-46, 1955-57, 1962-63, 1966-73, and 1976-83) witnessed at least one and generally two internal coups or armed confrontations. It should also be compared to Brazil's more legally constituted regime (1964-1985), also devoid of violent internal squabbles for power.

In Brazil, the tradition of conservative constitutionalism was very strong since the nineteenth century, even though applicable to a small urban minority, floating over the sea of an immense rural illiterate population, seen as potentially very menacing. And a rough-riding program of capitalist development, with low standards of living even for urban labor, could be imposed with relatively little resistance from civil society. This ease of social control facilitated in Brazil the launching of a major industrialization program, reminiscent of conditions in East Asian countries at the time.

By contrast, Argentina, since the early part of the century, had an experience of prosperity and labor scarcity. This set the conditions for the early formation of trade unions and popular and middle-class parties, like the Radicals or the Socialists, without an equivalent in Brazil, where the Communist Party was reduced to small elites. The historical success of the Argentine agricultural export-oriented model gave strength to the large landholders of the fertile Pampas, also without an equivalent in Brazil despite an approximation in the coffee areas. Those Argentine agrarian elites could claim to represent a model which had produced widespread prosperity, and thus resist the demands for industrialization, a risky and not sufficiently tried-out path. In Brazil there was no alternative to it.

In Argentina, as a result of the important presence of an organized working class, social power was more evenly spread among social classes than in Brazil. The popular sectors could usually manage to oppose and scuttle excessively unilateral programs supported by the dominant classes. The latter were, moreover, not at all united, because of the usual differences between branches of production, of which one, as mentioned above, the agrarian exporters, was remarkably strong. So it may be hypothesized that the strange instability of the Argentine dictatorships was due to the fact that there were many pressure groups in the country with contrasting projects, both among the bourgeoisie and the middle and lower strata, making it difficult for any non-consensual model to succeed.[14]

In Chile, there was, as in Brazil, a strong conservative/liberal constitutionalist tradition, but based on a society that was more egalitarian, and more functionally diversified and organized, with relatively high levels of education and urban culture. The diversity of pressure groups, therefore, approximated the Argentine situation, though with its working-class sectors channeled into socialist rather than populist expressions.

Social discipline and respect for superiors has always been much higher in Chile than in Argentina, the latter being marked more by the egalitarian attitudes of an immigrant and frontier society. This is not incompatible with the greater presence of the Left in Chile. In fact, the contrast resembles the one existing between Great Britain and the United States, the former being a more deferential society, and therefore sporting a solid Conservative party, more traditional than its Republican counterpart, but at the same time with a Labor rather than a Democratic party. *Mutatis mutandis*, Chile is closer to British patterns, and Argentina to those prevalent in the United States. It should not be surprising, then, that Chile has a solid Socialist movement, by now quite akin to British Labor, while Argentina has among its popular classes a Peronist movement, increasingly similar to the North American Democrats.

It is also significant that despite Pinochet's persistence in power, he soon proposed a constitution for Chile that, however distorted, did give some guarantees to the opposition, and that was ratified by a plebiscite in 1980. Finally, in 1988, and with greater freedom of expression, another plebiscite rejected the attempted perpetuation of Pinochet for a further eight-year term. The dictatorship, by now quite mellowed, bowed to public opinion, which in the following year's election started an era of democratic rule, with many limitations, but still involving a radical change with the past.[15]

The End of the Uruguayan Switzerland

In Uruguay, the Colegiado system ended in 1966, killed by a referendum in which the majority, now composed of both Blanco and Colorado sectors, decided to return to classical presidentialism. In the ensuing elections, the executive post was obtained by General Oscar Gestido, an independent Colorado, who had as his running mate the traditionalist Jorge Pacheco Areco. Gestido, a sort of Uruguayan Eisenhower, very soon died in office, leaving the vice president in charge but without much legitimacy. Pacheco had been trying to cultivate a strongman profile, and he continued along those lines, with a considerable response among some popular sectors.

The economic crisis, largely fueled by a catastrophic fall in wool prices, was beginning to erode the prosperity and the social services the country had become accustomed to. The Cuban model was, at the same time, seen as a realistic alternative for intellectual elites and university students. Frustration in Uruguay, as in Argentina, was particularly intense among them, because those two countries had the highest standard of living in the region, with the corresponding institutional and cultural development, and a more complex division of labor and availability of modern career patterns. When the prospects offered by this situation began to falter, frustration was particularly intense, and a general feeling of decrease in the international standing of the two countries stimulated a search for radical substitutes among the youth, often at the upper-middle class level.

Thus a propitious breeding ground was created for urban guerrillas or radical sympathizers, in Uruguay's case forming the Tupamaro organization (very active from 1968 to 1972), along Marxist lines, as there was no equivalent of a Peronist movement, and nationalism never had caught on. There was thus no connection to a massive popular movement, as in the Argentine case. The founder of the Tupamaros (a name harking back to Túpac Amaru's times) was Raúl Sendic, who had started as an organizer of strikes and agrarian protests in the northern sugar area. The underground Tupamaros had as their surface organization a Movimiento 26 de Marzo, or M-26. Repression was much easier than in Argentina, due to the above-mentioned lack of connections to a preexisting popular party.[16]

Pacheco's successor was Juan María Bordaberry, a Colorado of ruralista origins in Nardone's ("Chicotazo") current. The Colorado Party won the election (1971) by a small margin over the Blancos, who had spawned a moderate but significant left under the leadership of Wilson Ferreira Aldunate, in what became one of the main factions of the *lema*. On the independent Left a very broad coalition was formed, the Frente Amplio, including the Communists, the Socialists (very much radicalized since in 1961; the younger elements had defeated the old leadership of moderates such as Emilio Frugoni), and the Christian Democrats, who also had split from an older organization. In the Frente Amplio, dissident factions of the Colorados and Blancos were also included, as well as more radicalized and pro-guerrilla groups. In total, they got 18 percent of the popular vote, a remarkable increase over their traditionally modest levels. In Montevideo, however, they soared to 30 percent, arriving in second place, ahead of the Blancos, a major blow to the traditional two-party system. The violence generated by the Tupamaros had been accompanied by intense agitation among wide sectors of the population, who sympathized to various degrees with the guerrilla tactic, even if they did not engage in armed action.

This scenario stimulated a military coup which proceeded in a gradual manner, seeking consensus among a wide sector of public opinion. To begin with, in 1973 Congress was disbanded, and the president allowed to continue as a figurehead, a role he accepted because he basically agreed with the *golpistas*. This gave rise to the neologism *bordaberrización* to refer to such use of a political figure. Repression mopped up the remains of the guerrilla movement, which was already quite deteriorated at the time of the coup in 1973.

Before finishing his time in office, Bordaberry came into conflict with the military and resigned. Apparently, he wished to introduce permanent, authoritarian changes in the political system, while the armed forces preferred a gradual return to the usual constitutional practices. The military had created a Council of State, with civilian handpicked personalities, usually well respected among conservative circles of both traditional parties. This Council, together with the military top brass, formed a Consejo de la Nación. This Council appointed Aparicio Méndez, a Colorado lawyer, as chief executive (1976-1981) and afterwards replaced him with General Gregorio Álvarez (1981-1985). There were rumors about possible "Peruvianist" tendencies among some of the middle and even upper ranks of the armed forces, but nothing happened in that direction, and finally Álvarez decided to become the architect of a transition to democracy.[17]

The Democratic Experience in Colombia and Venezuela

In Colombia, the alternation in office of Conservatives and Liberals, as stated in the Frente Nacional pact, was ended in 1978. The first genuinely competitive elections saw the Liberals as victors, but after another four years a rejuvenated Conservative Party, adopting Social-Christian values, earned the presidency for Belisario Betancur. Economic development surged ahead with vigor, and with little foreign debt.

Violence, however, was far from eradicated; it started getting involved with drug traffic. The more extreme sectors of moribund Rojas Pinillismo had formed a guerrilla organization, the M-19, with wide sympathies among the popular classes. Marxists had their own structures, extending insecurity to all strata of society. And both major parties, as usual, had numerous internal currents. In the Liberal ranks, there was a significant social democratic faction, responsible for taking the party into the fold of the Socialist International. Among the Conservatives two magnets attracted quite a few people, in opposite directions: the progressive Social Christians, and the radical nationalist hardliners, headed by Álvaro Gómez, son of the legendary Laureano. Conditions were being created for a major challenge to the party system, second only to the one posed by Gaitán decades earlier.

In Venezuela, by contrast, violence was eliminated, and guerrilla groups, reprieved by Caldera (1968-1973), became integrated into civil society as political parties. The most important one in terms of electoral response was the Movimiento al Socialismo (MAS), capable of occasionally getting up to 10 percent of preferences. It included many erstwhile Communists and other Marxists who had earlier taken the path of armed resistance and were now very clearly converted to peaceful means, under the inspiration of Teodoro Petkoff. They aimed to become the real social democratic pole, replacing the faltering and allegedly corrupt Acción Democrática. The other group, the Movimiento de Izquierda Revolucionaria (MIR), with AD roots, never got much prominence. As for trade unionism, in its largest numbers it remained faithful to Acción Democrática.

At various points there were attempts at launching political options independent of the "two and a half" party system (that is, including the MAS as half). One of them was headed by writer Arturo Uslar Pietri, who in 1963 had a large following, but fell short of dislodging the dominant system, and soon he was forgotten. In 1968 Acción Democrática suffered a split from a more leftist group (which later returned to the party), and thus made it possible for the Social Christian Rafael Caldera to come into office, with only 27 percent of the popular vote.

An oil bonanza coincided with the administration of Caldera's successor, the *adeco* (as AD members are known) Carlos Andrés Pérez, who initiated a huge program of infrastructure building and launched spectacular industrialization schemes, under state supervision and tariff protection. He also took the very risky decision of nationalizing the oil industry. Corruption had ample room to thrive, and it did so, thus beginning a decline of the prestige and legitimacy of the democratic system, paradoxically at its most prosperous and expansive moment.[18]

In any case, peaceful party alternation in power was widely seen as consolidated, immune to military takeovers, and a model for the rest of the continent. Business groups, though mostly identified with COPEI, were pragmatic enough to finance both parties. Labor unions were solidly Adeco in their leadership, with a minority following Communist or other independent Left lines, and some militants were influenced by social Catholic ideas.

In Mexico Social Tensions Accumulate

In Mexico, the rapid industrial growth of the sixties and seventies was changing the country, swelling its cities and creating an impoverished mass which was more visible than when it remained in the countryside. It also had now a greater capacity to make an impact on public life, but few chances of being really integrated. Education, despite its deficits, kept producing secondary and university-educated strata shorn of any possibility of finding jobs commensurate to their aspirations. This scenario was typical of most Latin

American and also other third world countries, but in Mexico it took peculiar forms due to the coexistence, in the same country, of growth poles of great dynamism and prosperity, with stagnant areas and impoverished urban masses. Contrasts and subsequent frustrations were therefore much more intense than in places like Chile or Argentina, where conditions were relatively more egalitarian, with a wider middle class capable—at the time—of absorbing to a greater extent its own discontents. It was also the case that Mexico, having a much faster rate of growth, created a demonstration effect that frustrated those left outside, much more than what would have taken place if economic development had been slower.

The explosion happened in 1968, under the influence of the Parisian student revolt. A mass demonstration exceeded the limits normally tolerated by the government, and violent repression was exerted, leaving some 400 people dead. This "massacre of Tlatelolco" became a paradigm of disregard for human rights, and the Mexican government was branded as another example of the more openly dictatorial military regimes on the rest of the continent.

However, public indignation prompted some corrective reaction within the ruling circles themselves. Interior Minister Luis Echevarría, who was where the buck stopped in terms of responsibility for the massacre, evolved towards more *aperturista*, and actually progressive and even leftist ideas, becoming the next candidate of the PRI, and thus the chief executive (1970-1976). His term created great hopes for change, as he was surrounded by a zealous reformist team, which—following an inveterate tradition—soon became coopted and fully immersed in the classical PRI machine.

The seventies were blessed by the discovery and exploitation of huge oil deposits, which transformed Mexico into a new Venezuela, with similar results, both in terms of quick growth, and extended corruption. The worst of it was that the new level of aspirations thus created impelled the government to undertake new projects, using the then easily available international financial funds, confident that the debt would be repaid with the permanently high oil prices. When the bubble was pricked, in the early 1980s, a critical juncture had to be faced. The all-out state intervention and tariff protection of national industry was seen as detrimental to its health, as it had lasted much longer than what an infant industry argument might justify. The agricultural panorama was also being reconsidered, as the small collectively held and ill-financed plots given to individual peasants were seen as incapable of greater productivity, and thus demanded reprivatization. The menace of expropriation that still hanged over larger farms, vulnerable to agrarista activism, also created barriers to investment. But it was not easy to introduce changes in such delicate area, central to the revolutionary ideology which continued to be the basis of PRI solidarity, and of its impact on public emotions, even if by now only perfunctorily voiced by its leaders.[19]

Notes

1. François Bourricaud, *Poder y sociedad en el Perú contemporáneo*; Francisco Miró Quesada, *La ideología de Acción Popular*; A. Dietz, "Political Participation in the Barriadas, An Extension and Reexamination"; José Matos Mar, *Yanaconaje y reforma agraria en el Perú*.
2. Teobaldo Pinzas García, *La economía peruana, 1950-1978, un ensayo bibliográfico*; Cynthia McClintock and Abraham Lowenthal, eds, *El gobierno militar, una experiencia peruana, 1968-1980*; José Matos Mar et al., *Perú, hoy*; Vivián Trías, *Perú, Fuerzas Armadas y revolución*; Víctor Villanueva, *Nueva mentalidad militar en Perú*; Alfred Stepan, *The State and Society, Peru in Edarative Perspective*; Anfbal Quijano, *Nacionalismo, neoimperialismo y militarismo en el Perú*; Oscar Delgado, *El proceso revolucionario peruano: testimonio de lucha*.
3. James M. Malloy and Richard Thorn, eds., *Beyond the Revolution: Bolivia since 1952*; Herbert Klein, *Bolivia: The Evolution of a Multiethnic Society*; Mario Rolón Anaya, *Política y partidos en Bolivia*; Guillermo Lora, *De la Asamblea Popular al golpe fascista*.
4. Domingo Rivarola, *Estado, campesinos y modernización agrícola en Paraguay*; Werner Baer and Melissa Birch, "La expansión de la frontera económica, el crecimiento paraguayo en los años setenta"; Fran Gillespie, "Comprehending the Slow Pace of Urbanization in Paraguay between 1950 and 1972"; Andrew Nickson, "Brazilian Colonization of the Eastern Frontier Region of Paraguay."
5. Maria Vitória de Mesquita Benevides, *O governo Kubitschek: desenvolvimento económico e estabilidade política* and *O governo Jánio Quadros*; Mário Beni, *Adhemar*.
6. The subject of Parliamentary versus presidentialist systems of governance has been treated exhaustively, and will not be dealt with at large here. See Scott Mainwaring and Mathew S. Shugart, eds., *Presidentialism and Democracy in Latin America*; Juan Linz and Arturo Valenzuela, eds., *The Failure of Presidential Democracy. 1, Comparative Perspectives; 2, The Case of Latin America*.
7. In the Brazilian interior the local landowners, and other notables, were known as "coroneis," because since the previous century they had been usually appointed colonels of the National Guard in order to perform order-maintaining operations at the head of their subordinates. See Francisco Weffort, *O populismo na política brasileira*; Muniz Bandeira, *O governo João Goulart: as lutas sociais no Brasil*.
8. Thomas Skidmore, *Politics in Brazil, 1930-1964, An Experiment in Democracy*.
9. Leoncio Martins Rodrigues, *Conflito industrial e sindicalismo em Brasil*; Hélio Jaguaribe, *Brasil, crisis y alternativas*; Vamireh Chacon, *História das idéias socialistas no Brasil*; Irving L. Horowitz, Josué de Castro and John Gerassi, eds., *Latin American Radicalism*; Michael L. Conniff, *Latin American Populism in Comarative Perspective*.
10. Denis de Moraes, *A esquerda e o golpe de 64*; Carlos Castello Branco, *Os militares no poder*; Alfred Stepan, *The Military in Politics: Changing Patterns in Brazil*, and his edited book *Authoritarian Brazil*; Ronald Schneider, *The Political System of Brazil: Emergence of an Authoritarian "Modernizing" Regime, 1964-70*; Peter Flynn, *Brazil: A Political Analysis*; Iain S. Maclean, *Opting for Democracy? Liberation Theology and the Struggle for Democracy in Brazil*.
11. Juan Carlos Agulla, *Diagnóstico social de una crisis: Córdoba, mayo de 1969*; Francisco Delich, *Crisis y protesta social: Córdoba 1969-1973*; Beba and Beatriz

Balvé, *El 69: huelga política de masas*; James Brennan, *El Cordobazo: las guerras obreras en Córdoba, 1955-1976*.
12. Juan José Hernández Arregui, *Peronismo y socialismo*; Oscar Terán, *Nuestros años sesentas: la formación de la nueva izquierda intelectual en la Argentina, 1956-1966*; Guido Di Tella, *Perón-Perón;* Juan Carlos Torre, *Los sindicalistas en el poder, 1973-1976*.
13. Alain Joxe, *Las Fuerzas Armadas en el sistema político de Chile*; Norbert Lechner, *La democracia en Chile*; Ted Córdova-Claure, *Chile sí?*; Manuel Castells, *La lucha de clases en Chile*; Arturo Valenzuela, *Chile*.
14. Carlos Waisman, *Reversal of Development in Argentina: Postwar Counterrevolutionary Policies and Their Structural Consequences*; Paul H. Lewis, *The Crisis of Argentine Capitalism*; Donald Hodges, *Argentina, 1943-1987: The National Revolution and Resistance*; Daniel James, *Resistance and Integration: Peronism and the Argentine Working Class, 1946-1976*.
15. Douglas Chalmers, Atilio Borón and Maria do Carmo Campelo de Souza, eds, *The Right and Democracy in Latin America*.
16. Carlos Bañales and Enrique Jara, *La rebelión estudiantil*; Roberto Copelmayer and Diego Díaz, *Montevideo, 1968: la lucha estudiantil*; Eleuterio Fernández Huidobro, *Historia de los Tupamaros*; *Actas Tupamaras*.
17. Gustavo Varela, *De la República liberal al Estado militar*.
18. Howard R. Penniman, *Venezuela at the Polls: The National Elections of 1978*; *Politeia/1980*; Steve Ellner, *Los partidos políticos y su disputa por el control del movimiento sindical en Venezuela, 1936-1948*.
19. Roger Hansen, *La política del desarrollo mexicano*; José Luis Reyna and Richard Weinert, eds., *El autoritarismo en Mexico*; John C. Cross, *Informal Politics: Street Vendors and the State in Mexico City*.

6

The Central American and Caribbean Cauldron

The Central American and Caribbean "backyard" has proven to be a more complex and conflicted region than what might have been supposed given a rather simple evolutionist or even Marxist perspective. In chapter 3 this subject was treated as requiring a "theoretical revision." This chapter in turn will be devoted to an analysis of the region up to the present, always keeping a comparative approach to the rest of the continent.

El Salvador

In El Salvador, the reformist military takeover of 1944 was followed, after a few months, by a more classical, but unstable authoritarianism. After four years of this, a new expression of discontent among the military reasserted itself, in what came to be known as the "Revolution of 1948," bent on a program of progressive reforms under strict control, so as to avoid popular mobilization. In other words, for the people, but not by the people. Ministries were entrusted to young technocrats, and an effort made to control death squads, paramilitary groups, and the rural as well as the urban police. A new political party was formed, which in time became the Partido de Conciliación Nacional (PCN), a pallid copy of the Mexican PRI.

This regime passed through ballot box legitimation, not very credibly, when it won the contest by 93 percent of the votes. Repression of violent and non-violent resistance reached extremes of intensity, prompting a corrective military coup in 1960, followed by another one after a few months that restored the authorities and continued the experience of the "Revolution of 1948."

Towards the end of the sixties, the opposition grew in strength, and in 1972 formed a Unión Nacional Opositora, with the Christian Democrats, the social democrats of the Movimiento Nacional Revolucionario (MNR) and the Communist-dominated Unión Democrática Nacional (UDN). Christian Democrat José Napoleón Duarte was its candidate, with pro-Communist Guillermo Ungo as running mate. The Right was divided between the official Partido de Conciliación Nacional, bent on an *aperturista* policy, and other more hardline sectors. Elections were again fraudulent, and the opposition tried to counter with a general strike, but it was not successful. A situation of military anarchy continued unabated, and a strong guerrilla movement formed, whose two main forces were the Frente Farabundo Martí de LIberación Nacional (FMLN) and the Ejército Revolucionario del Pueblo (ERP).

The rural scene had become complicated by the development of the southern littoral, where an unprecedented expansion of large-scale capitalist cotton cultivation was pushing peasants off of their traditional holdings. The syndrome of 1932 appeared to be repeating itself, this time with cotton instead of coffee as the culprit.

Church authorities, usually very moderate if not conservative, joined a civilian resistance which, despite violence, still had some space to organize and express itself, even if often at the risk of death. The writing on the wall came with the downfall of Somoza in Nicaragua (1979) and Jimmy Carter's accession in the United States. Once again, a reformist sector of the armed forces took the opportunity and established a junta, with the participation of Christian Democrats, Social Democrats, and even Communist sympathizers, though soon internal squabbling ousted the more leftist elements.

Conservative opinion, both national and North American, was alarmed at the spectacle of military factions endlessly replacing each other, oscillating between genocidal repression and desperate attempts at coopting the rebels through social reform. It was feared that El Salvador was the next domino to fall, soon to be followed by equally chaotic Guatemala.

Guerrilla activity continued, while in the ruling junta José Napoleón Duarte continued to participate, in the expectation of changing things "from inside," even at moments when the repressive atmosphere was suffocating. Among the revolutionary forces there were those more intent on armed struggle, inevitably of an elitist type, and others who preferred a more broadly based mass movement, with roots among trade unions, barrio dwellers, and peasants. These various tendencies converged into a unified Frente Democrático Revolucionario.

American pressure forced the regime to sanction rather far-reaching land reform, though it was never very seriously applied. However, thousands of peasants did get a piece of land, diminishing to some extent their sympathies for the guerrillas. In 1982, the junta appointed Duarte as its provisional chairman, and held elections for a Constituent Assembly, where a majority was secured by an alliance of the traditional Partido de Conciliación Nacional (PCN) and a new organization led by Major Roberto D'Aubuisson, branded by an American ambassador as "a compulsive criminal." Despite that fact, he was surrounded by an aura of popularity, partly as a reaction by many people against the violence of the rebel forces. Military anarchy, in any case, continued to thrive.[1]

After the adoption of a new charter by the Assembly, elections were held, and this time they were won by Christian Democrat Duarte, who thus saw the crowning of his protracted efforts and complex strategies. His period in office (1984-1989), however, was no less contradictory, as he was forced to proceed with the harshest of repressions against anybody suspected of guerrilla connections, while economic circumstances did not allow him much scope for social reforms.

When the next contest was due, the Christian Democrats' discredit was quite widespread, and the tiredness of many gave a majority to the Alianza Renovadora Nacional, ARENA, the party put together by D'Aubuisson, now converted to constitutional rule, who in order to refurbish his image had as his running mate the young entrepreneur Alfredo Cristiani (1989).

Finally, the least expected outcome materialized: negotiations between the government and the guerrillas, with full granting of amnesties on all sides and the forgetting of past misdeeds. The rebel forces had to surrender their arms, and were free to continue their struggle by other means, forming a political party, which is what they did.

This strategy, which was successful, seems to be a case of the "Nixon in China" syndrome. That is, often the more adamant opposers of a certain policy are those who can implement it, once they become convinced of its inevitability. They are not hampered, as are the more genuine reformers, by the danger of being accused by more extremist sectors on their own side of giving in to the enemy. The sobering record of a Batista or a Somoza overthrown despite everything was, of course, another major factor in determining the Salvadorean Right to accept the risks involved in this policy of pacification.

Risks there were, in fact, and the erstwhile guerrillas, by now quite converted to reformist aims and strategic alliance-seeking, developed positions of great influence, gaining the mayoralty of the capital city and several others, and a relative majority in Congress. ARENA retained the presidency in the 1999 elections, but for quite some time opinion polls appeared to favor the Frente Farabundo Martí de Liberación Nacional (FMLN), which was weakened by some internal dissensions between the "comandantes" and their civilian friends. El Salvador, in any case, seems quite on its way toward a bipolarity. There is a clearly conservative party, opposed by a socialist one in the process of evolution from the espousal of violence to a social democratic organization, or maybe an Aprista-like one. But electoral participation is low, usually well below 50 percent, indicating the disenchantment or disinterest of a large part of the population, and the potentiality that something new might appeal to their imagination.[2]

Guatemala

The accumulation of social tensions in Guatemala, that Central American Bolivia, was, as in the Andean country, very serious. A group of young officers, similar to those who had come to power in El Salvador, but more responsive to the democratic atmosphere at the end of World War II, overthrew Ubico in 1944. They immediately called Juan José Arévalo, an exiled teacher with socialist ideas who was living in Argentina, and the following year he was elected (1945-1950). He started a program of radical reforms, piloted by his Partido Revolucionario Guatemalteco, in a climate of shared power between the military and a group of quite leftist intellectuals.

New elections in 1950 brought Colonel Jacobo Arbenz to the presidency. He had already become the regime's power behind the scenes, and now he came out into the open. He intensified the pace of reforms, hitting landowners and the foreign-owned banana companies. The Communist Partido Guatemalteco del Trabajo (PGT), a very well-organized minority group, was used as a vehicle for popular participation and mobilization.

Reaction came from abroad, with strong U.S. support. A small mercenary troop, trained in Honduras, invaded the country under Colonel Carlos Castillo Armas, and was joined by the national military, most of whom disliked the spate of reforms being introduced, and particularly the agitational role played by the Communists. The new regime organized from the top down a so-called Movimiento de Liberación Nacional, and engaged in dire repression. In 1957, a bullet cut short Castillo Armas' life, and various other military regimes followed suit, in a rather unstable and anarchic fashion.

In most of Central America the sixties and seventies witnessed an apparently unstoppable slide into state terrorism and guerrilla fighting of greater intensity than in the rest of the continent. In the Guatemalan case, the guerrilla movement had been started by two military officers, lieutenants Luis Turcios and Marco Antonio Yon Sosa, and then converged with other radical groups.

The armed forces in 1966, after establishing what they thought would be a more permanent regime (along Brazilian lines), opened the way to the polls, believing they could now control the process, having reduced very drastically the extent of guerrilla activity. The result was a return to power of a modified version of Arévalo's Partido Revolucionario Guatemalteco (PRG), led by Julio César Méndez Montenegro. But he could not escape the control of his mentors, who practically shared governmental functions with the civilian authorities. This discredited the PRG, which became a rubber stamp, and its more resolute members formed a new, Social Democratic Party.

In the 1970 contest the Right put forth an alliance between what remained of Castillo Armas's MLN and a new Partido Institucional Democrático (PID) organized by Colonel Carlos Arana Osorio, who had had a major role in the repression of the guerrillas. The opposition was divided between the dwindling PRG, its alternate, the Social Democratic Party, and the newly formed Christian Democrats, who became the main channel for reform forces. Arana Osorio won the contest in a hardly clean competition and in the same way four year later transmitted his post to a colleague. In 1978, another ritual of this sort was to be performed, in the midst of continued guerrilla and state terrorism, but now apparently some guarantees existed for fair counting of ballots. Public opinion gave as a sure winner General Efraín Ríos Montt, a man converted to fundamentalist Protestantism (which practically included half the national population), who had the support of the Christian Democrats, which in this manner expected to drive a wedge between the ruling circles. Fraud was so open and scandalous that discontent became widespread also among the armed forces, but the official candidate won the race. Meanwhile, violation of human rights continued unabated, in an internal war which during its whole course (up to the pacification of 1996) claimed some 200,000 victims.

The military regime was becoming vulnerable to criticism even among conservative groups, but it managed to renew its mandate once again in another fraudulent election in 1982, when the opposition consisted not only of the Christian Democratic Party, but also of two right-wing groups. At this moment, a sector of the armed forces with some receptivity to new ideas came into the open, overthrew the government, and offered the chief post to General Ríos Montt, who was considered the moral victor of the 1978 elections.

Ríos Montt could have led a normalization process, but instead he struck an alliance with some rightist groups, dissolved Congress, and appointed directly all mayors. Genocidal warfare started encompassing Indian zones where the guerrillas were now getting more support.

At the end of their tether, the armed forces once again took power, overthrowing Ríos Montt, and trying out a mixture of repressive and more nationalist policies. This antagonized some sectors of American public opinion, which exerted pressure so as to return to more stable conditions. The regime was then forced to grant fair elections, which were won in a landslide by Vinicio Cerezo, of the Christian Democratic Party (1986-1990). This seemed to start a slow process of social reform, but at the end of his term his party, discredited by allegations of corruption, lost to a conservative challenger. In this way the Right, after having been in power through the armed forces during the long years of violence, was coming back in civilian garb.[3]

In fact, there were several conservative parties. The main two were the Partido de Avanzada Nacional (PAN), led by wealthy businessman Alvaro Arzú, and the Frente Republicano Guatemalteco (FRG), of Ríos Montt. The Christian Democrats, after having a moment of glory, were reduced to almost nothing. The more moderate sector associated with the guerrilla movement, the Unión Nacional Revolucionaria de Guatemala, set up a legal electoral group, the Frente Democrático Nueva Guatemala, which had a modest show of strength in the contest of 1995, from which Arzú emerged the winner.

Once in power, Arzú, feeling well supported by a tired public opinion, started peace negotiations with the guerrillas, which were successfully completed by the end of 1996. The pacification process took quite some time to implement as it had to overcome resistances in both camps. By 1998, it had been almost completed, with the appointment of a Comisión para el Esclarecimiento Histórico, which would carefully delve into the past, with the cooperation of United Nations organizations.

In 1999, the fight was again mostly between the two conservative forces, and this time Ríos Montt's party came on top, without him as the candidate, but allowing him to be the power behind the throne. The pacified guerrillas only got 12 percent of the vote, contrasting to what happened in El Salvador, where they eventually came to have a dominant position. It must be taken into account that Ríos Montt, always within his conservative position, had a relatively progressive image in terms of social issues and could claim that he had tried to change the system a few years earlier, with the cooperation of the Christian Democrats. He also benefited from the support of the Protestant sectors, very numerous and widely distributed among the popular strata. A very conservative but civilianist political spectrum was becoming consolidated, with a small presence for the erstwhile guerrillas, whose "excesses" were also condemned by a exhausted public opinion.

Honduras

In contrast to "Bolivian" Guatemala, Honduras had a social structure with rather "Paraguayan" traits, that is, its social tensions were far fewer. Carías's dictatorship had ended in 1948, replaced by a successor more ready to open up the political scene. So much so, that in 1957 the progressive Liberal Ramón Villeda Morales came to power, leaning to the left.

His almost sure successor was Modesto Rojas, also a Liberal, accused of pro-Communist sympathies. True or not, this prompted the military to intervene, combining, as in the later Peruvian case, a distrust of popular participation with a determination to introduce some needed changes. Thus Colonel Osvaldo López Arellano started a series of "Nasserist" reforms, but soon veered to the right, and had himself legalized as president, with the backing of the conservative Nacional Party (1965-171).

During his time the "Football War" against El Salvador took place, in fact stimulated by the irritation caused in Honduras by the large numbers of Salvadoran immigrants who were taking advantage of the grater availability of land in the neighboring country. The end of the short conflict was followed by the mass expulsion of those immigrants, relieving pressures in Honduras at the cost of grievously increasing them in El Salvador.

In 1972 there was another coup, which like the one in 1963, started with reformist aspirations and projects of land reform, but soon channeled into cooperation with the Nacional Party. The new authoritarian experience, however, was relatively mild, in stark contrast with those in the rest of the region. Guerrilla activities were practically non-existent.

This stable authoritarianism lasted nine years (1972-1981), and after an internal coup which displaced its more "Peruanista" sector, the road to normality was undertaken, and a Liberal, Roberto Suazo Córdoba, from the right wing of his party, was elected. With this an era of civilian constitutional practices was inaugurated, up to the present, under Liberal hegemony, and loyal opposition from the Nacionales, who finally regained power in 2002.[4]

Nicaragua

In Nicaragua, the atmosphere of liberalization accompanying the end of World War II forced an opening of the regime. Somoza, who had already cultivated Communist support in 1944, gave in to a strong demand for renovation, coming even from sectors of his faithful National Guard. He allowed the candidacy of an old and venerable but easily pliable member of the conservative class. But when that man was in office he took his role seriously, naming erstwhile opposition figures to the ministries, which earned him a coup a month after his inauguration (1945). A search for substitutes and provisional solutions ended when, in 1948, an uncle of the strongman was elected by Congress, but he died after two years.

Meanwhile, Somoza acted as a careful owner of his estate, promoting economic development, mainly for himself but also for the country at large. He also tried to imitate the promotion of social legislation which other authoritarian regimes in search of legitimation were attempting at the time, notably Perón.

The system was able to survive the death of its founder, replacing him with his son Luis (1957-1963), then with the very reliable René Schick (1963-1967) and finally with the other son, Anastasio, Jr. (1967-1971). Under Anastasio, Jr. a personalistic and repressive slide of the system took place, till its demise in the revolutionary victory of 1979.

The Nicaraguan armed forces were named, as in the Dominican Republic and several other parts of the region, the National Guard, a result of the role played by the United States in their creation. The idea was that a real army was not necessary, and that it was better to concentrate on internal police functions. The Somozas shared this opinion, and were always apprehensive about the role a professionalized military might perform. The excessive predominance of the reigning family finally antagonized the local bourgeoisie, whose business ventures were constantly interfered with. Capitalist development in the rural areas, mostly in cotton and sugar, also had a fatal impact on many subsistence farmers, as in Guatemala and El Salvador (though not in Honduras, nor, as we shall see, in Costa Rica).

A first signal that not everything was right appeared in 1967, when the Conservatives, Independent Liberals, and Social Christians formed a Unión Nacional de la Oposición (UNO) to prevent Somoza's return to power after René Schick's relatively bland rule (1963-1967). During the ensuing contest an opposition crowd was fired upon, resulting in some five hundred deaths.

Under these evil auspices Anastasio, Jr. entered into the practically hereditary presidential office. When finishing his first term in 1971 he attempted to coopt the more dialogue-prone sector of the Conservatives, the so called "zancudos," passing on the executive office to a triumvirate under the control of that group, while he retained the more important command of the National Guard. As will be noted, during all this time constitutional formalities were more or less maintained. The Somozas' party was, by inheritance or cooptation, the Liberal one that had been the vehicle of their rise to power, and which was renamed Liberal Nacionalista. Anastasio, Jr. succeeded in dividing the opposition, but in 1973, when he returned to power, the regressive countdown was started. The previous year's earthquake, which practically destroyed the capital city, helped in discrediting the regime, as corruption and shady deals among the ruling groups became rampant.

The Frente Sandinista de Liberación Nacional (FSLN) was started in exile, in Honduras, in 1961, by Carlos Fonseca Amador, Silvio Mayorga, and Tomás Borge, the latter the only one to survive the first struggles. The early years saw scarce activity, mostly attempts to establish a liberated zone, or *foco*, in the eastern, mostly uninhabited lowlands. Later on they had the good fortune of trapping a whole bag of foreign diplomats (1974), forcing the government to negotiate a ransom and give them access to the media.

Within the FSLN there were three tendencies, often at odds with each other, and during some years acting separately:

1. The Tendencia Proletaria adopted an essentially Marxist-Leninist conception, favoring a working-class organization. Jaime Wheelock, Luis Carrión and Carlos Núñez were among its leaders.
2. The Guerra Popular Prolongada line preferred a tactic of creating rural *focos*, knowing that they would take a long time before giving fruits, so that it was necessary to be prepared for a long struggle. Tomás Borge was its main representative.
3. The insurrectional current, also known as Tercerista, favored a massive uprising, based on an interclass convergence as wide as possible, even if it was thought that in the long run only the peasant and proletarian segments would remain faithful. Daniel and Humberto Ortega advocated this approach, which is the one that prevailed, and in practice was the more moderate of the three, as it involved tactical alliances with sectors of the dominant classes.

In 1977, after Somoza had a heart attack, there was a reactivation of insurrectionary activity. A general strike obtained great support, even if trade unions were controlled by the government, and even those leaders following the Communist Party line did not set much store on overthrowing the regime by force.

In 1978, the director of the oppositionist Conservative paper *La Prensa*, Joaquín Chamorro, was assassinated, a fact that convinced wavering sectors of the upper classes that the government was no longer capable of controlling its own extremists. Nor could it keep down the guerrillas, who for a few hours occupied the National Palace itself. Finally, a prominent businessman, Alfonso Robelo, formed a Movimiento Democrático Nicaraguense (MDN), which staged a series of agitations and lockouts, together with Chamorro's widow, Violeta, and other very moderate groups, which were considering a coalition with the Sandinistas.

The signs of new times were all over the place. The numerous flock of liberation theology joined the guerrillas; the bishops themselves declared the right of the people to rebel, and to top it all, Jimmy Carter cut the supply of armaments. In July 1979, the capital city was occupied by the Sandinistas, swept to power by the combined effects of armed struggle, massive protests and strikes, and acquiescence of centrist groups well connected to the establishment.

The revolutionary government in Nicaragua first established a junta in which power was shared between the leftist guerrillas and the moderates who had joined them. Coexistence was not easy. Among the Sandinistas, despite the somewhat populist tendencies of the Ortega brothers, the Marxist-Leninist ideologues pushed for a reproduction of the Cuban single-party model. But the moderates sharing power expected that soon, once agrarian reform had been implemented, there would be a return to a basically capitalist pattern of development, as in Mexico.

The radicals got the upper hand, though, and pushed for further confiscation of private property. The moderates withdrew from the ruling coalition, becoming an "internal" opposition, to which was added an "external" one, made up of exiled members of the Guardia Nacional and other Somozistas, based in Honduras with North American help, known as Contras. The economic embargo imposed by the United States hindered the revolutionary regime, which had difficulty in creating new mechanisms of capital accumulation and work discipline to replace the old ones.

The elections finally held in 1984 gave a great victory to the Sandinistas, under conditions which the opposition and much of independent opinion judged scarcely competitive. The pressure towards a single-party system was then intensified, and led among other things to the closing of the influential newspaper *La Prensa*. However, internal as well as external resistance, and the discrediting of the Cuban model, made its reproduction difficult. And when new elections were held in 1990 the deterioration in living standards led to a lack of enthusiasm for the Sandinista cause, and to a victory for Violeta

Chamorro, at the head of the revived Unión Nacional Opositora (UNO), where many different and often conflicting ideological families existed.

Against what could be expected, the revolutionary government bowed to the popular verdict, not without serious internal wranglings as to whether to give in to petty-bourgeois prejudices. The Sandinistas struck a pact with the new authorities, to respect the continuity of the chief commandant of the armed forces, Humberto Ortega, who thus became the guarantor of the revolutionary conquests, against the foreseeable onslaught of the Conservatives now in power. It was also agreed that most of the sales of property to members of the revolutionary elite by their panicked owners, the so-called "piñata," were to be respected. Thus a swift transition was engineered, inaugurating a long-term coexistence between a civilian government representing the Right, and armed forces defending the Left.

In 1996, Arnoldo Alemán, at the head of a Liberal Alliance, supported by Violeta Chamorro, won the elections against Daniel Ortega of the Sandinista FSLN by 51 percent versus 37 percent. This basic pattern is complicated by the splintering of the anti-Sandinista forces, which include some participants in the Somoza regime and in the Contra civil war. On the Sandinista side, a group led by long-term revolutionary Sergio Ramírez has formed a separate, more clearly social democratic organization, but without much success. In 2002 again, the official party won against the Sandinistas by a comfortable margin, even if dissension within its ranks jeopardized its control of Congress. All in all, the country is heading, like El Salvador, towards a bipolarity and the real possibility of alternation in office.[5]

Costa Rica

In Costa Rica the war years saw a reform-oriented conservative party (Republicano Nacional) in power, with Rafael Calderón Guardia (1940-1944) at the helm. But in trying to apply some of the teachings of the Catholic Church, even if at the time they were not all that radical, he antagonized sectors of the Establishment, and in search of allies he approached Vanguardia Popular, the local name for the Communist Party. At the end of his time in office he paved the way for his protégé, Teodoro Picado (1944-1948), to keep the chair well guarded till his return.

In 1948, the polls gave an unexpected majority to the opposition, but the government alleged that there had been fraud on the part of the supposedly independent electoral tribunal. This argument of fraud committed by the opposition was not very credible, and it generated great resistance. The victorious candidate, Otilio Ulate, had been able to unify a part of the Conservative/Liberal vote with other factions of a reformist orientation but strong anticommunist attitudes. One of these was a social democratic study group launched by José Figueres, who decided to step into a more active public life and organized armed resistance against the invalidation of the electoral results. Thus a civil war was started (1948), with the support of the reformist youth and some labor groups organized by Benjamín Núñez, a priest not averse to radical action. In its search for allies, the contradictory Calderón looked for support across the border, to Anastasio Somoza, with whose regime he had some points of contact, in the field of establishing elements of a social policy, and even of using the Communists when necessary.

The Costa Rican civil war was of short duration, with Figueres victorious. He then organized a revolutionary junta which remained in power for two years so as to clean up the scene, but promising to transfer power to Ulate, whom he considered having been properly elected. During those two years a number of reforms were enacted, including the disbanding of the small national army, the nationalization of banks, and a property tax, thus antagonizing Ulate's followers who were basically conservative.

The ensuing elections for a Constituent Assembly gave a large majority to Ulate's partisans, because Calderón declared his abstention. The following year, the revolutionary process being considered closed, new elections gave a majority to an alliance between Figueres and Ulate, the latter being appointed president.

In 1951 Figueres formed his Movimiento de Liberación Nacional (MLN), with the members of his social democratic study groups, and the support of more pragmatic politicians. When in 1953 a renewal of authorities was scheduled Figueres finally reached the top post, with almost two-thirds of the votes, a figure made possible by yet another Calderonista abstention.

At the end of Figueres's administration, in 1958, the miracle of an opposition victory happened, now based on the coalition of Calderonismo with Ulate's forces, strongly backed by the business community and the conservative press, while the MLN had suffered a serious split. When this was healed, in 1962, the Liberacionistas came back to power. A two-coalition pattern was being established, approaching a two-party system, but with occasional complications and divisions.

One of these two poles is hegemonized by the Liberacionistas, who are the largest and best organized party, with an Aprista-like ideology tending towards social democracy. The other pole is built on the Calderonistas, who have adopted Christian Democratic principles. Often splinter groups from both main parties complicate the panorama, and there is also a Left, which oscilates in its attitudes.

Liberacionismo is strong among the small coffee producers and the urban middle classes, as well as among some labor sectors. Calderonismo combines a conservative support with the capacity to mobilize some popular sectors behind a caudillo figure. There is also a Left with roots among other working-class groups, particularly among port workers and the banana coastal plantations, where there is an important component of black population originating in the British Caribbean.[6]

Alternation in office has continued up to the present. At one point (1994) the MLN had as its candidate José Figueres's son, José, who won by a small margin against its traditional rival, which had changed its name to Partido Unión Social Cristiana. In 1998 luck went the other way, in a poll where there was a 40 percent abstention, a high figure for Costa Rica, where it is usually nearer to 20 percent. In 2002 the PUSC retained office, helped by a split among MLN supporters, which meant it wouldn't control Congress, thus forcing an element of coalition government.

Panama

In Panama the liberal oligarchical regime had been broken by Arnulfo Arias and his populism in 1940, as a result of the radicalization of the reformist movement he and his brother Harmodio had nurtured since the twenties. Their ideology, as in many other such cases, combined authoritarian and popular themes. In this case it included a special rejection of the quite numerous Asian and black minorities, the latter mostly anglophone and identified with the North Americans. Arias had been in Germany and harbored some sympathies for the Nazi experience, which gave arguments to his opponents, often concerned with other issues, and a military coup ousted him one year after his inauguration (1941).

A long time out of power, under various dispensations, was thus begun, till in 1948 he won another election but was barred from office by a coup led by Colonel José Antonio Remón with the support of the Right. A chaotic situation followed, and for a time Arias was allowed in the presidential post, but he was again demoted in 1951. His popular following remained firmly intact, however, while the political contest began being three-pronged. The participants were the civilian Right, with its main organization, the Liberal Party; militarism led by Remón, with some mobilizational tendencies inspired by Batista and Perón; and Arias, with a more mellowed populism.

Remón took over in 1952, but was assassinated in 1955, thus cutting short his attempt at becoming the new popular leader in the well-known military-authoritarian pattern, which was considered more menacing by the upper classes than Arias's older formula. Another chaotic five years followed, and finally in 1959 elections were held. Arias, knowing he would be barred, became in any case king maker, ordering his followers to vote for the Liberal Roberto Chiari, in exchange for a free run in 1964, when according to most evidence he in effect won the contest by a wide margin, though open fraud kept him out. Never losing his nerve, he again competed in 1968, and this time he was able to sit in the palace, but only for two weeks.

Of course, he had been overthrown by the Guardia Civil, and its commander was none other than Colonel Omar Torrijos, bent on a program of social reforms, but without Arias, and with popular mobilization under his strict control. The whole process was a caricature of the Peruvian duel between the military and Haya de la Torre, and had elements of Velasco Ibarra's fate in Ecuador.

Torrijos consolidated his regime, with a wide appeal to the popular classes, which started abandoning Arnulfo Arias. Torrijos had a solid supporter in Manuel Antonio Noriega, military commander of the banana region, where he was a popular personality. Torrijos's period in power (1968-1981) more or less coincided with that of the Peruvian Revolution, and was equally complex and contradictory in its ideological stance and its array of friends. Describing himself as a "cholo," he came from the rural middle class and had studied in a teachers' college, where he absorbed some progressive ideas before entering the military academy. He then passed through several courses organized by the United States forces, and others in Brazil and Peru, where he learned about antisubversive methods.

The ideology he developed through these experiences was highly synthetic, and not necessarily in line with what his teachers expected. Once in power he acted in an authoritarian manner, and never seriously thought of consulting the population about what had to be done, but his repressive methods were mild by the standards of the region. During most of his time in power he did not attempt to form a political party—in this following the Peruvian example—though he tried towards the end, when it was too late.

His dislike for elections did not rob him of sympathies among leftist circles, who did not put much store on that kind of formalism. Many, even members of the Communist Partido del Pueblo, participated in Torrijos's governing team, during its first, more progressive stage, up to 1974.

The 1972 Constitution, written and promulgated by Torrijos, gave him, as Jefe de la Revolución, the power to appoint the members of the Judiciary and also of Congress, which had only a consultative role. Another House of Representatives included one member for each county, popularly elected, but it met only one month per year, and had few responsibilities apart from that of electing the chief executive. A Dirección General para el Desarrollo de la Comunidad watched over relationships with barrio dwellers and their associations, obviously inspired in the Peruvian SINAMOS. Political parties were outlawed.

After 1974 the regime became more conservative, and towards 1978 changes were introduced so as to make the Congress more similar to its liberal namesakes, parties and all. Torrijos organized his own, the Revolucionario Democrático, hoping to follow the Mexican prototype.

Torrijos died in an accident in 1981, so he could not see the completion of his handiwork, nor the transition towards a more genuinely representative system. His successor lost the reformist vision that had inspired him, and corruption extended in an uncontrollable way, especially under Manuel Noriega, up to the United States intervention in 1989, when an armed force abducted him and jailed him on charges of drug trafficking. After this quick operation, a triumvirate remained in charge, and paved the path for a return to a normal constitutional system, with Guillermo Endara as its first president.[7]

The party system remained very fluid, with such initiatives as that of salsa singer Rubén Blades, who returned from the United States to form his Partido Papa Egoró ("Mother Earth"), and seemed well positioned for a while, but later declined. Old loyalties persisted, though. In 1999, a poll revealed that 52 percent of Panamanians would vote for Torrijos if he lived, and 35 percent for Arnulfo Arias. It so happened that the dictator's son, Martín, was at the head of a party of his own, and he was the frontrunner in opinion polls. Mireya Moscoso, widow of Arnulfo, also headed an Arnulfista party, and though she was not taken very seriously at the beginning, finally she staged a comeback and won the presidency.

Cuba

The two first years of the revolutionary government were dedicated to disassembling the Batista regime, which required the shooting of numerous agents of the repressive apparatus. Increasing elements of state property were meanwhile introduced, till in 1961 Fidel made a declaration of socialist objectives, which implied the elimination, except for minor areas, especially in the countryside, of private property of means of production.

In early 1961 Eisenhower, in the last stretch of his mandate, projected an attack on Cuba, using exiled volunteers, with strong logistic support from the CIA. When Kennedy took office in late January 1961 he allowed the operation to proceed, and thus a landing in the Playa de Girón or the Bay of Pigs took place (April 1961), meeting a complete failure, as the expected help from the local population did not materialize.

The provisional political system, during its early years, consisted of Fidel's own Movimiento 26 de Julio, the Directorio Estudiantil, and the Partido Socialista Popular (PSP), the name under which the Communists had been operating. Despite the hegemony of the 26 de Julio movement, the greater organizational capacity and Soviet backing of the PSP inclined the scales in its favor. The main countervailing power was the armed forces, headed by Fidel's brother, Raúl Castro.

Aníbal Escalante, long-time leader of the PSP, took the responsibility of forging a unified structure with the various revolutionary components. The new entity, first known as Organizaciones Revolucionarias Integradas, and then Partido de Unidad Revolucionaria Socialista, adopted in 1956 the Communist name. With this Fidel acknowledged Soviet hegemony, though really retaining control for himself, even on matters that might produce friction with the friendly world power.

In 1963 some alternatives to the Soviet model were explored, especially through the influence of Ernesto "Che" Guevara, who was intent on establishing a system of non-economic moral stimuli to work, and radical reductions of income differentials. This period saw a significant coolness in the rapport with the Soviet Union, and led to a demotion and later exile of their man Escalante.

Despite the purge of several Communist militants, many others remained in place, as economist Carlos Rafael Rodríguez, who led the agrarian reform program. But in 1966 there was another clean-up of "sectarian" elements, and Escalante got eighteen years in jail for antiregime activities.

The year 1968 saw the apex of these ideological innovations, combined with the influence of Mao Tse Tung. This phase lasted till 1970, when a return to more orthodox practices was undertaken. This was partly a reaction to failure to export the revolution, which Guevara had tried to start in Bolivia, where he met his death in 1967.

The new pragmatic approach went along with a rapprochement with the Soviet Union, and a greater amount of power granted to local enterprise managers, always within the public sector. The economy was growing rapidly (official statistics claimed a 12 percent annual rate between 1971 and 1977), partially fanned by the high prices of sugar, which from 5 cents a pound in 1970 jumped to 65 in 1974 in the international market. But by 1977 the boom had vanished, sugar falling to the more realistic values of 7 or 8 cents, though the USSR kept buying it at 30 cents, and sent subsidized oil.[8]

Fidel Castro's pro-Soviet orientation coincided with a clampdown at home against dissidents, like poet Heriberto Padilla (1971), who was forced to confess a series of scarcely credible crimes, maybe even exaggerating them himself as a coded message to international public opinion.

As for trade unions, during the early years, including the Guevarista period, they were not given much importance, as it was thought they had no place in a classless society. Since the new policies were put into effect, around 1970, unions were charged with the representation of sectorial interests, though always under close the Party's close vigilance. They also had to put up with strict controls against "vagrancy," aimed at controlling absenteeism, which reached the 20 percent mark in many areas. For a long time economic growth proceeded at a high rate, and even during the eighties, when the rest of Latin America was falling behind, the economy managed to grow. Social indices, such as infant mortality, life expectancy, and education and health, were among the best in the region.

The electoral system did not merit much attention, as it was believed that Fidel Castro's leadership replaced any absence of formal mechanisms. Meanwhile, the Party was consolidating its grip, and was becoming a channel of upward mobility, which could not but distort its social composition. In 1965, two-thirds of its Central Committee (of about a hundred members) belonged to the armed forces. Membership grew considerably, reaching 7 percent of the labor force in 1975.[9]

Only in 1975 was the first party congress held, and approved a draft Constitution, submitted to a referendum the following year. The new chart established Popular Power Organizations (OPP), elected at municipal level, which in an indirect manner would select provincial OPPs and a national one, which would function as a Congress. The Congress, in turn, formed a State Council with more permanent functions, because the national OPP would only meet for a couple of months each year, following in this the Soviet model. Though there would be no freedom to organize alternative parties, an effort would be made to have competing candidates at each level, as a method to check public opinion, though none could take really oppositionist attitudes.

The seventies also saw the expansion of the international role of the Cuban armed forces, sent to Angola in 1975 and later to Ethiopia. In total as many as 20,000 troops were stationed abroad.

During the whole duration of the Cuban revolutionary regime there has been plentiful emigration, largely in its early phase, but afterwards on several occasions when Fidel thought it advisable to relieve internal pressure. The number of political prisoners has also been quite high, though often jails were opened to allow some inmates to go to the United States.[10]

With the collapse of the Soviet Union the situation became quite critical, and some experiments in giving scope to private initiative were undertaken, but only in peripheral matters. However, during the nineties the economy deteriorated, putting in jeopardy some of the achievements in the social areas.

The regime does not have any programs for a change of the constitutional provisions for a single-party system, while internal challenges do not seem to be very strong. One big enigma in the future is whether the authorities will be able to proceed along some form of transition before it is too late and a more violent outcome is chosen by an internal opposition or a sector of the armed forces on the basis of a widespread malaise.[11]

Dominican Republic

In the Dominican Republic, Trujillo's dictatorship had started in 1930, on the basis of his role in the National Guard during North American occupation, and it was prolonged, directly or through cronies until his assassination in 1961. His regime was paradigmatic of one of the variants of authoritarianism, like Somoza's, and contrasting with the military anarchy rampant in several other places. Repression was ghastly, but concentrated on some individuals or in short-lived episodes. Thus, Jesús Galíndez, a Basque Republican emigré who had taken refuge on the island for several years and had later written a scathing denunciation of the dictator's rule, was kidnapped in New York and thrown into a ship's boiler. In another instance a mass killing of illegal Haitian immigrants was ordered. But nothing approached the level later reached in Guatemala or El Salvador.

On the other hand, both in Nicaragua and in the Dominican Republic the dictator administered the country rather carefully as his private property, promoting development and even adopting some progressive policies. Trujillo established elements of a welfare state, and the mere fact of maintaining order and stability after an agitated previous history earned him quite ample support. In some cases he also stood firm against North American requests.[12]

When a bullet ended his stay in power (1961), there was a military intervention and a call to free elections. The victor was the Partido Revolucionario Dominicano (PRD), of what can be called a leftist Aprista ideology, headed by long-term exile Juan Bosch (1962). However, Joaquín Balaguer, a trusted high official of the old regime, got a good proportion of the vote.

Bosch, driven by his more radical supporters, confronted the established interests without considering the consequences, and soon a military coup intervened, followed by popular rebellion with the participation of some army men. Thus the specter of military anarchy, or a series of ineffectual governments, was raising its head. To avoid the prospect of a new Cuba, the United States intervened in 1965, sending a military force with the participation of some other countries, and after one year new elections were held, this time giving the prize to Joaquín Balaguer and his Partido Reformista.

Bosch's radicalization led him to break away from the party he had created and of which he had been the unchallenged and charismatic leader. Proving the fact that such leadership is not exactly what it appears—as the leader can lead only at the cost of doing what his followers wish—Bosch was forced to create a new structure, the Partido de Liberación Dominicana (PLD), which got only a scant response at the polls. Frustrated by the incapacity of a fair democratic system to take root, Bosch opted for what he called a dictatorship with popular support. In a book of this title and in other works he even went to the length of considering the fallen dictator's followers less dangerous, given their allegedly popular character, than the moderates controlling the PRD, mostly supported by the middle classes, and who believed in the functioning of merely formal democratic institutions.[13]

As for the PRD, now clearly moderate and reformist, it has shared power alternately with Balaguer, eternal candidate of his party and several times winning the race, even when he was over ninety years old and practically blind. Balaguer's strength has been based on combining an appeal to the upper classes' conservatism with the memories a certain popular sector still harbors of the benefits they earned during Trujillo's time in power. The main labor concentration, in the dominant sugar industry, favors some form of radical leftism, whether of the PRD, Bosch's PLD, or Marxist parties. There has been no guerrilla movement, partly due to the island's geography, but particularly because channels exist for the expression of different sectorial interests, legitimately disputing supremacy at the polls.

The Balaguerista Reform Party and the PRD have long been quite equilibrated in voting strength, apparently heading towards a two-party pattern. This system was shaken in 1996 by an unexpected pact between the Balagueristas and the followers of Bosch's PLD. The PLD's candidate, Leonel Fernándeez, was voted by the Balagueristas, to thwart the PRD, who had a black man, José Francisco Peña Gómez, as its candidate. This coalition between what would appear as opposites resembles those forged in Bolivia between the MIR and Banzer. They were to some extent also foreshadowed by Bosch's theory that there was more compatibility between his party and the erstwhile Trujillistas, than with the middle-class-dominated PRD. This compatibility may be highly debatable, but the fact is that the alliance was established, and thus the PLD came to occupy the executive, and control Congress with the support of its old enemies.

Leonel Fernández (1996-2000) led a modernizing program, with support among the business community despite the leftist origins of his party. Many areas of the country were declared "zonas francas," enclaves where American products could enter free of any customs duties, and leave into the United States after being worked upon, in the same way. This caused a wide expansion of industrial exports, generating some employment and benefits for entrepreneurs located in such zones. In 2000, new elections returned power to the PRD, which maintains its popular base, while Balaguer's party was reduced to a quarter of the electorate. A three-pronged party system is developing, with the strange possibility that the "modernizing" PLD will become the main channel for the representation of business interests, leaving aside the more traditional and personalistic Reformistas, who in 2002 lost their leader. The PRD is positioned as the main expression of the popular organizations, a mixture between Aprista and Peronist models.

Haiti

Haiti was much less happy in its development, though it had also its equivalent of the Trujillo phenomenon, namely, François Duvalier. This small-town medical doctor had participated, during the thirties, in a black nationalist group called "les Griots" (the "sour ones"), in a sense a forerunner of the concept of *négritude* coined later by the Senegalese Léopold Sedar Senghor. It had mostly progressive traits, and challenged the hegemony of the mulatto upper class, which in an alternation of civilian and military regimes ruled with the occasional assistance of United States interventions.

Duvalier, like Somoza, created his own dynasty, and tried to govern in an authoritarian but developmental fashion, which he did only partially (1957-1971). The brutal excesses of his special police, the "Tontons Macoutes," made any form of national or international legitimation impossible. Finally, his less able son and successor succumbed to a military coup, inaugurating a stretch of military anarchy.[14]

This interregnum seemed to be at its end in 1991, when the charismatic Liberation Theology Catholic priest Jean Baptiste Aristide was elected. Once in power, he was not careful about methods for dealing with the opposition, and his followers inflicted maltreatment and tortures on those who stood on their way. The result was yet another military coup a few months after his accession.

This setback induced a diplomatic intervention by the Organization of American States and most governments of the area. As an indication of the complexity of alliances and criss-crossing, the prime minister favored by the local military as a provisional authority, considered a moderate by comparison to Aristide, was a member of the Communist Party. It was necessary for the United States to send an armed force, with the approval of some Latin American countries, to force the military to withdraw and allow free elections. The result was a victory by René Préval, of Aristide's party L'Avalas (the Avalanche) though at odds with his leader, who wished to be reinstated and complete his term. Préval confronted a stormy situation, closing Congress in early 1999, but promising to hold elections in 2001. At that time Aristide come back to power, apparently reconciled to more peaceful methods, but unable to really stop national disintegration.

Puerto Rico

In Puerto Rico, Luis Muñoz Marín had formed, in 1938, a Partido Popular Democrático, of a moderate reformist orientation, and closely connected with the Democrats in the United States and such other regional leaders as Haya de la Torre, Betancourt, and Figueres. He was elected governor repeatedly from 1949 to 1963, inaugurating in 1952 the special status of Associated Free State. He shunned independence, which was prodded by the Partido Independentista, of political sufferer Pedro Albizu Campos, which did not have much appeal to voters. On the right there was a party urging full incorporation into the United States, and closely associated with the mainland Republicans.

Economic and social progress were promoted by Muñoz Marín, and mass emigration abated internal social tensions. After the old leader's retirement party competition became more equal, the conservative New Progressive Party alternating in power with the Populares.

During a long period Puerto Rico was taken as a model of the application of pragmatically oriented reform policies, undertaken by a well-grounded local leadership cultivating excellent relations with the imperial power. This model was quite prestigious among moderate left and Aprista circles, up to the coming of the Cuban revolution, which channeled many sentiments and hopes along very different lines.[15]

Jamaica and Trinidad

In Jamaica, while under British domination, a party based on local trade unions had been formed, strong in sugar and bauxite areas. It was named the Labor Party, and was led by a caudillo figure, who also appealed to other interests, Alexander Bustamante. As with other islands of the British or French Caribbean, sugar generated a great concentration of manpower, easily accessible and organized into a working-class political party. The peasantry, on the other hand, was not at all numerous on this and other islands, by contrast with the Central American scenario, or bigger islands, like Cuba, or in the Guianas. Thus the existence of a classical conservative party was impeded.

The Right was forced to rely more directly on colonial authorities, or base its hopes on a restricted franchise after independence, which, given the spirit of the times, was unrealistic. The Jamaican Labor Party (JLP) won the first universal suffrage elections under colonial rule in 1944. Among the middle strata and the intelligentsia created by educational expansion, who were more sensitized to modern socialist ideas, a Peoples' National Party (PNP) was formed, led by a lawyer, Norman Manley. In 1955 this group won at the polls, but in 1962 it was Labor's turn again, inaugurating a ten-year stint at the head of the by now independent nation (1962-1972).

An important mutation happened in 1972 when the PNP, under the direction of Michael Manley, son of the founder, got a majority in favor of a very radical program of social change, patterned on the Chilean model. This program was followed during the next eight years (1972-1980), generating very serious social tensions, risking an armed intervention, from within or from outside the country. But the system stood firm, and by 1980 power returned to the by-now clearly conservative and business-supported Labor Party under its new leader Edward Seaga, of Syrian origin. Yet again, in 1988 another change brought to office a much more moderate Michael Manley, intent on accepting some of the dictates of the neoliberal nostrum. Since then, alternation with the Labor Party has become established.

Both parties, the JLP and the PNP, have a trade union sector, the latter more among qualified strata, while the JLP has an element of populism, based on the lowermost impoverished strata, some of whom are influenced by Rastafarianism, a religious-political group acknowledging the Ethiopian Emperor as its leader.[16]

In Trinidad and Tobago, sugar and oil also created a highly concentrated and unionizable working class, though divided along ethnic and ideological lines. The very numerous Asian Indian population, mostly among peasants and field workers, contrasted with the industrial labor of the sugar mills and other urban activities. Several leaders of an intellectual and cultural renaissance during the thirties, among them historian Eric Williams, abandoning their earlier stricter Marxism, launched a nationalist, multiclass party (Peoples' National Movement) for the 1956 elections, the first ones to form an autonomous government, though still under British supervision. The polls gave it a slight majority, and controlled access to office. The British authorities had the power to appoint some representatives to the local legislature, but refrained from annulling the PNM's majority, intent on giving the new forces a try.

There were some opposition parties, notably one organized after Alexander Bustamante's model, and associated with the Jamaican into a common front, when it was thought that a West Indies Federation would be the new independent nation, a project that soon failed, exploding into a thousand pieces.

At the same time that this supposedly "labor" party, clearly supported by the local business community, was being formed in Trinidad, a move to the left was taking place among the PNM, under the influence of the respected Marxist theoretician C.L.R. James, and also under the mirage of the Cuban Revolution. This upsurge of militancy lasted for only a couple of years, and soon the PNM returned to its pragmatism, preparing itself to assume full power at independence in 1962. In the transitional arrangements, a Senate was established as a control instance, where twelve members appointed by the popularly elected prime minister would be accompanied by two from the leader of the opposition, and seven from the governor, to give an assured representation to business, cultural or religious groups which did not have much of a chance to get electoral backing. The elections were among the more violent ones in the country's history, and could have easily degenerated into ethnic violence. This was avoided, the PNM came to power, and the island inaugurated an era of constitutional and democratic evolution.[17]

Guiana and Surinam

In Guiana, a two-party system had developed rather early, based along ethnic lines. Cheddi Jagan, of Asian Indian origin, led a leftist Peoples' Progressive Party (PPP), under heavy Marxist influence, with roots among the peasants, most of them also of Indian parentage. The black community, urban and including some commercial and professional elements, was for the most part behind Forbes Burnham's Peoples' National Congress (PNC).

With Guiana still under British rule in 1957, full franchise elections had allowed Jagan to become prime minister. This feat was repeated in 1961, though by a small margin over Burnham's PNC. There was a third group, potentially arbiter between the other two, Peter D'Aguiar's United Front (UF), supported by business groups, where many ethnic elements were present along with Indians and Africans.

At this time there was an upsurge of violence, combining ethnic with class confrontation. Thus in 1964 the sugar workers struck against Jagan, prodded by the main labor organization, the Trades Union Congress (TUC), which had a black majority. This resulted in almost two hundred dead, prompting Great Britain's intervention, welcomed by a wide spectrum of opinion, wary of the potential extension of ethnic strife once the colonial power was absent.

In this context, foreign investors and the United States government sided with Burnham, seen as basically moderate despite his trade union support, which contrasted with the openly flaunted Marxism-Leninism of Jagan's followers. The elections, held almost immediately, gave a slight majority to Jagan (46 percent) against Burnham's 41 percent and center-right D'Aguiar's 12 percent. The coalition between the latter two allowed Burnham a taste of office.

Under this new predicament independence was granted, in 1966, and since then the government increased its recourse to authoritarian methods, at the same time moving to the left. It declared a "Cooperative Republic," and established close contacts with Fidel Castro. The opposition accused Burnham of resorting to ever-more flagrant fraud, and of having little respect for human rights.

In 1971, bauxite mines were nationalized, and foreign investment was restricted. This produced a certain rapprochement with Jagan, also stimulated by Soviet and Cuban pressures. However, coexistence of the two leaders was not easy, and in 1977 they fell apart again, rekindling the sources of violent clashes. In 1980 the country was converted into a republic, and Burnham became its president till his death in 1985.

When in 1984 direct secret voting was established for trade union elections, Burnham's PNC lost the control it had traditionally held in that sector. Conditions became more stable, and in 1992, a few years after Burnham's death, a completely changed Jagan came back to power to implement an orthodox program of adjustment and retrenchment, while still paying lip service to Marxist-Leninist tenets.[18]

Economic growth accompanied his period in office, up to his death in 1997. He was succeeded by his wife, Janet, born in the United States. The country seemed to be heading towards a more consensual politics, though the ethnic chasm continued to be paramount.

Surinam became independent in 1975, but since 1965 it had enjoyed autonomy. The ethnic mosaic was even more extreme than in Guiana: in the countryside there was a major presence of Asian Indians (35 percent of the national total), Javanese (15 percent) and erstwhile runaway slaves (11 percent), who had a different identity from the rest of the black or mulatto population, more urban and professional, comprising 32 percent, to all of which influential minorities of Portuguese, Chinese, and Arabs should be added.

In the early twentieth century, gold had provided the main export product, to which afterwards sugar, timber, and rubber were added and, after the forties, bauxite. The standard of living was somewhat higher than in other parts of the area, including the northern states of Brazil.

Already, during Dutch times, a political party system had been formed, with a moderate National Party of Surinam (NPS), based on the mulatto elite and the upwardly mobile blacks ("Creoles"). It held governmental positions, first with a restricted franchise and later with the help of a distorted drawing of single-member constituencies. In the opposition there was a party representing the poorer sectors of the black population, and another two connected respectively to the Asian Indian and the Javanese population.

The last years of colonial rule were prosperous, under a government which reflected a coalition between the creole elite of the NPS and some other minority groups, plus the Indians, who had greater organizational and political experience than the Javanese. At the same time, nationalist groups were springing up, some of them favoring the adoption (or creation) of a national language and the study and respect of autochthonous traditions, with few votes but influence among strategically important groups.

After independence there was a spate of violent clashes between ethnic groups, and radical militancy among black activists. Three leftist parties were formed, vying with each other for more correct and uncompromising revolutionary values. The Indian community, fearing for the future, started emigrating, and this weakened their position. Tension increased when the 1980 elections were being prepared. But before that Dersi Buterse, a black non-commissioned officer trained in Holland, staged a coup, which had a wide support among the public, as the armed forces were one of the institutions with greater ethnic equilibrium. But immediately an interplay of alliances and strategic moves started, which recalls to some extent the Cuban situation of 1933, with Buterse playing the role of Batista, and the leftist forces that of Grau San Martín.

The coup was particularly supported by the new industrial and commercial business class, but also, surprisingly, by the bigger of the three leftist movements mentioned above, with populist tendencies, the Party of the People (VP), and some trade unions influenced by it. A consultative National Military Council was formed, with nine members, whose leadership was entrusted to one of the more left-leaning officers. To deflect ethnic suspicions, the post of prime minister was given to a person of Chinese origin. The plan was to hold elections after some prudential time had elapsed and passions subsided, but fate would not have it so. An unprecedented military anarchy started, which combined with the ethnic mosaic, and the prevalence of extreme leftist groups, formed an explosive mixture.

The drama started when Buterse led another coup, in August 1980, six months after his first one, now under the banner of "Surinamism," a new ideology whose contents can be easily imagined, and with full support from the Netherlands and the United States because of his pragmatism. But the following year he took another unexpected decision: he became reconciled with leftist officers he had jailed, and declared himself in favor of a "socialist society," causing consternation among foreign observers who had been celebrating the end of ideology in yet another land. The formation of Peoples' Committees and civic militia followed, with the support of the leftist parties, enthused by the idea of reproducing the experience of Allende in Chile. Relations with Cuba became very cordial.

The Right, of course, tried to react to this, supporting in 1982 a military coup, which failed and its chief shot. Then the opposition tried to organize a civic resistance, with the participation of the old political parties and some trade unions. They gathered a huge crowd in the main plaza, bigger than the officially-sponsored one that greeted Grenada's prime minister, Maurice Bishop, invited by Buterse and also following a policy of radicalization (his country was later invaded by United States forces). Violent clashes ensued, culminating in the assassination, by armed paramilitary bands, of fifteen well-known opposition leaders. Labor unions were also persecuted, and they joined in opposition, together with the conservative forces, forming an Association for Democracy, against Buterse's radicalized version of populism. The government responded by terrorism, burning several opposition head offices and assassinating a further dozen of their leaders, including trade unionists and some military.

Now, confronting indignant international protests and a Brazilian diplomatic intervention, Buterse attempted a moderate turn, getting rid of some of his more radical advisers and expelling the Cuban ambassador. After a year of unstable equilibrium, a strike at the Alcoa bauxite mines, provoked by leftist activists, spelled the end of their influence in ruling circles.

Buterse then tried an alliance with labor unionists, who were demanding a mixture of democracy and corporatism. A hastily convened Constituent Assembly was created by government fiat, with fourteen delegates from the ruling party (by now named Movement 25 February), eleven from the unions (till the day before in the opposition) and six from business organizations. This composition was an insult to the latter, who refused to participate. Buterse was forced to the negotiating table, with ethnic and religious representatives, as well as the traditional political parties. A two-year normalization program was launched, which was to lead to competitive elections and a civilian government in 1987.

The transition was marred by widespread rebellions of Maroons and Amerindians, brutally repressed, but causing a temporary breakdown of bauxite production. Finally, in 1987 the elections gave a large majority to an alliance of traditional parties over Buterse's National Democratic Party, which was now pleading for socialism and brotherhood among ethnic groups.

In 1990, a conflict that started with Buterse's resignation from his army command, led to another coup by his successor, who however promised new elections. These were held in 1991, leading again to a victory for the coalition of traditional parties, to which a small Labor group had been added, forming the New Democracy and Development Front. This coalition has remained in power after the 1996 renewal of authorities, in what seems to be a democratic normalization, with the prevalence of a rather stable moderate coalition including diverse ethnic groups. Buterse's party has been reduced to an ineffectual minority, reconciled with standard electoral practices.[19]

Notes

1. Michael McClintock, *State Terror and Popular Resistance in El Salvador*, pp. 283, 296; Jorge Cáceres B., Rafael Guidos Béjar and Rafael Menjívar Larín, *El Salvador: una historia sin lecciones*.
2. Terry Karl, "Imposing Consent? Electoralism vs Democratization in El Salvador"; Fermán Cienfuegos, *Veredas de audacia: historia del FMLN*, and his edited book *Visiones alternativas sobre la transición*; Joaquín Villalobos, *Una revolución en la*

izquierda para una revolución democrática; Jeffery M. Paige, *Coffee and Power: Revolution and the Rise of Democracy in Central America.*
3. Ronald M. Schneider, *Communism in Guatemala, 1944-1954*; Peter Calvert, *Guatemala: A Nation in Turmoil*; Susanne Jonas, *The Battle for Guatemala*, and *Of Centaurs and Doves: Guatemala's Peace Process*; Jennifer Schirmer, *The Guatemalan Military Project: A Violence Called Democracy.*
4. Arturo Fernández, *Partidos políticos y elecciones en Honduras en 1980*; Daniel Slutzky and Esther Alonso, *Empresas trasnacionales y agricultura: el caso del enclave bananero en Honduras*; James A. Morris, *Honduras: Caudillo Politics and Military Rule.*
5. Thomas Walker, ed., *Nicaragua: The First Five Years,* and *Nicaragua Without Illusions: Regime Transition and Structural Adjustment in the 1990s*; David Close, *Nicaragua: Politics, Economics and Society*; Harry Vanden et al., eds., *Democracy and Socialism in Sandinista Nicaragua*; Henry Patterson, "The 1996 Elections and Nicaragua's Fragile Transition"; Jorge Domínguez and Abraham Lowenthal, eds, *Constructing Democratic Governance: Mexico, Central America and the Caribbean in the 1990s*; Orlando Núñez Soto, *Transición y lucha de clases en Nicaragua 1979-1986.*
6. Charles D. Ameringer, *Don Pepe: A Political Biography of José Figueres of Costa Rica*; John Patrick Dell, *Crisis in Costa Rica: The 1948 Revolution*; Jacobo Schifter, *La fase oculta de la guerra civil en Costa Rica*; Fabrice Edouard Leboucg, "Class Conflict, Political Crisis and the Breakdown of Democratic Practices in Costa Rica: Reassessing the Origins of the 1948 Civil War"; John Booth and Mitchell Seligson, eds., *Elections and Democracy in Central America*; John Booth, *osta Rica: Quest for Democracy.*
7. Omar Torrijos, *La batalla de Panamá*; Sharon Collazos, *Labor and Politics in Panama.*
8. Carmelo Mesa Lago, *Dialéctica de la Revolución Cubana,* and *La economía en Cuba socialista*; Robert M. Bernardo, *The Theory of Moral Incentives in Cuba*; Maurice Halperin, *The Rise and Decline of Fidel Castro*; Mona Rosendal, *Inside the Revolution: Daily Life in Socialist Cuba.*
9. Mesa Lago, *Dialéctica*, pp. 111-115.
10. Edward González, *Cuba under Castro: The Limits of Charisma*; Maurice Zeitlin, *Revolutionary Politics and the Cuban Working Class*; Pedro Ramón López Oliver, *Cuba: crisis y transición*; Amnesty International, *Political Imprisonment in Cuba.*
11. Peter Schwab, *Cuba: Confronting the United States Embargo*; Joseph Tulchin et l., *Cuba and the United States: Will the Cold War in the Caribbean End?*
12. Ramón Emilio Saviñón M., *Memorias de la Era de Trujillo 1916-1961*; Eric Paul Roorda, *The Dictator Next Door*; José Moreno, *Barrios in Arms: Revolution in Santo Domingo*; Víctor Grimaldi, *Golpe y Revolución: El Derrocamiento de Juan Bosch y la Intervención Norteamericana.*
13. See Juan Bosch, *The Unfinished Experiment: Democracy in the Dominican Republic,* and his *El próximo paso: dictadura con respaldo popular* as well as *Capitalismo, democracia y liberación nacional*; G.Pope Atkins and Larman C. Wilson, *The Dominican Republic and the United States: From Imperialism to Transnationalism*; Amaury Justo Duarte, *Partidos políticos en la sociedad dominicana (1844-1998.)*
14. Lorimer Denis and François Duvalier, *Le problème des classes sociales a travers l'histoire d'Haiti*; Leslie Manigat, *Ethnicité, nationalisme et politique: le cas d'Haiti,* and *De un Duvalier a otro: itinerario de un fascismo de subdesarrollo.*
15. Kelvin A. Santiago-Valles, *"Subject People" and Colonial Discourses: Economic Transformation and Social Disorder in Puerto Rico, 1898-1947*; Justin Daniel, ed., *Les îles Caraïbes: modèles politiques et stratégiques de développement.*

16. J.H. Parry, P.M. Sherlock and A.P. Maingot, *A Short History of the West Indies*; Michael Craton and James Walvin, *A Jamaican Plantation: History of Worthy Park, 1670-1970*; Orlando Patterson, *The Sociology of Slavery: An Analysis of the Origins, Development and Structure of Negro Slave Society in Jamaica*; Adam Kuper, *Changing Jamaica*; John D. Forbes, *Jamaica: Managing Political and Economic Change*; Philip Sherlock and Hazel Bennett, *The Story of the Jamaican People*.
17. Bridget Brereton, *A History of Modern Trinidad, 1783-1962*; Perry Mars, *Ideology and Change: The Transformation of the Caribbean Left*.
18. Kemp Ronald Hope, *Guyana: Politics and Development in an Emergent Socialist State*; Andrés Serbin, *Guyana*; Rita Giacalone de Romero, ed., *Guyana hoy*.
19. Henk E. Chin and Hans Buddingh', *Surinam: Politics, Economics and Society*; Betty Sedoc Dahlberg, ed., *The Dutch Caribbean: Prospects for Democracy*; F.S.G. Ledgister, *Class Alliances and the Liberal Authoritarian State: The Roots of Post-Colonial Democracy in Jamaica, Trinidad and Tobago, and Surinam*.

7

The Workings of Democracy: From the Eighties to the New Century

In Brazil, the military regime began to feel strong pressures for change at the end of the seventies, when a notable economic development had changed the country, or at least the more central parts of it. The possibility that, if no reforms were initiated, violent protests might spread was certainly on the minds of the regime's more thoughtful elements. As a sign of the search for new methods one may take nationalist General Afonso Albuquerque Lima's Plano Rondon, which offered university students a year of work and community service in the most inhospitable places, in lieu of military service. It was hoped that this local version of the Peace Corps would cement a new solidarity between the armed forces and the future intelligentsia, cured of unrealistic revolutionary ideas through the discovery of the "real Brazil." The project was quite risky, as the Peruvian example might suggest, and it is surprising that it was accepted at all. It was applied, but never got really off the ground, and it involved only a few people.

At higher levels, General Golbery do Couto e Silva, an expert in geopolitics, planned the best way to transfer power without really losing it. The economic downturn, partly a result of the two major oil crises of 1973 and 1979, didn't help. Ernesto Geisel (1974-1979), as we have seen, took the first steps in the direction of *abertura*, after the harsh years of his predecessor Garrastazu Médici. Censorship was scrapped, and freedom of association restored, except for very extremist groups. The solid majorities to which ARENA had become accustomed started to disintegrate. It seemed as if the members of the Varguista right, their apprehensions having been assuaged after the dismantling of the revolutionary Goulartian bases, would rejoin the mainstream of what remained of the old alliance, that is, the MDB.

In Greater São Paulo the old corrupt union leaders (*pelegos*) had difficulty in controlling the younger and more skilled workers, who in a pragmatic way wished to have better representatives to discuss bread-and-butter issues with the employers. Thus a new brand of leaders emerged, who because of their youth did not have a police record, and thus could pass through the screening process still in effect. Among them, pride of place was soon earned by Inácio Lula da Silva, a qualified mechanic, who at the start of his career had North American unionism as his model, with little if any ideology appended.

He survived continued harassment by employers and police, for whom it was too late to push him fully aside under the new dispensation, as he had become quite popular, and enjoyed the support of the by now numerous progressive sectors of the Catholic Church. Soon he found himself surrounded by all sorts of leftist activists, from Fidelistas to Maoists and Trotskyits, to whom were added for good measure the increasingly radical liberation theology priests and laymen. The main exception were the Communists, who had more union cadres than the rest combined, and who did not set much store on this combination of "yellow" Catholicism, bread and butter unionism and infantile leftism.[1]

In the MDB, which saw its voting strength swell with any new election, the prospect of eventually coming to power within historical time attracted increasing numbers of politicians. This included Communists, who, their party being still outlawed, preferred to infiltrate bourgeois structures rather than waste their time with the more extremist challengers of the regime. To prevent the consolidation of a united opposition, chief strategist Couto e Silva convinced the authorities to abandon the two-party rigid scheme, and allow any number of flowers to bloom, preferably on the decomposing body of the MDB, which was widely considered a bag of cats. This ploy succeeded beyond expectations.

ARENA, held together by the glue of official dispensation, remained practically intact, though it changed its name to that of Partido Democrático Social (PDS), a name which meant nothing, and was intended to make people believe it had something to do with the old Varguista PSD (which was true only to a minor degree, as its supporters came mostly from the UDN).

In contrast, the MDB suffered the expected proliferation. Its main stem kept together and adapted its name to that of Partido do Movimiento Democrático Brasileiro (PMDB), thus practically retaining its increasingly popular logo. But the more "authentic" sectors of old Trabalhismo, both in and out of Congress, formed the Partido Democrático Trabalhista (PDT), led by firebrand Leonel Brizola, brother in law of Goulart and his political heir. They were unable to retain the old name because Ivette Vargas registered it earlier, and then used it as a rubber stamp offered for a consideration to politicians of any hue wishing to have some formal backing.

Further to the left were Lula and his constellation of Marxist and Catholic friends. Though these ideological groups and parties were yet unable to get recognition, they did flock around Lula and his union militants, who formed a Partido dos Trabalhadores (Workers' Party), with very radical principles, absorbed by Lula from his new comrades. The Communists again opted for remaining within the womb of the PMDB. On its right, the MDB also suffered the departure of some well-heeled members, who formed, together with a fraction of ARENA, the Partido Popular, which was the least popular of them all, and was fondly nicknamed the bankers' party, but soon it was dissolved. So finally the situation remained as follows, from right to left, leaving aside the irrelevant new PTB.[2]

1. PDS, transmutation of ARENA, which in turn had been formed by the UDN and a majority of Kubitshek's PSD.
2. PMDB, main current of the MDB, which had been mostly based on the old PTB, that is, the Varguista left, plus some sectors of the PSD. Now the PMDB retained its more moderate elements, acquiring some back from their stint in ARENA.
3. PDT, splitting from the MDB, basically channeling its more militant members, mostly from the old PTB, parliamentary and extraparliamentary.
4. PT, with new people, plus some minor sectors of the MDB.

The Brazilian Transition

The system continued to liberalize, increasingly giving more areas of expression to the opposition, despite the ruses and the attempts at dividing it. Divided it was, and particularly important for the PMDB was the loss of the PDT. Brizola was considered a potential mass leader, capable of reaching the still not fully aroused masses of the vast interior, and especially those of the larger urban centers.

In 1982 direct elections for governors were allowed, and gave a majority to the PMDB, which despite its losses was becoming the main national party. There was a wide popular demand to have direct elections also for president, but this was too much, and the very forceful campaign of "diretas já!" did not move the government. The designation of the chief executive continued to be in the hands of an Electoral College, based on the full Congress, to which now six extra representatives for each state (appointed by local legislatures) were added, so as to give more weight to the small, backward, and conservative regions.

The PMDB was confronted with the option of accepting the challenge in the Electoral College, legitimizing the unfair proceedings, or else rejecting such participation and seeking redress through wider popular agitation, hoping to get some echo among the military. The more radical elements of the PMDB (always a highly undisciplined party), plus practically the whole PDT and PT, refused to play the game. The main current of the PMDB did accept the rules, and chose its more moderate, almost conservative leader, Tancredo Neves, as its candidate, hoping to attract wavering elements from the PDS. This strategy paid off, and produced a permanent split in the PDS, where a very hard-line, though civilian candidate had been adopted, Paulo Maluf. Incensed, the more *aberturista* members of the regime now formed their own organization, the Partido da Frente Liberal (PFL), which happened to include the vice president and several other high-ranking officials. Then an alliance was struck between them and the PMDB, which offered to appoint one of their number, José Sarney, as Neves's running mate. With the triumph of this unexpected last-minute coalition in the electoral college the military regime came to its end. What had happened was another instance of the typical method of changing governments under authoritarian or semi-authoritarian conditions: a division of the ruling party. Of course, such divisions do not occur simply because of unmanageable personal ambitions, but reflect deeper tensions, or changes in the economic and social infrastructure.

In fact, the decision of the Electoral College was only the first step in an arduous and contorted route. Neves died before taking office and left Sarney, a man who had occupied high positions during the military regime, in charge of affairs. It was a re-run of the Quadros-Goulart charade, in reverse. Sarney lacked legitimacy, even if he governed with the victorious coalition, in which the PMDB had prime of place. But economic problems proved to be intractable, inflation, which had been controlled under the dictatorship, returned in full force, and economic growth never recovered the high levels of the "Brazilian miracle."

Sarney's term (1985-1990) saw a deterioration of the image of the majority party, the PMDB, which had been expected to take its leader, Ulysses Magalhaes, to the top post, but instead broke into many pieces. Already in 1988, a Constituent Assembly had established direct elections for the chief executive and the governors, plus many other detailed provisions which were more appropriate to a party program than for a Constitution, like reducing interest rates to a maximum of 12 percent, job security for all state employees, prohibition of selling off state enterprises in strategic areas, and so on.

Freedom for organizing new parties was now total, and the divisive process especially affected, once again, but this time dramatically, the PMDB, which came weakened to the contest of December 1989. A group of distinguished technicians and professionals who had joined the PMDB without much political experience, including sociologist Fernando Henrique Cardoso, broke away, and formed the small Partido da Social Democracia Brasileira (PSDB), with social democratic ideas but without the organizational structures, mainly trade unions, that usually sustain such ideological groups. However, having inherited from the mother party some experienced and pragmatic politicians, they did net some 10 percent of the vote. The PMDB also lost many regional structures, led by local sons who fashioned diverse parties, with meaningless names, known by their initials, and with no known party platform. On the left, both PT and PDT got each some 15 percent of the vote, a fraction more for the PT.

An unsuspected phenomenon, due largely to the main national TV station, was the launching to fame of Fernando Collor de Mello, an obscure politician from the small Northeastern sugar state of Alagoas, where he was a major local figure and wealthy entrepreneur. He created another rubber stamp party called the Partido da Renovação Nacional (PRN) and got 35 percent of the vote in the first turn. Obviously, the population was tired of the old faces and wanted to have someone new, which they got, though things would not be changed so easily. A second turn was necessary, and it was fought between Collor, clearly supported by the Right and Center, and Lula, who was defeated by a moderate margin, as he picked not only the PDT's, but also half the PSDB's and some other independent votes. Now the problem was that Collor had next to no support in Congress, which was not renovated at the same time as the executive. When after a few months, legislative elections were held, however, Collor's charisma did not extend to this level, and he got only a paltry bloc in Congress, so he had to rely on alliances in order to govern. This difference between preferences expressed for presidential and for congressional candidates was and continues to be typical of Brazil, though to a diminishing degree, and had already been in effect during Goulart's days.

Collor's appeal has been branded as populist by many observers and the media. The concept of populism, though, is better reserved for political movements which are aimed against the Establishment and appeal to popular sentiments, even if they are not based on autonomous working-class organizations. By these standards, Varguismo (post-1945), Aprismo, and Peronism do qualify, but Collor's movement does not. It did have a popular following, as most conservative parties of any significance do. Collor inveighed against the privileges of the upper rungs of the state bureaucracy, which was a very minor part of the really privileged classes, against which he didn't utter a word. The conservative sectors of the population clearly understood his purpose, and voted for him, already in great numbers in the first round, temporarily abandoning their traditional parties, which by now were the PDS and the PFL. They did so overwhelmingly in the second turn, to stop Lula.

In power, Collor was unable to curb inflation, mostly because of the weakness of his party. At times Collor managed to get a majority in Congress on the basis of his conservative allies, plus a shifting array of centrist and regional groups, easily bought, and of what remained of the PMDB. His economic policies, of a neoliberal, free market orientation, met the stiff opposition of the popular parties (PT and PDT) and their unions, which made life impossible for him.

Finally, in September 1992, after an accumulation of scandals about corruption in high places, the president was impeached, and replaced by the vice president, Itamar Franco, who led a lame duck regime till the end of 1994, bringing in sectors of the opposition, notably the PSDB, one of whose main representatives, Fernando Henrique Cardoso, was made minister of economy.[3]

The success of Cardoso in controlling inflation made him seem an economic wizard, and paved the way for his election in 1994, when he got the support of the Center and the Right as a bulwark against Lula's PT. His government proved effective in keeping inflation down, and in proceeding along the path of privatization. Social inequities, deeply rooted in the social structure of the country, could not be seriously dealt with, and as a result some movements of social protest sprang up, notably the agitation of the Sem Terra (landless) who, demanding land, occupied large estates, with the support of a considerable sector of the Catholic Church.

In 1998 Cardoso was reelected, with an increasing support from the Right and from his own small centrist party. Lula's PT, in alliance with Brizola's PDT, became the main opposition. Between these two poles a vast number of small, often regionalist parties operate, rivaling the legendary Marais during the French Revolution, and mockingly known as *fisiológicos* because of their constant demand for handouts in exchange for their votes in Congress.[4]

How Cardoso was able to control inflation remains a puzzling sociological enigma. It must be said that he had the Argentine example, where the Peronists' minister of economy, Domingo Cavallo, had succeeded in killing the monster in 1991, at the price of overvaluing the peso, pegging it to the dollar, causing a temporary recession, and soon creating high unemployment. In Argentina, the government had many trump cards in its hand, as it had the confidence both of the trade unions and of the business community, the latter having been coopted by Menem. With such backing, which had not been the privilege of any government before him, not even the military dictatorships, Cavallo held a powerful weapon, and he played it masterfully. He did irritate some Peronist supporters, notably the unions, but because they felt the government was "their" government they did not stage a frontal fight against it. It cannot be said that Cavallo was more of an economic wizard than his many predecessors during both civilian and military regimes who tried similar recipes but failed to get them through. What Cavallo did have in his favor was a convergence of various sectors of public opinion and interest groups, who were alarmed at the hyperinflation that had recently gripped the country.

Cardoso, first as Itamar Franco's minister of economy, and then as president, did not have such solid social support, especially because there was no equivalent of the Peronist party to channel support from the popular classes. Far from that, he had to face a determined opposition from the Socialist/Populist alliance of PT and PDT. Rather than a solid party behind him, he had to manage an unstable congeries of dissimilar groups, though with strong backing from the entrepreneurial groups and their two parties, the PFL and the PDS (later renamed PPB). Admittedly, Brazil had also gone through the equivalent of major hyperinflation, which even if it didn't reach the Argentine mark of 200 percent per month, was for years at an approximately 40 percent monthly figure. It is also true that the opposition from the popular classes was weaker than in Argentina, and more heterogeneous. The combination of PT and PDT was never very solid, and the trade union nucleus around Lula, though strong, was only powerful in the highly industrialized areas, a smaller percentage of the population in Brazil than in Argentina. Because of the radicalization of the PT and its unions (also an alternative trade union structure) the Força Sindical, was organized, which even if it was not enthusiastic about Fernando Henrique Cardoso's policies, did contribute to weaken the trade union front.

Cardoso was successful in controlling Congress through constant negotiation with the *fisiologistas*, going ahead in the privatization process, and maintaining dynamic growth. Inflation was also under control. He also managed to have a constitutional change accepted, enabling him to seek a second term, and eliminating some of the rigidities of the 1988 Constitution. The contest of 1998 was practically a rerun of the 1984 race, with Cardoso now solidly supported by the two conservative parties, the more market-oriented Partido Pogressista Brasilerio (PPB) and the more regional Partido da Frente Liberal (PFL) plus most of the PMDB and smaller groups. On the opposite side, Lula remained as his main contender.

Cardoso's second term was full of problems, beginning with a world speculation against the local currency, the *real*, which had to be strongly devalued. The president's popularity, which had been quite high, plummeted now and remained low, making it difficult for him to pass on his charisma to a successor. As the 2002 national elections approached, Lula was well ahead in the opinion polls, and a conservative alternative, the PFL's Roseana Sarney, who was very well positioned, was caught in a corruption scandal and reduced to nonentity. The Right was in a shambles, incapable of putting up a credible candidate, with the official PSDB's José Serra running third or fourth. By mid-year Ciro Gomes, an erstwhile member of the PSDB, who had veered somewhat to the left, came from nowhere and started equaling Lula in popular preferences. He had actually become the candidate of the Partido Popular Socialista, the absolutely moderate and re-christened old Communist Party. In practice, he started attracting conservative votes, and even followers of the party in power took him as a "lesser evil" than Lula. Others, including important sectors of the industrial establishment, organized in the Federação de Industrias do Estado de São Paulo (FIESP), were ready to negotiate with the now more moderate erstwhile trade unionist, which had established alliances with some conservative groups, especially a small but significant party based on the evangelicals, mostly on the right in law-and-order and family values, but representing a very deprived constituency.

The elections gave a handsome victory to Lula, with 47 percent of the vote in the first round, against 24 percent of his main rival, the government-sponsored Jose Serra. Not having reached the 50 percent mark, a second turn was necessary, though the result was obvious, as he got the support of the other two main candidates apart from Serra. However, his own party fell far short of gaining a majority in Congress; many people voted for him for the presidency, but for other parties for Congress. So he needs to build coalitions, mostly with other leftist, and center-left parties, but he has also come to an understanding in cooperating in basic reforms with the right-wing Partido Progressista Brasileiro (PPB).

Lula's first actions were extremely moderate, gaining recognition from the national and international business communities. He has been successful in many of the first challenges, but has inevitably lost some support among the left of his own party, and among the more extreme sectors of activists, especially the Sem Terra, and some state employees who may suffer a reduction of their privileges.

On the international scene, Lula has stated his priority for the consolidation of the regional market, Mercosur, with Argentina, Paraguay, and Uruguay, and a weaker association with Chile and Bolivia. He has established a solid understanding with presidents Ricardo Lagos of Chile, and Nestor Kirchner, of Argentina, forming a trio that might evolve towards some local form of the "Third Way."

Diversity of Transitions: Peru, Ecuador, Bolivia, and Paraguay

Peru

In Peru the military regime was in danger by the mid-seventies, unable to consolidate its system of popular mobilization, and hit by an economic crisis sparked by the withdrawal of the *anchovetas*, the basis of the fish meal fertilizer industry, deep into the Pacific. In 1975 an internal coup removed Velasco Alvarado and put in his place the more conservative Francisco Morales Bermúdez, who decided to seek a reconciliation with political parties and plan a very gradual return to normality.

Thus elections were held for a Constituent Assembly in 1978, where Aprismo got a majority, signaling its impending coming to power. Its majority, however, was partly due to the abstention of Acción Popular, who cultivated a more determined oppositional role. But Haya de la Torre would not see his dream fulfilled; he died before the elections of 1980, leaving his party in disarray and divided, thus paving the way for a second term for Belaúnde Terry, who this time was able to finish it. In contrast with the Apra's continued weakness and internal squabbling, a new force was coming into being, the Izquierda Unida, where a great number of Marxist and radical parties were conjoined.

Izquierda Unida, which included the Communists, was a serious contender for working-class preferences against the Apra, having established solid enclaves among student and labor groups. But at the same time a very determined guerrilla group was being formed, the Sendero Luminoso, which was much more radical than the subversive groups of the sixties. It followed supposedly Maoist dictates, but to a larger extent it incorporated ancient Inca millenarian traditions, and a nationalist Marxism based on Mariátegui's teachings.[5]

The fact that Belaúnde was elected to replace the military regime eased the changeover, because if the Izquierda Unida had won the contest, surely the military would have thwarted it. Even an Aprista victory would have been difficult to swallow, despite the increased moderation of its leadership. The test, however, came at the end of Belaúnde's administration (1985), when everything pointed to a sure victory of the Apristas, now led by Alan García, one of Haya's disciples, and very determined to renovate the movement, giving it a slightly more leftist hue, and at the same time making it more compatible with peaceful competition with others. He was extremely successful in this overhauling of old structures, and got the maximum share of the votes the party had ever garnered, some 50 percent of the total, followed by the Izquierda Unida with about 20 percent. Belaúnde's Acción Popular, down to 8 percent, formed a conservative rump, where the Partido Popular Cristiano had a major role.[6]

Despite the favorable political conditions under which he initiated his mandate, Alan García did not perform adequately. He aimed at maintaining himself within the populist and state-interventionist parameters of his party's ideology, confronting the international monetary establishment, and going to the length of nationalizing the banks. Reigning economic conditions made this policy impossible, and he had to change his course, with much loss of prestige. On the other hand, he was unable to control corruption, and lost approval from a population that had placed its faith in him and now felt betrayed.

When his term came to an end in 1990, a major mutation of the Peruvian political spectrum was underway. The Right had always been poor in votes, but now it was buttressed by its incorporation of Mario Vargas Llosa, converted to neoliberalism and prepared to head a new party dedicated to those ideas. With ample business support, he formed a coalition between his own makeshift Movimiento Libertad and the two more experienced center-right forces, Belaúnde's Acción Popular and the Popular Cristianos. Given the discredit of the Apra, his victory seemed assured, as the Izquierda Unida had great difficulty in venturing very far from its citadels among ideologically sensitized workers and intellectuals, despite having contributed to the election of Lima's mayor, Alfonso Frijolito Barrantes.

But there was another new element in this constellation: the sudden appearance of Alberto Fujimori, an engineer and academic administrator with little if any political experience. He jumped into public view through the mass media, in a sense like Collor in Brazil, though with much less help from the Establishment. Moreover, as a *chino* (actually, of Japanese ancestry) he posed as a *cholo*, a man of the people, set against the bigwigs backing the neoliberal coalition. Surprisingly, he came very close to Vargas Llosa in the first round (29 percent against 33 percent), with Apra trailing behind with 23 percent, and the severely battered Izquierda Unida in fourth place. In the second turn, Fujimori gathered most of the anti-Vargas Llosa vote and won the presidency. What had happened was that most Aprista and leftist voters, intent on beating the Right, had rallied to him, in what appeared to be a typical and probably short-lived populist movement.

Fujimori, whose appeal was mostly personal (the party he created was called Cambio 90) lacked sizeable support in Congress, and had to face mounting economic problems and the challenge of Sendero Luminoso, constantly gathering new recruits, and terrorizing the non-committed public and even the very peasants among whom they were trying to establish a solid base. He finally couldn't resist applying his technocratic methods, ordered an *autogolpe*, that is, a coup d'état planned from the government, and closed down Congress (1992). However, facing serious resistance at home and abroad, he soon called a Constituent Assembly, in which most opposition parties did not participate, and afterwards held legislative elections, where he obtained a majority despite the efforts of the various opposition groups, unable to come together.[7]

Fujimori's economic policies, despite the nature of his early electoral support, veered to the neoliberal pole, getting increasing acceptance from the conservative sectors that had been his main opponents. Political parties were passing through an unprecedented disarray, and in each election voter preferences shifted wildly. In 1993, municipal elections were won practically throughout the country by independents, mostly locally based. But that same year a referendum on the newly sanctioned Constitution, which had introduced many neoliberal ideas, was approved nationwide, particularly on the basis of its support in Lima while in the provinces most people rejected it.

For the 1995 renovation Fujimori had few if any rivals. He came out on top with 64 percent of the popular votes, against Javier Pérez de Cuéllar, a member of the traditional upper class who had been secretary general of the United Nations but had no popular appeal. The volatility of the electorate showed again in the ensuing municipal contest, where independents again got most of the posts.[8]

Towards the latter part of his second term, Fujimori's star seemed to be on its way down, his popularity sagging ominously, and a new reelection being constitutionally impossible. However, he fought back, and, twisting the arm of the law, presented himself to the verdict of the citizenry for the year 2000. There were several opposition candidates, including as frontrunner, Lima's mayor, an independent. Suddenly a new man sprung up from nowhere, Fujimori-style, Alejandro Toledo, a foreign-trained man of heavily Indian ancestry. Popular associations organized protests against Fujimori's methods and economic policies, notably the Confederación General de Trabajadores del Perú (CGTP) which stopped the country in late 1999. In the first round of the new elections, Fujimori managed to get almost 50 percent, though according to many observers with quite a bit of ballot box juggling. His main runner-up, Toledo, got 40 percent. The popular reaction against Fujimori's methods and corruption in high places finally created a situation of ungovernability, and Fujimori had to leave the country and take refuge in Japan. An interim administration held new elections, this time with Toledo as the victor, based on his wide appeal to the Indian and mestizo electorate. Surprisingly, the Apra, with Alan García, who had been also forced into exile due to legal proceedings against him, and was now back, came in second, with a heavy vote, leaving right-of-center Lourdes Nano a far-behind third.

Fujimori's creation, a party that changed name in each election, was running strong for some time, though by now it has been annihilated by its leader's disgrace. While prosperous, it appeared as a new form of populism, replacing the worn out Apra, which survived decades of persecution but not a stint in government. Fujimori's following, after his first couple of years in establishing his regime, was very much the multi-class integrative type, having retained the support of many of his early voters, to which he added important sectors of the business community. His movement, however, was not based, as in Mexico or India, on a long struggle, but rather on manipulation from the top. Finally it petered out, though it may yet come back transformed into a clearly conservative party with the support of the upper and middle classes, but with little if any lower down the social pyramid.[9]

Toledo's government has proved to be unstable, orienting itself in economic matters to the right, and facing widespread popular protests. Apra, as the main opposition, is biding its time, playing a responsible role but keeping away from coalition government. If bipolarity is in store for Peru, it seems that the Apra is quite well positioned to occupy its left-of-center hemisphere, but it is not clear who, if anyone, will replace the unsuccessful experiences of Vargas Llosa and Fujimori.

Ecuador

In Ecuador, Velasco Ibarra's fourth term (1968-1972) passed without much novelty, except that towards its end it was becoming evident that Assad Bucaram would be the victor. As this was an unacceptable outcome for the military, they intervened, but this time without any intention of returning power quickly to the civilians. Peru was on their minds as a model. In fact, their administration was at first very innovative, but later it lost steam. Despite the prosperity generated by the discovery and exploitation of large oil deposits, instability continued, with internal struggles adding to a period of military anarchy. Elections were finally held in 1978.

The problem continued to be Bucaram, who was vetoed as a candidate. But then his son-in-law Jaime Roldós took his place, and came ahead of everybody with 27 percent of a very dispersed vote. The Right was divided between Liberals and Social Christian Conservatives, both together reaching to almost half the electorate. On the left, or popular side, the newly formed Izquierda Democrática garnered 10 percent of the vote. In the second round, Roldós was triumphant, with an impressive 68 percent, that is, he gathered not only the anti-status quo sectors of public opinion but quite a few from the right-of-center.[10]

Roldós's premature death passed his office to the vice president, who was able to finish his term. In 1984, with a highly splintered electorate, the Right, with León Febres Cordero (1984-1988), heading a Conservative party by now very heavily imbued with Social Christian ideas, won the contest. Oil prosperity was over, but it had changed the country considerably.

Trade unions and other progressive sectors, tired of traditional parties and excessively personalist populism, converged around Izquierda Democrática, which was finally successful in 1988, taking its leader Rodrigo Borja to the chief executive chair. His main opponent was the Guayaquil populism of the Bucarams, now headed by nephew Abdala. The Izquierda's expected reform program could not be implemented, due to economic circumstances common to most countries in the region, forcing it to adopt neoliberal recipes.

Finally, in 1992 political fragmentation reached its apex, with two candidates from the Right competing against each other. Between both they absorbed most of the traditionalist vote (33 percent against 25 percent), leaving Abdala Bucaram in third place (22 percent), and far behind a dwindling Liberalism and an equally discomfited Izquierda Unida.

The Abdala Bucaram's turn came in 1996, when he won the elections with the help of several leftist groups and the increasingly vocal Indian communities. He had an anti-privatization program, but no solid organizational support, which he compensated for with a wild demagogic appeal, including singing for money on the radio while he was in office, and promising to those who didn't like it to shut up for a consideration. He also put his whiskers up for public auction. More seriously, he proposed to declare the state multinational, to encompass the Indian ethnic groups. He was finally impeached, while popular agitation was showing its head, with some new Marxist groups and the Indian Pachakutik-Nuevo País movement taking to the streets.

In 1998, a conservative dissident, Jamil Nahuad, was elected by a small margin against the Roldosista (that is, Bucaramista) Alvaro Noboa, a wealthy Guayaquil banana grower. Economic conditions were becoming intractable, the new president suggested adopting the dollar as national currency, and managed to antagonize all sectors of public opinion.

Then a new phenomenon occurred, probably a harbinger of things to come in other parts of the continent: a convergence of radical Indian groups with army personnel, staging a coup and setting up a junta to start transforming the country, or rather the various nations Ecuador was purportedly made of. But it was not to be, for the moment at any rate: Another general dissolved the junta and recalled the vice president to finish his constitutional mandate. The Indian activists saw themselves betrayed by their armed friends, and prepared for a new round of confrontation.

Bolivia

In Bolivia Banzer's regime, started in 1971 as a reaction against the excesses of the Asamblea Popular and General Torres's mobilizational tactics, felt sufficiently confident to call competitive—if not fully honest—elections in 1978, two years earlier than announced. The actual results were never disclosed, nor will they probably ever be known. The authorities stated that their man, General Juan Pereda, had won by a wide margin. Public opinion was convinced that a fraction of the MNR, known as MNR de Izquierda (MNRI), led by veteran Hernán Siles Suazo, had won the contest, in coalition with the Christian leftists of the Movimiento de Izquierda Revolucionaria (MIR) and the Communist Party.

Civic protest forced the Electoral Tribunal to invalidate the poll and ask the citizenship to express itself against their will. Herewith the offended Pereda took over, displacing his mentor Banzer, but soon another military faction overthrew him and again held elections the following year (1979) and confirmed the victory of the above-alluded leftist alliance, known as the Unión Democrática y Popular (UDP). In second place was the MNR Histórico (MNRH) of Paz Estenssoro, and finally Banzer's newly formed Acción Democrática Nacionalista (ADN).

The electorate seemed to be jelling into three tiers, rather equilibrated. As no one had obtained an absolute majority, Congress had to decide, launching frantic negotiations. Anything could happen because the option was between the *three* major competitors. This awkward system ended in a civilian anarchy, which brought as much discredit to the democratic system as the previous military anarchy had to the armed forces. Given the impossibility of reaching an agreement, Congress chose the moderate erstwhile *movimientista* Walter Guevara Arce as a provisional caretaker, with the task of calling for yet another expression of public preferences.

Immediately, General Alberto Natusch Busch staged a coup, though he confronted serious civilian and tradeunion resistance. A brief period of stark repression ensued, but finally Natusch was forced to negotiate, passing on provisional power to the MNRH's Lydia Gueiler, and calling again for an electoral solution. The same results were patent, and this time the political parties hastened to declare Siles Suazo the winner.

To no avail. General Luis García Meza overthrew the authorities, prohibited any political party activity, and started a massive persecution of oppositionists in La Paz and in the mining centers, which were repeatedly bombarded. Marcelo Quiroga Santa Cruz, who had formed another Socialist Party (which in order to distinguish itself from its namesakes called itself Socialista Uno, PS-1), was assassinated. The country had seldom if ever descended to such depths, but they were surpassed by two further short-lived internal coups, destined to show that the country was not actually ruled by narco-traffic, of which García Mesa was considered a representative.

After this chaos the solution was to admit the validity of the latest elections, and thus Siles Suazo and his running mate, *mirista* Paz Zamora, were inaugurated. With this decision an era of both civilian and military anarchy was left behind. But the economic situation continued to degenerate, and it exploded into an uncontrollable hyperinflation, of almost Weimar German dimensions.

In 1985, Banzer's candidacy was seen as quite strong, while the Left in power had lost credibility and was internally divided. The polls gave a majority to the old leader of the MNR (now known as the MNRH, but later again becoming the sole bearer of the historical name) Paz Estenssoro, who entered again the Palacio Quemado after signing a pact of governability with his old enemy Banzer and a small group representing the Christian Democratic right (PDC).

During this new stint in power the MNR adopted the most orthodox policies imaginable, becoming the model neophyte of the International Monetary Fund and the world bankers. At the end of its mandate it seemed that Paz Estenssoro's protégé Gonzalo Sánchez de Losada might replace him, on the basis of the success in combating inflation. However, that result had been obtained at an excessively high social price. The MNR had lost much of its popular appeal, and though the business community had become reconciled with its leader, it still preferred Banzer, owner of the legitimate merchandise, rather than the MNR's ersatz.

The elections were practically a draw between the MNR Histórico and General Banzer, with 23 percent each, very closely followed by the MIR, now the main representative of the Left, because Siles's MNRI had practically disappeared. The more extreme parties, Lechín's PRIN, the Trostskyite POR and the Communist Party, could boast influence in some mining enclaves, which despite their economic and social significance did not represent more than 3 percent of the national labor force, and thus did not have much electoral presence. The peasantry was divided between the classical populism of Paz Estenssoro, and a popular conservatism headed by Banzer, seen as protecting both the freedom of their market operations, and the scarcely orthodox property titles given by the Bolivian Revolution. In a sense, he was seen as an heir of Barrientos.

As there was no absolute majority, the game of alliances began again. The result, to shock true believers, was that the supposedly leftist Paz Zamora accepted the support of Banzer's ADN, just to avoid the continuation of MNR rule (1989). The economic policy, however, was basically maintained, under the vigilant control in Congress of the ADN.

The difficult process of coexistence between the various factions was getting wide sectors of public opinion used to the inevitability of pragmatism. Others, however, reacted with disdain and looked for miraculous solutions. These they found in a spate of new populist agitators, active particularly on the municipal scene, and from there launched to the national arena. One of them was beer manufacturer Max Hernández, at the head of a Unión Cívica Solidaridad (UCS) and the other the folk singer Carlos Palenque, who owned a radio station and launched his Conciencia de Patria.

In 1993 Sánchez de Losada got his chance. He prepared for it, overcoming his rather strict neoliberal attitudes, and built a coalition between his revamped MNR and the indigenous Movimiento Revolucionario Túpac Katari de Liberación (MRTKL), whose leader Víctor Hugo Cárdenas became his running mate. To this later the UCS and a social democratic Movimiento Bolivia Libre were added. He swept the polls, ahead of the unholy alliance of Banzer and Paz Zamora. Bolivia was now clearly on the road of restructuring, with control of inflation and stability, but at a high cost in terms of unemployment and popular well-being.

The political scenario remained highly volatile. In the capital city, the neo-populist Condepa won the mayoralty against the major national parties. In 1997 there was a variant of what was becoming a classical three-pronged contest. This time Banzer came on top, with only 22 percent, but sure of becoming president, with the support of the MIR (now classified third), which was returning the favor from eight years earlier. He also included in his government the Conciencia de Patria movement, now led by the self-assumed *chola* Remedios Loso. The MNR came in second place, and fourth was Max Hernández's UCS. Banzer, returning now as a democrat, expanded his support to include several small parties and the disintegrating UCS, whose founder Max Hernández had died. There appeared to be a chance for a bipolarity (or a two-and-a-half system) to emerge, with Banzer as the leader of a regenerated and somewhat modernized Right, and new forces, some of them of Indian identity, others of a populist character, becoming the more determined opposition.

However, Banzer's movement was excessively personalistic, and with his illness and death the party practically disappeared. In the 2002 elections a new right was formed, led by Manfred Reyes Villa, the Nueva Fuerza Republicana (NFR), competing with the MNR's Sánchez de Lozada, clearly following a neoliberal model. On the left there was a Indian leader, Evo Morales, at the head of a nativist Movimiento al Socialismo (MAS) supported by coca growers, while the MIR remained as a purportedly left-of-center formation.

Sánchez de Lozada came in first place, but with scarcely more than a quarter of the electorate, closely followed by Evo Morales, who had been unwittingly helped by the American ambassador's strictures against voting for him. Reyes Villa was third, and the MIR fourth. Now Congress had to decide between the two (no longer three) front runners, and there Sánchez de Lozada was anointed, with the help of the MIR.

It is tempting to compare Bolivia's MNR with Mexico's PRI, two parties with some common roots and traits. Both had a revolutionary past, a long period in power, and were evolving towards incorporating important sectors of the newly created upper classes. In Mexico, the PRI has lost a lot of that support, which had clearly gone to the PAN, a party with solid structures and a long history, while the left jelled into the PRD. In Bolivia, there is no clear equivalent of the PAN. Banzer's Acción Democrática Nacionalista could have been one, but it did not. The Nueva Fuerza Republicana is a possible candidate for that role, though it doesn't seem to have much clout. There remains the MNR itself, following a path which some PRI leaders would like to tread, but which does not appear available to them. On the moderate left, there is the rather discredited MIR, and new movements on the radical fringe or with Indian nativist programs, like Evo Morales' MAS. One factor to take into account is that the Indian presence is much greater in Bolivia than in Mexico, and this could make the difference. It is highly likely that in the future ethnically based Indian parties will arise, changing beyond recognition the situation in such countries as Ecuador (where the phenomenon has already occurred) or in Peru and Guatemala, where it is not yet so prominent.[11]

Paraguay

The convulsive end of Bolivian authoritarianism is a tragic example of one of the types of transitions that also occurred in the Caribbean and Central America. It contrasts sharply with the gradual though still clouded process in Paraguay.

In Bolivia, there was a combination of extremely high repressive violence, with governmental incapacity to establish a permanent regime. Dictators were like blind persons banging in the dark, with much bloodshed, but incapable of solidly imposing their will. This was probably due to the existence of strong nuclei of popular resistance, notably the mines and other concentrations of labor, which created dissension among ruling circles as to how to deal with them. There was also an intense frustration among the middle classes, where the chasm between aspirations and occupational gratifications was greater than in other countries with a similar level of development, like Paraguay. The clash of sectorial interests in Bolivia, turned red-hot by economic decay, also created among the higher bourgeoisie discontented groups ready to appeal to any means to defend their interests. To complete the picture one must add the ethnic abyss between the upper and the lower classes.

In Paraguay, Stroessner's authoritarian rule had been more solid than any in Bolivia, and was accompanied by an economic expansion of which it was, in turn, cause and effect. The greater simplicity and homogeneity of Paraguay's social structure made the country much more governable. The democratic transition thus took a more Spanish path, though with some native traits added.

A palace coup, led by General Andrés Rodríguez, the brother-in-law and up till then protégé of Stroessner, started a process that aimed at reestablishing public freedoms without actually losing power. This was made possible by the populist character of the political machine which had been at their service, the Colorado Party.[12]

That support was paradoxically due to a large extent to the repression and terrorism applied during decades to the opposition. There were also a lot of benefits to be had by joining the official party. However, in other places such methods are far from producing popular support. In Paraguay, as was seen earlier, the populist nature of the regime was backed by a dynamic policy of land distribution, using fiscal property.

Thus it was that Coloradismo was able to continue providing popular support to Rodríguez, who came out on top in relatively free elections. The Colorado Party, always divided into factions, had displaced the *Stronista* elements, even if in its majority it is still traditionalist, that is, wary of democratic practices and electoral transparency. The Liberal Party (named Liberal Radical Auténtico as a result of successive splits, later mended) is the main opposition, while to its left there was a group calling itself Paraguay para Todos, capable of winning the mayoralty in Asunción, but later decaying. Another party, the Encuentro nacional, has been formed by a wealthy entrepreneur and member of a traditional political family, Guillermo Caballero Vargas, hoping to replace the Liberals as a modern, businesslike alternative.[13]

In 1993 freer elections still gave the Colorados a victory, with their reformist candidate Juan Carlos Wasmosy, a wealthy industrialist, who got, however, only 43 percent of the popular vote, followed by the Radical Liberals (30 percent) and the Encuentro Nacional (20 percent). There was no second turn contemplated in the Constitution, but in Congress the opposition had a majority. So Wasmosy called its leaders, arranging for a governability pact, and giving them, after some further alternatives, some ministries. Thus coalition government, an absolute novelty, was being introduced in Paraguay.

Within the Colorado Party there was a fierce struggle between various currents, including those who longed for a return of Stroessner. There were the traditionalists, headed by Luis María Argaña; the modernizers, with Wasmosy; the more democratic sector of the Movimiento Popular Colorado (MOPOCO) and a new group headed by General Lino Oviedo, a popular figure, who had been instrumental in Rodríguez's coup against Stoessner.

In 1996, Oviedo, who harbored high aspirations but was threatened with removal from his military high command, attempted a coup d'état, which failed and landed him in prison. From there he continued scheming his moves within the party, and in 1997 was able to compete in internal polling for the post of party chief, where he defeated traditionalist Luis Argaña. He was again jailed in 1998, so as to investigate further his role in the attempted coup, but really to invalidate any attempt at becoming a candidate. For that year's elections his delegate, Raúl Cubas, got the nomination of the party, again against Argaña, who was, in any case, appointed running mate. This formula overcame that of the coalition of the Radical Liberals with Encuentro Nacional (which had incorporated the erstwhile leftist Paraguay Para Todos).

Social tensions were increasing, with a wave of strikes and some violence. In this setting, the vice president, Argaña, sworn enemy of Oviedo, was assassinated. As public suspicion pointed to the hand of the Oviedistas, Cubas was made to resign, replaced by the speaker of the senate, also a Colorado of more neutral orientation. Oviedo, who had been freed recently, asked for asylum in Argentina and later in Brazil, from where he would continue to plot his return.

The Unexpected Breakdown of the Argentine Dictatorship

In Argentina, the military regime never had the degree of stability and institutionalization of its peers in Brazil or Chile. The attempt to depersonalize the regime was not successful. True enough, General Videla was a *primus inter pares*, surrounded by a triumvirate made up of the chiefs of the three branches of the armed forces, that is, the army, the navy, and the air force. But when that triumvirate had to select a successor to Videla, in 1981, it couldn't make up its mind for over a month, which was the time it had publicly set itself to accomplish the task. Finally, given the astonishment of public opinion, which suspected a break in the internal solidarity of the regime, the ruling junta appointed, by a "two-thirds majority," General Roberto Viola as president, causing the resentment of the navy, whose chief Emilio Massera had higher ambitions.

Massera, in search of allies and of a new political formula, went to the length of exploring a connection with the almost moribund Montoneros, who had a very pragmatic wing, but to no avail. In any case, from being the main violator of human rights he became an opponent of the regime, and was thought by many, including a Peronist faction, capable of becoming the wedge that would divide and finally undo the dictatorship. The elements of a military anarchy were accumulating, and anybody conversant with the history of the continent knew the dangers involved.

Within this context, aggravated by the persistence of the economic crisis and unstoppable inflation, as well as the accumulation of an enormous foreign debt, General Leopoldo Galtieri led an internal coup and occupied the supreme position towards the end of 1981. The dictatorship was already quite debilitated by that time, and a sector of opinion that had been favorable to it as a bulwark against subversion saw no need to continue with that kind of government now that the guerrillas had been practically wiped out.

As may be inferred, it was in order to surmount this predicament that Galtieri ordered the invasion of the Falkland/Malvinas islands in April 1982. This desperate gesture had the well-known result, causing the final deterioration of the regime. An internal movement deposed Galtieri, replacing him with low-profile General Reynaldo Bignone, who started the process of reconstitutionalization, with full recognition of the Peronists and the Left.

The military regime had been defeated by a combination of internal feuds and popular resistance. The latter had a trade union-cum-Peronist wing, increasingly determined to resort to strikes and demonstrations, and a human rights wing, with activists like the Madres de Plaza de Mayo, who defied repression, demanding information about their disappeared sons and daughters, of which there were, according to estimates, between 10 and 30,000.[14]

Of course the final blow was the defeat in war, as had happened earlier to the Greek colonels over the Cyprus adventure. But there was another fact. By invading the islands the regime was thumbing its nose at the international financial community, which had been its dedicated backer for years. The very influential Anglo-Argentine community was feeling worried, its school-going children being made to repeat in front of TV cameras "las Malvinas son Argentinas" to show they were also part of the flock. If through an unlikely loss of nerve by Margaret Thatcher Galtieri had been able to get away with his feat, he might still be at the head of a completely new coalition, as a populist leader inveighing against world capitalism. For the bourgeoisie it was high time to realize that the military, even if their intervention might be necessary in extreme cases, were not reliable defenders of the system. So they too became democrats. Like most Argentines, democrats by default, but in due time their behavior may seep into their conscious attitudes.

For the 1983 elections, everybody thought the Peronists would win, as always happened when there were no restrictions. However, this was not the case, partly because of the disarray caused by the death of their leader, and also because of the new strategies deployed by Raúl Alfonsín, at the head of the Unión Civica Radical (UCR).

Alfonsín had been fighting for years to bring some fresh air to the old structures of his party. In doing so, he surrounded himself with people from the most varied origins, mostly from the moderate left, but also including many who had been involved with Peronism in its more extreme and violent factions, and who after profound soul-searching were converted to social democratic methods and ideals.

As his candidacy grew with a significant number of new adepts, Alfonsín became a credible match for the Peronists, and he started attracting also the moderate-right and center factions, who didn't like very much his new friends, but whose main concern was to avoid a Peronist takeover. Thus Afonsín put together an electoral coalition of a very disparate nature, ranging from moderate Right to Center and Left, amounting to over 50 percent of the vote, against the Peronist's 40 percent. The rest was divided among small groups of the more independent Right and Left.

The Radical victory facilitated the transition, for two reasons, one obvious, the other more debatable. The obvious one is that the UCR was the party with clearer democratic credentials in the country. The less obvious is that it posed a lesser menace to the military-civilian establishment.

This interpretation has to be confronted with the often expressed one, according to which there was an entente between the military and the Peronists, both of them believing that it was possible to regenerate the alliance between the army and the people forged during the halcyon days of World War II. In fact, among the Peronists there were many who believed this possible, and who were constantly looking for potential friends among the armed forces. The presence within the Peronist movement of clearly fascist and extreme-right factions also pointed in the same direction. However, by far the greater part of the military and the business community were solidly anti-Peronist, and considered Radicalism as a lesser evil, from which not much was to be feared. Thus they were impelled to vote for Alfonsín, with some qualms, easily overcome by the nightmarish vision of a return, with Peronism in power, of the convulsions of the 1970s.[15]

During his term in office, Alfonsín started by taking a hard attitude towards the chiefs of the so-called *Proceso*, and had them all jailed, through a judicial prosecution, some for life, on charges of gross violations of human rights. This was harsher than what the Peronists would have dared to do. Paradoxically, it was possible because of the basically moderate characteristic of the Radicals, who were not seen as a menace to any significant social group. Any similar action by the Peronists might have smacked of revenge, and rekindled the fears of the upper classes.

On the trade union front the government made an attempt at legislating reform of the abusive practices rampant in that area, but the adamant resistance of the labor leaders and their activist teams, plus the Senate's adverse vote (where Peronists plus some provincial allies held a majority) killed the project.

The economy was a particularly difficult bone of contention, even if the Plan Austral, applied in 1985, had a temporary success in stopping inflation, and paid off in the ensuing elections. But after a couple of years the temptation to yield to popular demands fired inflation again, and the results in the mid-term elections of 1987 were catastrophic, foreshadowing a Peronist victory in 1989.

In that same year 1987, the military scene was again agitated by a rebellion of middle ranks (so-called "carapintadas" because of the war camouflage they wore). This group was concerned about the extension of legal proceedings against all personnel who had had anything to do with repression, which was an enormous number. Alfonsín overcame the challenge because of the support—however little heartfelt—he had from top brass, which in any case demanded something in return. This was the sanctioning by Congress of an "Obediencia Debida," and later a "Punto Final" law, which in effect suspended most proceedings. However, still there were other two rebellions, during 1988, but with a diminishing intensity as most officers considered it unnecessary to seek greater safeguards, even if some of the more aberrant cases kept coming to the courts.

Peronism, meanwhile, was in a process of renovation, led by the highly respected leader Antonio Cafiero, with the support of several others, among them Carlos Menem, governor of the interior province of La Rioja. In 1988 the re-democratized party held for the first time in its life internal elections to appoint its candidate, and then the unexpected happened. Carlos Menem, who had parted ways with Cafiero, and rejoined some of the more traditional dinosaurs among the political and the trade union ranks, won the poll. The continuing economic crisis, and two-digit monthly inflation figures foretold of dismal prospects for the ruling party. Anti-Peronist fears among the business and intellectual elites were rampant, particularly because Menem had resorted to a wildly agitational campaign. It was thought that he would revert to old practices, combining inflation with price controls, freezing of rents, and in general playing havoc with market mechanisms and private property, not to speak of constitutional niceties.

This panorama was one of the more solid causes of the hyperinflation that was unleashed when the electoral result became known. Panic set in, and a rate of 200 percent in a month was reached in June, forcing an early transfer of power, which normally would have had to wait a few more months.

The prospect of Menem in the Casa Rosada led many to believe that a period of intense social strife was again in the offing, as during Isabelita's days, or—with a different ideology but similarly intense confrontation—Allende's in Chile. It is quite likely that had Menem tried to implement his program a military coup would have quickly cut short his experiment. In any case, he opted for a full about-face, and made a deal with the economic and political Right, including, of course, the military, and for good measure the Church. Given the lack of a believable party of the Right, Menem went to the biggest private corporation in the country, the Bunge y Born group, the nearest thing to an Argentine-based multinational, with industrial, agrarian, and commercial interests, and offered it to take the responsibility of managing the economy.

The reaction among national and international business circles was jubilant, though with an aura of suspicion as to whether this was simply another ruse from this "Turco" sharp dealer, soon ready to revert to old habits. But as his policies continued, and cost him the support of the more militant sectors of his following, a peaceful coexistence was achieved between the establishment and Peronism, soon converted into an open alliance.

On the left, and among labor and Peronist party militants, this was seen as a betrayal, soon to meet its due. However, a majority of trade unions did not join the protest and continued to negotiate with the government. In the next legislative elections Peronism slid from its 50 percent mark in 1989 to 40 percent, but still outdistanced Radicalism by a safe margin.

The lost votes went to various groups of the right and left. Surprisingly, a good chunk of this protest vote was netted by the "carapintadas," who had formed a Movimiento de Dignidad Nacional (MODIN) claiming to be at the same time a law-and-order guarantor and the genuine representative of the classical popular-nationalist pennants now falling from Peronist hands. In some areas of greater Buenos Aires, where low-income groups were concentrated, the MODIN reached the 30 percent mark, and 10 percent in the province of Buenos Aires as a whole.

It is significant that the Left, in its many variants, from moderate to highly adversarial, could not capture much of the existing discontent. This was partly because such popular feelings were still expressed, despite everything, along Peronist lines, seen as more reliable than little-known parties with a tradition of anti-Peronism. On the other hand, the more destitute sectors of the popular classes still had a need for a strongman, and this could be fulfilled more easily by a military officer like Aldo Rico, the MODIN chief and erstwhile golpista, than by run-of-the-mill politicians or even union leaders.

Menem's first term in office was successful, having adopted after some trial and error Domingo Cavallo as his economic wizard, who was able to stop inflation though at the cost of overvaluing the local currency and pegging it to the dollar by law. There was also increasing unemployment and foreign indebtedness, but these effects took some time to appear. Preparing for a second term (prohibited by the Constitution), Menem struck a deal with his Radical rival Alfonsín, who gave his support for a change in the basic law. This was done in the so-called Pacto de Olivos, which cost Alfonsín a lot of popularity, as it was believed to be a sellout. In fact, he had obtained important concessions, especially changes in the judiciary, and the adoption of second runs for presidential elections, where the expected pattern was for Peronists to have only a relative majority, and their opponents to be unable to unite in the first round but not in the second. This deal was not understood by the electorate, which rebelled against the Radicals and flocked to a newly formed coalition, the Frente País Solidario (Frepaso) where the classical Left had got together with important Peronist dissidents. In the 1995 presidential elections Menem got his second term. He again reached the 50 percent mark he had attained in his earlier bid, but now with a different composition. He probably lost 10 percent of the national total to the Frepaso, but he collected a similar quantity from conservative or neoliberal opinion, now reconciled to this surprisingly effective new representative of their views. On the opposite side, the Frepaso finished in second place, leaving the Radicals behind. Apparently, the classical bipartisan structure was entering a transformative crisis.

The full crisis was avoided by the Radicals getting together with the Frepaso to form a coalition, the Alianza, which on paper looked quite like Chile's Concertación, with the Radicals playing the role of the middle-class centrist Christian Democrats, and the Frepaso substituting for the Socialists. The main difference, though, was that they lacked serious trade union and lower-class support. On the other hand, their opponent was not a classical Right, as in Chile, but the very peculiar combination of various currents and social groups Menem had built around Peronism. Was Peronism then, or the Menemista coalition, Argentina's Right? This does not seem to have been the case. It is quite common for a popular party to adopt neoliberal, or conservative economic policies, as an option or as a result of international financial pressures. That does not convert them into the Right of their countries. More important than the economic policy applied is their sources of organizational strength and social class grounding.

The fact is that Peronism has always been a very complex combination of disparate elements, welded together through various means. Menem added new materials, and at a time it looked as though he was approaching the multiclass integrative pattern of the Mexican PRI. This didn't happen, though. And in the 1999 elections, when it was impossible for him to run, Peronism reacquired some of its more classical colors. The business sectors that had been involved with Menem kept their distance, and fielded their own man, Domingo Cavallo. Cavallo got 10 percent of the electorate, taking it from the Peronist candidate, who thus was defeated by the Alianza's Fernando de la Rúa.

In opposition, Peronism is undergoing a further change. Its trade union wing, now unrestrained, has gained in militancy; and the governors of the more important provinces have come forth to challenge Menem, who would like to remain in control and plan his return to the Casa Rosada in 2003. But this doesn't seem very likely, as the party is evolving into a less *verticalista* structure, with a greater federalist component, while retaining much of its popular following.

The new bipolarity present in Argentina by the end of the twentieth century, however, is quite different from Western European or Chilean models. There still is no clear representative of the Right with much vote-gathering capacity. A comparative perspective may suggest that at some moment a more typical Right/Left scenario will emerge. This would need a consolidated Right, including pieces of Menemista Peronism and fractions of the Radicals, plus several provincial forces which are clearly conservative but lack a national dimension. This would leave on the other side the Alfonsinista Radicals and the Frepaso, plus a sector of Peronism linked to progressive and trade union circles. Many observers would deem this new combination impossible, refusing to believe that events similar to those occurring in Chile or Italy, where erstwhile enemies have come to share power in rather tight coalitions, can happen in Argentina.

Events at the end of 2001 rocked the political spectrum, moving it in this direction, though not yet clearly. The accumulation of economic problems, notably the very heavy foreign debt, high interest rates, and rising unemployment, caused the De la Rúa government to lose the legislative midterm elections in October. By December it had become necessary to take drastic measures to stop a bank run, and private deposits were frozen, while a default on the foreign debt was obviously in the offing. Public reaction combined a protest by the middle-class shorn of its savings, with violence and looting by unemployed and other marginal elements, with repression causing some thirty deaths.

This fact, added to the lack of a majority in Congress, determined the president to resign. Congress had to select a replacement, and after some hesitations decided for Eduardo Duhalde, who had been the defeated candidate in 1999, and decided to let the peso sink to its true, or panic-driven level.

New presidential elections were held in April 2003, with three Peronist candidates competing with each other. The Radical Party also lost a sector that went to the Right and another one that moved to the left. The three Peronists were Carlos Menem, hopeful of a comeback; Adolfo Rodriguez Saa, a traditional leader of a small province; and Nestor Kirchner, heading a renovated fraction of the party. Kirchner and Menem came on top of the poll, with practically the same support (22 percent and 24 percent). A second turn was necessary, but Menem decided not to compete. President Kirchner now needs to build a coalition, so as to get support in Congress. He must begin by trying to reunify the Peronist Party, but also seek the cooperation of some center-left groups. [16]

Political Openings in Uruguay and Chile

Uruguay

Among the Uruguayan armed forces there was always a moderate sector, of greater weight than in other countries of the area, partly due to the slighter sense of menace felt by the dominant classes. Democratization could therefore proceed in a swifter way, though to a large extent this was also due to the demonstration of what was happening in its two big neighbors.

In 1980 a referendum was held, to validate a highly authoritarian constitutional project. Despite very limited freedom of the press and of association, a majority rejected the new charter, initiating the breakdown of the regime. Gregorio Álvarez (1981-1985), appointed by the Consejo de la Nación, was forced to implement a slow return to normality. He initiated contacts with political parties, and launched a process of reorganization of their structures, via massive affiliation campaigns and internal elections, inspired by North American primaries.

The new party authorities, thus legitimized, became valid interlocutors for the regime, but they did not accept anything but return to pre-coup constitutional practices. They were, however, prepared to shelve any investigations about abuses committed during the dictatorship. This was agreed upon in the "Pacto del Club Naval," signed by representatives of the Colorado Party and of the Frente Amplio. The Blancos refused to participate, in an attempt to outflank their rivals, and to remove their image of being the more conservative of the three.[17]

In the 1985 elections the Colorado Party came out on top, with somewhat more than 40 percent of the vote, though it was divided between the center-left current led by Julio Sanguinetti, the now neoliberal group around Jorge Batlle, and the clearly conservative Jorge Pacheco Areco. Through the operation of the Ley de Lemas these three formulas, plus other lesser ones, added their strength, thus outdoing the Blancos, whose main candidate got more direct votes than Sanguinetti. The main leader of the renovating effort in the Blanco Party, Wilson Ferreira Aldunate, seen as an irresponsible enemy by the military, was barred from participating, and this facilitated the Colorado victory. The Frente Amplio arrived in third place, with 24 percent of the vote, highly concentrated in the Montevideo area.

Sanguinetti, without a solid majority in Congress, had to enter into unstable alliances with other forces, which demanded a high price for reasonableness on their part. Trade unionism, very radicalized in its intermediate levels, maintained a strident resistance against the new economic policy, which could never satisfy popular aspirations.

In 1990, towards the end of Sanguinetti's administration, the democratic system had become quite consolidated, though the ruling party had suffered a loss of prestige. Thus the Blancos won the next election, with a rather conservative candidate, Luis Lacalle Herrera, great-nephew of the traditional *caudillo*, though in his party other more leftist groups existed, mostly those created by the deceased Ferreira Aldunate.

The Frente Amplio once again increased its support, and won the mayoralty of the city of Montevideo, though without an absolute majority, which forced it to engage in continuous haggling with minor forces, as happens also at the national level. Despite these difficulties, the national party system is in good health, and its leaders have avoided falling into mere obstructionism.

After a change to the Colorados in 1995, with Sanguinetti in his second term, the political scenario began to change, as the solidity of Frente Amplio representation made a coalition between the two traditional parties mandatory. In fact, due to the well-known heterogeneous character of the parties, what took place was a coalition between fractions of the Colorados and Blancos. This was repeated for the contest of 1999, where the Frente Amplio came in first place, with over a third of the electorate. In the re-run there was a more explicit Colorado-Blanco alliance, leading yet another member of the Batlle family, Jorge, to the chief executive post.

Chile

In Chile, the transition was slower and fraught with greater obstacles, due to the solidity of its military regime, and its success in achieving economic transformation and expansion, even if at a high social cost, not to speak of the repression of its early years. The contrast with Argentina is apparent, and so it is with Brazil, though less starkly.

In Brazil, after the boom of the sixties and early seventies, an economic downturn had occurred. In Chile almost the contrary happened, allowing the authorities to remain more in command of the democratization process, which recalls what happened in Spain. In 1980 a constitutional text was presented to the electorate, and was approved under conditions of press censorship and intimidation, though there was no actual interference with the counting of ballots. According to this text, in 1988 another referendum was to be held, to determine whether Pinochet would be granted a further eight years at the helm, or else elections for a new executive would be held. This time, with much greater freedom of expression, the opposition managed to reject the official proposal. The example of the changes in the rest of the region, and not least, the new orientation of United States foreign policy, reversing it support of the coup in 1973, were, of course, also important factors. The elections thus programmed saw the victory of the opposition, based on an alliance of the erstwhile enemies, the Christian Democrats and the Socialists. The latter, deeply divided during most of the Pinochet years, finally had come together, revising their traditional distrust of social democracy, and engaged along the new path of reform and coalition politics.[18]

The more radically Socialist left remained outside of the party, though it later revised its position and joined the mainstream. The Communists, defying Moscow's preferences, engaged during the last stretch of the dictatorship on a subversive course, implemented by a Frente Manuel Rodríguez (named after a nineteenth-century populist rebel), but with no success. They then returned to peaceful means, having lost much of their following, though retaining important enclaves among university students and some trade unions.

Patricio Aylwin, a moderate Christian Democrat, was the winning presidential candidate of the coalition, named Concertación; a Socialist in the Moneda would have been unacceptable. The Right, reorganized into two parties, the more traditional Renovación Nacional (PRN) and the Unión Democrática Independiente (UDI), got a sizeable portion of the electorate, thus retaining its condition of potential challenger for future contests.

One of the prices of the Spanish-style transition was the acceptance of the many antidemocratic features of the 1980 Constitution, mainly the presence in the Senate of some 20 percent of seats reserved for "institutional" representatives, appointed by the president for eight-year terms, or by the armed forces in conjunction with the Supreme Court. The electoral law ensured a disproportionately high presence for the minority, giving it a strong basis of resistance against dictates of the majority. This actually was intended to give guarantees to Pinochet's friends in the foreseeable case of a Concertación victory at the polls. The armed forces also acquired autonomy, almost equivalent to that of the Catholic Church, with authority resulting from promotion within the ranks, rather than interference from the executive. They were also assured of a fixed proportion of copper exports.

As in Spain, Peru, and Argentina, in Chile also the coming to power of a centrist party facilitated the transition, even if it was allied to leftist forces. The Christian Democratic-Socialist alliance, on the other hand, reproduced to some extent the Italian pattern, where power has been shared between a sector of the old Christian Democratic Party and the renamed and born-again Communists, a convergence which would have been unthinkable a decade earlier.[19]

The economic policies adopted have to a large extent accepted the restructuring brought about by the military regime. This was obviously the result of international conditions, and of the desire not to rock the boat with more basic changes. However, as time passes the rule of law is becoming more solid, and despite legally accepted reprieves of human rights violators, aberrant cases are coming to be judged. A social safety net of more solidity than in neighboring Argentina has also been constructed.

Aylwin was succeeded by Eduardo Frei Ruiz-Tagle (son of the former president), who steered Chile nearer to the Mercosur, establishing a free-trade connection, though not yet full membership. Greater integration is made difficult by Chile's very low existing tariffs, and by the alternative some sectors entertain, of joining the North Atlantic Free Trade Area (NAFTA). Time will tell which of these roads is more realistic.

For the 1999 renovation, primaries were held by the Consertación, and this time Ricardo Lagos, leader of the Socialist Party (and of its twin the PPD) got the nomination. This alarmed some moderate sectors, and prompted the Right to increase its efforts at offering a very moderate, even popular, image, disassociating itself from the "excesses" of the Pinochet regime and cultivating a clientele among low income groups. The first round of elections resulted practically in a draw (46 percent each, Lagos half a point ahead). The second round was won by Lagos, mostly by getting the unsolicited Communist vote (3 percent). His inauguration went ahead with no problems, auguring a further normalization of the Chilean political system, and changes in the Constitution are being contemplated, so as to remove some of its authoritarian residues.[20]

Party Bipolarity under Attack in Venezuela and Colombia

Venezuela

In Venezuela, the alternation between social democrats and Christian democrats became for decades the basis of the political system, and under it in 1989 Carlos Andrés Pérez returned to the presidency, on the basis of the popularity he had earned during the prosperous years of his first term. Now, oil prices having dipped seriously, a different policy was necessary. Following the dictates of international pundits and the IMF, a strict fiscal policy and retrenchment were adopted, and to begin with the prices of some subsidized consumer staples, utilities, and public transport were increased. The result was an explosion of popular anger, the barrios of the periphery disgorging their population into Caracas's streets on a rampage, later known as the Caracazo, and when confronted by the police leaving over a hundred dead. This violent resistance must be contrasted with what happened in Argentina, where at the same time Menem was implementing similar policies, but without an equivalent popular response. To understand this difference it is necessary to take into account the fact that Argentine standards of living are quite higher than in Venezuela, and its party system proved to be more solid, grounded in a more dynamic civil society, with greater organizational experience.[21]

Neoliberal policies remained in effect, despite the many resistances, not only coming from the popular classes but from business groups, which had grown accustomed to state protection and subsidies. In February 1992 another unexpected event took place, even more shocking than the Caracazo: a group of middle-rank military officers, led by Hugo Chávez, mutinied, demanding a correction of the economic reforms being adopted, and a stop to the devouring corruption. Some popular and student circles, at a loss as to how to combat those policies, joined the military during the few days the movement lasted, menacing the convergence of disparate ideologies, a well-known phenomenon on the continent. Towards the end of that same year another similar event took place, also easily foiled. But an increasing wave of expectations was surging, combining elements of the most diverse origins.

In 1993, as a result of allegations of wrongdoing and corruption, or misdirection of funds, Pérez was impeached. Some new leftist groups were sprouting, one of them Causa-R, led by a steelworker from the new industrial center of Ciudad Bolívar, Andrés Velázquez, who appeared as a Venezuelan version of the Brazilian Lula. The party system fell into total disarray. Strangely enough, Rafael Caldera, one of the founders of the system, was the first to challenge it. He broke with COPEI, forming a new movement, in alliance with several leftist groups, especially the MAS, and in practice drawing on much of the wide resentment and disappointment. He was successful, in a much divided electorate, with Causa-R his runner up, while COPEI and AD maintained important bases. In the early period of his government Caldera tried to stop the trend towards liberalization of markets undertaken by Pérez. He found a barrage of resistance from national and international financial circles, and was forced to change course. For his new programs, oriented in a much more "orthodox" manner, he chose none other than Teodoro Petkoff, the former guerrilla leader of the MAS.[22]

Economic conditions, partly due to continued low prices of oil and to the weight of foreign debt, made it difficult to assuage the widespread discontent. When new elections were due, at the end of 1998, Caldera's popularity was at its lowest point and all parties divided and were discredited. Political leaders attempted to rise to visibility by breaking away from either main party, to launch new personalistic appeals. An erstwhile Miss Universe, who was mayor of a wealthy suburb of Caracas, became for a while the front runner in opinion polls. But soon the new phenomenon arose, along the most classical canons of populism: Hugo Chávez, at the front of a makeshift Movimiento Bolivariano

Quinta República, surged to great popularity. People didn't mind his past or rather extolled it, indicative of an early rejection of the neoliberal package. Both major leftist parties, the MAS and Causa-R, split, with important factions joining Chávez in an alliance, in a sense repeating the Chilean phenomenon of Ibáñez supported by the Partido Socialista Popular half a century earlier.

The opposition to Chávez was concentrated in a party calling itself Proyecto Venezuela, led by Enrique Salas Römer, who had left COPEI and in practice channeled conservative opinion. The COPEI and Acción Democrática got little response, and the new electoral system even reduced it to nullity. Chávez went on appealing to the people, with referenda and elections to form a new Constituent Assembly, and then to get elected again under its terms. This permanent mobilization was beginning to tire many people, but expectations still ran high, as many believed he could stop the continent-wide drift towards free market globalization. However, the ranks of his followers were quite heterogeneous, and he started losing the support of several of his leftist allies, and also of one of his military comrades, who became a noted oppositionist.

Under existing constitutional provisions Chávez has still several yeas ahead of him, but popular protest is forcing him to reconsider. Massive demonstrations have been organized by a combination of the top employer organization, Fedecámaras, with union leaders (who have resisted efforts to unseat them) and middle-class opinion. In one of those protests repression caused several deaths, causing increased anger, and a short-lived military coup by top officers, who put the president of the business organization in charge of the Executive. This highly unorthodox attempt, condoned by traditional political parties and much international opinion, was quickly foiled by loyal armed sectors, mostly grounded among medium ranking personnel. Protests continued, demanding the resignation or radical shortening of Chávez's stint in office.[23]

Colombia

In Colombia, the Liberal César Gaviria was elected in 1990, facing dangerous party fragmentation. The Liberals had maintained a remarkable presence at the polls, and a capacity to discipline their forces, though there was a tug of war between a social democratic and a more orthodox liberal wing. Conservatives suffered a serious schism. Their mainstream group had adopted Christian Democratic traits, adding the word Social to its name. The followers of Álvaro Gómez broke away, searching for new ideological formulas and the revamping of the political system, calling themselves Salvación Nacional. And a Nueva Fuerza Democrática also spun off, adopting all-out free market and neo-liberal laissez-faire tenets, posing as the modern alternative, and taking votes away from both main parties.

But outside this traditional gamut the erstwhile guerilla group M-19 positioned itself, rechristened as Movimiento Democrático M-19, surprisingly integrated itself into party politics, and engaged with gusto in coalition politics. Soon after coming down from the mountains they got strong support at the polls, which permitted them, in an unholy alliance with Álvaro Gómez's Salvación Nacional, to push for the convening of a Constituent Assembly. In it the above-mentioned alliance between what apparently were the more extreme right and left was maintained, as both shared anticapitalist sentiments, and they mustered a majority. The new Constitution did not introduce many innovations, and soon politics went back to normal, the two main parties coming back to their traditional positions of preeminence, and the M-19 fading away.[24]

Despite pacification attempts, guerrilla activities and narco-traffic remain considerable, challenging the rule of the state in ever-wider areas of the country. It is difficult to make an optimist forecast under these conditions. In the 2002 elections a new movement was organized by a splinter group from the Liberal Party, led by hard-line, law-and-order Álvaro Uribe, who in practice garnered a lot of Conservative votes, that party having been reduced to a small rump, while the official Liberals maintained a significant presence, flanked by various smaller groups. Apparently, the classical two-party system is undergoing a severe crisis. Even if several others have been surpassed in the past after a period of turmoil, it would be surprising indeed if the system did not start changing for good.

Mexico's Search for a Change

In Mexico, the more alert members of the PRI have been quite conscious that changes must be introduced in order to avoid a violent explosion, but it was thought not to be easy to do without provoking major turmoil and the specter of military or civilian anarchy. In fact, the PRI's continued stint in power increasingly reminds observers of the Porfiriato, despite the obvious differences, notably the forced renovation of the person heading the Executive. As long as double-digit growth indices continued to appear, the problem could be sidetracked, but as the economy ground to a halt due to falling oil prices and to the increased burden of the foreign debt, the search for new solutions was intensified.

For the presidential contest of 1988 the opposition had an unexpected trump card, Cuauhtémoc Cárdenas. The son of the revered national icon left the PRI and formed, in alliance with the many minuscule Marxist or "authentic" revolutionaries, a Frente Democrático Nacional, later fused into a single organization, the Partido Revolucionario Democrático (PRD). Alarm spread among ruling circles, as widespread popular sympathies accompanied the new emerging leader. Cárdenas' contacts in the PRI machine gave him much greater chances than those traditionally reserved to the many leftist parties.

At the time of voting, according to most observers, the usual fraud was rampant, allowing the PRI to maintain its power, now administered by Carlos

Salinas de Gortari, an American-trained technocrat with far-reaching neoliberal and privatizing projects. He got only 51 percent of the vote, a very low figure by PRI standards, against 30 percent for Cárdenas. The PAN came in third place, consolidating its center-right roots, and updating its ideology, also oriented to free market reforms, and strongly backed by some industrialists.

The new president's team was determined to revamp the system, controlling corruption, stopping subsidies, and confronting some labor leaders, like the mythical boss of the Tampico oil workers, who could not resist the onslaught. This show of force earned Salinas the support of a good portion of public opinion, enthused at the idea of a major revamping of outworn habits without the risks of a change of government, always feared in Mexico as the harbinger of violence and chaos. Salinas promised a greater transparency in future elections, with foreign observers and extended guarantees. The result was much-increased grass-roots activity in the ruling party, which consolidated its position in the legislative renewal. Maybe the old machine had not yet approached the moment of being scrapped.

The next test was due in 1994, but the year before already the PRI had as one of its main candidates Donaldo Colosio, a well-connected modernizer. Apparently, he was trying to renovate the PRI with an excessive zeal, and he was assassinated, public opinion pointing to members of his own party as the culprits.

In 1993 the NAFTA treaty was signed, to enter into a free trade association with the United States and Canada, against the opposition of the left and many trade unionists. The very day the treaty was going to be inaugurated, a rebellion exploded in the heavily Indian and very poor state of Chiapas, where an Ejército Zapatista de Liberación Nacional had been formed. This group was able to control a significant area, and resist military intervention. Soon there were pacification efforts, which culminated in 1996, but a tense situation has been maintained since.[25]

The new president, Ernesto Zedillo, continued the liberalization efforts of his predecessor. Salinas, however, had finished his mandate amid a corruption scandal including his brother and possibly himself, which forced him into voluntary exile. The need to revamp the system remained on top of the agenda. Guarantees to the opposition were given for the counting of votes, but some pro government changes were introduced, giving a benefit to first minorities (i.e., the PRI, hopefully) when no candidate got 50 percent, with no need for a second turn.

In 1997, by-elections gave increasing support to the opposition. Cárdenas was elected governor of the capital city, but in general the PAN was positioning itself ahead of the PRD. If both parties could find a common candidate they might win, but such an alliance was thought to be impossible, as the two parties were on opposite ends of the spectrum. Their association would, among other things, antagonize their more convinced supporters, and thus lose them votes. In practice, such a convergence did not take place, except for occasional tactics in Congress. The PRD is still very much under the influence of radical groups who reject Third Way or social democratic solutions as too moderate, but they are not capable of eroding the PRI's organized peasant and labor machines, who prefer a familiar evil to an uncertain good.

By mid 2000 the unbelievable happened: the PRI lost a presidential election, and accepted the verdict of the ballot boxes. The PAN, much renewed, with solid entrepreneurial sympathies, and shedding its authoritarian Catholic past, came first past the post, so near 50 percent that a second run was not necessary. A part of the leftist PRD electorate, with the hope of putting an end to PRI hegemony, voted for the PAN, and some of the party leaders were coopted into the new government. However, President Vicente Fox lacked a majority in Congress, so he had to rely on support from the more amenable opposition groups. A faction in the PRI, having absorbed neoliberal economic tenets, tends to seek an alliance with the PAN, or to position itself as a better representative of business interests than the inexperienced PAN. Other groups, mostly among the PRI's still strong trade union and peasant organizations, would prefer a populist alternative, eventually seeking coincidences with the PRD. For the moment, a "three-thirds" pattern is present, with some similarities to the classical pre-1973 Chilean system. One may hypothesize that with time a bipolarity will emerge in Mexico as in Chile and in most more developed countries. It is however difficult to predict whether this potential bipolarity will rest on a PAN-PRD contraposition, destroying or splitting apart the PRI (as happened to the Chilean Radical Party), or alternatively the PRI might recoup its popular traditions and left-of-center programs or at least image, eroding the support base of the PRD, which would be reduced to a radicalized rump.[26]

Notes

1. Scott Mainwaring, *The Catholic Church and Politics in Brazil, 1916-1985*; Michael Novak, *Will it Liberate? Questions About Liberation Theology*.
2. Bolivar Lamounier and Fernando H. Cardoso, eds., *Os partidos e as eleições no Brasil*; Olavo Brasil de Lima Junior, ed., *Sistema eleitoral brasileiro, teoria e prática*; Ricardo Antunes, *A rebeldia do trabalho: o confronto operário no ABC paulista, as greves de 1978/80*; Jacob Gorender, *Combate nas trevas: a esquerda brasileira, das ilusões perdidas á luta armada*; Moacir Gadotti and Otaviano Pereira, *Pra qué PT: origem, projeto e consolidação do Partido dos Trabalhadores*; Leôncio Martins Rodrigues, "A composição social das lideranças do PT," and *CUT: os militantes e a ideologia*.
3. Alfred Stepan, ed., *Democratizing Brazil, Problems of Transition and Consolidation*.
4. Peter R. Kingston and Timothy S. Porver, eds., *Democratic Brazil: Actors, Institutions and Processes*; Maria D'Alva G. Kinzo and Simone Rodrigues da Silva, "Politics in Brazil, Cardoso's Government and the 1998 Re-election"; Victor Bulmer-Thomas, ed., *The New Economic Model in Latin America and its Impact on Income Distribution and Poverty*; Scott Mainwaring, *Rethinking Party Systems in the Third Wave of Democratization, The Case of Brazil*.

5. Gustavo Gorriti Ellenbogen, *Sendero, historia de la guerra milenaria en el Perú*; David Scott Palmer, *Shining Path of Peru.*
6. Augusto Zimmermann Zavala, *Los últimos días del General Velasco: ¿quién recoge la bandera.*
7. E. Ferrero Costa, "Peru's Presidential Coup."
8. There was a 30 percent abstention, and a 13 percent blank or null vote. See Joseph Tulchin and Gary Bland, eds., *Peru in Crisis: Dictatorship or Democracy?*; Maxwell Cameron, *Democracy and Authoritarianism in Peru: Political Coalitions and Social Change*; John Crabtree, *The 1995 Elections in Peru: The End of the Line for the Party System.*
9. Giorgio Alberti, "'Movimientismo' and Democracy: An Analytical Framework and the Peruvian Case Study"; Kenneth Roberts, "Neoliberalism and the Transformation of Populism in Latin America: The Peruvian Case."
10. Nick D. Mills, *Crisis, conflicto y consenso: Ecuador, 1979-1984*; Amparo Menéndez Carrión, *La conquista del voto en el Ecuador: de Velasco a Roldós.*
11. Donna Lee Van Cott, ed., *Indigenous Peoples and Democracy in Latin America.*
12. Domingo Rivarola et al., *Militares y políticos en una transición atípica.*
13. Paul Lewis, *Paraguay Under Stroessner*; Domingo Rivarola, ed., *Estado, campesinos y modernización agrícola en el Paraguay*, and *Los movimientos sociales en el Paraguay*; Werner Baer and Melissa Birch, "La expansión de la frontera económica, el crecimiento paraguayo en los años setenta"; Fran Gillespie, "Comprehending the Slow Pace of Urbanization in Paraguay Between 1950 and 1972."
14. Juan E. Corradi, Patricia Weiss Fagen and Manuel Antonio Garretón, eds., *Fear at the Edge: State Terror and Resistance in Latin America.*
15. Oscar Oszlak, ed., *Proceso, crisis y transición democrática*; Liliana de Riz, *Retorno y derrumbe*; Pablo Giussani, *Los días de Alfonsín*; Alejandro Horowicz, *Los cuatro peronismos*; Vicente Palermo, *Democracia interna en los partidos: las elecciones partidarias de 1983 en el radicalismo y justicialismo porteños*; James W. McGuire, *Peronism Without Perón: Unions, Parties and Democracy in Argentina.*
16. James P. Brennan, ed., *Peronism and Argentina*; Torcuato S. Di Tella, "Evolution and Prospects of the Argentine Party System."
17. Juan Rial, "Los partidos tradicionales, restauración o renovación," and with Carina Perelli, "El discreto encanto de la social-democracia en el Uruguay"; Arturo Porzecanski, *Uruguay's Tupamaros: The Urban Guerrilla*; Luis Roniger and Mario Sznajder, "The Legacy of Human Rights Violations and the Collective Identity of Redemocratized Uruguay."
18. During the first democratic elections internationally-denominated parties were not allowed, and thus the Socialists created a Partido por la Democracia (PPD). Later on, when they could return to their old name, they readopted it, but retaining the PPD, so as to have a greater appeal to the electorate. See Jorge G. Castañeda, *Utopia Unarmed: The Latin American Left at the End of the Cold War.*
19. Sergio Bitar, *Chile, Experiment in Democracy*; Manuel Antonio Garretón, *The Chilean Political Process.*
20. Peter M. Siavelis, *The President and Congress in Postauthoritarian Chile*; Kenneth M. Roberts, *Deepening Democracy? The Modern Left and Social Movements in Chile and Peru.*
21. Carlos Rangel Guevara, *Del buen salvaje al buen revolucionario*; Ramón Escovar, *Evolución política de Venezuela*; José Antonio Gil Yepes, *The Challenge of Democracy*; Daniel C. Hellinger, *Venezuela's Tarnished Democracy*; Luis J. Oropeza, *Tutelary Pluralism;* .
22. Steve Ellner, *Los partidos políticos y su disputa por el control del movimiento sindical en Venezuela, 1936-1948*; Gerhard Wahlers, *Nace una alternativa: CLAT, historia de una internacional sindical latinoamericana.*

23. Terry Karl, *The Paradox of Plenty: Oil Booms and Petro-States*; George Philip, "Venezuelan Democracy and the Coup Attempt of February 1992"; Deborah Norden, "Democracy and Military Control in Venezuela, From Subordination to Insurrection"; Richard Gott, *In the Shadow of the Liberator: Hugo Chávez and the Transformation of Venezuela*; Heinz Sonntag and Thaís Maingón, *Venezuela: 4-F 1992. Un análisis sociopolítico*; Freddy Carquez, *Crítica a la experiencia histórica del 23 de enero*.
24. For the various currents within traditional parties see Belisario Betancur, *Despierta, Colombia*; Virgilio Barco, *Lucha partidista y política internacional*; Alfonso López Michelsen, *Parábola del retorno*; Carlos Holmes Trujillo, *Colombia: drama y esperanza*.
25. Robert Wasserman, *Class and Society in Central Chiapas*; Neil Harvey, *The Chiapas Rebellion: The Struggle for Land and Democracy*; Enrique Florescano, *Etnia, Estado y Nación: ensayo sobre las identidades colectivas en México*; Willibald Sonnleitner, *Los indígenas y la democratización electoral: una década de cambio político entre los tzotziles y tzeltales de Los Altos de Chiapas, 1988-2000*.
26. Donald Schulz and Edward J. Williams, eds, *Mexico Faces the XXIst Century*; Riordan Roett, ed., *Political and Economic Liberalization in Mexico*; Gregorio Vidal, *Grandes empresas, economía y poder en México;* Soledad Loaeza, *El Partido Acción Nacional: la larga marcha, 1939-1994 Oposición leal y partido de protesta*; Joaquín Osorio Goicoechea, *Fox: a un año de la alternancia*.

8

Continuity and Change in Latin American Party Systems

One of the main problems any democratic regime must confront is the integration of its more dispossessed sectors into the political system. That has been the challenge Latin American nations have had to cope with for most of the twentieth century and up to the present, though each in a different manner.

During the earlier stages of industrial development the popular classes tended to assume violent and highly antagonistic attitudes toward the established order. It is often said that nowadays, in contrast, the role of social class in party support has diminished notably. This is a highly overstated assumption. In fact parties have never been based on clear-cut class cleavages, but in most industrialized countries there is a bipolarity, pitting a conservative, business-backed party or coalition against a working-class opponent. Around this pattern several complicating features often exist, notably in the United States, where the popular movement includes important minorities of the upper classes.

John Stuart Mill had argued, in his *Representative Government*, that in a modern community, if not divided along ethnic, language or nationality lines, there is a basic confrontation between the entrepreneurial groups and the working class. Mill believed that manual workers and those in similar positions, that is, artisans, the self-employed, and peasants, would normally muster a majority in free and equal elections. He also expected they would vote in a homogeneous manner. He feared that if a social class acquired an excessively solid control over all spheres of government, the other sectors of society would not feel adequately protected. This would be bad, we may surmise, for two reasons. One was that if minority interests, especially those in industry and commerce, did not possess a set of guarantees, they would not perform their functions efficiently. The other point was that in order to protect their menaced positions they would start plotting, using their contacts with the armed forces. In order to avoid those dangers Mill proposed a qualitatively differentiated vote, giving more weight to the educated and managerial classes.

Historical experience showed that a balance between social classes could be attained without qualified voting. This was so because economic growth generated numerous middle strata, and the power of the upper classes allowed them to exert their influence over the mass of the population. This arithmetic, of course, expressed itself through political parties.

But are political parties really all that necessary? Couldn't there be elections without professional politicians? Perhaps public affairs could be managed through meetings of concerned citizens, eventually appointing representatives on their individual merits and not through party networking.

These fantasies, so common, explicitly expressed or not, in times of parliamentary crises or corruption scandals, are nothing new. No less a figure than George Washington in his Farewell Address voiced them, as is well known. Also the authors of the Federalist Papers were wary of political parties, though they considered them an inevitable by-product of a free society. In any case, they devised a series of checks and balances precisely in order to stop a given party — seen as a faction, or a cabal — from taking control of government.

At that time, Great Britain was the main example of a society dominated by parties, and many believed that these were destroying the country through their intrigues and corruption. The tragic experience of Antiquity was there to chastise the optimists. William Hogarth, the popular English painter and engraver, drew in one of his most impressive compositions the "fire of faction" as a monster devouring a helpless citizenry.

So a rehabilitation of political parties was, and remains, an uphill task. Edmund Burke was one of the earlier writers to make a doctrine of the need for such institutions, in order to stop the tyrannical tendency of kings or, worse still, the potential alliance of "king and people."

In Latin American history and thought the prestige of political parties has never been very great. And in order to counteract their fissiparous tendencies often a local equivalent of the "king and people" alliance was often proposed: the caudillo, the strongman, capable of overcoming anarchical factions, whether determined to support the social order or to subvert it. But the accumulated experience of a full century or more has demonstrated that such remedies are ineffectual. In fact, even anti-party leaders have ended up forming political parties, some of them quite long-lived.

When during the fifties and sixties North American scholars started looking at the newly independent countries of Asia and Africa, and reconsidering also their view of Latin American societies, it became evident that under conditions of underdevelopment it was very difficult to establish a democratic system. Less obvious was the assumption, which some entertained, that it was useless to expect a democratic government to take root, and it might be better to have developmental dictatorships for some time, till conditions became more favorable. This school of thought had many followers in Latin America, not necessarily among the social science community.

Cross-national collections of data by James Coleman and others, reproduced by Seymour Martin Lipset in his *Political Man*, gave statistical support to the relationship between economic development and democracy. However, such a correlation between two variables can show at most a scattergram, and if only two or three dots are taken, a contrary association may seem to emerge. In the early seventies Guillermo O'Donnell, in a very influential book, noticed that there were indeed several cases which seemed to mark a contrary tendency, more significant than the usual chance scattering of dots around a main line. As the countries involved happened to be the major ones in South America, he searched for additional variables that might explain this seemingly paradoxical fact. His conclusion was that a strategic hurdle was encountered when countries at middle levels of economic growth had to face "deepening" industrialization. At that point they were likely to have a large working class, menacingly concentrated in large enterprises and cities, capable of organizing but deprived of material benefits, and thus ready to violently challenge the system. The extra effort of accumulation and disciplining of the labor force required a strong power, so as to curb the foreseeable resistance of the popular classes. This was not a dictatorship arising in extremely underdeveloped regions, but rather one taking hold of the more advanced areas of the periphery. If the regime — branded as bureaucratic-authoritarian — tried to liberalize itself, soon the agitation of the popular classes would resume, and cause another military intervention.[1]

The policy implications of this anaysis were not unambiguous. One interpretation, in line with the above-alluded widespread view of the best way for underdeveloped countries to prosper, was that at this higher level authoritarian rule was necessary, or unavoidable. This was not the intent of the author, nor of most of his readers, who rather took the thesis to be an indictment of "associated dependent capitalism." If there were going to be a series of economic expansions, partial liberalizations, menacing popular furor, and renewed clampdowns, sooner or later a successful social revolt might break out. In the more central parts of the world, by contrast, greater wealth allowed avoidance of the above fatal cycle.

For practically twenty years this analysis seemed to be supported by the proliferation of military takeovers, beginning in 1964 in Brazil and soon followed by similar events in Argentina (1966), Peru (1968), Chile (1973), and Uruguay (1973). The Argentine recurrent sequences of ineffectual dictatorship, internal coup and short-lived partial democratization was particularly impressive.

History eventually moved in another direction, as has been described in the previous chapters. The revolutionary forces based on the working class were not all that strong, they existed if at all, and the authoritarian regimes finally had to give in to internal and external pressures. Basically, they had been successful in eradicating the subversive menace, which unquestionably did exist, though not necessarily based on a freely organized working class. Some of those dictatorships, notably the Brazilian and Chilean, were quite successful in restructuring the economy and increasing the national product, even if at the cost of repression and gross inequality. In other cases, especially Argentina, the economic failure was evident. And even more importantly, at the time of Galtieri's invasion of the Falklands/Malvinas, it became evident that the military might be quite irresponsible, and changeable in their loyalties, as had already been seen in the Peruvian Revolution.

So redemocratization set in, not necessarily under conditions of increased wellbeing for the masses. Even in successful Brazil, the majority of the population continued to live in dire poverty. In its large industrial centers a new autonomous working-class organization sprang up, the Partido dos Trabalhadores, but it did not have subversive potential, despite its rhetorical leftism.[2]

The fact is that the concept of menace to the social order needed reconsideration. It is true that at many points in the history of Latin America that menace has been quite high, beginning with the massive revolts at the end of the eighteenth century. However, the formation of an industrial working class does not necessarily involve an increase in that menace, but often the opposite.

The new scenario of transitions to democracy was again subjected to theoretical interpretation. The excessive determinism of the previous paradigm was given up, as it was realized that "anything can happen," as a result of an interplay of strategies from the various sectors in government and in opposition. There were hawks and doves on both sides, and the maintenance or recovery of democracy required, basically, an understanding between the moderates of whatever origin, in a complex game of political chess. This was a more realistic approach, which has been by now quite widely accepted among Latin Americanists in their efforts at understanding the forces that make a free society possible.[3]

One may point out, though, that the concept of menace to the dominant social order has been unjustifyably sidetracked. Serious menace did exist at some important points, including in Brazil under Goulart, in Argentina at the height of Montonero agitation, and in Chile during Allende's years. That menace was not simply the result of a freely organized working class, but of a constellation of factors. These factors may recur in the future under new forms, or in different countries.

To complete the story, a classification will be attempted now of the parties thus formed, and of the systems encompassing them. To make the text more fluid, in some cases party systems rather than individual parties are taken as items in this list. Broadly speaking, the following groups can be discerned:[4]

(a) The Classical Conservative/Liberal Polarity

Typically this system held sway for long in Colombia, Ecuador, Chile, in the early history of Cuba and Central America, and in imperial Brazil. A Conservative party, associated with the Catholic Church and to landowning interests, confronted a Liberal one, anticlerical and linked to the emerging middle classes, as well as to some rural sectors, often regionalist or export-oriented. The placing of the commercial groups within this dichotomy depended on context. In most cases they opted for Liberalism but they could also be the basis of a more urban Conservatism, particularly when they came from the colonial power, as in nineteenth-century Brazil.

Often Conservatism had a greater capacity than Liberalism to mobilize the lower popular strata, through the Church and some caudillo figures, and also as a result of its greater understanding of the protectionist needs of the artisans. For the same reasons it could obtain the support of industrialists who competed against foreign manufactures.

Within Conservatism there was often a line of progressive social thought based on Church encyclicals, while Liberalism had on its margins currents favoring some form of moderate socialism.

A somewhat differentiated version of this model existed in Uruguay with the Blanco or Nacional party, rural and Catholic, and the Colorados, more urban and anticlerical, almost up to the present, when a third element has appeared, the leftist Frente Amplio.

The Latin American Conservative/Liberal dichotomy is similar — under quite different social conditions — to the one prevailing in England during the nineteenth century. It implies that the more salient conflicts oppose sectors of the upper and middle classes. Popular groups act as a support, or clientele, with little autonomous organization; as they acquire such organization, they tend to express themselves independently, searching new channels of political action.

(b) The Conservative/Liberal System Expanded towards Radicalism and Socialism

With urban, industrial, and educational development the countries where a Conservative/Liberal dichotomy had been established tended to amplify it to incorporate first a middle-class Radical and then a working-class Socialist or Communist party. The latter two were based to a large extent on labor unions autonomously organized by working-class activists. In the paradigmatic English case a Radical party did not emerge, its place being taken by a more progressively oriented Liberalism under Lloyd George's leadership.

In Latin America, the most typical instance is Chile. The middle class, as it became more numerous and acquired confidence in its strength, formed its own political party, associated also with some business groups, especially in peripheral areas, though not to a majority of them. Socialism emerged somewhat later, closely linked to trade unions, whose leaders, coming from proletarian ranks, maintained a position in social space quite near to their constituents, that is, they did not constitute a very strong bureaucratic structure.[5]

In Chile the Radical party was eventually replaced, as a representative of the middle classes, by the Christian Democrats, given the diminution of anti-clerical feelings once the Catholic church had renovated itself. In France the Radical party was replaced by the short-lived post-war experience of the Christian Democrat MRP, which eventually lost its electorate to right and left.

(c) The Right/Left Polarity

This scheme is a simplification of the one above. Often, confronting the surge of labor or socialist forces, the bourgeois electorate concentrates on one of the establishment parties, abandoning the other. Thus in Great Britain the Conservative/Liberal/Labor trio, corresponding to model *b*, was replaced by a basic bipolarity, with the disappearance or notorious weakening of one of the erstwhile major parties, in this case the Liberal. There remain, then, one party mostly based on the organized capitalist sectors, capable of coopting most of the middle classes and the rural population; and another one grounded on the trade unions, sectors of the intelligentsia, and a progressive sector of the middle classes.

In highly developed countries this scheme is the more often seen, especially in Western Europe, Israel, Australia, New Zealand, and Japan. Sometimes instead of one party two or even three permanently allied exist on one of the sides, as in France with the two groups of Gaullist parentage, or in Sweden the trio formed by Conservatives, Liberals, and Agrarians, or Centrists, who for decades have worked in combination. This dichotomy does not mean that there is a clear class composition on each side. Actually, both recruit among various social strata, especially among the middle class and the working-class tories. But the vast majority of the really upper-class groups and their business associations favor the Conservative side, while the equaly vast majority of union leaders and activists are on the opposite side. This is not necessarily the case of passive union members, or unaffiliated lower classes, but this fact does not detract from the basic class grounding of the leading elements on each sides of the cleavage line. However, in cases where there are serious religious, national, or language conflicts, they often take precedence over the class lines, thus making the system depart from this model.[6]

In Latin America, the Right/Left bipolarity is not often found in its more classical form. It may be hypothesized, though, that Chile and Uruguay are on the verge of reaching this stage. In Uruguay the Frente Amplio is likely to continue its electoral growth, and in 1999 has already challenged the united front of the two traditional parties, which won by a slight margin at the price of forging a coalition, a complete innovation in their ages-long practice. If those two parties, Colorados and Blancos, were to unite permanently, or one of them fades away, maybe through an internal division, the bipolar modern system would be achieved.

In Chile, the pattern appears to be somewhat different. The solid rightist alliance (which in the 2000 elections lost the presidency by a slight margin) confronts the quite permanent coalition of Christian Democrats and Socialists, while the extreme left has been reduced to an insignificant minority. So the bipolarity is not between parties but between coalitions, as in several European countries, notably Italy.

This bipolarity also exists in the United States, but there the popular or left side of the dichotomy is not occupied by a labor or social democratic party, but by the highly heterogeneous Democrats, with a strong trade union basis, but an otherwise highly mixed electorate. In some countries, like Spain, the Right was fragmented and weak at the time of transition, up till some years ago, but has since been consolidated, becoming a permanent rival to the Socialists.

(d) Multiclass-Integrative Parties

The typical case of a party that encompasses strong organized sectors from many diverse social strata is the Mexican PRI. It is not only that it has adherents recruited among various stratification levels, which happens to practically any political movement capable of winning an election. What is typical of this kind of parties is that very important organized groups, from the business as well as the popular classes, urban or rural, as well as the middle strata, are welded into a single political structure, even if within it they maintain different attitudes.

When revolutionary conditions are created, as a result of internal civil war or the fight for independence against a colonial power, it is highly likely that such a multiclass integrative party will be generated. Apart from the archetypical PRI, this is also true of India's Congress Party, and of many Middle East and African governments, where Arab socialism or other such ideologies prevail. In most cases these regimes are not willing to pass a genuine electoral test, but there is much evidence that they can be quite popular and integrative, at least in their initial stages, as in Egypt or Algeria.

In Brazil, the almost permanent alliace between the two Varguista wings, the PSD plus the PTB, while it lasted, was a similar case of a party structure, or rather an alliance, of a multiclass integrative kind. It differed from its Mexican counterpart in that, as there had not been a radical revolution, in Brazil the Right retained much more strength. Thus the clearly right-of-center UDN was a strong oposition, much more significant than what the Mexican right-wing PAN has been able to become up to the present.

In Paraguay also, the Colorado Party has some elements of a multiclass integrative organization, and the same seems to be the case with the strange phenomenon of Peru's Fujimorismo. Fujimori started as an anti-status quo figure, but after reaching power he became reconciled with the Right, in a move reminiscent of Menem's in Argentina, though with much less backing of a significant party he can call his own. After years in office, his contacts with the dominant classes have increased, so much so that the ideological left considers him simply an incarnation of the Right. However, his is more likely a variety of a multiclass, integrative party, again patterned on the PRI as far as social support is considered, but without a strong organization, and lacking the cement provided by the million dead of Mexico.

In a country where such a coalition is dominant, it is usual, if electoral competition is at least formally allowed, to have relatively minor parties at the right and left of the main one, as in Mexico with the PAN and the PRD, or in India with the religious conservatives and the Marxist Left. If the hold of the dominant party falters, as has already happened in India and might become the case in Mexico, a three-pronged system may emerge, as it did in Chile from the 1930s up to the 1970s. This involves going back to model *b*, but, for the time being at least, with a relative stronger Center than what was the case in Chile with the Christian Democrats.

Multiclass integrative parties, when they have revolutionary or antiimperialist roots, have usually passed through an early period when their composition was more popular, more similar to those we will later see as Aprista or Social Revolutionary (models *e* and *h*). With the consolidation of the revolution the new ruling class formed during the process (industrial bourgeoisie or top bureaucracy) manages to control the movement.

(e) Middle-Class Populist Parties ("Aprista")

In countries at intermediate levels of development it is usual to find a popular party rooted in a convergence of insecure middle classes — often provincial — with intellectuals, workers, and peasants. It may be called middle-class populist, not because the middle class is its main support (in that case, it shouldn't be called populist) but because the middle class is its main organizational base, with more weight and experience than the trade unions and peasant groups, though their inclusion is essential. In contrast to the previous multiclass integrative type it lacks support among the upper-middle and upper classes. I have called it "Aprista" in reference to the party that has more classically represented the group, and which has made more of a theory of it. If these parties lose a significant grounding among labor unions or lower strata — beyond occasional setbacks — they change into a different category, that of middle-class centrist parties (model *j*).

Apart from the Peruvian Apristas, in this group it is possible to include Venezuela's Acción Democrática, Costa Rica's Liberación Nacional, Arévalo's Partido Revolucionario Guatemalteco, the equally named Dominican Party, and Bolivia's MNR. Most tend to adopt a social democratic ideology, and are affiliated to the Socialist International, even if they differ from the European,

Australian, or Japanese varieties (referred to in model *g*). The latter have a relatively greater basis among the unionized workers than among the middle classes, which being more affluent and secure flock rather to the Right.

(f) Working-Class Populist Parties ("Peronist")

This type has some similarities to those listed above — that is why I have also called it populist — and includes the archetypical Argentine Peronism, Brazil's Trabalhismo, and possibly a more recent arrival, Venezuela's Chávez's movement, though it is still too early to really include it.

In these cases, the backbone is the trade union movement, which brings in cadres and organizational structures, even though the real leadership comes from above, and from quite higher stratification levels. These parties, because of their origins and social bases, express a clearer, though not necessarily more violent, class confrontation than the Aprista group. They lack, proportionally, support among the middle classes, which are central in the Aprista variety. But they are differentiated from the socialist workers' parties, which we will see presently, in that they have significant support among sectors of the upper classes, often industrialists and military, which are a minority within their categories, but are strategically important for the formation of the party. It is from their ranks that the charismatic leadership, which is essential in this type, is derived, and which does not exist in working-class socialist parties.

Peronism is a case that better fits this description. Brazilian Trabalhismo should also be included, during Vargas's later days and under Goulart's leadership. In more recent times the party (renamed PDT) has retained its mobilizational capacity, and its charismatic leadership, but restricted to a few states, and with little union support, which foretells its further decline. It seems that in Brazil intense industrialization has generated, at least in its peak areas, a new working class that shuns populist involvements, and heads in a socialist direction, as in Lula's Partido dos Trabalhadores (not to be confused with Trabalhismo).

I have called parties in this group working-class populist to point to two of their main traits. It is not, of course, that they are only grounded in the working class. Far from it; they have important backing higher up in the social pyramid, and therefore they are quite multiclass in their composition, and to some observers they may even seem local versions of the Mexican PRI. There is a great diference, though, namely, that in the PRI there is, and particularly was during its classical era, apart from the popular support a vast incorporation of top business groups and middle classes, relatively absent from Peronism. Within the latter there have always existed minorities from the top layers of the pyramid, but they are normally at odds with the majority of their class, with little legitimation among them, and treated as black sheep.

These parties may change with time into a multiclass integrative structure. Admittedly, this seemed to be happening under Menem, but it appears that it was more a tactical convergence than a solid party formation, and this shows in the fact that the conservative groups that had supported him have now for the most part abandoned the ship, to flock after Cavallo's Acción por la República. In countries like Argentina, with quite an organized and strong civil society, there is a tendency for social groups to become differentiated according to their basic social class composition. That is, it is very difficult, if not impossible, to have *within the same party* relevant groups of businessmen and trade unionists. International comparative experience —not logic or common sense — suggests such a statement. The formation of tactical alliances is something else, and it occurs also to socialist workers parties, as in Spain where Felipe González was for long allied to the very bourgeois Catalan regionalists, or his counterparts in Germany with the Free Democrats. It is also necessary to differentiate between class composition and programmatic moderation. The latter is happening all over the world to popular or socialist parties, as a result of national and particularly international economic pressures, from the first to the third worlds.

(g) Working-Class Socialist Parties ("Social Democrat")

This type was created in Europe, a byproduct of the industrial revolution and the widening of the suffrage. A convergence then set in between the ideological concerns of intellectuals and the economic struggle of the organized workers. The state, in practically all cases, was foreign to this, though it often tried to negotiate, and help channel this movement into moderate and peaceful ways.

These parties developed attitudes of vigorous confrontation toward the dominant classes and the state, fired by their conception of an ideal society. This led them to seek the opportunity for a violent revolution, which was sometimes attempted, and in any case believed to be a neessary result of the social tensions and combustible materials capitalism, left to itself, would accumulate.

As is very well known, these revolutionary outbursts were only successfull in countries of the periphery, and in some particularly explosive enclaves. It was understandable, then, that the social forces engineering those changes were quite different from those that the revolutionaries' own theories predicted, and which were in operation in the more industrialized countries, though soon taking there the road of reform.

After such experiences as those of the Second World War and the totalitarian degeneration of the Soviet Union, the alternative, basically moderate strategy was increasingly adopted, but retaining the capacity to represent mostly working-class feelings and interests. Under this orientation, the political parties which because of their origin can be called working-class socialist have acquired in Europe, Australia, and Japan a particular profile, which is usually known as social democratic, and which also applies increasingly to the Communist parties of those areas (in contradistinction to those of the Third World), even to those that have not yet made the full change.[7]

In Latin America, this type of party has been difficult to ground. The main historical examples are the Socialist parties of Chile, Uruguay, and Argentina, of which the Chilean is still vigorous, and the Uruguayan hegemonizes the very dynamic Frente Amplio, while the Argentinean has been reduced to a rump after the advent of Peronism. The Chilean Communists also come near to this model, as do their Uruguayan comrades, and less clearly the Brazilian, who had their moment of glory right after the Second World War, and later declined markedly. Their place was temporarily taken by the Varguista PTB, and later, and more permanently, by Lula's PT. The Partido dos Trabalhadores is based, as is wont to happen to social democratic organizations, on two pillars: the highly organized industrial working class (including low-paid state employees and teachers), and the intelligentsia, in this case heavily loaded with radical Catholic elements. The latter are the Brazilian equivalent of the British Methodists and other dissident sects. Admittedly, the heavy involvement of these Catholic Church sectors (most of them higher in social space that the British Methodists) has added an element of populism to the party, which also has happened at various moments to the Chilean Socialists, but does not detract from their being included into the type we are now describing.

This group must not be confused with others, mostly the Apristas (model *e*), despite their having adopted social democratic values. This is because, as was mentioned above, their organization is basically different, with a much greater middle-class component and above all a caudillista leadership.

Maybe precisely that differece is what has given the Aprista pattern of organization its greater rootedness in the region, as stated by their theoreticians. But following that same line of argument it may be stated that after a certain level of development is reached the time for a working-class socialist model will have passed.

Admittedly, though, one must be careful in applying simplistic evolutionary schemes to this matter. It is also true that even in the more developed parts of the world new economic and social conditions force social democratic parties to diminish their earlier class character. There might be even a tendency for them to approximate the structure of the American Democratic Party, which is also based on the two pillars of an organized working class and an intelligetsia, but also rests on other foundations, due to the peculiarities of the United States, notably deep regional divisions and the ethnic cleavage, which do not exist to such an extent in European countries and much less in Japan. One party which may be soon nearing the American Democratic type is Peronism, after the disappearance or fading away of its charismatic leaders, and its becoming somewhat less working-class based, more permanently incorporating segments of the national or regional upper classes.[8]

(h) Social-Revolutionary Parties ("Fidelista")

In countries in early stages of capitalist development, and with great internal inequalities, it is often the case that the challengers of the status quo adopt a radical version of the socialist ideology. In those cases, however, their social bases are located more among the frustrated middle classes and the intelligentsia, rather than on an autonomously organized working class, whose relative weight is rather small. On the other hand, for those elites to adopt such an ideology it is necessary for them to be more alienated from the system than in countries where they follow an Aprista path.

Something similar happens in countries where cultural conditions, or the peculiarities of their history, favor, instead of radical socialism, an equally radical and fundamentalist version of an established religion. But the consequent connection with a major ecclesiastical structure, like Islam, favors a more conservative version of the revolutionary force engendered, nearer to the multiclass integrative pole (model *d*). In Latin America, these parties do not exist, given the fact that Catholicism, in its present stage of development, does not stimulate extremist positions, except in some very special circumstances, as in Northern Ireland, which have no parallels in the area.

Social revolutionary parties in Latin America have been often started with much less ideological homogeneity than in the paradigmatic cases of Russia and China. In Cuba, at its inception, Fidel Castro's 26 de Julio movement looked more like an early version of Aprismo. It may be even hypothesized that, had the United States adopted a more flexible attitude, the Cuban regime would have followed those lines, rather than falling into the orbit of the Soviet Union, with the inevitable internal consequences. A social revolutionary organization need not always adopt the Marxist-Leninist ideology. Some attempts of forming this kind of movements have derived from populist fractions, as the Montoneros in Argentina or the M-19 in Colombia. The future might even have in store the formation of new violent expressions of the aboriginal population, as seem to be burgeoning in Mexico, Ecuador, and in Bolivia, but is is still too early to say whether they will follow the more radical alternative or a more moderate, possibly Aprista, or even multiclass integrative road.

On the other hand, given certain conditions, a formerly very radical social revolutionary movement can take a moderate path, as happens to the Sandinistas in Nicaragua and to their comrades in Guatemala and El Salvador after pacification. If they come to power in a more permanent way, as in Cuba, social revolutionary regimes tend to consolidate the domination of a new bureaucratic class, rather than the classless society they theoretically favor. They therefore become a multiclass integrative party, integrating, of course, the post-revolutionary classes, which are not simply the peasantry and the working class. If they do not reach power, or lose it, as the Central American cases referred to above, it is highly probable they will adopt an Aprista or social democratic format, as has more cleary already happened to the Colombian M-19 and the Venezuelan MAS.

(i) Variants of Parties of the Right

There is a rightist tradition in Latin America which has manifested itself in military or personalistic dictatorships, without practically any party veneer, as with Vicente Gómez in Venezuela, or the military in Argentina and Uruguay. In other cases similar authoritarian regimes do have a party basis, as during the nineteenth century those of Porfirio Díaz in Mexico or Guzmán Blanco in Venezuela, or more recently and covertly Pinochet in Chile. Some of them have survived in post-dictatorial stages, under Conservative, Liberal, National, or other names, such as PDS and PFL in Brazil, or PRN and UDI in Chile. In such instances they perform a role identical to the one they have in more developed and democratic countries, where an important Right exists, and is an essential component of the political game.

In other cases, like Roca's Partido Autonomista Nacional (PAN) in Argentina or the various state Republican parties in pre-Vargas Brazil, they were elitist organizations which, despite fraudulent manipulation of the ballot boxes and other abuses, contributed to lay the ground of liberal institutions, with considerable freedom of the press and of association. They obviously channeled the participation of the upper classes in the political process, creating a circulation of elites between the private and the public spheres.

In many parts of the continent there have been long stretches of time when conservative parties, by that or any other name, were particularly weak, a fact that requieres explanation, as it is far from obvious that such should be the case. It certainly did not happen in the classical European, North American, Australian, or Japanese cases. By conservative, or rightist, I mean parties which fulfill two requirements: (a) they are supported by a majority of the upper classes, or a solid sector thereof; and (b) they have an ideology that gives pride of place to the interests of those classes, and to the requirements of the accumulation of capital.

Given the absence or weakness of such conservative parties, their role has been taken often by the military (who, however, are an unreliable substitute) or by center parties, like Acción Popular in Peru. In other cases, a movement is suddenly contrived around an appealing personality, as Vargas Llosa in Peru or Collor de Mello in Brazil, though for different reasons none has proved to be permanent.

In countries such as Mexico the interests of the upper classes can be represented either by a clearly conservative party, the PAN, or by the multiclass integrative PRI, despite the latter's revolutionary origins. It is not impossible that a tripartite scheme develops for a time, with the PRI performing a centrist role, though it might also regild its revolutionary traditions and displace the PRD as the main representative of the preferences of the popular classes.

Another point to take into account is the difference between a well-grounded conservative party and a popular one with conservative or even fascist elements in it, that has adopted moderate and even conservative policies, as Peronism under Menem. Also in the European case it is necessary to distinguish between a genuinely conservative party as Aznar's Partido Popular in Spain, and a moderate, conservatized if you will, popular party as Felipe González's Socialists. In the Peronist case, however, the increased normalization of the political system most probaby will make the continued coexistence of rightist and trade union forces in that party impossible, because of the excessive weight of the former.[9]

(j) Variants of Middle-Class Centrist Parties

In Latin American countries with medium to high levels of economic, urban and educational development it is common to find political parties based on the middle classes, with a centrist and democratic mentality. Sometimes they may have some populist traits, or leftist currents, but basically they are moderate. The middle strata which form their bedrock are far from being as frustrated and disinherited as those that turn to Aprista, not to speak of Fidelista solutions.

The Chilean and Argentine Radicals are paradigmatic cases, and so are the Uruguayan Colorados, and less cleary that country's Blancos. Christian Democracy has taken over this role in several places, as in Chile. Venezuela's COPEI is often considered to be another case in point, but most of the time it has performed the role of being the counterweight, supported by the upper classes, to Acción Democrática's populism. In Chile, though Christian Democracy does have some conservative sectors, there is a massive presence of a really conservative electorate to its right, and this is the main factor defining its center-left position. This social grounding is more important in defining its ideological position than the policies adopted by it in government, which are the result of international and local pressures above anybody's capacity to overcome — till something occurs, at any rate. In Brazil today the main representative of the centrist and mostly middle-class position is what remains of the Partido do Movimento Democrático Brasileiro (PMDB).[10]

On the other hand, if middle-class populist parties under given circumstances lose their trade union and peasant support, they may transform themselves into members of this more predominantly middle class model. In first world countries, parties of this centrist type are not now very strong. They did have more presence before the Second World War, or immediately afterwards, as the French Radicals and the Christian Democrat Mouvement Républicain Populaire (MRP), both of which had their electorate eventually swallowed up by the Gaullist and Liberal Right, or by the Socialist Left. Also in Great Britain Lloyd George's radical variety of Liberalism, and in Germany the Catholic Zentrum were significant up to the twenties, but later disappeared as first-line players, or became absorbed into a larger conservative structure.

What has happened is that the continued growth of trade unionism and Labor or socialist forces has pushed the middle classes into the defensive, throwing them generally into the arms of a renovated Right, by that or any other name, but fulfilling the two requirements outlined when referring to the conservative type, in point *i* above.

Paradoxically, in those very countries the centrist mentality is predominant, including ever-greater sections of the population and the political class, so that there is a policy convergence of the (moderate) Right with the (equally moderate) Left. This does not mean, however, that policy differences between them have disappeared, and their social bases remain quite differentiated, particularly if, instead of simply counting votes, the nature of the organizational elites that influence them is considered. If Latin America does not face major catastrophes in its economic and cultural development it is quite likely that this bipolar pattern will become increasingly common.

***

Antagonisms and tensions are the daily stuff of politics, and they express themselves mostly through parties, which are not simply or even mainly the result of a competition between aspiring individuals, but reflect structural cleavages. The study of these changing cleavages, and of the political parties that can be built around them, is one of the main components of a study of the conditions for democracy.

This I have tried to do, delving into the whole twentieth-century experience, focusing on hundreds of encounters, as though it were memorable chess games, from which one can learn strategies and rules of behavior that may apply also in other circumstances. The players of those games are to a large extent political parties, and in order to systematize the study of their behavior I have classified them into the categories outlined in this chapter. Further work has to be done in specifying in greater detail these types, and seeing to what extent the social movements and political parties that may appear in the twenty-first century fit into these categories. Some may become simple reminders of the past, others will have to be constructed to reflect new fears or hopes.

Notes

1. Guillermo O'Donnell, *Modernización y autoritarismo*.
2. Terry Lynn Karl, "Dilemmas of Democratization in Latin America," and with Philippe Schmitter, "Modes of Transition in Latin America, Southern and Eastern Europe."
3. Guillermo O'Donnell and Philippe Schmitter, "Tentative conclusions for uncertain democracies." See also, for the changeability of electoral fortunes, Kenneth Roberts and Erik Wibbels, "Party Systems and Electoral Volatility in Latin America: A Test of Economic, Institutional and Structural Explanations."
4. For other classifications, or ideas about typologies, see Ruth Berins Collier and David Collier, *Shaping the Political Arena: Critical Junctures, the Labor Movement, and Regime Dynamics in Latin America*; Scott Mainwaring and Timothy R.

Scully, eds., *Building Democratic Institutions: Party Systems in Latin America*; J. Samuel Valenzuela, "Movimientos obreros y sistemas políticos: un análisis conceptual y tipológico"; Paul Drake and Eduardo Silva, eds., *Elections and Democratization in Latin America, 1980-1985*; Liliana de Riz, "Política y partidos. Un ejercicio de análisis comparado: Argentina, Chile, Brasil y Uruguay"; Richard Gott, ed., *Guide to the Political Parties of Latin America*; Jean Pierre Bernard et al., *Tableau des partis politiques en Amérique du Sud*; Ian Roxborough, "The Analysis of Labour Movements in Latin America: Typologies and Theories."

5. See about the internal government of trade unions, Seymour Martin Lipset, *Political Man*, ch. 4 and 12.
6. Seymour Martin Lipset and Stein Rokkan, eds, *Party Systems and Voter Alignments*; Ronald J. Johnston, "Lipset and Rokkan Revisited: Electoral Cleavages, Electoral Geography, and Electoral Strategy in Great Britain"; Seymour Martin Lipset, "The Significance of the 1992 Election"; David Croteau, *Politics and the Class Divide: Working People and the Middle Class Left*; Michael Hout, Clem Brooks and Jeff Manza, "The Democratic Class Struggle in the United States, 1948-1992." Regarding the impact of racial issues on the class character of voting in the U.S. see Thomas Byrne Edsall with Mary D. Edsall, *Chain Reaction: The Impact of Race, Rights and Taxes on American Politics*.
7. Frances Fox Piven, *Labor Parties in Post Industrial Societies*.
8. For a revision of the concept that economic development makes democracy more likely to flourish, due not so much to the growth of the middle classes as to that of trade unions and other popular organizations. See Dietrich Rueschemeyer, Evelyne Huber Stephens and John D. Stephens, *Capitalist Development and Democracy*.
9. Douglas Chalmers, Atilio Borón and Maria do Carmo Campelo de Souza, eds., *The Right and Democracy in Latin America*.
10. For the "fight for the center," contrasted with the occasional tendency towards extremist polarization, see Anthony Downs, *An Economic Theory of Democracy*; Giovanni Sartori, *Parties and Party Systems: A Framework for Analysis*.

Bibliography

Acker, Alison. *Honduras: The Making of a Banana Republic.* Boston: South End Press, 1988.
Actas Tupamaras, 3rd ed. Mexico: Diógenes, 1981.
Adelman, Jeremy, ed. *Essays in Argentine Labor History, 1870-1930.* London: Macmillan, 1992.
Agor, Weston. *The Chilean Senate.* Austin: University of Texas Press, 1971.
Aguilar Camín, Héctor. *La frontera nómade.* Mexico: Siglo XXI, 1977.
Agulla, Juan Carlos. *Diagnóstico social de una crisis: Córdoba, mayo de 1969.* Córdoba: Editel, 1969.
Alape, Arturo. *El Bogotazo, memorias del olvido.* Bogotá: Fundación Universidad Central, 1983.
Alberti, Giorgio. "'Movimientismo' and Democracy: An Analytical Framework and the Peruvian Case Study," in Eli Deniz, ed. *O desafio da democracia na América Latina.* Rio de Janeiro: Instituto Universitario de Pesquisas de Rio de Janeiro, 1996: 253-289.
Alessandri, Arturo. *Recuerdos de gobierno,* 3 vols. Santiago: Nascimiento, 1967.
Alexander, Robert. *Labor relations in Argentina, Brazil and Chile.* New York: McGraw Hill, 1962.
Alexander, Robert. *Rómulo Betancourt and the Transformation of Venezuela.* New Brunswick, NJ: Transaction Publishers, 1982.
Alexander, Robert, ed. *Aprismo, The Ideas and Doctrines of Víctor Raúl Haya de la Torre.* Kent, OH: Kent State University Press, 1973.
Alonso, Paula. *Between Revolution and the Ballot Box: The Origins of the Argentine Radical Party.* Cambridge: Cambridge University Press, 2000.
Ameringer, Charles D. *Don Pepe: A Political Biography of José Figueres of Costa Rica.* Albuquerque: University of New Mexico Press, 1978.
Amnesty International. *Political Imprisonment in Cuba.* Washington, DC: The Cuban American National Foundation, 1987.
Anderson, Thomas P. *Matanza: El Salvador's Communist Revolt of 1932.* Lincoln: University of Nebraska Press, 1971.
Antunes, Ricardo. *A rebeldia do trabalho: o confronto operário no ABC paulista, as greves de 1978/80.* Sao Paulo and Campinas: Ensaio/Unicamp, 1988.
Antunes, Ricardo. *Classe operária, sindicatos e partido no Brasil, da revolução de 30 até a Aliança Nacional Libertadora,* 2nd ed. Sao Paulo: Cortez Editora, 1988.
Arango, Mariano. *Café e industria, 1850-1930.* Bogotá: Carlos Valencia Editores, 1977.
Ares Pons, Roberto. *El Paraguay del siglo XIX.* Montevideo: Nuevo Mundo, 1987.
Arguedas, Alcides. *Obras completas,* 2 vols. México: Aguilar, 1959.
Aricó, José, ed. *Mariátegui y los orígenes del marxismo latinoamericano.* Mexico: Pasado y Presente, 1980.
Artaza, Policarpo. *Ayala, Estigarribia y el Partido Liberal.* Buenos Aires: Ayacucho, 1946.
Atkins, G.Pope, and Larman C. Wilson. *The Dominican Republic and the United States: From Imperialism to Transnationalism.* Athens: The University of Georgia Press, 1998.

Baer, Werner, and Melissa Birch. "La expansión de la frontera económica, y el crecimiento paraguayo en los años setenta." *Revista Paraguaya de Sociología* 20 (September-December 1983): 7-36.

Balbis, Jorge, et al. *El primer batllismo: cinco enfoques teóricos.* Montevideo: Banda Oriental, 1985.

Balestra, Juan. *El 90: una evolución política argentina.* Buenos Aires: Fariña, 1959.

Balvé, Beba and Beatriz. *El 69: huelga política de masas.* Buenos Aires: Cicso-Contrapunto, 1989.

Bandeira, Muniz. *O governo João Goulart: as lutas sociais no Brasil.* Rio de Janeiro: Civilização Brasileira, 1977.

Bañales, Carlos, and Enrique Jara. *La rebelión estudiantil.* Montevideo: Arca, 1968.

Baptista Gumucio, Mariano. *Historia Contemporánea de Bolivia, 1930-1978.* La Paz: Gisbert y Cía, 1980.

Baraona, Rafael, Ximena Aranda and Roberto Santana. *Valle de Putaendo: estudio de estructura agraria.* Santiago: Instituto de Geografía, Universidad de Chile, 1961.

Barbosa Cano, Fabio, ed. *La CROM, de Luis Morones a A.J. Hernández.* Puebla: Universidad Autónoma de Puebla, 1980.

Barco, Virgilio. *Lucha partidista y política internacional.* Bogotá: Carlos Valencia Editores, 1981.

Barrán, José Pedro, and Benjamín Nahum. *Batlle, los estancieros y el imperio británico,* 7 vols. Montevideo: Banda Oriental, 1985-1986.

Barrán, José Pedro, and Benjamín Nahum. *Historia rural del Uruguay moderno,* 7 vols. Montevideo: Banda Oriental, 1967-1978.

Barrett, Rafael. *Lo que son los yerbales paraguayos.* Montevideo: Claudio García Editor, 1926.

Barría, Jorge. *El movimiento obrero en Chile.* Santiago: Universidad Técnica del Estado, 1971.

Barros, João Alberto Lins de. *Memórias de um revolucionário,* 2nd ed. Rio de Janeiro: Civilização Brasileira, 1954.

Basadre, Jorge. *Historia de la República, 1822-1899.* Lima: Librería e Imprenta Gil, 1939.

Basadre, Jorge. *La multitud, la ciudad y el campo en la historia del Perú,* 2nd ed. Lima: Huascarán, 1947.

Bates, Robert H. *Open-Economy Politics: The Political Economy of the World Coffee Trade.* Princeton, NJ: Princeton University Pres, 1997.

Beiguelman, Paula. *Formação política do Brasil,* 2 vols. Sao Paulo: Pioneira, 1967.

Benevides, Maria Vitória de Mesquita. *O governo Jánio Quadros,* 2nd ed. Sao Paulo: Brasiliense, 1982.

Benevides, Maria Vitória de Mesquita. *O governo Kubitschek: desenvolvimento económico e estabilidade política.* Rio de Janeiro: Paz e Terra, 1976.

Benevides, Maria Vitória. *A UDN e o udenismo.* Rio de Janeiro: Paz e Terra, 1981.

Bengoa, José. *Historia del pueblo mapuche: siglo XIX y XX,* 6th ed. Santiago de Chile: LOM, 1985.

Beni, Mário. *Adhemar.* Sao Paulo: Grafikor, no date.

Bergquist, Charles. *Labor in Latin America: Comparative Essays on Chile, Argentina, Venezuela, and Colombia.* Stanford, CA: Stanford University Press, 1986.

Bernard, Jean-Pierre et al. *Tableau des partis politiques en Amérique du Sud.* Paris: Armand Colin, 1969.

Bernardo, Robert M. *The Theory of Moral Incentives in Cuba.* University: University of Alabama Press, 1971.

Betancourt, Rómulo. *Venezuela, política y petróleo.* Mexico: Fondo de Cultura Económica, 1956.

Betancur, Belisario. *Despierta, Colombia.* Bogotá: Tercer Mundo, 1970.
Bitar, Sergio. *Chile, Experiment in Democracy.* Philadelphia, PA: Ishi, 1986.
Blanchard, Peter. *The Origins of the Peruvian Labor Movement, 1883-1919.* Pittsburgh, PA: University of Pittsburgh Press, 1982.
Blanksten, George. *Ecuador: Constitutions and Caudillos.* Berkeley: University of California Press, 1951.
Booth, John. *Costa Rica: Quest for Democracy.* Oxford: Westeview Press, 1999.
Booth, John, "Rural Violence in Colombia, 1948-1963." *Western Political Quarterly* 27 (December 1974): 657-679.
Booth, John, and Mitchell Seligson, eds. *Elections and Democracy in Central America.* Chapel Hill: University of North Carolina Press, 1989.
Borde, Jean, and Mario Góngora. *Evolución de la propiedad rural en el valle del Puangue*, 2 vols. Santiago: Editorial Universitaria, 1956.
Bosch, Juan. *Capitalismo, democracia y liberación nacional.* Santo Domingo: Alfa y Omega, 1983.
Bosch, Juan. *El próximo paso: dictadura con respaldo popular.* Santo Domingo: Publicaciones Max, 1971.
Bosch, Juan. *The Unfinished Experiment: Democracy in the Dominican Republic.* London: Pall Mall, 1966.
Botana, Natalio. *El orden conservador: la política argentina entre 1880 y 1916.* Buenos Aires: Sudamericana, 1977.
Bourricaud, François. *Poder y sociedad en el Perú contemporáneo.* Buenos Aires: Sudamericana, 1967.
Brandi, Paulo. *Vargas: da vida para a história*, 2nd ed. Rio de Janeiro: Zahar, 1985.
Brennan, James. *El Cordobazo: las guerras obreras en Córdoba, 1955-1976.* Buenos Aires: Sudamericana, 1996.
Brennan, James, ed. *Peronism and Argentina.* Wilmington, DE: SR Books, 1998.
Brereton, Bridget. *A History of Modern Trinidad, 1783-1962.* Oxford: Heinemann International, 1981.
Brown, Jonathan, ed. *Workers' Control in Latin America, 1930-1979.* Chapel Hill: University of North Carolina Press, 1997.
Browning, David. *El Salvador: Landscape and Society.* Oxford: Clarenon Press, 1971.
Buchrucker, Christian. *Nacionalismo y peronismo: la Argentina en la crisis ideológica mundial, 1927-1955.* Buenos Aires: Sudamericana, 1987.
Bulmer-Thomas, Victor, ed. *The New Economic Model in Latin America and its Impact on Income Distribution and Poverty.* New York: St. Martin's, 1996.
Bulnes, Francisco. *El verdadero Juárez y la verdad sobre la intervención y el imperio.* Paris: Viuda de Bouret, 1904.
Bulnes, Francisco. *La guerra de Independencia: Hidalgo, Iturbide.* México: El Caballito, 1982 (1st ed. 1910).
Burbano de Lara, Felipe, and Carlos de la Torre Espinosa, eds. *El populismo en el Ecuador.* Quito: Ildis, 1989.
Caballero, Ricardo. *Hipólito Yrigoyen y la revolución radical de 1905.* Buenos Aires: Libros de Hispanoamérica, 1975.
Cáceres B., Jorge, Rafael Guidos Béjar and Rafael Menjívar Larín. *El Salvador: una historia sin lecciones.* San José, Costa Rica: Flacso, 1988.
Caetano, Gerardo, and Raúl Jacob. *El nacimiento del terrismo, 1930-1933*, 2 vols. Montevideo: Banda Oriental, 1989.
Calvert, Peter. *Guatemala: A Nation in Turmoil.* Boulder, CO: Westview, 1985.
Camargo, Aspásia, et al. *O golpe silencioso: as origens da república corporativa.* Rio de Janeiro: Rio Fundo, 1989.

Cameron, Maxwell. *Democracy and Authoritarianism in Peru: Political Coalitions and Social Change.* New York: St. Martin's, 1994.
Camp, Roderick. *Intellectuals and the State in Twentieth Century Mexico.* Austin: University of Texas Press, 1985.
Campero Prudencio, Fernando, ed. *Bolivia en el siglo XX: la formación de la Bolivia contemporánea.* La Paz: Harvard Club de Bolivia, 1999.
Campobassi, José S. *Mitre y su época.* Buenos Aires: Eudeba, 1980.
Cano, Wilson. *Raízes da concentração industrial em Sao Paulo,* 3rd ed.: Sao Paulo: Hucitec, 1990.
Cardoso, Ciro F.S. "La formación de la hacienda cafetalera en Costa Rica." *Estudios Sociales Centroamericanos* no. 6 (September-December 1973).
Cardoso, Fernando Henrique. *Ideologías de la burguesía industrial en sociedades dependientes: Argentina y Brasil.* Mexico: Siglo XXI, 1971.
Carone, Edgard. *A Primeira República.* Sao Paulo: Difel, 1969.
Carone, Edgard. *A República Velha,* 2 vols. Sao Paulo: Difel, 1978.
Carone, Edgard. *Movimento operário no Brasil, 1877-1944.* Sao Paulo: Difel, 1979.
Carone, Edgard. *O PCB,* 2 vols. Sao Paulo: Difel, 1982.
Carquez, Freddy. *Crítica a la experiencia histórica del 23 de enero.* Caracas: Ediciones de a Biblioteca, Universidad Central de Caracas, 1989.
Carr, Barry. *El movimiento obrero y la política en México, 1910-1929,* 2 vols. Mexico: Sepsetentas, 1976.
Carrera Damas, Germán. *Formulación definitiva del proyecto nacional: 1870-1900,.*Caracas: Cuadernos Lagoven, 1988.
Carvalho, José Murilo de. *A construção da ordem: a elite política imperial.* Brasilia: Universidade de Brasília, 1980.
Casalecchi, José Enio. *O Partido Republicano Paulista, 1889-1926.* Sao Paulo: Brasiliense, 1987.
Castañeda, Jorge G. *Utopia Unarmed: The Latin American Left at the End of the Cold War.* New York: Vintage, 1993.
Castello Branco, Carlos. *Os militares no poder,* 3 vols. Rio de Janeiro: Nova Fronteira, 1977-79.
Castells, Manuel. *La lucha de clases en Chile.* Buenos Aires: Siglo XXI, 1974.
Castro, Daniel, ed. *Revolutions and Revolutionaries: Guerrilla Movements in Latin America.* Wilmington, DE: SR Books, 1999.
Chacon, Vamireh. *História das idéias socialistas no Brasil,* 2nd ed. Fortaleza/Rio de Janeiro: Universidade Federal do Ceará and Civilizaçao Brasileira, 1981.
Chacon, Vamireh. *História dos partidos brasileiros,* 3rd ed. Brasilia: Editora Universidade de Brasília, 1998.
Chalmers, Douglas, Atilio Borón and Maria do Carmo Campelo de Souza, eds. *The Right and Democracy in Latin America.* New York: Praeger, 1991.
Chang Rodríguez, Eugenio. *La literatura política de González Prada, Mariátegui y Haya de la Torre.* Mexico: Studium, 1957.
Charlín, Carlos. *Del avión rojo a la República Socialista.* Santiago: Quimantú, 1972.
Chin, Henk E., and Hans Buddingh'. *Surinam: Politics, Economics and Society.* London: Frances Pinter, 1987.
Ciccarelli, Orazio. *The Sánchez Cerro regime in Peru, 1930-1933.* Microfilm, unpublished doctoral dissertation, University of Florida, Gainesville, 1969.
Cienfuegos, Fermán. *Veredas de audacia: historia del FMLN.* San Salvador: Arcoiris, 1993.
Cienfuegos, Fermán, ed. *Visiones alternativas sobre la transición.* San Salvador: Sombrero Azul, 1993.

Ciria, Alberto. *Partidos y poder en la Argentina moderna, 1930-1946*, 2nd ed. Buenos Aires: Hyspamérica, 1986.
Clementi, Hebe. *El miedo a la inmigración*. Buenos Aires: Leviatán, 1984.
Clementi, Hebe. *El radicalismo, trayectoria política*. Buenos Aires: Siglo XX, 1982.
Clementi, Hebe. *El radicalismo: nudos gordianos de su economía*. Buenos Aires: Siglo XX, 1982.
Close, David. *Nicaragua: Politics, Economics and Society*. London: Pinter, 1988.
Cockcroft, James D. *Intellectual Precursors of the Mexican Revolution, 1900-1913*. Austin: University of Texas Press, 1968.
Collazos, Sharon Phillips. *Labor and Politics in Panama: The Torrijos Years*. Boulder, CO: Westview, 1991.
Collier, Ruth Berins, and David Collier, *Shaping the Political Arena: Critical Junctures, the Labor Movement, and Regime Dynamics in Latin America*. Princeton, NJ: Princeton University Press, 1991.
Comisión de Homenaje. *El Presidente Ortiz y el Senado de la nación*. Buenos Aires: Buenos Aires Herald, 1941.
Conniff, Michael L. *Latin American Populism in Comparative Perspective*. Albuquerque: University of New Mexico Press, 1982.
Conniff, Michael L. *Urban Politics in Brazil: The Rise of Populism, 1925-1945*. Pittsburgh, PA: University of Pittsburgh Press, 1981.
Copelmayer, Roberto, and Diego Díaz. *Montevideo 1968: la lucha estudiantil*. Montevideo: Diaco, 1969.
Córdova-Claure, Ted. *Chile sí?* Buenos Aires: De la Flor, 1973.
Corradi, Juan E., Patricia Weiss Fagen and Manuel Antonio Garretón, eds. *Fear at the dge: State Terror and Resistance in Latin America*. Berkeley: University of California Press, 1992.
Cosío Villegas, Daniel, ed. *Historia moderna de México*, 10 vols. Mexico: Hermes, 1984.
Cossío del Pomar, Felipe. *Haya de la Torre, el indoamericano*, 2nd ed. Lima: Nuevo Día, 1946.
Cotler, Julio. *Clases, Estado y nación en el Perú*, 4th ed. Lima: Instituto de Estudios Peruanos, 1987.
Crabtree, John. *The 1995 Elections in Peru: The End of the Line for the Party System*. Occasional Paper no. 12, London: Institute of Latin American Studies, University of London, 1995.
Craton, Michael, and James Walvin. *A Jamaican Plantation: History of Worthy Park, 1670-1970*. London: W. Allen, 1970.
Cross, John C. *Informal Politics: Street Vendors and the State in Mexico City*. Stanford, CA: Stanford University Press, 1998.
Cross, Malcolm, and Gad Heuman, eds. *Labour in the Caribbean: From Emancipation to Independence*. London: Macmillan, 1988.
Croteau, David. *Politics and the Class Divide: Working People and the Middle Class Left*. Philadelphia, PA: Temple University Press, 1995.
Cueva, Agustín. "Interpretación sociológica del velasquismo." *Revista Mexicana de Sociología* 32 (May-June 1970).
Cueva, Agustín. *El proceso de dominación política en el Ecuador*. Quito: Solitierra, 1973.
Cúneo, Dardo. *Comportamiento y crisis de la clase empresaria*. Buenos Aires: Pleamar, 1967.
Cuvi, Pablo. *Velasco Ibarra: el último caudillo de la oligarquía*. Quito: Instituto de Investigaciones Económicas, 1977.
D'Araujo, Maria Celina Soares. *O segundo governo Vargas, 1951-1954: democracia, partidos e crise política*. Rio de Janeiro: Zahar, 1982.

Dahl, Robert A., ed. *Regimes and Oppositions*. New Haven, CT: Yale University Press, 1973.

Dahlberg, Betty Sedoc, ed. *The Dutch Caribbean: Prospects for Democracy*. New York: Gordon and Breach, 1990.

Dalton, Roque. *Miguel Mármol, los sucesos de 1932 en El Salvador*. San José: Editorial Universitaria Centroamericana, 1972.

Daniel, Justin, ed. *Les îles Caraïbes: modèles politiques et stratégiques de développement*. Paris: Karthala, 1996.

Davies, Thomas M., and Víctor Villanueva, eds. *Trescientos documentos para la historia del APRA*. Lima: Horizonte, 1978.

De Marco, Miguel Angel, and Oscar Luis Ensinck. *Historia de Rosario*. Rosario: Museo Histórico Provincial de Rosario, 1978.

De Riz, Liliana. "Política y partidos. Un ejercicio de análisis comparado: Argentina, Chile, Brasil y Uruguay." *Desarrollo Económico* 25 (January.-March 1986): 659-682.

De Riz, Liliana. *Retorno y derrumbe*. Mexico: Folios, 1981.

Dean, Warren. *A industrialização de Sao Paulo*. Sao Paulo: Difel, 1971.

Degler, Carl. *Neither Black nor White: Slavery and Race Relations in Brazil and the United States*. New York: Macmillan, 1971.

Delgado, Oscar. *El proceso revolucionario peruano: testimonio de lucha*. Mexico: Siglo XXI, 1972.

Delich, Francisco. *Crisis y protesta social: Córdoba 1969-1973*. Mexico: Siglo XXI, 1974.

Dell, John Patrick. *Crisis in Costa Rica: The 1948 Revolution*. Austin: University of Texas Press, 1971.

Denis, Lorimer, and François Duvalier. *Le problème des classes sociales a travers l'histoire d'Haiti*. Port au Prince: Les Griots, 1948.

Deutsch, Karl. "Social Mobilization and Political Development." *American Political Science Review* 55 (September 1961): 493-514.

Deutsch, Sandra McGee. *"Las derechas": The Extreme Right in Argentina, Brazil and Chile, 1890-1939*. Stanford, CA: Stanford University Press, 1999.

Devoto, Fernando, and Gianfausto Rosoli, eds. *La inmigración italiana en la Argentina*. Buenos Aires: Biblos, 1985.

Devoto, Fernando, and Gianfausto Rosoli. *L'Italia nella società argentina*. Rome: Centro Studi Emigrazione, 1988.

Di Tella, Guido. *Perón-Perón*. Buenos Aires: Hyspamérica, 1985.

Di Tella, Torcuato S. "Evolution and Prospects of the Argentine Party System," in Joseph Tulchin and Allison Garland, eds. *Argentina: The Challenges of Modernization*. ilmington, DE: Wilson Center and SR Books, 1998: 117-32.

Di Tella, Torcuato S. "El impacto inmigratorio sobre el sistema político argentino." *Estudios Migratorios Latinoamericanos* 1 (August 1989): 211-230.

Di Tella, Torcuato. *Latin American Politics: A Theoretical Approach*, 2nd ed. Austin: Texas University Press, 2001.

Di Tella, Torcuato. *Perón and the Unions: The Early Years*. London: Institute of Latin American Studies, Research Paper # 55, 2002.

Díaz de Molina, Alfredo. *José Figueroa Alcorta, de la oligarquía a la democracia, 1898-1928*. Buenos Aires: Panedile, 1979.

Díaz Machicao, Porfirio. *Historia de Bolivia: Toro, Busch, Quintanilla*. La Paz: Juventud, 1957.

Dietz, A.. "Political Participation in the Barriadas: An Extension and Reexamination." *Comparative Political Studies* 18 (October 1985): 323-55.

Dix, Robert. *Colombia: The Political Dimensions of Change*. New Haven, CT: Yale University Press, 1967.

Domínguez, Jorge, and Abraham Lowenthal, eds. *Constructing Democratic Governance: Mexico, Central America and the Caribbean in the 1990s.* Baltimore, MD: The Johns Hopkins University Press, 1996.

Domínguez, Jorge. *Cuba: Order and Revolution.* Cambridge, MA: Belknap Press, 1978.

Donoso, Ricardo: *Alessandri, agitador y demoledor,* 2 vols. Mexico: Fondo de Cultura Económica, 1952.

Donoso, Ricardo: *Las ideas políticas en Chile.* Mexico: Fondo de Cultura Económica, 1946

Dorfman, Adolfo. *Cincuenta años de industrialización en la Argentina, 1930-1980.* Buenos Aires: Solar, 1983.

Dornbusch, Rudiger, and S. Edwards, eds. *The Macroeconomics of Populism in Latin America.* Chicago: Chicago University Press, 1991.

Anthony Downs. *An Economic Theory of Democracy.* New York: Harper and Row, 1957.

Drake, Paul, and Eduardo Silva, eds. *Elections and Democratization in Latin America, 1980-1985.* San Diego: University of California, 1986.

Drake, Paul. *Socialism and Populism in Chile.* Urbana: University of Illinois Press, 1978.

Dulles, John W.F. *Getúlio Vargas: biografia política.* Rio de Janeiro: Renes, 1974.

Dumoulin, John. *Azúcar y lucha de clases, 1917.* Havanna: Editorial de Ciencias Sociales, 1980.

Dumpierre, Erasmo. *Mella, esbozo biográfico.* Havanna: Academia de Ciencias de Cuba, 1965.

Dunkerley, James. *Power in the Isthmus: A Political History of Modern Central America.* London: Verso, 1988.

Echaiz, René León. *Evolución histórica de los partidos políticos chilenos,* 2nd ed. Buenos Aires: Francisco de Aguirre, 1971.

Echavarría Olázaga, Felipe. *Colombia, una democracia indefensa: la resurrección de Rojas Pinilla.* Rome: 1965.

Eckstein, Susan, ed. *Power and Popular Protest: Latin American Social Movements.* Berkeley and Los Angeles: University of California Press, 1989.

Edsall, Thomas Byrne, with Mary D. Edsall. *Chain Reaction: The Impact of Race, Rights and Taxes on American Politics.* New York: W.W. Norton, 1991.

Edwards Vives, Alberto. *La Fronda aristocrática en Chile.* Santiago: Editorial Universitaria, 1984.

Ellner, Steve. *Los partidos políticos y su disputa por el control del movimiento sindical en Venezuela, 1936-1948.* Caracas: Universidad Católica Andrés Bello, 1980.

Enrique Mosconi. *La batalla del petróleo.* Buenos Aires: Ediciones Problemas Nacionales, 1957.

Erikson, Kenneth. *The Brazilian Corporative State and Working Class Politics.* Berkeley: University of California Press, 1977.

Escobar, Antonio, and Sonia E. Alvarez, eds. *The Making of Social Movements in Latin America: Identity, Strategy and Democracy.* Boulder, CO: Westview, 1992.

Escobar, Antonio, Sonia E. Alvarez and Evelina Dagnino, eds. *Cultures and Politics, Politics and Cultures.* Boulder, CO: Westview Press, 1998.

Escovar, Ramón. *Evolución política de Venezuela.* Caracas: Monteávila, 1975.

Etchepareborda, Roberto. *Tres revoluciones, 1890, 1893, 1905.* Buenos Aires: Pleamar, 1968.

Etkin, Alfredo. *Bosquejo de una historia y doctrina de la Unión Cívica Radical.* Buenos Aires: Ateneo, 1928.

Eyzaguirre, Jaime. *Chile durante el gobierno de Errázuriz Echaurren, 1896-1901,* 2nd ed. Santiago: Zig Zag, 1957.

Fals Borda, Orlando. *Campesinos de los Andes: estudio sociológico de Saucío*. Bogotá: Iqueima, 1961.
Fals Borda, Orlando. *El hombre y la tierra en Boyacá: desarrollo histórico de una sociedad latifundista*, 2nd ed. Bogotá: Punta de Lanza, 1973.
Fals Borda, Orlando. *La subversión en Colombia*. Bogotá: Departamento de Sociología, Universidad Nacional, 1967.
Faoro, Raymundo. *Os donos do poder: formação do patronato político brasileiro*, 8th ed. Rio de Janeiro: Globo, 1989.
Fausto, Boris. *A revolução de trinta: historiografia e história*. Sao Paulo: Brasiliense, 1970.
Fernandes, Florestan. *A integração do negro na sociedade de classes*, 3rd ed. Sao Paulo: Ática, 1978.
Fernández Huidobro, Eleuterio. *Historia de los Tupamaros*, 3 vols. Montevideo: Tae, 1986-87.
Fernández, Arturo. *Partidos políticos y elecciones en Honduras en 1980*. Tegucigalpa: Guaymuras, 1981.
Figueiredo, Eurico de Lima, ed. *Os militares e a revolução de 30*. Rio de Janeiro: Paz e Terra, 1979.
Fleet, M. *The Rise and Fall of Chilean Christian Democracy*. Princeton, NJ: Princeton University Press, 1985.
Florescano, Enrique. *Etnia, Estado y Nación: ensayo sobre las identidades colectivas en México*. Mexico: Aguilar, 1996.
Flynn, Peter. *Brazil: A Political Analysis*. Boulder, CO: Westview Press, 1978.
Forbes, John D. *Jamaica: Managing Political and Economic Change*. Washington, DC: American Enterprise Institute, 1985.
Forjaz, Maria Cecília Spina. *Tenentismo e Aliança Liberal, 1927-1930*. Sao Paulo: Livraria Editorial Polis, 1978.
Foweraker, Joe. *Theorizing Social Movements*. London: Pluto Press, 1995.
Freyre, Gilberto. *Casa grande y senzala*, 2 vols. Buenos Aires: Ministerio de Justicia e Instrucción Pública, 1942.
Gadotti, Moacir, and Otaviano Pereira. *Pra qué PT: origem, projeto e consolidação do Partido dos Trabalhadores*. Sao Paulo: Cortez, 1989.
Gallo, Ezequiel. *Farmers in Revolt*. London: Athlone Press, 1976.
Gálvez, José. *Vida de Don Gabriel García Moreno*. Buenos Aires: Difusión, 1942.
Gálvez, Manuel. *Vida de Hipólito Yrigoyen*. Buenos Aires: Club de Lectores, 1976.
García, Antonio. *La rebelión de los pueblos débiles*. La Paz: Editorial Juventud, 1955.
Garretón, Manuel Antonio. *The Chilean Political Process*. Boston: Unwin Hyman, 1989.
Geddes, Barbara. *Politican's Dilemma: Building State Capacity in Latin America*. Berkeley: University of California Press, 1994.
Germani, Gino. *Política y sociedad en una época de transición: de la sociedad tradicional a la sociedad de masas*. Buenos Aires: Paidós, 1968.
Germani, Gino. "El surgimiento del peronismo, el rol de los obreros y los migrantes internos," *Desarrollo Económico* 13 (October-December 1973): 435-88.
Gerson, Brasil. *O sistema político do Império*. Bahia: Progresso Editora, 1970.
Giacalone de Romero, Rita, ed. *Guyana hoy*. Mérida, Ven.: Corpoandes, 1982.
Gil Yepes, José Antonio. *The Challenge of Democracy*. New Brunswick, NJ: Transaction Publishers, 1981.
Gil, Federico. *El sistema político de Chile*. Santiago: Andrés Bello, 1969.
Gillespie, Fran. "Comprehending the Slow Pace of Urbanization in Paraguay between 1950 and 1972." *Economic Development and Cultural Change* 31 (January 1983): 355-75.

Giussani, Pablo. *Los días de Alfonsín.* Buenos Aires: Legasa, 1986.
Gomes, Angela M. de Castro. *A invenção do trabalhismo.* Sao Paulo: Vértice/Iuperj, 1988.
Gomes, Angela M. de Castro, ed. *Regionalismo e centralização política: partidos e Constituinte nos anos 30.* Rio de Janeiro: Nova Fronteira, 1980.
Gómez Quiñones, Juan. *Porfirio Díaz, los intelectuales y la revolución.* Mexico: El Caballito, 1981.
Gonzales, Michael J. *Plantation Agriculture and Social Control in Northern Peru, 1875-1933.* Austin: University of Texas Press, 1985.
González, Edward. *Cuba under Castro: The Limits of Charisma.* Boston: Houghton and Mifflin, 1974.
González Casanova, Pablo. *La democracia en México.* Mexico: Era, 1965.
González Miranda, Sergio. *Hombres y mujeres de la Pampa: Tarapacá en el ciclo de expansión del salitre,* 2nd ed. Santiago: Lom, 2002.
Gorender, Jacob. *Combate nas trevas: a esquerda brasileira, das ilusões perdidas á luta armada,* 3rd ed. Sao Paulo: Atica, 1987.
Gorriti Ellenbogen, Gustavo. *Sendero, historia de la guerra milenaria en el Perú.* Lima: Apoyo, 1990.
Gott, Richard, ed. *Guide to the Political Parties of Latin America.* Middlesex: Penguin Books, 1973.
Richard Gott. *In the Shadow of the Liberator: Hugo Chávez and the Transformation of Venezuela.* London: Verso, 2000.
Graham, Richard. "Causes for the Abolition of Negro Slavery in Brazil: An Interpretive Essay." *Hispanic American Historical Review* 46 (May 1966): 123-37.
Grandin, Greg. *The Blood of Guatemala: A History of Race and Nation.* Durham, NC: Duke University Press, 2000.
Grayson, George. *El Partido Demócrata Cristiano Chileno.* Buenos Aires: Francisco de Aguirre, 1968.
Grela, Plácido. *El grito de Alcorta: historia de la rebelión campesina de 1912.* Rosario: Editorial Tierra Nuestra, 1958.
Grimaldi, Víctor. *Golpe y revolución: el derrocamiento de Juan Bosch y la intervención norteamericana,* 2ªed. Santo Domingo: Corripio, 2000.
Gros Espiell, Héctor. *Esquema de la evolución constitucional del Uruguay.* Montevideo: Facultad de Derecho y Ciencias Sociales, Universidad de la República, 1966.
Gudmunson, Lowell. "Peasant, Farmer, Proletarian: Class Formation in a Small Holder Coffee Economy, 1850-1950." *Hispanic American Historical Review* 69 (May 1989): 221-257.
Guerra y Sánchez, Ramiro. *Azúcar y población en las Antillas,* 2nd ed. Havanna: Cultural S.A., 1935.
Guerra, François Xavier. *México, del Antiguo Régimen a la Revolución.* Mexico: Fondo de Cultura Económica, 1988.
Gurr, Ted Robert. *Handbook of Political Conflict: Theory and Research.* New York: The Free Press, 1980.
Guzmán Campos, Germán, Orlando Fals Borda and Eduardo Umaña Luna. *La violencia en Colombia,* 2 vols. Bogotá: Iqueima, 1963-64.
Hall, Carolyn. *El café y el desarrollo histórico-geográfico de Costa Rica.* San José, Editorial Costa Rica, 1976.
Halperin, Maurice. *The Rise and Decline of Fidel Castro.* Berkeley: University of California Press, 1974.
Halperín Donghi, Tulio. *La democracia de masas.* Buenos Aires: Paidós, 1972.
Hansen, Roger. *La política del desarrollo mexicano,* 8th ed. Mexico: Siglo XXI, 1978.

Hart, John M. *El anarquismo y la clase obrera mexicana, 1860-1931.* Mexico: Siglo XXI, 1980.
Harvey, Neil. *The Chiapas Rebellion: The Struggle for Land and Democracy.* Durham, NC: Duke University Press, 1998.
Haya de la Torre, Víctor Raúl. *Obras completas,* 7 vols. Lima: García Baca, 1976-77.
Haya de la Torre, Víctor Raúl. *Treinta años de aprismo.* Mexico: Fondo de Cultura Económica, 1956.
Heise González, Julio. *Chile, el período parlamentario,* 2nd ed. Santiago: Andrés Bello, 1987.
Hellinger, Daniel C. *Venezuela's Tarnished Democracy.* Boulder, CO: Westview Press, 1991.
Hernández Arregui, Juan José. *Peronismo y socialismo.* Buenos Aires: Ediciones Hachea, 1972.
Herrera Soto, Roberto, ed. *Antología del pensamiento conservador en Colombia,* 2 vols. Bogotá: Instituto Colombiano de Cultura, 1982.
Hilton, Stanley. *A rebelião vermelha.* Rio de Janeiro: Record, 1986.
Hippolito, Lucia. *De raposas e reformistas: o PSD e a experiéncia democrática brasileira.* Rio de Janeiro: Paz e Terra, 1985.
Hodges, Donald. *Argentina, 1943-1987: The National Revolution and Resistance.* Albuquerque: University of New Mexico Press, 1987.
Hoetink, H. *The Dominican People, 1850-1900: Notes for a Historical Sociology.* Baltimore, MD: The Johns Hopkins University Press, 1982.
Holmes Trujillo, Carlos. *Colombia: drama y esperanza.* Bogotá: Plaza and Janés, 1987.
Hondagneau-Sotelo, Pierrette. *Gender Transitions: Mexican Experiences of Immigration.* Berkeley and Los Angeles, University of California Press, 1994.
Hope, Kemp Ronald. *Guyana: Politics and Development in an Emergent Socialist State.*Oakville, Ontario: Mosaic Press, 1985.
Horowicz, Alejandro. *Los cuatro peronismos.* Buenos Aires: Legasa, 1985.
Horowitz, Irving L., Josué de Castro and John Gerassi, eds. *Latin American Radicalism.* New York: Random House, 1969.
Horowitz, Joel. *Argentine Unions, the State, and the Rise of Perón, 1930-1945.* Berkeley: Institute of International Studies, University of California at Berkeley: 1990.
Ionescu, Ghita, and Ernest Gellner, eds. *Populism: Its Meanings and National Characteristics.* London: Weidenfeld and Nicholson, 1969.
Jaguaribe, Hélio. *Brasil: crisis y alternativas.* Buenos Aires: Amorrortu, 1976.
James, Daniel. *Resistance and Integration: Peronism and the Argentine Working Class, 1946-1976.* Cambridge: Cambridge University Press, 1988.
Jaramillo Uribe, Jaime. *El pensamiento colombiano en el siglo XIX,* 2nd ed. Bogotá: Temis, 1974.
Johnston, Ronald J. "Lipset and Rokkan Revisited: Electoral Cleavages, Electoral Geography, and Electoral Strategy in Great Britain," in R.J. Johnston, F.M. Shelley and P.J. Taylor, eds. *Developments in Electoral Geography.* London: Routledge, 1990.
Jonas, Susanne. *Of Centaurs and Doves: Guatemala's Peace Process.* Boulder, CO: Westview Press, 2000.
Joxe, Alain. *Las Fuerzas Armadas en el sistema político de Chile.* Santiago: Editorial Universitaria, 1968.
Justo Duarte, Amaury. *Partidos políticos en la sociedad dominicana, 1844-1998.* Santo Domingo: Editora Universitaria-UASD, 1998.
Kairnes, Thomas. *The Failure of Union: Central America 1824-1975.* Tempe: University of Arizona Press, 1976.
Kamman, William. *A Search for Stability: United States Diplomacy toward Nicaragua, 1925-1933.* Notre Dame, IN: University of Notre Dame Press, 1968.

Kantor, Harry. *Ideología y programa del movimiento aprista.* Mexico: Humanismo, 1955.
Karl, Terry. "Dilemmas of Democratization in Latin America." *Comparative Politics* 23 (October 1990): 1-21.
Karl, Terry. "Imposing Consent? Electoralism vs Democratization in El Salvador," in Paul Drake and Eduardo Silva, eds. *Elections and Democratization in Latin America, 1980-1985.* San Diego: Center for Iberian and Latin American Studies, University of California at San Diego, 1986.
Karl, Terry. *The Paradox of Plenty: Oil Booms and Petro-States.* Berkeley: University of California Press, 1997.
Karl, Terry, and Philippe Schmitter. "Modes of Transition in Latin America, Southern and Eastern Europe." *International Social Scence Journal* 43 (May 1991): 269-284.
Kingston, Peter R., and Timothy S. Porver, eds. *Democratic Brazil: Actors, Institutions and Processes.* Pittsburgh, PA: Pittsburgh University Press, 2000.
Kinzo, Maria D'Alva G., and Simone Rodrigues da Silva. "Politics in Brazil: Cardoso's Government and the 1998 Re-election." *Government and Opposition* 34 (Spring 1999): 243-262.
Klarén, Peter. *Modernization, Dislocation, and Aprismo: Origins of The Peruvian Aprista Party, 1870-1932.* Austin: University of Texas Press, 1972.
Klarén, Peter F. *Peru: Society and Nationhood in the Andes.* New York: Oxford University Press, 2000.
Klein, Herbert S. *Orígenes de la Revolución Nacional boliviana, la crisis de la generación del Chaco.* La Paz: Juventud, 1968.
Klein, Herbert. *Bolivia: The Evolution of a Multiethnic Society.* New York: Oxford University Press, 1982.
Klein, Herbert. *Slavery in the Americas: A Comparative Study of Virginia and Cuba,* Chicago: Chicago University Press, 1967.
Klein, Herbert. "La integración de inmigrantes italianos en Argentina y los Estados Unidos." *Desarrollo Económico* 21 (April-June 1981): 3-27.
Knight, Alan. *The Mexican Revolution,* 2 vols. Cambridge: Cambridge University Press, 1986.
Knight, Franklin W. *Slave Society in Cuba during the XIXth Century.* Madison: University of Wisconsin Press, 1970.
Krauze, Enrique. *Caudillos culturales en la Revolución Mexicana.* Mexico: Siglo XXI, 1976.
Krauze, Enrique. *Plutarco Elías Calles.* Mexico: Fondo de Cultura Económica, 1987.
Krauze, Enrique. *Venustiano Carranza, puente entre siglos.* Mexico: Fondo de Cultura Económica, 1987.
Kruijt, Dirk, and Menno Velinga. *Labor Relations in Multinational Corporations: The Cerro de Pasco Corporation in Peru (1902-1974).* Assen, Netherlands: Van Gorcum, 1979.
Kuper, Adam. *Changing Jamaica.* London: Routledge & Kegan Paul, 1976.
Kvaternik, Eugenio. *Crisis sin salvataje: la crisis político-militar de 1962-63.* Buenos Aires: Ides, 1987.
Lamounier, Bolivar, and Fernando H. Cardoso, eds. *Os partidos e as eleições no Brasil,* 2nd ed. Rio de Janeiro: Paz e Terra, 1978.
Landerberger, José, and Francisco Conte, eds. *La Unión Cívica: origen, organización y tendencia.* Buenos Aires: 1890.
Larra, Raúl. *El General Baldrich y la defensa del petróleo argentino.* Buenos Aires: Editorial Mariano Moreno, 1981.
Larra, Raúl. *Mosconi, general del petróleo.* Buenos Aires: Futuro, 1957.

Leboucq, Fabrice Edouard. "Class Conflict, Political Crisis and the Breakdown of Democratic Practices in Costa Rica: Reassessing the Origins of the 1948 Civil War." *Journal of Latin American Studies* 23 (February 1991): 37-60.
Lechner, Norbert. *La democracia en Chile*. Buenos Aires: Signos, 1970.
Ledgister, F.S.G. *Class Alliances and the Liberal Authoritarian State: The Roots of Post-Colonial Democracy in Jamaica, Trinidad and Tobago, and Surinam.* Trenton, NJ: Africa World Press, 1998.
Lehmbruch, Gerhard, and Philippe Schmitter, eds. *Patterns of Corporatist Policy Making.* Sage Modern Politics Series, vol. 7. Beverly Hills, CA: Sage, 1982.
Levine, Robert M. *O regime de Vargas: os anos críticos, 1934-1938.* Rio de Janeiro: Nova Fronteira, 1980.
Lewis, Paul H. *The Crisis of Argentine Capitalism.* Chapel Hill: University of North Carolina Press, 1990.
Lewis, Paul. *Paraguay Under Stroessner.* Chapel Hill: University of North Carolina Press, 1980.
Lewis, Paul. *Socialism, Liberalism and Dictatorship in Paraguay.* Stanford, CA: Hoover Institution, 1982.
Leyburn, James. *The Haitian People.* New Haven, CT: Yale University Press, 1941.
Liévano Aguirre, Indalecio. *Los grandes conflictos sociales y económicos de nuestra historia*, 2nd ed. Bogotá: Tercer Mundo, 1966.
Liévano Aguirre, Indalecio. *Rafael Núñez.* Bogotá: Cromos, 1946.
Lima Junior, Olavo Brasil de, ed. *Sistema eleitoral brasileiro: teoria e prática.* Rio de Janeiro: Rio Fundo/Iuperj, 1991.
Lima Barbosa, Sobrinho. *Presença de Alberto Torres.* Rio de Janeiro: Civilização Brasileira, 1968.
Linz, Juan, and Arturo Valenzuela, eds. *The Failure of Presidential Democracy. 1, Comparative Perspectives; 2, The Case of Latin America.* Baltimore, MD: The Johns Hopkins University Press, 1994.
Lipset, Seymour M. *Political Man*, 2nd ed. London: Heinemann, 1983.
Lipset, Seymour M., and Stein Rokkan, eds. *Party Systems and Voter Alignments: Cross National Perspectives.* New York: Free Press, 1967.
Liss, Sheldon B. *Marxist Thought in Latin America.* Berkeley: University of California Press, 1984.
Liss, Sheldon B. *Radical Thought in Central America.* Boulder, CO: Westview, 1991.
Liss, Sheldon. *Roots of Revolution: Radical Thought in Cuba.* Lincoln: University of Nebraska Press, 1987.
Loaeza, Soledad. *El Partido Acción Nacional: la larga marcha, 1939-1994 Oposición leal y partido de protesta.* México: Manlio Fabio Fonseca Sánchez, 1999.
López Michelsen, Alfonso. *Parábola del retorno.* Bogotá: Tercer Mundo, 1988.
López Oliver, Pedro Ramón. *Cuba: crisis y transición.* Coral Gables, FL: Research Institute for Cuban Studies/North South Center, University of Miami, 1992.
Lora, Guillermo. *De la Asamblea Popular al golpe fascista.* Buenos Aires: El Yunque, 1972.
Lucchini, Cristina. *Apoyo empresarial en los orígenes del peronismo.* Buenos Aires: Cedal, 1990.
Lumbreras, Luis G. et al. *Nueva historia general del Perú*, 4th ed. Lima: Mosca Azul, 1985.
Maclean, Iain S. *Opting for Democracy? Liberation Theology and the Struggle for Democracy in Brazil.* New York:Peter Lang, 1999.
Madsen, Douglas, and Peter Snow. *The Charismatic Bond: Political Behavior in Times of Crisis.* Cambridge, MA: Harvard University Press, 1991.

Mainwaring, Scott. *The Catholic Church and Politics in Brazil, 1916-1985*. Stanford, CA: Stanford University Press, 1986.
Mainwaring, Scott. *Rethinking Party Systems in the Third Wave of Democratization, The Case of Brazil*. Stanford, CA: Stanford University Press, 1999.
Mainwaring, Scott, and Mathew S. Shugart, eds. *Presidentialism and Democracy in Latin America*. Cambridge: Cambridge University Press, 1997.
Mainwaring, Scott, and Timothy R. Scully, eds. *Building Democratic Institutions: Party Systems in Latin America*. Stanford, CA: Stanford University Press, 1995.
Malloy, James M. and Richard Thorn, eds. *Beyond the Revolution: Bolivia since 1952*. Pittsburgh, PA: Pittsburgh University Press, 1971.
Malta, Octavio. *Os tenentes na revolução brasileira*. Rio de Janeiro: Civilização Brasileira, 1969.
Manigat, Leslie. *De un Duvalier a otro: itinerario de un fascismo de subdesarrollo*. Caracas: Monteávila, 1982.
Manigat, Leslie. *Ethnicité, nationalisme et politique: le cas d'Haiti*. New York: Editions Connaissance d'Haiti, 1974.
Mariátegui, José Carlos. *El alma matinal y otras estaciones del hombre de hoy*, 7th ed. Lima: Amauta, 1981.
Mariátegui, José Carlos, *Defensa del Marxismo*, 11th ed. Lima: Amauta, 1981.
Mariátegui, José Carlos. "Henri de Man y la 'crisis' del Marxismo." in *Defensa del marxismo:* 19-23.
Mariátegui, José Carlos, "El problema de las elites." in *El alma matinal y otras estaciones del hombre de hoy*: 48-53.
Mariátegui, José Carlos, "Sentido heroico y creador del socialismo." in *Defensa del Marxismo:* 71-74.
Mariátegui, José Carlos. *Obras*, 2 vols. Havanna: Casa de las Américas, 1982.
Mars, Perry. *Ideology and Change: The Transformation of the Caribbean Left*. Detroit, MI: Wayne State University Press, 1998.
Martínez Peláez, Severo. *La patria del criollo*, 10th ed. Ciudad Universitaria Rodrigo Facio, Costa Rica: Editorial Universitaria Centroamericana, 1985.
Martz, John D. *Acción Democrática: Evolution of a Modern Political Party in Venezuela*. Princeton, NJ: Princeton University Press, 1966.
Martz, John. *Ecuador: Conflicting Political Culture and the Quest for Progress*. Boston: Allyn and Bacon, 1972.
Matos Mar, José, et al. *Perú, hoy*. Mexico: Siglo XXI, 1971.
Matos Mar, José. *Yanaconaje y reforma agraria en el Perú*. Lima: Instituto de Estudios Peruanos, 1976.
Mayer, Frederick. *Interpreting NAFTA: The Science and Art of Political Analysis*. New York: Columbia University Press, 1998.
McClintock, Cynthia, and Abraham Lowenthal, eds. *El gobierno militar, una experiencia peruana, 1968-1980*. Lima: Instituto de Estudios Peruanos, 1983.
McClintock, Michael. *State Terror and Popular Resistance in El Salvador*, vol. 1 of *The American Connection*, 2 vols. London: Zed Books, 1985.
McGuire, James W. *Peronism Without Perón: Unions, Parties and Democracy in Argentina*. Stanford, CA: Stanford University Press, 1997.
Mella, Julio Antonio. *Qué es el ARPA* [sic]. Lima: Editorial Educación, 1975 (1st ed. Mexico 1928).
Mellafe, Rolando. *La esclavitud en Hispanoamérica*. Buenos Aires: Eudeba, 1984.
Melo Franco, Virgílio A. de. *Outubro 1930*, 5th ed. Rio de Janeiro: Nova Fronteira, 1980 (1st ed. 1931).
Méndez, Joaquín. *Los sucesos comunistas en El Salvador*. San Salvador: Imprenta Funes Ungo, 1935.

Menéndez Carrión, Amparo. *La conquista del voto en el Ecuador: de Velasco a Roldós.* Quito: Corporación Editora Nacional, 1986.

Mercadante, Paulo. *A consciencia conservadora no Brasil,* 3rd ed. Rio de Janeiro: Nova Fronteira, 1980.

Mesa Lago, Carmelo. *Dialéctica de la Revolución Cubana.* Madrid: Editorial Playor, 1979.

Mesa-Lago, Carmelo. *La economía en Cuba socialista.* Madrid: Editorial Playor, 1983.

Meyer, Jean. *La Cristíada,* 3 vols. Mexico: Siglo XXI, 1973-74.

Millar Carvallo, René. *La elección presidencial de 1920.* Santiago: Editorial Universitaria, 1981.

Millett, Allan Reed. *The Politics of Intervention, The Military Occupation of Cuba, 1906-1909.* Columbus: Ohio State University Press, 1968.

Mills, Nick D. *Crisis, conflicto y consenso: Ecuador, 1979-1984.* Quito: Editora Nacional, 1984.

Miró Quesada, Francisco. *La ideología de Acción Popular.* Lima: Tipografía Santa Rosa, 1964.

Molina, Gerardo. *Las ideas liberales en Colombia,* 3 vols. Bogotá: Tercer Mundo, 1970-77.

Montero Moreno, René. *La verdad sobre Ibáñez,* Buenos Aires: Freeland, 1953.

Mora y Araujo, Manuel, and Peter Smith, eds. *El voto peronista.* Buenos Aires: Sudamericana, 1980.

Moraes, Denis de. *A esquerda e o golpe de 64,* 2nd ed. Rio de Janeiro: Espaço e Tempo, 1989.

Moreno Fraginals, Manuel. *El ingenio: el complejo económico social cubano del azúcar,* 2nd ed. Havanna: Editorial de Ciencias Sociales, 1978.

Moreno, José. *Barrios in Arms: Revolution in Santo Domingo.* Pittsburgh, PA: University of Pittsburgh Press, 1970.

Morris, James A. *Honduras: Caudillo Politics and Military Rule.* Boulder, CO: Westview., 1984.

Moya Pons, Frank. *Manual de historia dominicana,* 6th ed. Santo Domingo: Universidad Católica Madre y Maestra, 1981.

Moya Pons, Frank. *El pasado dominicano.* Santo Domingo: Fundación J.A. Caro Álvarez, 1986.

Murmis, Miguel, and Juan Carlos Portantiero. *Estudios sobre los orígenes del peronismo.* Buenos Aires: Siglo XXI, 1971.

Murmis, Miguel, ed. *Clase y región en el agro ecuatoriano.* Quito: Editora Nacional, 1986.

Nicholls, David. *From Dessalines to Duvalier: Race, Colour and National Independence in Haiti.* Cambridge: Cambridge University Press, 1979.

Nieto Arteta, Luis Eduardo. *Economía y cultura en la historia de Colombia,* 2nd ed. Bogotá: Tercer Mundo, 1962.

Norden, Deborah. "Democracy and Military Control in Venezuela, From Subordination to Insurrection." *Latin American Research Review* 33 (1998): 143-165.

Novak, Michael. *Will it Liberate? Questions About Liberation Theology.* New York: Paulist Press, 1986.

Nunn, Frederick. *Chilean Politics, 1920-1931: The Honorable Mission of the Armed Forces.* Albuquerque: University of New Mexico Press, 1970.

Núñez Soto, Orlando. *Transición y lucha de clases en Nicaragua, 1979-1986.* México: Siglo Veintiuno, 1987.

O'Connor, James. *The Origins of Socialism in Cuba.* Ithaca, NY: Cornell University Press, 1970.

O'Donnell, Guillermo. *Modernización y autoritarismo*. Buenos Aires: Paidós, 1972.
O'Donnell, Guillermo, and Philippe Schmitter. *Tentative conclusions for uncertain democracies*, part IV of Guillermo O'Donnell, Philippe Schmitter and Lawrence Whitehead, eds. *Transitions from Authoritarian Rule: Prospects for Democracy*. Baltimore, MD: The Johns Hopkins University Press, 1986.
O'Leary, Juan E. *El Mariscal Solano López*, 3rd ed. Asunción: Casa América/Moreno Hnos, 1970.
Oddone, Juan A. *La formación del Uruguay moderno: la inmigración y el desarrollo económico-social*. Buenos Aires: Eudeba, 1966.
Oliveira Filho, Moacyr de. *Um operário no poder: a insurreição comunista de 1935 vista por dentro*. Sao Paulo: Alfa-Omega, 1985.
Oliveira Vianna, Francisco José. *Evolução do povo brasileiro*. Sao Paulo: Monteiro Lobato, 1923.
Oliveira Vianna. *O idealismo da Constituiçao*, 2nd ed. Sao Paulo: Editora Nacional, 1939.
Oliveira Vianna, Francisco José. *Instituções políticas brasileiras*, 2nd ed., 2 vols. Rio de Janeiro: José Olympio, 1955.
Oropeza, Luis J. *Tutelary Pluralism*. Cambridge, Mass: Center for International Affairs, Harvard University, 1983.
Orrego, Claudio, et al. *Siete ensayos sobre Arturo Alessandri Palma*. Santiago: Instituto Chileno de Estudios Humanísticos, 1979.
Ortiz, Fernando. *Contrapunteo cubano del tabaco y el azúcar*, 2nd ed. Havanna: Consejo Nacional de Cultura, 1963.
Osorio Goicoechea, Joaquín. *Fox: a un año de la alternancia*. Jalisco: Amaroma, 2001.
Ospina Vásquez, Luis. *Industria y protección en Colombia*. Medellín, ESF, 1955.
Oszlak, Oscar, ed. *Proceso, crisis y transición democrática*, 2 vols. Buenos Aires: Cedal, 1984.
Oved, Iaacov. *El anarquismo y el movimiento obrero en la Argentina*. Mexico: Siglo XXI, 1978.
Paerregaard, Karsten. *Linking Separate Worlds, Urban Migrants and Rural Peru*. Oxford and New York: Berg, 1997.
Paige, Jeffery M. *Coffee and Power: Revolution and the Rise of Democracy in Central America*. Cambridge, MA: Harvard University Press, 1997.
Palacios, Marco. *El café en Colombia, 1850-1970*. Bogotá: Presencia, 1979.
Palermo, Vicente. *Democracia interna en los partidos: las elecciones partidarias de 1983 en el radicalismo y justicialismo porteños*. Buenos Aires: Ides, 1986.
Palma Zúñiga, Luis. *Historia del Partido Radical*. Santiago: Editorial Andrés Bello, 1967.
Palmer, David Scott. *Shining Path of Peru*, 2nd ed. New York: St. Martin's Press, 1994.
Parry, J.H., P.M. Sherlock and A.P. Maingot. *A Short History of the West Indies*. London: Macmillan Caribbean, 1956.
Paso, Leonardo. *Historia del origen de los partidos políticos en la Argentina, 1810-1918*. Buenos Aires: Ediciones Centro de Estudios, 1972.
Pastore, Carlos. *La lucha por la tierra en el Paraguay*, 2nd ed. Montevideo: Antequera, 1972.
Patterson, Henry. "The 1996 Elections and Nicaragua's Fragile Transition." *Government and Opposition* 32 (Summer 1997): 380-398.
Patterson, Orlando. *The Sociology of Slavery: An Analysis of the Origins, Development and Structure of Negro Slave Society in Jamaica*. London: McGibbon & Kee, 1967.
Peloso, Vincent C. *Peasants on Plantations: Subaltern Strategies of Labor and Resistance in the Pisco Valley, Peru*. Durham, NC: Duke University Press, 1999.

Penniman, Howard R. *Venezuela at the Polls: The National Elections of 1978*. Washington, DC: American Enterprise Institute, 1980.
Pérez Brignoli, Héctor. *Breve historia de Centroamérica*. Madrid: Alianza, 1985.
Pérez Jr, Louis A. *Army Politics in Cuba, 1898-1958*. Pittsburgh, PA: University of Pittsburgh Press, 1976.
Pérez Jr, Louis A. *Cuba under the Platt Amendment, 1902-1934*. Pittsburgh, PA: Pittsburgh University Press, 1986.
Petras, James, and Maurice Zeitlin. *El radicalismo político de la clase trabajadora chilena*. Buenos Aires: Cedal, 1969.
Philip, George. "Venezuelan Democracy and the Coup Attempt of February 1992." *Government and Opposition* 27 (Autumn 1992): 455-469.
Picón Salas, Mariano et al. *Venezuela independiente, 1810-1960*. Caracas: Fundación Eugenio Mendoza, 1962.
Pinheiro, Paulo Sérgio. *Estratégias da ilusão: a revolução mundial e o Brasil, 1922, 1935*. Sao Paulo: Companhia das Letras, 1991.
Pinzas García, Teobaldo. *La economía peruana, 1950-1978: un ensayo bibliográfico*. Lima: Instituto de Estudios Peruanos, 1981.
Pivel Devoto, Juan E. *Historia de los partidos políticos en el Uruguay*, 2 vols. Montevideo: Atlántida, 1942-1943.
Piven, Frances Fox. *Labor Parties in Post Industrial Societies*. Cambridge, MA: Polity, 1991.
Politeia/1980. Caracas: Instituto de Estudios Políticos, Universidad Central de Venezuela, 1980.
Pollack, Benny. "The Chilean Socialist Party, Prolegomena to its Ideology and Organization." *Journal of Latin American Studies* 10 (1978): 117-152.
Poppino, Rollie. *International Communism in Latin America, A History of the Movement, 1917-1963*. New York: Free Press, 1964.
Porzecanski, Arturo. *Uruguay's Tupamaros: The Urban Guerrilla*. New York: Praeger, 1973.
Potash, Robert. *El ejército y la política en la Argentina*, 2nd ed., 2 vols. Buenos Aires: Hyspamérica, 1986.
Potash, Robert. *Perón y el GOU, los documentos de una logia secreta*. Buenos Aires: Sudamericana, 1984.
Powell, John Duncan. *Political Mobilization of the Venezuelan Peasant*. Cambridge, MA: Harvard University Press, 1971.
Przeworski, Adam. *Capitalism and Social Democracy*. Cambridge: Cambridge University Press, 1985.
Purnell, Jennie. *Popular Movements and State Formation in Revolutionary Mexico: The Agraristas and Cristeros of Michoacán*. Durham, NC: Duke University Press, 1999.
Quijano, Aníbal. *Nacionalismo, neoimperialismo y militarismo en el Perú*. Buenos Aires: Periferia, 1971.
Quintero, Rafael. *El mito del populismo en el Ecuador*. Quito: Flacso, 1980.
Rama, Germán. *El club político*. Montevideo: Arca, 1971.
Ramírez Necochea, Hernán. *Historia del movimiento obrero en Chile: antecedentes, siglo XIX*. Santiago: Austral, 1956.
Ramírez, Sergio. *El pensamiento vivo de Sandino*, 2nd ed. Caracas: Centauro, 1981.
Rangel Guevara, Carlos. *Del buen salvaje al buen revolucionario*. Caracas: Monteávila, 1976.
Remmer, Karen L. *Party Competition in Argentina and Chile: Political Recruitment and Public Policy, 1890-1930*. Lincoln: University of Nebraska Press, 1984.

Reyes Abadie, Washington, ed. *Crónica de Aparicio Saravia*, 2 vols. Montevideo: El Nacional, 1989.
Reyna, José Luis, and Richard S. Weinert, eds. *El autoritarismo en México*. Mexico: 1981.
Rial, Juan. *Los partidos tradicionales, restauración o renovación*. Montevideo: Documentos de Trabajo, Centro de Informaciones y Estudios del Uruguay, 1984.
Rial, Juan, and Carolina Perelli. *El discreto encanto de la social democracia en el Uruguay*. Montevideo: Documentos de Trabajo, Centro de Informaciones y Estudios del Uruguay, 1985.
Riker, William. *The Theory of Political Coalitions*. New Haven, CT: Yale University Press, 1962
Rivarola, Domingo. *Estado, campesinos y modernización agrícola en Paraguay*. Asunción: Centro Paraguayo de Estudios Sociológicos, 1982.
Rivarola, Domingo, ed. *Los movimientos sociales en el Paraguay*. Asunción: Centro Paraguayo de Estudios Sociológicos, 1986.
Rivarola, Domingo, et al. *Militares y políticos en una transición atípica*. Buenos Aires: Grupo de Trabajo de Partidos Políticos (CLACSO), 1991.
Roberts, Kenneth M. *Deepening Democracy? The Modern Left and Social Movements in Chile and Peru*. Stanford, CA: Stanford University Press, 1998.
Roberts, Kenneth. "Neoliberalism and the Transformation of Populism in Latin America: The Peruvian Case." *World Politics* 48 (October 1995): 82-116.
Roberts, Kenneth, and Erik Wibbels. "Party Systems and Electoral Volatility in Latin America: A Test of Economic, Institutional and Structural Explanations." *American Political Science Review* 93 (September 1999): 575-590.
Rock, David. *Argentina 1516-1987: From Spanish Colony to Alfonsín*. Berkeley: University of California Press, 1985.
Rock, David. *Politics in Argentina, 1890-1930*. Cambridge: Cambridge University Press, 1975.
Rodrigues, Edgar. *Os libertários*. Petrópolis. Vozes, 1988;
Rodrigues, Leôncio Martins. "A composição social das lideranças do PT," in *Partidos e sindicatos*. Sao Paulo: Ática, 1990: 7-33
Rodrigues, Leôncio Martins. *Conflito industrial e sindicalismo em Brasil*. Sao Paulo: Difel, 1966.
Rodrigues, Leôcio Martins. *CUT: os militantes e a ideologia*. Rio de Janeiro: Paz e Terra, 1990.
Rodrigues, Leôncio Martins. *Partidos: ideologia e composição social*. Sao Paulo: Editora da Universidade de São Paulo, 2002.
Rodrigues, Leôncio Martins. "O PCB, os dirigentes e a organização," in *História Geral da Civilização Brasileira*, directed by Sérgio Buarque de Holanda and Boris Fausto, 3 books in 11 vols. Rio de Janeiro: Difel, 1963-86, book 3, vol. 3, ch. 8: 361-443.
Roett, Riordan, ed. *Political and Economic Liberalization in Mexico*. Boulder, CO: Lynne Rienner, 1993.
Rolón Anaya, Mario. *Política y partidos en Bolivia*. La Paz: Librería Editorial Juventud, 1966.
Romero, José Luis. *A History of Argentine Political Thought*. Stanford, CA: Stanford University Press, 1963.
Romero, Luis Alberto. *Breve historia contemporánea de la Argentina*. Buenos Aires: Fondo de Cultura Económica, 1994.
Roniger, Luis, and Mario Sznajder. "The Legacy of Human Rights Violations and the Collective Identity of Redemocratized Uruguay." *Human Rights Quarterly* 19 (1997): 55-77.

Roorda, Eric Paul. *The Dictator Next Door*. Durham, NC: Duke University Press, 1998.
Ropp, Stephen C. *Panamanian Politics: From Guarded Nation to National Guard*. New York: Praeger, 1982.
Roseberry, William. *Coffee and Capitalism in the Venezuelan Andes*. Austin: University of Texas Press, 1983.
Rosendal, Mona. *Inside the Revolution: Daily Life in Socialist Cuba*. Ithaca, NY: Cornell University Press, 1997.
Ross, Stanley. *Francisco Madero: Apostle of Mexican Democracy*. New York: Columbia University Press, 1955.
Rouquié, Alain. *Poder militar y sociedad política en la Argentina*, 2nd. ed., 2 vols. Buenos Aires: Hyspamérica, 1986.
Roxborough, Ian. "The Analysis of Labour Movements in Latin America: Typologies and Theories." *Bulletin of Latin American Research* 1 (October 1981): 81-95.
Rueschemeyer, Dietrich. Evelyne Huber Stephens and John D. Stephens. *Capitalist Development and Democracy*. Chicago: University of Chicago Press, 1992.
Ruiz, Ramón. *The Great Rebellion, Mexico, 1905-1924*. New York: W.W. Norton, 1980.
Sábato, Hilda, and Ema Cibotti. "Inmigrantes y política, un problema pendiente." *Estudios Migratorios Latinoamericanos* 2 (December 1986): 475-482.
Sábato, Hilda, and Ema Cibotti. *Hacer política en Buenos Aires: Los italianos en la escena pública porteña, 1860-1880*. Buenos Aires: Cisea-Pehesa, 1988.
Salamanca, Luis, ed. *Los pensadores positivistas y el gomecismo*, 3 vols. Caracas: Congreso de la República, 1983.
Salazar, Rosendo. *La Casa del Obrero Mundial*. Mexico: B. Costa-Amic, 1962.
Sales, Alberto. *A pátria paulista*, 2nd ed. Brasilia: Universidade de Brasília: 1983.
Salgado, René. "Economic Pressure Groups and Policy-Making in Venezuela: The Case of Fedecámaras Reconsidered." *Latin American Research Review* 22 (1987): 91-105.
Sánchez Albornoz, Nicolás. *La población de América Latina desde los tiempos precolombinos al año 2000*. Madrid: Alianza Editorial, 1973.
Sánchez, Luis A. *Haya de la Torre y el Apra*. Santiago de Chile: Editorial del Pacífico, 1955.
Sanguinetti, Horacio. *Los socialistas independientes*. Buenos Aires: Editorial de Belgrano, 1981.
Santa Cruz Schuhkrafft, Andrés de. *Cuadros sinópticos de los gobernantes de la República de Bolivia y de la del Perú*. La Paz: Fundación Universitaria Simón Patiño, 1956.
Santiago-Valles, Kelvin A. *'Subject People' and Colonial Discourses: Economic Tranformation and Social Disorder in Puerto Rico, 1898-1947*. Albany, NY: SUNY Press, 1994.
Sartori, Giovanni. *Parties and Party Systems: A Framework for Analysis*. Cambridge: Cambridge University Press, 1976.
Saviñón M., Ramón Emilio. *Memorias de la Era de Trujillo 1916-1961*. Santo Domingo: Amigo del Hogar, 2002.
Schifter, Jacobo. *La fase oculta de la guerra civil en Costa Rica*, 2nd ed. San José: Editorial Universitaria Centroamericana, 1981.
Schirmer, Jennifer. *The Guatemalan Military Project: A Violence Called Democracy*. Philadelphia: University of Pennsylvania Press, 1998.
Schmitter, Philippe. *Interest Conflict and Political Change in Brazil*. Stanford, CA: Stanford University Press, 1971.
Schmitter, Philippe, and J. Grot. *Corporative Sisyphus*. Florence: European University Institute, 1997.
Schmitter, Philippe, and Terry Lynn Karl. "What Democracy Is, and Is Not." *Journal of Democracy* 2 (Summer 1991):75-88.

Schmitter, Philippe, and Gerhard Lehmbruch, eds. *Trends Toward Corporatist Intermediation.* London: Sage, 1979.
Schneider. Ronald M. *Communism in Guatemala, 1944-1954.* New York: Praeger, 1955.
Schneider, Ronald. *The Political System of Brazil: Emergence of an Authoritarian "Modernizing" Regime, 1964-70.* New York: Columbia University Press, 1971.
Schulz, Donald, and Edward J. Williams, eds. *Mexico Faces the XXIst Century.* Westport, CT: Praeger, 1995.
Schvarzer, Jorge. *Empresarios del pasado: la Unión Industrial Argentina.* Buenos Aires: Cisea-Imago Mundi, 1991.
Schwab, Peter. *Cuba: Confronting the United States Embargo.* New York: St. Martin's Press, 1999.
Scully, Timothy R. *Rethinking the Center: Cleavages, Critical Junctures and Party Evolution in Chile.* Stanford, CA: Stanford University Press, 1992.
Seligson, Mitchell. *El campesino y el capitalismo agrario en Costa Rica.* San José, Costa Rica: Editorial Costa Rica, 1980.
Selser, Gregorio. *Sandino, general de hombres libres.* Buenos Aires: Abril, 1984.
Semo, Enrique et al., eds. *Historia de la cuestión agraria mexicana,* 4 vols. Mexico: Siglo XXI and Centro de Estudios de Historia del Agrarismo en México, 1988.
Serbin, Andrés. *Guyana.* Caracas: Brughera, 1979.
Sharpless, Richard. *Gaitán of Colombia: A Political Biography.* Pittsburgh, PA: Pittsburgh University Press, 1978.
Sherlock. Philip, and Hazel Bennett. *The Story of the Jamaican People.* Kingston: Ian Randle Publisher, 1998.
Shumway, Nicolas. *The invention of Argentina.* Berkeley: University of California Press, 1991.
Siavelis, Peter M. *The President and Congress in Postauthoritarian Chile.* University Park: Pennsylvania State University Press, 2000.
Silva, Hélio. *A ameaça vermelha: o plano Cohen.* Porto Alegre: L&PM, 1980.
Skidmore, Thomas. *Politics in Brazil, 1930-1964. An Experiment in Democracy.* New York: Oxford University Press, 1967.
Slutzky, Daniel, and Esther Alonso. *Empresas trasnacionales y agricultura: el caso del enclave bananero en Honduras.* Tegucigalpa: Editorial Universitaria, 1982.
Snow, Peter. *El radicalismo chileno: historia y doctrina del Partido Radical.* Buenos Aires: Francisco de Aguirre, 1972.
Soares, Glaucio Dillon. "The Brazilian Political System: New Parties and Old Cleavages." *Luso-Brazilian Review* 19 (1982): 39-66.
Soares, Gláucio Dillon, and Nelson do Vale Silva. "Urbanization, Race and Class in Brazilian Politics." *Latin American Research Review* 22 (1987): 155-176.
Solberg, Carl. *Immigration and Nationalism: Argentina and Chile, 1890—1914.* Austin: University of Texas Press, 1970.
Sonnleitner, Willibald. *Los indígenas y la democratización electoral: una década de cambio político entre los tzotziles y tzeltales de Los Altos de Chiapas, 1988-2000.* México: 2001.
Sonntag, Heinz, and Thaís Maingón. *Venezuela, 4-F 1992: un análisis sociopolítico.* Caracas: Nueva Sociedad, 1992.
Sosa Abascal, Arturo, et al. *Gómez, gomecismo y antigomecismo.* Caracas: Universidad Central de Venezuela, 1987.
Sosa Abascal, Arturo, and Eloi Lengrand. *Del garibaldismo estudiantil a la izquierda criolla: los orígenes marxistas del proyecto AD, 1928-1935.* Caracas: Centauro, 1981.
Sosa, Ignacio. *Conciencia y proyecto nacional en Chile, 1891-1973.* Mexico: Unam, 1981.

Stavenhagen, Rododolfo. *Siete tesis equivocadas sobre América Latina.* Turrialba, Costa Rica: Instituto Interamericano de Ciencias Agrarias, 1972.
Stepan, Alfred, ed. *Authoritarian Brazil.* New Haven, CT: Yale University Press, 1973.
Stepan, Alfred, ed. *Democratizing Brazil: Problems of Transition and Consolidation.* New York: Oxford University Press, 1989.
Stepan, Alfred. *The Military in Politics: Changing Patterns in Brazil.* Princeton, NJ: Princeton University Press, 1971.
Stepan, Alfred. *The State and Society: Peru in Comparative Perspective.* Princeton, NJ: Princeton University Press, 1978.
Stone, Laurence. "The English Revolution." In Robert Foster and Jack P. Greene, eds. *Preconditions of Revolution in Early Modern Europe.* Baltimore, MD: Johns Hopkins University Press, 1970: 55-108.
Strawbridge, George. *Ibáñez and Alessandri: The Authoritarian Right and the Democratic Left in XXth Century Chile.* Buffalo, NY: SUNY Press, 1971.
Stryker, Sheldon, and Anne Statham Macke. "Status Inconsistency and Role Conflict." *Annual Review of Sociology* 4 (1978): 57-90.
Suárez, Andrés. *Cuba: Castroism and Communism, 1959-1966.* Cambridge, MA: MIT Press, 1967.
Taylor, Philip B. Jr. *The Venezuelan Golpe de Estado of 1958: The Fall of Marcos Pérez Jiménez.* Washington, DC: Operations and Policy Research, 1968.
Terán, Oscar. *Nuestros años sesentas: la formación de la nueva izquierda intelectual en la Argentina, 1956-1966.* Buenos Aires: Punto Sur, 1991.
Tilly, Charles. *From Mobilization to Revolution.* Reading, MA: Addison-Wellesley, 1978.
Tirado Mejía, Álvaro. *Aspectos políticos del primer gobierno de Alfonso López Pumarejo, 1934-1938.* Bogotá: Pro Cultura/Instituto Colombiano de Cultura, 1981.
Torre, Juan Carlos. *Perón y la vieja guardia sindical.* Buenos Aires: Sudamericana, 1990.
Torre, Juan Carlos. *Los sindicalistas en el poder, 1973-1976.* Buenos Aires: Cedal, 1983.
Torres, Alberto. *A organização nacional*, 2nd ed. Sao Paulo: Editora Nacional, 1938.
Torres, Alberto. *O problema nacional brasileiro.* Sao Paulo: Editora Nacional, 1938.
Torrijos, Omar. *La batalla de Panamá.* Buenos Aires: Eudeba, 1973.
Trías, Vivián. *Perú: Fuerzas Armadas y revolución.* Montevideo: Banda Oriental, 1971.
Trindade, Hélgio. *O Integralismo: o fascismo brasileiro na década de 30.* Sao Paulo: Difel, 1979.
Tulchin, Joseph, and Gary Bland, eds. *Peru in Crisis: Dictatorship or Democracy?* Boulder: Lynne Rienner and Woodrow Wilson Center, 1994.
Tulchin, Joseph, et al. *Cuba and the United States: Will the Cold War in the Caribbean End?* Boulder, CO: Lynne Rienner, 1991.
Valencia, Elmo. *Libro rojo de Rojas.* Bogotá: Ediciones Culturales, 1970.
Valenzuela, Arturo. *Chile.* Baltimore, MD: The Johns Hopkins University Press, 1976.
Valenzuela, Carlos. *Frustraciones y realidades políticas en América Latina: del APRA al MNR.* Buenos Aires: Peña Lillo, 1961.
Valenzuela, J. Samuel. "Movimientos obreros y sistemas políticos: un análisis conceptual y tipológico." *Desarrollo Económico* 23 (October-December. 1983): 339-368.
Van Cott, Donna Lee, ed. *Indigenous Peoples and Democracy in Latin America.* New York: St. Martin's Press, 1995.
Vanden, Harry E. *National Marxism in Latin America, José Carlos Mariátegui's Thought and Politics.* Boulder, CO: Lynne Rienner, 1986.
Vanden, Harry E., et al., eds. *Democracy and Socialism in Sandinista Nicaragua.* Boulder, CO: Lynne Rienner, 1993.
Vanger, Milton I. *José Batlle y Ordóñez, el creador de su época, 1902-1907.* Buenos Aires: Eudeba, 1968.

Vanger, Milton I. *El país modelo*. Montevideo: Banda Oriental, 1982.
Varela, Alfredo. *Revoluções cisplatinas: a República Riograndense*, 2 vols. Porto: Chardron, 1915.
Varela, Gustavo. *De la República liberal al Estado militar: Uruguay 1968-1973*. Montevideo: Nuevo Mundo, 1968.
Vasconcelos, José. *Memorias*, 2 vols. Mexico: Fondo de Cultura Económica, 1982.
Vazeilles, José. *Los socialistas*. Buenos Aires: Jorge Alvarez, 1967.
Vega Centeno, Imelda. *Aprismo popular: mito, cultura e historia*. Lima: Tarea, 1986.
Vega Centeno, Imelda. *Ideología y cultura en el aprismo popular*. Lima: Tarea, 1986.
Vega Ugalde, Silvia. *La gloriosa: de la revolución del 28 de mayo de 1944 a la contrarrevolución velasquista*. Quito: El Conejo, 1987.
Vidal, Gregorio. *Grandes empresas, economía y poder en México*. México: Plaza y Valdés, 2000.
Villalobos, Joaquín. *Una revolución en la izquierda para una revolución democrática*. San Salvador: Arcoiris, 1992.
Villanueva, Víctor. *Nueva mentalidad militar en Perú*. Buenos Aires: Replanteo, 1969.
Villanueva, Víctor. *La tragedia de un pueblo y un partido*. Santiago: 1954.
Waisman, Carlos. *Reversal of Development in Argentina: Postwar Counterrevolutionary Policies and Their Structural Consequences*. Princeton, NJ: Princeton University Press, 1987.
Wahlers, Gerhard. *Nace una alternativa: CLAT, historia de una internacional sindical latinoamericana*. Miami, FL: Saeta Ediciones, 1991.
Walker, Thomas, ed. *Nicaragua Without Illusions: Regime Transition and Structural Adjustment in the 1990s*. Wilmington, DE: SR Books, 1997.
Walker, Thomas, ed. *Nicaragua: The First Five Years*. New York: Praeger, 1985.
Wasserman, Robert. *Class and Society in Central Chiapas*. Berkeley: University of California Press, 1983.
Weffort, Francisco. *O populismo na política brasileira*. Rio de Janeiro: Paz e Terra, 1978.
Williams, John Hoyt. *The Rise and Fall of the Paraguayan Republic, 1810-1870*. Austin: University of Texas Press, 1979.
Witker, Alejandro. *Los trabajos y los días de Recabarren*. Mexico: Nuestro Tiempo, 1977.
Womack. John. *Zapata y la Revolución Mexicana*. Mexico: Siglo XXI, 1969.
Wurth Rojas, Ernesto. *Ibáñez, caudillo enigmático*. Santiago: Editorial del Pacífico, 1958.
Zeitlin, Maurice. *Revolutionary Politics and the Cuban Working Class*. New York: Harper and Rowe, 1970.
Zimmermann Zavala, Augusto. *Los últimos días del General Velasco: ¿quién recoge la bandera?*. Lima: Talleres Humboldt, 1978.
Zum Felde, Alberto. *Proceso histórico del Uruguay: esquema de una sociología nacional*. Montevideo: Maximino García, 1919.

Index

ABC, Cuba,64
Abertura, Brazil, 147, 150
Acción Communal, Panama, 67
Acción Democrática, Venezuela, 28-29, 62-63, 92, 94, 117, 174, 175
Acción Democrática Nacionalista (AND), Bolivia, 160, 162
Acción Popular, Peru, 87, 154, 155
Agrupación Nacional Democrático-Social, Uruguay,54
Agrupación Nacional Ecuatoriana (ARNE),89
Aldunate, Wilson Ferreira, 115, 171
Alemán, Miguel, 96
Alemán, Arnoldo, 130
Alessandri, Arturo, 31-32, 33, 51
Alessandri, Jorge, 86, 111
Alfaro, Eloy, 8
Alfonsín, Raúl, 165, 166, 168
Aliança Nacional Libertadora (ANL), Brazil, 48
Aliança Renovadora Nacional (ARENA), Brazil,106, 107, 123, 147, 148, 149
Alianza, Argentina, 168
Alianza Nacional Popular (ANAPO), Colombia, 95
Alianza Popular Ervolucionaria Americana (APRA), Peru, 22, 29
Allende, Salvador, 84, 86, 111, 112-113
Alliance for Progress, 112
Almeida, José Américo de, 49
Alonso, José, 109
Alvarado, Manuel Velasco, 100, 154
Álvarez, Gregorio, 116, 170
Álvarez, Waldo, 56
Alvear, Marcelo T de, 43, 52, 72
Amador, Carlos Fonseca, 128
Amaral, Antonio José Azevedo do, 49

Anarchists, Anarchy, 17-18, 34, 56, 60
Andino, Tiburcio Carias, 28
Angarita, Isaías Medina, 62
Aperturista, 36, 107, 118, 122, 150
Aprismo, Apra, 22, 26-27, 29, 58, 49, 60, 61, 65, 86, 87, 94, 95, 99-100, 108, 136, 138, 154, 155, 157
Aprista parties, definition, 188-189
Arais, Arnulfo, 67, 132, 133, 134
Arais, Harmodio, 67, 132
Aramburu, Pedro E., 78
Araujo, Arturo, 66
Arbenz, Jacobo, 124
Arce, Armando, 56
Arce, Walter Guevara, 83, 159
Areco, Jorge Pacheco, 115, 171
Arellano, Asvaldo López, 126
Arévalo, Juan José, 124
Argaña, Luis María, 163, 164
Argentina, 12-13, 33-37, 43-46, 52-53, 71-74, 76-79, 108-111, 114, 164-170
Argentinian Revolution, influence of, 109-110
Arguedas, Alcides, 9, 56, 57
Aristide, Jean Baptiste, 138, 139
Armas, Carlos Castillo, 124
Arosemena, Juan Denóstenes, 67
Arraes, Miguel, 105
Arzú, Alvaro, 125, 126
Associação Integralista Brasileria (AIB), 49
Ayala, Eusebio, 26, 58
Aylwin, Patricio, 172, 173

Balaguer, Joaquín, 137
Balbín, Ricardo, 78, 79
Baldivieso, Enrique, 25, 55, 56, 57
Baldomir, Alfredo, 54-55
Balmaceda, José Manuel, 11, 31

Barrantes, Alfonso Frijolito, 155
Barrientos, René, 83, 84, 101
Barrios, Justo Rufino, 5
Barros, Adhemar de, 103, 105
Barros, João Alberto Lins de, 47, 48
Batista, Fulgencio, 65, 93, 94, 132, 134, 143
Batista, Pedro Ernesto, 47
Batlle, Jorge, 170-171
Batlle y Ordóñez, José, 14, 37, 38, 39, 53-54
"Bay of Pigs," Cuba, 134
Bermúdez, Francisco Morales, 154
Berres, Luis Batlle, 80
Betancourt, Rómulo, 28, 92, 93, 139
Betancur, Belisario, 116
Bignone, Reynaldo, 164
Billinghurst, Guillermo, 8, 24-25
Blades, Rubén, 134
Blanco Party, Uruguay, 37-38, 53, 54, 80, 114, 170, 171
Bolivia, 9, 24-25, 55-58, 81-84, 101-103, 159-162
Bolivian Revolution, influence of, 83
Bordaberry, Juan María, 115
Borge, Tomás, 128
Borja, Rodrigo, 158
Bosch, Juan, 137, 138
Bosque, Pío Romero, 65
Branco, Humberto Castelo, 105, 107
Brazil, 10-11, 29-31, 46-50, 74-76, 103-107, 113-114, 147-154
Brizola, Leonel, 148, 149, 152
Bucaram, Assad, 89, 157
Burham, Forbes, 141, 142
Burke, Edmund, 182
Busch, Alberto Natusch, 159
Busch, Germán, 55, 56, 57, 81, 83
Bustamente, Alexander, 140
Bustamente y Rivero, José Luis, 86
Buterse, Dersi, 143, 144

Caballero, Bernardino, 58
Cabrera, Manuel Estrada, 5, 28
Cafiero, Antonio, 165, 167
Caldera, Rafael, 92, 117, 174
Calles, Plutarco Elías, 18, 19, 20, 21, 63
Camacho, Manuel Ávila, 63, 96
Camargo, Alberto Lleras, 95
Cambio, 90, Peru, 156
Campisteguy, Juan, 39
Cámpora, Héctor, 110, 111

Campos, Francisco, 47
Campos, Pedro Albizu, 139
Capitalism, associated dependent, 183
Cárdenas, Cuauhtémoc, 176
Cárdenas, Làzaro, 21, 63, 72
Cárdenas, Victor Hugo, 161, 177
Cardoso, Fernando Henrique, 150, 151-152, 153
Carranza, Venustiano, 19
Carter, Jimmy, 129
Casa del Obrero Mundial, 19
Castillo, Ramón, 53
Castro, Cipriano, 7-8, 28
Castro, Fidel, 93, 94, 105, 111, 134, 135, 142
Castro, Raúl, 134
Catholicism, influence of, 2, 20, 49, 63, 77, 85-86, 89, 92 105, 107, 122, 130, 148, 152, 172, 185
Causa-R, Venezuela, 174, 175
Cavallo, Domingo, 152, 168, 169
Célula Socialista Revolucionaria, 56
Cerda, Pedro Aguirre, 51
Cerezo, Vinicio, 125
Cerro, Luis Sánchez, 59
Céspedes, Augusto, 25, 56, 57, 64
Chamorro, Joaquín, 129
Chamorro, Violeta, 129, 130
Chávez, Hugo, 174, 175
Chiari, Roberto, 132
Chibás, Eduardo, 93
Chile, 11-12, 31-33, 50-53, 84-86, 111-114, 171-173
Civilista Party, Civilismo, 8
Clube Tres de Outubro, Brazil, 47
Colby, Bainbridge, 27
Colegiado, Uruguay, 38, 55, 80
Coleman, James, 183
Colombia, 6-7, 29, 61-62, 94-96, 116-117, 175-176
Colorado Party, Uruguay, 26, 37-38, 53-54, 80, 81, 103, 108, 114-115, 116, 162-163, 164, 170, 171
Colosio, Donaldo, 177
Comité de Organización Política Electorial Independiente (COPEI), 92, 117, 174, 175, 174, 175
Communist Party; Communism, influence of 24, 26, 28-29, 44, 47-48, 51-52, 56, 61, 64-66, 67, 75, 81, 84, 87, 89, 105, 135, 136, 148
Conciencia de Patria, Bolivia, 161

Index 221

Concordancia, Bolivia, 82
Confederación General de Trabajadores del Perú (CGTP), 156
Confederación Nacional Obrera de Cuba (CNOC), 26-27
Confederación Obrera Boliviana (COB), 102
Confederación Socialista de Bolivia (CSB), 55, 56
Consejo de la Nacion, Uruguay, 116
Consertación, Chile, 173
Conservative Party, definition, 91-92, 185
Constituent Assembly, Brazil, 48
Constitution of 1857, Mexico, 1
Contras, Nicaragua, 129, 130
Contreras, Eleazar López, 62
Cook, John William, 109
Cordero, León Febres, 158
Córdoba, Roberto Suazo, 127
Corporación de Fomento de la Producción (CORFO), 52
Corporatist doctrines, Brazil, 49
Costa Rica, 4, 130-132
Costas, Robustiano Patrón, 53, 71
Costa e Silva, Artur de, 107
Couto e Silva, Golbery, 147, 148
Cristero War, 20
Cristiani, Alfredo, 123
Cuba, 3-4, 26-27, 63-65, 93-94, 134-136
Cuban Revolution, influence of, 89
Cubas, Raúl, 163, 164
Cuéllar, Javier Pérez, 156

D'Aguiar, Peter, 141
D'Aubuisson, Roberto, 122-123
Diaz, Porfiro, 1-2, 17, 18, 96
Directorio Estudiantil Universitario (DEU), Cuba, 64, 134
Dominican Republic, 4, 136-138
Dorticós, Osvaldo, 111
Drago Doctrine, Venezuela, 8
Duarte, José Napoleón, 122, 123
Dutra, Eurico Gaspar, 75
Duvalier, François, 138

Echevarría, Luis, 118
Ecuador, 8, 60-61, 88-89, 157-158
Ejécito Revolucionario del Pueblo (ERP), Argentina, 111, 122
Ejécito Revolucionario del Pueblo (ERP), El Salvador, 122
Ejécito Zapatista de Liberación Nacional, 177

El Salvador, 5, 28, 65-67, 121-123
Encuentro Nacional, Paraguay, 163
Escalante, Aníbal, 134-135
Estado Novo, Brazil, 31, 49, 50, 74
Estenssoro, Victor Paz, 25, 56, 57, 82, 83, 102, 159, 160
Esteves, Gomes Freire, 58
Estigarribia, José Félix, 58

Falange Nacional, Chile, 86
Falange Socialista Boliviana, 57, 83, 102
Falkland/Malvinas Islands, 164, 184
Federaçao de Industrias do Estado de São Paulo (FIESP), Brazil, 153
Federaciones Obreras del Trabajo, Bolivia, 55
Federación Sindical de Trabajadores Mineros de Bolivia (FSTMB), 81
Federal Revolution of 1899, Bolivia, 25
Fernández, Leonel, 137, 138
Figueres, José, 130-131, 132, 139
Flores, Venancio, 14
Força Sindical, Brazil, 153
Fox, Vicente, 178
Franco, Itamar, 151, 152
Franco, Rafael, 58
Frente Amplio, Uruguay, 115, 170, 171, 186
Frente Democrático Nacional, Mexico, 176
Frente Democrático Nueva Guatemala, 125
Frente Democrático Revolucionario, El Salvador, 122
Frente Farabundo Martí de Liberación Nacional (FMLN), El Salvador, 122, 123
Frente Manuel Rodríguez, Chile, 172
Frente Nacional, Colombia, 95, 116
Frente País Solidario (Frepaso), Argentina, 168
Frente Republicano Guatemaltco (FRG), 125
Frente Sandinista de Liberación Nacional (FSLN), Nicaragua, 128, 130
Frente Unico Socialista, Bolivia, 57
Frondizi, Arturo, 72, 78, 79, 108
Fujimori, Alberto, 155, 156, 157

Gaitán, Jorge Eliécer, 29, 61, 62
Galíndez, Jesús, 136
Galtieri, Leopoldo, 164, 165

Gallegos, Rómulo, 92
García, Alan, 155, 157
García, Antonio, 94
Gaviria, César, 175
Gay, Luis, 76
Geisel, Ernesto, 107, 147
Gestido, Oscar, 114-115
"Glorious 28th Day of May Revolution," Ecuador, 88
Gomes, Corp, 153
Gómez, Álvaro, 95, 116, 175, 176
Gómez, José Francisco Peña, 137
Gómez, José Miguel, 26
Gómez, Juan Vicente, 28, 62, 63
Gómez, Laureano, 62, 95, 116
Gortari, Carlos Salinas de, 176-177
Goulart, João, 76, 103, 104, 105, 148
Grauert, Julio C., 54
Grove, Marmaduke, 32, 33
Grupo Obra de Unificación (GOU), Argentina, 72
Guardia Civil, Panama, 132
Guardia Nacional, Nicaragua, 28, 129
Guardia, Rafael Calderón, 67, 130
Guarda Republicana, Bolivia, 25
Guatemala, 4-5, 28, 124-126
Gueiler, Lydia, 159
"Guerra de Diez Años," Cuba, 3
"Guerra de los Mil Días," Colombia, 6, 29, 61
Guevara, Ernesto "Che," 79, 104, 134, 135
Guiana, 141-142
Guido, José María, 79, 108

Haiti, 4, 138
Haya de la Torre, Víctor Raúl, 22, 23, 24, 27, 59, 60, 61, 86, 93, 94, 99, 132-133, 139, 154
Hernandez, Max, 161
Herrera, Enrique Olaya, 61
Herrera, Luis Alberto de, 53, 54, 80
Herrera, Luis Lacalle, 171
Heureaux, Ulises, 4
Huerta, Victoriano de la, 19
Hochschild, Mauricio, 57
Honduras, 5, 28, 126-127

Ibañez, Carlos, 32, 51, 84, 85, 86, 87, 175
Ibarra, José María Valasco, 60-61, 88, 89, 133, 157

Illia, Arturo, 108
Insurgencia, Mexico, 1
Intransigentes, Argentina, 52, 72, 110
Irigoyen, Bernado de, 37
Izquierda Cristiana, Peru, 112
Izquierda Democrática, Ecuador, 157, 158
Izquierda Unida, Peru, 154, 155, 156

Jagan, Cheddi, 141, 142
Jagan, Janet, 142
Jamaica, 139-140
Jamaican Labor Party (JLP), 139-140
James, C.L.R., 141
Jiménez, Marcos Pérez,92, 93
Julião, Francisco, 105
"July Revolution," Ecuador, 60
Junta Renovadora, Argentina, 76
Justo, Augustín, 44, 52
Juvetud Peronista, Argentina, 109

Kubishek, Juscelino, 76, 103
Kirchner, Nestor, 154, 170

L'Avalas, Haiti, 139
Lagos, Ricardo, 154, 173
"La Matanza," El Salvador, 66
Lamarca, Carlos, 107
Lanusse, Alejandro, 110
Latorre, Lorenzo, 37
Lebensohn, Moisés, 72
Lechín, Juan, 81, 83, 102
Left/Right polarity, definition, 186-187
Legion of Veterans, Bolivia, 55
Leighton, Bernardo, 85-86
Leguía, Augusto, 59
Levingston, Norberto, 110
Ley de Lemas, Uruguay, 53, 171
Liberal Doctrinario, Panama, 67
Liberal Nacionalista, Nicaragua, 128
Liberal Party, definition, 2, 185-186
Liberal Radical Auténtico, Paraguay, 163
Liga Agraria, Bolivia, 105
Lima, Alfonso Albuquerque, 147
Lins de Barros, João Alberto, 47-48
Lipset, Seymour Martin, 183
Llosa, Mario Vargas, 155, 157
Lonardi, Eduardo, 78
López, Francisco Solano, 9, 81
Lora, Guillermo, 102
Los Cientificos, Mexico, 2
Losada, Gonzalo Sánchez de, 160, 161

Loso, Remedios, 161
Lott, Teixeira, 76, 103

Machado, Gustavo, 27, 28, 63-64
MacIver, Enrique, 12
Madero, Francisco, 17, 18, 19, 36, 96
Magalhaes, Ulysses, 150
Magón, Ricardo Flores, 17
Maluf, Paulo, 150
Manley, Michael, 140
Manley, Norman, 140
Manrique, Francisco, 110
Marées, José González von, 51, 57
Mariátegui, Francisco, 24, 60
Marighela, José Carlos, 107
Marín, Luis Muñoz, 139
Martí, Farabundo, 66
Martí, José, 3, 93
Martínez, Maximiliano Hernández, 66, 93, 161
"Massacre of Chuspipata," Bolivia, 82
"Massacre of San Juan," Bolivia, 83-84
"Massacre of Tlateloco," Mexico, 118
"Massacre of Trujillo," Perú, 59
Massera, Emilio, 164
"Maximato," Mexico, 20, 63
Mayorga, Silvio, 128
Médici, Emílio Garrastazu, 107, 147
Mello, Fernando Collar de, 151
Méndez, Aparicio, 116
Mendieta, Carlos, 64
Menem, Carlos, 166, 167, 168, 169, 170
Menocal, Mario, 26, 27
Mesa, Luis García, 159
Metheun Treaty, 10
Mexico, 1-3, 17-22, 63, 117-118, 176-178
Mexican Revolution, 27, 82
Middle-class populist parties, definition, 188-189, 194-195
Mill, John Stuart, 181
Mitre, Bartolomé, 35, 37
MNR de Izquierda (MNRI), Bolivia, 159, 160
MNR Historica (MNRH), 159, 160
Montalva, Eduardo Frei, 85-86, 111
Montenegro, Carlos, 25, 56, 57
Montenegro, Julio César Méndez, 124
Montoneros, Argentina, 109, 111, 164
Montt, Efraín Ríos, 125, 126
Morales, Evo, 161
Morales, Ramón Villeda, 126
Moreno, Carlos Guevara, 88, 89

Moríñigo, Higinio, 59, 80
Morones, Luis, 19, 63
Moscoso, Mireya, 134
Movement 25 February, Surinam, 144
Movimiento 19 (M-19), Colombia, 96, 116
Movimiento 26 de Marzo (M-26), Uruguay, 115
Movimiento 26 de Julio, Cuba, 94, 134
Movimiento al Socialismo (MAS), Venezuela, 117, 161, 174, 175
Movimiento Bolivia Libre, 161
Movimiento Bolivariano Quinta Républic, 174-175
Movimiento de Acción Popular Unitaria (MAPU), Chile, 112
Movimiento Democrático Brasileiro (MDB), 106, 107, 148, 149
Movimiento Democrática M-19, Colombia, 175, 176
Movimiento Democrático Nicaraguense (MDN), 129
Movimiento de Dignidad Nacional (MODIN), Argentina, 167
Movimiento de Izquierda Revolucionaria (MIR), Bolivia, 102, 159, 160, 161
Movimiento de Izquierda Revolucionaria (MIR), Chile, 112
Movimiento de Izquierda Revolucionaria (MIR), Venezuela, 93, 117
Movimiento de Liberación Nacional (MLN), Costa Rica, 131, 132
Movimiento de Liberación Nacional, Guatemala, 124
Movimiento de Veteranos y Patriotas, Cuba, 64
Movimiento Libertad, Peru, 155
Movimiento Nacional Revolucionario (MNR), El Salvador, 121
Movimiento Nacionalista Revolucionario (MNR), Bolivia, 25, 57, 81, 83, 94, 102, 160, 161
Movimiento Nacionalista Revolucionario Auténtico (MNRA), Bolivia, 83
Movimiento Revolucionario Túpac Katari de Liberación (MRTKL), 161
Movimiento Popular Colorado (MOPOCO), Paraguay, 163
Multiclass-Integrative parties, definition, 187-188

Nacional Party, Honduras, 126-127
NAFTA Treaty, 177

Nahuad, Jamil, 158
Nardone, Benito "Chicotazo," 80
National Administrative Council, Uruguay, 38
National Committee for Economic Vigilance, Uruguay, 54
National Democratic Party, Surinam, 144
National Party of Surinam, 142
Nazi/"Naci," influence, 51, 57, 58, 85, 109, 132
Neves, Tancredo, 149, 150
New Democracy and Development Front, Surinam, 144
New Progressive Party, Puerto Rico, 139
Nicaragua, 5, 27-28, 66-67, 127-130
Nicaraguan Civil War, influence of, 28
Noboa, Alvaro, 158
Noriega, Manuel Antonio, 133
Nueva Fuerza Democrática, Colombia, 175
Nueva Fuerza Republicana (NFR), Bolivia, 161, 162
Nuñez, Benjamín, 131
Nuñez, Rafael, 7

Obregón, Álvaro, 18, 19, 20, 63
O'Donnell, Guillermo, 183
Odria, Manuel, 86-87, 92, 94, 99
Oncenio, Perú, 59, 60
Ongánia, Juan Carlos, 108, 109, 110
Organizaciones Revolucionarias Integradas, Cuba, 134
Ortega, Daniel, 130
Ortega, Humberto, 130
Ortiz, Roberto, 52
Osorio, Carlos Arana, 124-125
Ovando, Alfredo, 83, 102
Oviedo, Lino, 163-164

Padilla Heriberto, 135
Palenque, Carlos, 161
Palma, Tomás Estrada, 4, 26
Panama, 5-6, 67, 132-134
Panameñismo, 67
Paraguay, 9, 25-26, 58-59, 80-81, 102, 162-164
Paraguay por Todos, 163
Partido Acción Popular, Peru, 87
Partido Agrario Laborista (PAL), Chile, 84
Partido Autonomista Nacional (PAN), 12, 96, 177, 178

Partido Cooperativista, Mexico, 19
Partido da Frente Liberal (PFL), Brazil, 150, 152, 153
Partido da Renovaçao Naacional (PRN), Brazil, 151
Partido da Social Democracia Brasileira (PSDB), 150, 151
Partido de Acción Nacional (PAN), Mexico, 20
Partido de AvanzadaNacional (PAN), Guatemala, 125
Partido de Conciliación Nacional (PCN), El Salvador, 122
Partido de Izquierda Revolucionaria, Bolivia, 25
Partido de la Revolución Mexicana, 21
Partido de Liberación Dominicana (PLD), 137, 138
Partido de Unidad Revolucionaria Socialista, Cuba, 134
Partido de la Únion Republicana Socialista (PURS), Bolivia, 57
Partido del Pueblo, Cuba, 93, 133
Partido del Pueblo, Peru, 93, 133
Partido do Movimiento Democrático (PMDB), Brazil, 148, 149
Partido dos Trabalhadores (PT), Brazil, 148, 149, 150, 151, 152, 184
Partido Demócrata Nacional, Argentina, 44, 45, 71
Partido Demócrata Progresista, Argentina, 36, 44 ,45, 72
Partido Democrático, Brazil, 29, 48
Partido Democrático, Chile, 84
Partido Democrático Nacional, Venezuela, 28-29
Partido Democrático Social (PDS), Brazil, 148, 152
Partido Democrático Socialista, Bolivia, 57
Partido Democrático Trabalhista (PDT), Brazil, 148, 149, 150, 151, 152
Partido Guatemalteco del Trabajo (PGT), 124
Partido Independiente de Color, Cuba, 26
Partido Independentista, Puerto Rico, 139
Partido Institucional Democrático (PID), Guatemala, 124
Partido Laborista, Argentina, 19-20, 76, 85
Partido Laborista, Mexico, 19

Partido Laborista Mexicano, 17
Partido Liberal Constitucionalista, Mexico, 19-20
Partido Moderato, Cuba, 26
Partido Movimiento Democrático Brasileiro (PMDB), 153
Partido Nacional Revolucionario (PNR), Panama, 67
Partido Nacionalista, Bolivia, 25
Partido Obrero Revolucionario (POR), Bolivia, 25, 83, 102
Partido Pogressista Brasilerio (PPB), 153, 154
Partido Popular (PPB), Brazil, 149, 153
Partido Popular Cristano, Peru, 155
Partido Popular Cubano (PPC), 27
Partido Popular Democrático (PPD), Puerto Rico, 139
Partido Popular Socialista, Brazil, 153
Partido Renovación Nacional (PRN), Chile, 172
Partido Republicano Nacional (PRN), Chile, 172
Partido Republicano Nacional (PRN), Costa Rica, 130
Partido Republicano Paulista, Brazil, 29
Partido Republicano Riograndense, Brazil, 29
Partido Republicano Socialista, Bolivia, 56
Partido Revolucionario Cubano, 3
Partido Revolucionario Cubano Auéntico (PRCA), 65, 93, 94
Partido Revolucionario de Izquierda Nacionalista (PRIN), Bolivia, 83, 101, 160
Partido Revolucionario Democrático (PRD), Mexico, 176, 177-178
Partido Revolucionario Democrático, Panama, 133
Partido Revolucionario Dominicano (PRD), 137, 138
Partido Rèvolucionario Guatemalteco (PRG), 124-125
Partido Revolucionario Institucional (PRI), Mexico, 21, 72, 63, 96, 118, 121, 161, 176, 177
Partido Revolucionario Mexicano (PRM), 63
Partido Social Democrático (PSD), Brazil, 74, 75, 103, 104, 106, 149
Partido Socialista, Bolivia, 102
Partido Socialista, Chile, 33
Partido Socialista Obrero, Chile, 31
Partido Socialista Popular (PSP), Chile, 84, 85
Partido Socialista Popular (PSP), Cuba, 94, 134, 175
Partido Trabajador Nicaragua (PTN), 66
Partido Trabalhista Brasileiro (PTB), 74, 75, 76, 103, 105, 106, 149
Partido Único de la Revolución Nacional, Argentina, 77
Partido Unfon Social Cristiana (PUSC), Costa Rica, 132
Party of the People (VP), Surinam, 143
Pastrana, Misael, 95
Paulista politics, 46, 48
Peasant Congress, Bolivia, 81
Peña, Roque Sáenz, 35, 52
Peñaranda, Enrique, 57
People's Committees, Surinam, 143
People's Labor Party (PLP), Jamaica, 140
People's National Congress (PNC), Guiana, 141
People's National Movement (PNM), Trinidad and Tobago, 140, 141
People's National Party (PNP), Jamaica, 140
People's Progressive Party (PPP), Guiana, 141
Peralta, Jóver, 58
Pereda, Juan, 159
Pérez, Carlos Andrés, 117, 173, 174
Pérez, Mariano Ospina, 62
Perón, Evita, 74
Perón, Isabelita, 111
Perón, Juan Domingo, 72-74, 76, 77, 85, 87, 88, 89, 99, 109, 111, 132
Peronism, Peronists, 72, 76-79, 81, 108, 109, 110, 111, 138, 152, 165, 166, 167, 169
Peru, 8, 22-24, 59-60, 86-88, 100-101, 154-157
Peruvian Revolution, influence of, 100-101, 102, 133, 183
Petkoff, Teodoro, 117, 174
Picado, Teodoro, 130
Pietri, Arturo Uslar, 117
Pinedo, Federico, 45
Pinilla, Gustavo Rojas, 62, 92-93, 94, 95
Pinochet, Augusto, 113, 114, 115, 172

Platt Amendment, 3, 26, 64
Plaza de Mayo, 73, 77, 110, 164
Plaza, Galo, 89
Ponce, Camilo, 89
Popular Fronts, 50-51, 65, 66, 71, 73, 84
Popular Power Organizations (OPP), Cuba, 135, 136
Populism, definition, 80-85, 89-92, 151
Populist parties, middle-class (Aprista), definition, 188-189
Populist parties, working-class (Peronist), definition, 189-190
Porfiriato, Argentina, 36
Prado, Manuel, 59, 60,67, 86, 87, 88, 99
Prestes, Luis Carlos, 47, 48, 49, 75, 107
Préval, René, 139
Proyecto Venezuela, 175
Puerto Rico, 139
Pumarejo, Alfonso López, 61

Quadros, Jánio, 103, 104
Queremistas, Brazil, 74, 75
Quijano, Carlos, 54
Quiroga, José Cuadros, 57

Ramírez, Sergio, 130
Razón de Patria Lodge (RADEPA), Bolivia, 81
Recabarren, Luis Emilio, 11, 31
Rega, José López, 109
Regeneración, Colombia, 7
Remón, José Antonio, 132
República Parliamentaria, Chile, 32
Republicano Nacional, Costa Rica, 130
Republicanos Genuinos, Bolivia, 57
Resistancia, Argentina, 108
"Revolución en Libertad," Chile, 112
"Revolución en Marcha," Colombia, 61
"Revolución Libertadora," Argentina, 77, 78
Revoluciónio Auténtico, Cuba, 65
"Revolution of 1948," El Salvador, 121
Reyes, Bernardo, 17
Reyes, Cipriano, 76
Reyes, Hernán Siles, 25
Rico, Aldo, 168
Right/ Left polarity, definition, 186-187, 193-194
Robelo, Alfonso, 129
Roca, Julio A., 12, 36, 44
Roca-Runciman Pact, 45, 46
Rodríguez, Andrés, 162, 163

Rodríguez, Carlos Rafael, 135
Rojas, Isaac, 78
Rojas, Modesto, 126
Roldós, Jaime, 157, 158
Römer, Enrique Salas, 175
Roosevelt, Franklin, 64
Rosas, Juan Manuel de, 12, 36
Rosca mining consortium, Bolivia, 57, 82, 101
Ruiz-Tagle, Eduardo Frei, 173

Saa, Adolfo Rodriguez, 170
Saavedra, Bautista, 25, 55, 56, 57, 82
Sabattini, Amadeo, 72
Sacasa, Juan Bautista, 66
Salamanca, Daniel, 25, 55, 57
Salgado, Plínio, 49
Salvación Nacional, Colombia, 175-176
San Martin, Raúl Grau, 64, 65, 93, 143
Sandanistas, Nicaragua, 129-130
Sandino, Augusto César, 27-28, 65
Sanguinetti, Julio, 170-171
Santa Cruz, Marcelo Quiroga, 102, 159
Santos, Eduardo, 61
Santos, Máximo, 37
Sarney, José, 150
Sarney, Roseana, 153
Savaria, Aparicio, 14, 38
Schick, René, 127
Seaga, Edward, 140
Sem Terra, Brazil, 154
Sendero Luminoso, Peru, 154, 156
Sendic, Raúl, 115
Serra, José, 153
Silva, Inácio Lula da, 148, 150, 152, 154
Sistema Nacional de Movilización Social (SINAMOS), 100-101
Socarrás, Carlos Prío, 93, 94
Social order, dominant, 184
Social-revolutionary (Fidelista) parties, definition, 192-193
Socialista Nicaragüenese, 67
Socialistas Independientes, Bolivia, 57
Socialista Uno (PS-1), Bolivia, 159
Somoza, Anastasio, 28, 66, 122, 127, 128, 130-131, 136, 138
Somoza, Anastasio Jr., 127, 128
Somoza, Luis, 127
Stefanich, Juan, 58
Stroessner, Alfredo, 81, 103, 162, 163
Suárez, Hugo Banzer, 102-103, 138, 159, 160, 161, 162

Suazo, Hernán Siles, 55-56, 83, 159, 160
Surinam, 142-144

Taft, William, 26
Tamayo, Franz, 56
Tenetismo, Brazil, 30, 47, 48, 58, 60, 86, 88
Terra, Gabriel, 53, 54
Terry, Fernando Belaúnde, 87, 99, 100, 154-155
Toledo, Alejandro, 156, 157
Tomic, Radomiro, 85-86, 112
Tonton Macoutes, Haiti, 138
Toro, David, 56, 81
Torre, Lisandro de la, 36, 44
Torres, Alberto, 30, 31, 49
Torres, Camilio, 96
Torres, Juan José, 102
Torrijos, Omar, 67, 132-133, 134
Trades Union Congress (TUC), Guiana, 141
Trinidad and Tobago, 140-141
Trujillo, Rafael, 136, 138
Tupamaros, Uruguay, 115
Turcios, Luis, 124

Ubico, Jorge, 28, 124
Ugarte, Marcelino, 37
Ulate, Otilio, 130
Ungo, Guillermo, 122
União Democrática Nacional (UDN), Brazil, 74-75, 103, 106
Unidad Popular, Chile, 112, 113
Unión Cívica Radical (UCR), Argentina, 37, 44, 52, 72, 76, 78, 165, 166
Unión Cívica Radical del Pueblo (UCRP), Argentina, 78, 79, 108
Unión Cívica Radical Intransigente (UCRI), Argentina, 78, 79, 108, 164
Unión Cívica Solidaridad (UCS), Bolivia, 161
Unión Democrática, Argentina, 73
Unión Democrática, Bolivia, 82
Unión Democrática Independiente (UDI), Chile, 172
Unión Democrática Nacional (UDN), El Salvador, 121-122
Unión Democrática y Popular (UDP), Bolivia, 159
Unión Nacional de la Oposición, Nicaragua, 128
Unión Nacional Opositora (UNO), El Salvador, 121, 129-130
Unión Nacional Revolucionaria de Guatemala, 125
Unión Nacionalista, Cuba, 64
Unión Revolucionaria, Perú, 59
Unión Social Republicana de Asalariados de Chile (USRACH), 32
United Front (UF), Guiana, 141
United States, intervention by, 3, 27, 28, 64, 66, 94, 112, 113, 122, 124, 129, 133, 137, 139, 141, 161
Uribe, Àlvaro, 176
Uriburu, José Félix, 44
Uruguay, 37-39, 53-55, 80, 114-116, 170-171

Valle, Juan José, 78
Vandor, Augusto, 109
Vanguardia Popular, Costa Rica, 130
Vargas, Getúlio, 31, 47, 49-50, 74-76, 87, 103
Vargas, Guillermo Baballero, 163
Vargas, Ivette, 148
Vasconcelos, José, 20
Vega, Oscar Unzaga de la, 57
Velázquez, Andrés, 174
Velázquez, Fidel, 63
Venezuela, 7-8, 28-29, 62-63, 92-93, 117, 173-175
Vianna, Francisco José Oliviera, 30-31, 49
Videla, Gabriel González, 84, 164
Viera, Feliciano, 39
Villa, Manfred Reyes, 161
Villa, Pancho, 19
Villarroel, Gualberto, 81, 82
Viola, Roberto, 164
Violencia, Colombia, 62, 94

War of Independence, Cuba, 26
War of the Chaco, 25- 26, 55
War of the Pacific, 8, 10
War of the Triple Alliance, Paraguay, 9, 81
Wars of Reform, Mexico, 1
Washington, George, 182
Wasmosy, Juan Carlos, 163
Wells, Sumner, 64
Williams, Eric, 140
Working-class populist parties (Peronist), definition, 189-190

Working-class socialist parties (Social Democrat), definition, 190-191
World War I, influence of, 27, 65
World War II, influence of, 20, 74, 124, 127, 190-191

Yon Sosa, Marco Antonio, 124

Yrigoyen, Hipólito, 37, 43, 44, 72

Zamora, Paz, 160, 161
Zapata, Emiliano, 19
Zayas, Alfredo, 27, 64
Zedillo, Ernesto, 177
Zelaya, José Santos, 5